D0364554

SHOUTING IN
THE STREET

ADVENTURES AND MISADVENTURES
OF A FLEET STREET SURVIVOR

SHOUTING IN THE STREET

DONALD TRELFORD

Biteback Publishing

First published in Great Britain in 2017 by
Biteback Publishing Ltd
Westminster Tower
3 Albert Embankment
London SE1 7SP
Copyright © Donald Trelford 2017

ISBN 978-1-78590-252-9

10 9 8 7 6 5 4 3 2 1

A CIP catalogue record for this book is available from the British Library.

Set in Minion Pro

Printed and bound in Great Britain by
CPI Group (UK) Ltd, Croydon CR0 4YY

MIX
Paper from
responsible sources
FSC
www.fsc.org   FSC® C020471

For Claire

'He was fated, for many years, to be a defender as well as a crusader; a bruising role where he sometimes felt himself beset on all sides. But Trelford was first and foremost a journalist and an editor: multi-talented, hands-on, a master of sport as well as news, shrewd and decisive. The paper, through his years, may often have been under attack, but it also won many awards and gathered together brilliant teams of writers who kept the flame of Astor alive. And Trelford, at the end, was there to pass *The Observer* on, unbroken and unbowed.'
PETER PRESTON, EDITOR OF *THE GUARDIAN* 1975–95

'Donald is a journalists' editor. He appreciates good reporting and instantly recognises it when he sees it. And he has another great advantage over rival editors: he can write as well as his staff. He is an expert reporter with a sensitive ear for words and a nose for news that would do credit to a beagle. These gifts are priceless.

He also managed to lay out the front page and write many of the best headlines himself – something beyond most editors these days – while simultaneously taking bets from the staff on every big race or rugby international. The queue of people outside his office door after first edition, waiting to hand over fivers, was like Russian serfs paying tribute.'
GAVIN YOUNG, FOREIGN CORRESPONDENT FOR *THE OBSERVER* FROM 1960

'Donald Trelford is regarded by friend and foe as the Harry Houdini of journalism. Bound, gagged and tied to the rails and within seconds of the locomotive wheels, Trelford wriggles free from each succeeding crisis. There has scarcely been a dull month in all his years as editor.'
PETER McKAY, *DAILY MAIL* COLUMNIST, WRITING IN *TATLER*

'Trelford – the Rocky Marciano of newspaper politics.'
ALAN WATKINS, POLITICAL COMMENTATOR FOR *THE OBSERVER* 1976–93

'Donald Trelford has a remarkable capacity for staying upright in a shipwreck.'
LORD GOODMAN

'Donald feels that being editor of *The Observer* is an invitation to the cocktail party of life.'
TATLER

CONTENTS

FOREWORD

I decided to write this book on 29 April 2013, the day I was told I had prostate cancer. Being given such life-changing news naturally provokes dramatic, even melodramatic, thoughts. It was time, I thought, to get it all down before it was too late. I had been badgered for years by family, friends and former colleagues to turn my party-piece jumble of anecdotes into a coherent tale; one friend said I had reached my 'anecdotage'. Somehow, though, I never got round to it. I used to joke that I was enjoying life too much, living with my new family in the Majorcan sunshine, and didn't really fancy revisiting times when things were more troubled.

Many years ago, I received a substantial advance from a publisher for a book about my time as an editor, but I later paid it all back – something practically unheard of, I was told. I informed the publisher that I simply couldn't be bothered to write the book and couldn't imagine that anybody would be bothered to read it anyway. The second part may still be true, but I don't care so much about that now.

I was also prompted to put pen to paper (or finger to keyboard) by the birth of a son, Ben, when I was seventy-three – an age at which I had always expected to be dead, not changing nappies in the middle of the night. I realised with a chill, as I stared lovingly into his cot, that I would never know Ben as an adult. Then, three years later, Poppy turned up.

When she was two, Poppy made an unwelcome contribution to this book. Just as I had completed a chapter of about 20,000 words, mostly about Tiny Rowland, she came into my study to say goodnight. As she sat on my lap, she reached towards the keyboard and tapped a few strokes which, remarkably, 'disappeared' the whole chapter. Even computer experts failed to recover it, so I had to rewrite the chapter from memory. I sensed Tiny's ghostly hand from beyond the grave.

I thought that, one day, Ben and Poppy might be curious to know what their old dad had been up to in all those years before they were born. The same is probably true of my four older children – Sally, Tim, Paul and Laura – who didn't see much of me at home when I was working all hours as a journalist – and of my wife Claire, come to that, who only met me four years after I had stopped editing *The Observer*.

Even then, after making the decision to write the book, it took almost another three years to get down to it (during which time, thankfully, the cancer has gone away; so far anyway). I had always imagined that I would write in disciplined periods of intense work, like Jeffrey Archer, whom I see when he comes to Majorca to write his books. But Jeffrey doesn't have to do the school run, or take and collect children from judo or riding lessons, and I imagine he has someone to do his shopping and have the car checked out at the garage. Having two little ones makes it impossible to arrange a regular writing schedule – I have just had to snatch the odd hour here and there when I could, or even the odd few minutes to rewrite a passage or add a story I had just remembered.

This book is not an autobiography. It wasn't even meant to be about me, or at least not mainly so. But, after completing most of the book, I began to feel, rightly or wrongly, that readers might want to know who I was and what I had been doing in the twenty-eight years before I joined *The Observer*. So I introduced two chapters at the start about my family and some friends who'd had a strong influence on me at school and university. Really, however, this book is a portrait in action of some interesting people I got to know well, mainly through my three decades on *The Observer* or through my other, mostly sporting interests. Nearly all of them are more significant people than me. And I suppose something of my own personality may come through in the way I tell their stories and report on my dealings with them.

I started off thinking I would write about these major figures in my life in the style of a series of *Observer* profiles, but I found that I kept wandering off the central theme as one story reminded me of another. If the chronology seems rather jumbled at times, I'm sorry, but the memories of an old man can be a bit like that.

Readers of the chapter on Tiny Rowland, for example, may be surprised when Saul Bellow and the Queen turn up, or that the comic figure of Kenneth Williams intrudes into a chapter on David Astor. The chapter on Pamella Bordes was a late addition because I concluded that, if I were to omit that brief but heavily publicised episode in my life, some readers might wonder if I had something to hide.

I should admit that I was also impelled to write by some published accounts of my time at *The Observer*, especially about my relations with Lonrho and the paper's handling of the Harrods affair. Some of these accounts were not only inaccurate but malicious, sometimes quite ridiculous. I have not responded before to even the most outrageous of them. I thought it was time now to put the record straight.

The title of the book came to me after an incident in London on one of my occasional visits. I usually stay at the Garrick Club, and when I leave I pull my hand luggage through the streets of Covent Garden towards Embankment station on the way to Victoria, the Gatwick Express and the return flight to Majorca, where we have had a *finca* on the side of a mountain since 2003.

This route takes me past Zimbabwe House on the Strand, which is looking almost as run-down these days as the country it represents. I have some history, as they say, with President Mugabe, as will become clear within this book. Every time I passed the building I would utter a profane imprecation against the old monster.

On one such occasion, however, I had failed to notice that a policeman was right behind me (Charing Cross police station is just across the road). After hearing my cry, the policeman stopped me and asked me what I was doing. I explained to this young black man about Zimbabwe and Mugabe without getting any feeling that he knew or cared what I was talking about. Finally, he said in a patient though slightly exasperated tone: 'That's all very well, sir, but we can't have elderly gentlemen shouting in the street, now can we?'

CHAPTER 1

TOM

My father was born in the Aged Mineworkers' Home at Shincliffe, County Durham. I always fancied writing that sentence: having written it, however, I can see that it doesn't make much sense. How could a baby have been born in an Aged Mineworkers' Home? The answer, it turns out, is that my heavily pregnant grandmother had been caught short on a visit to friends in a neighbouring mining village and had been forced to throw herself on the mercy of the nearest place offering nursing care.

Her husband, Samuel Trelford, had left school at the age of ten because his father had decided to emigrate to Pennsylvania in search of work in the coal mines over there. By the time the family had sailed across the Atlantic, however, my great-grandmother had discovered she was pregnant again, so they decided to sail back home for the birth. Had this not happened, they would have settled in the United States and I would never have existed. On such tiny chances can human life depend.

When they returned, my grandfather didn't resume his interrupted schooling. Instead, he was sent down the mine at Tow Law (I still have his miner's lamp in my study). He gave up mining when he was in his early twenties. Even so, he coughed his way through life with what was thought to be asthma but which turned out, at a post-mortem after his death at the age of eighty, to be the dreaded miners' lung disease.

He opened a bicycle shop, of which I have an aged photo, in the pit village of Esh Winning. He taught himself to play the organ from an instruction book and became the local chapel organist. He was a voracious reader, always found ransacking the local library. I still have his marked copy of *Julius Caesar* dated 1906.

He studied languages, including Welsh (for no obvious reason, as far as I can tell, except that he liked the sound of it), which he would recite to me when I was a child. He would also take me on his knee and show me the effects of different sources of light on a Leonardo da Vinci painting. How he learned these things I don't know.

Grandad Trelford was to become a substitute father to me during the Second World War – for the first eight years of my life, in fact – and continued to be a strong presence throughout my period of growing up, urging me to make the most of the education he had never had. Because of our close ties, I was given compassionate leave from the RAF to attend his funeral.

Samuel Trelford doubtless lived a life of unblemished probity, but one curious incident raised a question about this. An *Observer* reader, having seen me on television, sent a photograph of her late father, pointing out that he had a distinct resemblance to me. I was inclined to send a polite, 'what a coincidence' sort of reply, until I studied the photograph more closely and saw the address on the letter.

It was from Consett, the mining village next to where Sam Trelford had been brought up, and the family likeness was certainly uncanny. I sent the letter and photograph on to my father. When he didn't respond after a couple of weeks I rang him about it. After a pause he said reluctantly: 'All I can say is that my father had a bicycle.'

• • •

My father, Tom, was born in 1911; my youngest son Ben was born in 2011. By an odd coincidence, my mother was born in 1914 and my daughter Poppy was born in 2014. When my father was eight, he nearly perished in an epidemic of diphtheria at the end of the First World War (another example of the tiny chances on which human life depends). In his early teens, his education was interrupted by the General Strike, which closed all the schools. Instead, one of his teachers taught him to play golf – a pastime that became an obsession until he was over eighty – and he never went back to school.

His father, badly shaken by his own experience underground, would not allow him to become a miner, even if he had wanted to. So, when he was seventeen, he was directed to work in a Coventry car factory and went to live on his own in the Midlands city, 200 miles away from home. This was Norman Tebbit's famous injunction to the unemployed – 'get on your bike' – put into action. He was given digs in King William Street, next to Coventry City's football ground, and developed a loyalty to the club and a love of football that he passed on to his son.

I sometimes wonder if my obsession with sport derives from my father's accidental placement next to a football ground in 1929. Being a lonely bachelor in a strange city, he had little else to do, except for playing billiards and snooker at the local Methodist boys' club – another obsession he passed on to his son.

Tom found factory life not to his liking, however, and soon got a job as a van delivery driver instead. His parents came to live in Coventry and my grandfather started a business called Trelford's Teas, selling a variety of exotic brands door-to-door from a van with the company's name on the side. Tom had kept in touch with my mother, Doris Gilchrist, whose family came from the same Durham mining village of Esh Winning, and in 1935 they were married.

Unfortunately for them, his old jalopy of a car broke down after the wedding and they had to spend their honeymoon with my father's religious and strictly teetotal parents. His mother, to adapt a phrase from P. G. Wodehouse, would never be mistaken for a ray of sunshine. The new bride later recalled how she had brought her a cup of tea in bed on the first morning and said: 'I don't suppose you'll be coming down for a few days.' My mother replied: 'Why ever not?' Her new mother-in-law explained: 'Well, think of the shame.'

The Trelfords didn't approve of the marriage, thinking my father had married beneath him. My mother came from a rough family of coal miners of mixed Irish and Scottish descent who liked a drink and, even worse, were not church- or chapel-goers. Her father had been a drover from the Scottish Borders before he went down the mines. Her mother's family, the Ryans, were Irish, and had worked as servants in Dublin Castle. Because her own mother had died young, my grandmother had brought up her younger brothers and sisters and never went to school herself, so she couldn't read or write.

•   •   •

Some years later, when my name became known, I had a letter from someone in Northern Ireland pointing out that the Trelford side of the family also had Irish connections. The Trelfords, in fact, are commemorated in a stained-glass window in the Anglican cathedral in Belfast, which I went to see. Until then I had known nothing of this branch of the family. I also discovered a Trelford Street in Belfast named after a prominent figure called Robert Trelford.

Evidently a couple of Trelford brothers had crossed to the north of Ireland with 'King Billy's Army' – the army that King William of Orange sent to defeat the deposed James II at the end of the seventeenth century. They appear to have stayed on as landowners, one of them moving to the south, from where some of his descendants emigrated to Canada (there is a concentration of Trelfords in Ontario) and one to Texas in the United States. One brother had stayed in the Belfast area, presumably the ancestor of Robert Trelford. (In fact, nearly all the male Belfast Trelfords seem to have been called Robert, back to 1720.)

My eldest son, Tim, once opened the door at our house in Wimbledon to find a stranger on the doorstep. 'My name's Tim Trelford,' said the stranger. 'So's mine,' said my son. The visitor was from Texas and had tracked us down.

• • •

My Gilchrist grandparents went on to have twelve children, two of whom died in infancy. My grandmother told me that for ten years she never ventured beyond her garden gate. They had met when he had driven cattle down from the Borders to Durham and then gone with his colleagues to the seaside at Seaton Carew. When she was in her nineties, my grandmother reminisced to me about that sunny afternoon in 1901 with a faraway look in her eyes: 'He and his friends dashed past us into the water. He was burned to a golden colour by the sun. He looked like a god.'

My mother was the first girl from their mining village to get a scholarship to Durham County High School for Girls – an honour that meant nothing to her illiterate parents. She used to get up at five o'clock in the morning to cadge the sixpenny bus fare to Durham from her brothers, who were putting on their hobnailed boots to go down the pits. Eventually she was made to give up school to go and help one of her sisters in domestic service near London. The sister couldn't cook and my mother had to go and take over in the kitchen.

My Gilchrist grandfather was a bit of a rebel. He had once been jailed overnight during the General Strike after joining a gang that threw the Bishop of Durham into the River Wear for preaching a sermon in which he told the miners to go back to work. He had a reputation as a troublemaker and the only work he could get was as a shot-firer, a dangerous job that in those days involved going down with a canary and one of his sons into unexplored areas of a mine, some of them just two or three feet high, to see if they were safe enough from gas leaks to bring them into use.

When I arrived in 1937, my parents were renting two rooms, heated and lit through a gas meter, at the top of a terraced house in the Earlsdon district of Coventry; I was born in the back bedroom at a time when home births were more common. They moved to a newly built house of their own in Radford, with three bedrooms and a garden front and back, when I was a few months old, and stayed there until my father died sixty-four years later. I was nearly two when the war came. My father volunteered first for the Fire Service and then for the army and I never saw him until he was discharged in 1946, when I was eight. I had no memory of him before then.

Our house in Coventry was damaged by bombing – it was a few hundred yards from the Daimler and Dunlop factories, both prime targets for the Luftwaffe. During the raids, we hid in an Anderson shelter in the garden. Children were made to lie on top of each other on the floor, which was flooded with water, and we emerged after the raid soaked to the skin.

On the night of the big blitz on Coventry in November 1940, the house of my Gilchrist grandparents, who had also moved to the city, was struck by fragments of a bomb that had landed in a neighbour's front garden. My grandfather had left the bomb shelter to go into the house and was thrown across the room by the blast. I remember my grandmother cutting a loaf of bread the next morning and finding a piece of glass inside it.

My grandfather never really recovered from the head injuries he suffered that night and died soon after the war. I remember him sitting silently in a rocking chair by the fire and teaching me to box. I would charge at him and he would send me crashing across the room with his huge miner's hands. When I wasn't at school, I used to take his billycan of tea to the village factory where he worked. His job was carrying heavy sacks – the only job he could get.

On the morning after the raid on Coventry, my Trelford grandfather put me onto the back seat of his Austin Seven – I still remember the registration number: OG7041 – and told me to stand up and look through the tiny rectangular back window while he drove round the devastated city. All he said was: 'I want you to remember this.' I was just over three years old by then and I believe this experience must have provided my first childhood memory.

I can still see the collapsed buildings, most dramatically the burning cathedral, with water running everywhere, fires still raging, the road-blocks and the piles of sand. There were large wrapped packages at the top of the rubble on each bombed house. It was only later that I realised these were dead bodies waiting to be collected.

My father was in Aldershot, preparing for embarkation overseas, when he heard about the bombing of Coventry. He asked for leave to go there, which was refused, but he went anyway. When he arrived, having walked and hitch-hiked all the way, he found all three family homes empty. We had all – my mother and me and both sets of grand-parents – been evacuated back to Durham, where both sides of the family had their roots, and we stayed there for the rest of the war.

My mother took us to live in a village called Stillington, near Stockton-on-Tees, which was dominated by a huge slag heap on which we used to try to fly our homemade kites. She had to live on twenty-two shillings a week and rented a tiny terraced house with two small bed-rooms and an unlit lavatory in the yard. The yard was so frighteningly dark in the evening that I would be in and out of the loo in seconds, a habit that has never left me. I have a vivid memory of visiting a young friend of my mother's to see her new baby in a house that had oil lamps and water running down the walls.

Looking back, the war must have been a terrifying ordeal for my mother, still in her mid-twenties and bringing up two young children – my sister Margaret had been born after my father's last embarkation leave and some years passed before he even knew of her existence. She was an unwanted child, which my mother took few pains to hide.

It was a difficult birth, which meant that my mother had to stay in hospital for three months while I was billeted with my Aunt Mary, who got married, with me as a page boy, while I was living with her. Although Margaret grew up with a loving husband and family, she had problems with depression in later life and is now in a care home with Alzheimer's disease.

My mother wouldn't have known if Great Britain would win the war or if her husband would ever return from it, or what would happen to her then. I will never forget an evening when I upset a pan of treacle that was being warmed on the open fire to make toffee and seeing my mother burst into tears. It wasn't so much the loss of the toffee that caused her such misery, I suspect – though the treat must have cost money she could barely afford – but her generally bleak and lonely situation.

I was always top of the class at the village school, which caused me to be bullied by the Mercer twins, a couple of village thugs. One day my maternal grandmother came to collect me from school – she of Irish descent – and saw the Mercer boys hitting me as they tried to pinch my sixpence pocket money. When I saw her, I crossed the road and rushed for safety into the haven of her skirts. Instead of cuddling me, however, she turned me round and told me to go back and punch them, which I did, thrashing at them through my tears. The Mercer boys never bullied me again.

An older boy took me to see some Italian prisoners of war breaking stones in a valley. When people jeered down at them, the Italians responded by smiling and waving. My guide said he knew where they were billeted, so after they were marched off we followed them to a field where they lived in huts.

Security must have been minimal – I suppose the authorities thought the Italians would rather sit out the war in safety than try to make a hazardous escape – and we got close enough to peep through the curtains into one of the huts. When we were seized by strong arms and carried inside, we were naturally terrified. But the prisoners came up and hugged us and plied us with sweets and chocolate. We obviously reminded them of the families they had left behind in Italy.

My mother was not best pleased when I reported this escapade. 'Fraternising with the enemy,' she said disapprovingly. 'You could have got yourselves hanged for that.'

Although we were living in an isolated village, we weren't very far from military targets in Stockton-on-Tees, Middlesbrough, Newcastle-on-Tyne and Darlington, and at night we could hear the enemy bombers massing overhead and could stand at the front door of the house and see the bombs dropping at an angle on the factories and shipyards. They were all some miles away, but were lit up eerily by the searchlights. For a child, it was like watching a fireworks display.

For my mother, however, it brought back such terrible memories of the bombing of Coventry that she was paralysed with fear – a fear that communicated itself to my little sister and me. She would sometimes take refuge in the tiny cupboard under the stairs, shaking uncontrollably, and would drag us in beside her.

It took me some time to overcome the sense of anxiety my mother had instilled in me – if, in fact, it ever really left me. Recently I came across a line in John le Carré's book about his life that had a special resonance for me: 'I remember a constant tension in myself that even in great age has not relaxed.'

I was especially fearful of the noise of aircraft overhead, because I had seen for myself what destruction they could cause. Even after the war, if I could hear the buzz of a plane while I was lying in bed, I would wait nervously until the noise had passed. It would then take some time for me to feel safe enough to go to sleep, just in case it came back.

There were only two books in the house, both free offers from *John Bull* magazine. One of them, called *How Much Do You Know?*, I devoured eagerly and could probably recite most of the facts from it now, seventy years later. The other, *How It Works and How It's Done*, was about scientific and technical matters. I never even opned it.

• • •

When the war ended, we returned to Coventry. At the junior school there I entered into a competition with other boys as to who had the tallest dad. All our fathers had been in the war, but none of us could remember them. I talked myself into being the winner. It was a source of some embarrassment, therefore, when my father was finally demobbed and turned out to be barely five feet tall.

My main achievement at Hill Farm junior school was playing Pau-Puk-Keewis in a performance of Longfellow's *Hiawatha*. The reason I mention this is that I had to do the wild Beggar's Dance, which Pau-Puk-Keewis performed at Hiawatha's wedding – and some elements of this frantic style may still be traced in my dancing as an adult.

My uninhibited style of dancing – so out of character really – has been much commented on, notably by *Private Eye*. It caused an embarrassing episode when I attended a party given by British Airways, where my wife Claire was then working for their television arm. In the course of one dance I threw out a leg and my shoe shot across the dance floor and almost hit the chief executive.

•   •   •

My father was a salesman for a wholesale tobacconist (later he moved indoors and became a manager) and sometimes he allowed me to go round with him as he called on his customers. I remember a particular occasion when I saw him talking to George Mason, who had been a legendary pillar of the Coventry City defence and became a publican on his retirement.

George was a giant of a man who towered over my father by at least a foot and a half, yet Tom never looked in the least embarrassed by the disparity in size between himself and every adult he met, and plainly regarded himself as the equal of any man. Being of under-average height myself (though a good six inches taller than him), I think I may have learned that lesson myself through watching the self-confident way in which my father conducted himself.

'Stop looking!' was the recurring household cry of my childhood when my father finally found his keys. Nobody had moved a muscle to search for them: we would roll our eyes and get on with eating our cornflakes. It is a classic Freudian cliché that someone who has mislaid their keys doesn't really want to go to work. No wonder really; as a non-smoker, it must have seemed strange to devote his career to selling cigarettes, and as a moral man it must have affected his view of himself when it became clear that smoking killed people.

•   •   •

Although I won a scholarship to Bablake School, this didn't cover all the fees and extras, and my father struggled to afford the amount he was required to pay. When I was sixteen and poised to enter the sixth form, he arranged for me to visit Alfred Herbert & Co., a factory in Coventry that made machine tools. He was clearly hoping that I would leave school and become an apprentice, but the noise of the factory horrified me; in any case, I was determined to stay on at school and go to university.

We argued about it. My father was naturally concerned about the money it would cost him if I stayed on at school. And, of course, no one on either side of my family had ever been to university. My father finally gave in after talking about my prospects to one of my teachers. He was forced to take on a second job to pay for it. After working all day from nine till five, he would have a quick meal at home then go off to work as a clerk at Pickford's, the removals firm, checking lorries in and out until ten at night. It was only later that I fully realised what a sacrifice he had made for me.

This prolonged absence from home, following six years away in the war, could hardly have helped his marriage, especially given that my parents were not temperamentally well suited to each other in the first place. He retained some of his parents' Methodist mentality – high-minded, hard-working, teetotal. I can still recall the dread I used to feel when I heard them arguing. My mother, with her Irish–Scots background, liked a bit of fun. There was a period when she got a job as a waitress in a restaurant known as Fishy Moores, near the bus station, and I have never known her to be so happy.

My father hated her working, regarding it in an old-fashioned way as some slight on himself, suggesting that he couldn't provide enough money to keep her. My mother loved the job – not only, I suspect, because it got her out of the house and allowed her to mix with people, but because she was earning her own money and not having to rely on her husband for pocket money, as women who stayed at home often had to do in those days.

Once, when I was earning a good salary, I decided that the best birthday present I could give her was cash. She was in her favourite armchair by the fire, where she would normally sit reading, knitting or doing a crossword. When I slipped her the wad of notes in a roll, it disappeared among her cushions like lightning before my father could see it.

They fell out badly over her love of bingo. She liked it mainly for the company it provided, but my father was shocked at her gambling and made his moral disapproval only too clear. But he couldn't prevent her leaving the house while he was at work, so he had to lump it. It turned out that she was quite successful at bingo, and at the fruit machines in the same casino, and one day she came home with so many coins in her handbag that she couldn't bear the weight and had to keep stopping and resting the bag on garden walls. This became a favourite family joke.

At the party to celebrate their sixtieth wedding anniversary, she was heard to interject at one point, while someone was extolling their wonderful marriage, saying: 'We've had our ups and downs, you know.' How much distress lay behind that remark we could only guess at.

•   •   •

While he was living on his own in Coventry as a young man, my father had developed a love for the music hall, where he would go to entertain himself. After the war, he used to take me to the Hippodrome, where the number of the act in the programme would be shown in lights by the side of the stage. I was entranced; it was such a colourful change from dreary village life in war-time County Durham.

I remember seeing Ted and Barbara Andrews – 'and little Julie', the future Hollywood star appearing at the age of ten; the Irish tenor, Cavan O'Connor ('I'm only a strolling vagabond…'); 'Two Ton' Tessie O'Shea with her little banjo; and a number of comedians, including Rob Wilton, Max Miller and Arthur English. Deep down, I sometimes think Tom would have liked to have shed the Methodist inhibitions instilled in him as a child and become a stand-up comedian.

His jokes could be pretty awful. I still remember the frozen look on the faces of some old ladies when he told them a slightly risqué tale. We knew a story was coming up when he uttered his favourite phrase: 'Funnily enough…' I thought of repeating some of his jokes here, but they might have made him sound (to use another favourite phrase of his) a bit barmy, which he certainly wasn't.

When Roy Hudd produced a book about the history of the music hall, my father wrote to him about the various acts he had seen. Hudd wrote back saying: 'You're luckier than me. I only write about these people. You actually saw them.' When he was in his eighties, he went to Birmingham for what was billed as an Edwardian music hall and attired himself accordingly. When it was pointed out to him that he was the only member of the audience who had dressed up for the occasion, he replied: 'I can't help it if other people don't know how to behave.'

When my parents came down to London to see me one weekend, I persuaded my father to join me and some *Observer* colleagues, mostly from the sports department, at a snooker club near the office called Duffer's. Casting aside any reservations about gambling he once had, he suggested playing for a small wager; my colleagues looked doubtful – he was quite old and barely high enough to see over the table. By the end of the evening, however, he had cleaned out their wallets.

Another time, both my parents came down to London to see Donald Sinden in a Westminster farce. It was a matinee and I arranged for them to meet the actor in his dressing-room after the performance. Whenever I bumped into Donald at the Garrick Club, where he was a prominent member, he would say: 'We Donalds must stick together.'

He thought we should have a lunch of Donalds, but with Bradman and Wolfit long gone we couldn't think of any other Donalds we wanted to dine with. (Funnily enough, Donald Trump's name never came up.) These conversations would usually end with Sinden saying: 'Ah well, we'd better have lunch together then.'

When I ushered my parents in to see the great man, he was in his usual effusive and deeply courteous mode, despite having just completed an energetic performance in which he had hurled himself around the stage at a time when, to put it mildly, he was some way past his first youth. He put his arm round my tiny mother and boomed down at her in his best stage baritone: 'There's a question I've always wanted to ask you, Mrs Trelford. Why did you call him Donald?' To which my mother replied shyly: 'I don't rightly know.'

• • •

Like many soldiers, my father always shied away from talking about the war, but he talked freely about some of the places where it had taken him, such as Cairo, Sicily, Milan, Rome and Trieste, and had photos of himself in some of them. When he was in his late eighties, I took him to the Churchill War Rooms in Whitehall, where he became absorbed in a map of war-time Europe and started pointing out the route he had taken through North Africa and Italy. We were amused to hear an astonished young Scandinavian student say to his backpacking friends: 'There's a man here who fought in the war!'

He had never been abroad until the army took him there, which was probably the case with nearly all British servicemen in the Second World War. My parents only went abroad together once, when I arranged for them to go to Venice for their golden wedding anniversary. My mother hated flying (a first experience for her at the age of seventy-one) and my father distrusted the food, so I don't think they had a very good time.

On one occasion, when I was leaving their house in Coventry after telling him I was about to pile my young family into an old Jag and drive them to the South of France, he waved goodbye at the garden gate – then, with a stricken look on his face, turned back and asked me to wind down the car window. I couldn't imagine what he was going to say, but it was a remark I have treasured ever since: 'You say you're going to France – how will you manage for food?'

After my mother died, we asked him where he would like to go for his birthday. He chose Jersey, because he had never been there. He took a bus from Coventry to Victoria coach station in London, where my wife and I met him and took him on to Gatwick airport. We hit a serious problem at customs. After he had set off the alarm on his way through, he was ordered to empty his pockets and out fell a whole jumble of knives, pocket scissors and other assorted sharp objects.

When he was told he couldn't take them on the plane, he got very cross, saying they were his property, he had owned them for over fifty years, and they had no right to take them from him. Tempers were frayed so badly that the head of security at Gatwick had to be summoned. She immediately berated my wife and myself for allowing him to bring all this stuff; but we hadn't been there when he'd dressed and packed.

One of the customs officers, more amused by the episode than his more senior colleagues, said to me: 'It's amazing how a man so old and so tiny can create such a rumpus.' Eventually a compromise was reached and my wife was allowed to go back air-side, as they call it, and send the items to his home in Coventry by parcel from the post office in the Gatwick terminal.

At the height of the row, the security people had taken a photo of the three of us. When my wife came back into departures and passed through various checkpoints before she could board the plane, she could see our photo coming up on all the computer terminals as her passport and boarding pass were checked. One official, looking at the picture, said: 'He must be the oldest terrorist suspect ever!'

Finally, Claire reached the plane, only just in time, and sat down beside us heaving for breath, having run most of the way. My father's comment did nothing for her temper: 'She took her time, didn't she?'

When I took my father into his hotel room in Jersey, he dug deep into a trouser pocket and fished out, with some satisfaction, yet another knife – used, he said, for taking stones out of horses' hooves or from the tyres of bicycles – which had somehow escaped detection. 'They think they're so clever, these people, but they never found this,' he said with some pride, as though he had won a major victory. I decided not to tell Claire about this.

He was always firing off letters to the local paper in Coventry about anything that annoyed him, usually local matters but sometimes wider national or international issues. The frequency of these letters increased after my mother died – either because he had more time on his hands or because she wasn't there to listen to his opinions or to tell him he was talking rubbish. When he died, the *Coventry Telegraph* ran a news story reporting the death of the paper's most prolific correspondent.

He had brought back two abiding memories from his army service in Italy: opera and gorgonzola cheese, which my sister and I were required to eat even though we hated it. While in Milan he had organised a visit for his company to La Scala opera house, where Beniamino Gigli was singing. The commanding officer at first vetoed it, but was then persuaded to change his mind and go along with them. I imbibed his love of opera, especially the romantic arias of Verdi and Puccini. At his funeral in 2002, he asked us to play the famous duet from *The Pearl Fishers* by Bizet.

· · ·

My father comes into conversations between my wife and myself almost every day, mainly because I inherited his weakness for corny jokes and even weaker puns. When I utter one of these, my wife gives me a warning look and says: 'Tom, stop it!' I suppose it's as good a way as any to be remembered.

CHAPTER 2

RICK

For some reason I can't explain (though a psychologist might), many of my friends throughout my life have been exceptionally tall. That was certainly true of my best boyhood friend, Rick Melville, whom I met at the age of eight as we were unloading furniture on our return to Coventry after being evacuated during the war. He was sitting on a wall nearby and watching us. We stayed in touch for the next sixty-six years.

Rick was brilliant at all sports and came close to winning an England cap at rugby football. When he retired from playing for Coventry, then one of the country's top clubs, he held the record for the number of tries scored in a career. He played in the same three-quarter line as two legendary England players, Peter Jackson and David Duckham. He was also a top-class sprinter, held the British junior long jump record for many years, and had a trial for Warwickshire at cricket.

I have a picture of the two of us standing outside our front door in our caps and school uniforms on our first day at Bablake School, after we had passed the eleven-plus, with me coming up to his armpit. It is a rare picture of me wearing a cap, as I have always tried to resist headgear, even when I was an officer in the RAF.

Rick's size came in useful on our first day. There was a tradition at the school called 'fuzzerising', an initiation rite in which new boys were subjected to various forms of discomfort, such as having one's head pushed down a flushing lavatory or being forced to sit on a piping-hot radiator. Because he was bigger than the bullies, Rick fought them all off and I avoided trouble by sticking close to him, as if to say: 'I'm with him.'

I had been firmly reminded of my lack of height when the headmaster picked me out from the front row at my first assembly. Clearly intrigued by my size, or lack of it, he asked me to join him on stage in front of the whole school. He asked me my name. 'Trelford, sir,' I declaimed loudly, to the amusement of the boys. 'And how tall are you?' he asked in apparent wonderment. 'Four foot and half an inch, sir,' I replied, puffing out my tiny chest in a way that provoked hysterical laughter.

The headmaster then placed his hand on my shoulder and announced solemnly to the assembly: 'Gentlemen, meet Mr Trelford, the smallest boy to be admitted to this school since it was founded by Queen Isabella in 1344.' Cue more laughter and applause. I thought afterwards: how could he have known that I was the smallest boy ever admitted to the school? Were records kept through all those centuries?

That wasn't to be the end of the taunting over my lack of inches, however. At the gym in the afternoon we were all required to strip to our shorts and vests and to run around in a circle. The PT master gradually pulled out normal-looking boys until only two of us were left: a very fat boy called Stubbs, whose bouncy breasts caused much amusement, and little me. He put his hand on my head and said: 'From now on this boy will be known as "Bruiser".'

I sometimes wonder what psychological effect these cruel barbs had on me. I wasn't greatly upset because of the lesson I had learned from watching my father talk to the giant footballer George Mason, a lesson which can be roughly summarised as: 'We may be shorter but we're just as good as the rest of them.'

But it may be no coincidence that I went on to make my mark on the school playing fields, especially at rugby. It was as though I had to prove myself in a physical way, to show that I was as tough, or even tougher, than the rest. It may also have sparked my ambition to be a pilot in the RAF. Who knows – if I had been left to myself and not singled out and mocked for my size, I might have eschewed virile pursuits and immersed myself in poetry or chamber music instead. I might have become a different man altogether.

Rick and I soon teamed up with two other boys, Ray Stone and Jack Pilbin, and over the next few years the four of us went on to dominate all the school sports teams, especially rugby, but also cricket and athletics. We went everywhere together and became well known as a quartet at school, at a church youth club and around the neighbourhood. As we all lived within a couple of streets of each other, we got to know each other's families too.

Rick's father had played centre-half for Blackburn Rovers and also appeared for Warwickshire at cricket. We went to watch him at Edgbaston after climbing aboard the train from Coventry as it slowed round a bend and stowing away until it reached New Street station in Birmingham, where we managed to slip through railings to avoid the guards. We had enough money to buy tickets for the game, but funded our lunch and return journey by collecting empty beer and lemonade bottles around the ground and returning them to a tent for two pence each.

Jack's father, a boozy though genial Geordie, took me to my first proper rugby match at Coundon Road, where I saw Coventry beat Aldershot Services by twenty-six points to three. I was hooked on the game for the rest of my life. Norman Pilbin took a shine to me and pronounced one day in front of the others: 'This is the one who'll go furthest in life. I'll bet he becomes the first Baron Radford [the suburb of Coventry in which we lived].' Sorry to have disappointed you, Norman.

Rick was a wing three-quarter, big and very fast; Jack a burly centre; while Ray and I built a close partnership at half-back – he as a talented stand-off and me as a nippy scrum-half. Ray and I developed such an intuitive understanding that I seemed able to find him with a pass wherever he was. All four of us went on to play for the county schools team and we all had trials for Coventry. Rick was the most successful, but the rest of us played rugby at a reasonable level.

When we were about seventeen, we started visiting country pubs – we had an older friend with an even older car. I still have a nightmare vision of several pints still waiting on a bar counter, with whisky chasers alongside, which I had to finish off or lose face with my mates. When I returned home and crept up to bed, I soon found I had to throw up. Alerted by the noise, my parents were standing outside the bathroom door in their dressing gowns when I emerged, with differing expressions on their faces.

My father, predictably, looked prim and rather shocked; my mother, however, seemed to have a smile close to the surface. When I tackled her about this some years later, she said: 'I was just so relieved to see that there was some Gilchrist in you and you weren't one of those strait-laced Trelfords.'

When I returned to Bablake for my last year, the headmaster asked to see me and walked me up the staircase to his room. He was a huge man called Seaborne, who seemed to model himself on Dr Arnold of Rugby School, swishing around the place in his gown as if Bablake was a grander school than it was – up there, if not with Eton and Harrow, then at least with places like Rugby.

'It would appear', he said, with ill-disguised reluctance, 'that I have no alternative but to make you head of the school. You were first in the public examinations, you are captain of cricket, editor of the school magazine, and you are the unanimous choice of the senior common room.' When we reached his office, he hinted at the source of his reservations: 'I want you to promise to get your hair cut. I don't want the captain of Bablake School looking like an advertisement for the Kleeneze brush company.'

He went on, as if musing to himself: 'Why is it that small men reach such positions of power? I'm thinking of people like Napoleon, Stalin, Hitler, Mussolini.' I was rather startled to find myself in such a galère of evil men, the last three of whom had died just a few years before.

I never got my hair cut short. Nor did I ever wear my school cap, which used to puzzle young boys when I punished them for failing to wear theirs.

The mention of the school magazine reminds me of the times I used to spend at the printer's, trying to put the edition together. Sometimes the printer would say to me: 'Don (I was always called Don, rather than Donald, until I joined *The Observer*), we're still a few inches short on this page,' and I would knock out a quick sonnet in biro on a scrap of paper to fit the page.

• • •

After school, I went into the RAF while Ray went to Imperial College in London and played rugby for Surrey. Whenever we were in Coventry we tried to get a game together for the Old Wheatleyans, the Bablake old boys' team. On one Saturday, however, Ray was due to play for nearby Kenilworth while I played for the Old Wheats. We arranged to meet after our respective games in Broadgate, the city centre, and go on to the pictures. I waited for over an hour for Ray, but he never turned up.

Or did he? At one point, as I was waiting, I was sure I saw him in a crowd of people that swept past me and went on through a passage at the side of the Owen Owen department store. He was wearing his usual raincoat. I shouted after him, but he didn't hear me. After a time, I gave up, bought a copy of the *Pink 'Un*, the *Coventry Evening Telegraph's* Saturday sports paper, and caught a bus back home.

Upstairs on the bus I looked up the reports of our matches. The report of Ray's match began: 'A minute's silence was observed before today's game in memory of the Kenilworth fly-half, Raymond Stone, aged twenty-one, who was killed last night when his car struck a tree near Stoneleigh Abbey.' I was naturally dumbfounded, not just by the tragic news itself, but by the fact that I had just seen him, or thought I had.

I know, I know, I was expecting to see him at any moment and was therefore easily misled into thinking I had seen him when somebody similar went by. My rational mind understands that, but part of me still says: 'I saw him. It was Ray.' When I wrote about this curious experience in *The Spectator* many years later, my story started being quoted in books about the paranormal. Alan Watkins, then my political columnist on *The Observer*, was heard to say: 'The editor's seeing ghosts.'

Jack Pilbin also met a tragic end. At the age of forty-five he hanged himself because he was hopelessly in debt. He didn't go gambling, so nobody, including the Coroner, could work out how his finances had got into such a terrible mess. I remember the night he met his wife. We had all gone to a Christmas dance where boys from Bablake and our rivals, King Henry VIII, mixed with girls from neighbouring schools. I met my first wife, Jan, at a similar dance when she was sixteen.

Jack was a rugged individual with a broken nose who smoked and swore a lot and seemed to model himself on Humphrey Bogart. We were all astonished when he took up with a girl from the local convent school who was simply exquisite. Neat, pretty and with the demeanour of a young nun, she seemed the very antithesis of everything about Jack Pilbin. Nonetheless, they married and were evidently happy until his sudden death.

I was driven up the M1 to his funeral from London by my *Observer* driver, Jimmy Rennie. We arrived late and joined the hundreds of people who couldn't get in to the overcrowded church and listened to the service through a loudspeaker outside. Jack had been a well-known Midlands rugby coach and I saw huge prop forwards crying uncontrollably. The irony was that a whip-round among these grieving friends would probably have solved the financial problem that drove Jack to his death.

Rick had suffered a serious back injury towards the end of his rugby career. My father had been one of the Red Cross ambulance volunteers who went on to the field to help carry him off during the match. The club doctor said to Rick in the dressing room: 'You'll probably be playing again within six weeks, but you'll really feel the effects of this injury in about thirty years' time.' Rick eventually contracted Parkinson's disease and died at seventy-four, leaving me as the only survivor of our schoolboy quartet.

●　●　●

When I went up from school for an interview at St Catharine's College, Cambridge, the cross-country trains from Coventry, via Bletchley, got me there several hours late, so that I missed my slot by a considerable margin. Undeterred by this, I turned up at the porter's lodge and said I had an appointment with Brigadier Henn, who was an English lecturer and also president of the college.

After knocking hesitantly on the door of his rooms, I heard a distant voice shout: 'Enter!' So I ventured into a large study, with books stacked to the ceiling on all the walls, to find it apparently empty. Then a booming voice asked: 'Who are you?' I managed to trace the voice to a bear of a man perched perilously on a ladder high up among the books.

When I explained who I was and how I had missed my interview that morning, I expected him to tell me to clear off. Instead, to my amazement, he recited the line, 'O lurcher-loving collier, black as night', then demanded that I finish the poem. Luckily, I was heavily into Auden at the time and was able to do as he asked.

Then came another quotation from the man on the ladder, whose face I still hadn't seen. '"There's no art to find the mind's construction in the face." What does the word "construction" mean in that sentence?' I recognised the line from *Macbeth* and explained that the word came from 'construe'. After a bit more of this literary ping-pong, he finally came down the ladder and shook my hand.

'I'm terribly sorry,' he said. 'I'm afraid we gave all our scholarships away this morning. But I know James Winny at Selwyn was very disappointed with his scholarship candidates today. I'll ask him over for tea to see if he has anything left. You wait outside.' In due course, Winny arrived, we had tea, and he offered me an Open Exhibition at Selwyn College without asking me a single question about English literature.

When I returned to school the next day, the headmaster called me in and said I had been offered a place at Pembroke College and an exhibition at Selwyn. He added: 'You will, of course, accept the kudos of the exhibition. I have informed the colleges accordingly.' He gave me a slip of paper saying that the school would have a day off in honour of my award. I had to carry this message round the school to be read out in every classroom. The clapping and cheers this evoked were some compensation, I reflected, for the mocking laughter that had greeted me on my first day at the school.

•   •   •

I was to enjoy the lectures of T. R. Henn, especially on his fellow Irishman Yeats, when I eventually got to Cambridge two years later, after my National Service, though he was treated as a bit of a joke by some students for his portentous voice and brisk military manner. He was described by F. R. Leavis as 'the red-faced brigadier of King's Parade'.

On one occasion, when Henn was lecturing on T. S. Eliot's *The Waste Land*, some loose pages from the ancient paperback book he was quoting from fell to the floor. This brought sniggering laughter from his listeners. I shall never forget the old Brigadier's response as he looked up from his haunches while gathering up the missing pages. 'You may laugh,' he cried in a passionate voice that was close to tears, 'but this was all that held body and soul together during the war.' The laughter stopped.

Over the years I have acquired more knowledge of life and learning from friends, who might be described these days as my gurus, rather than from my nominated teachers. At school it was Ken Osborne, another of my very tall friends, who introduced me to reading *The Observer*. He won a history scholarship to Oxford after writing an essay titled 'Red

Indians' that described the threat of Communism on the Indian sub-continent. He emigrated to Canada and I never saw him again.

In the RAF, I had a brief acquaintance in the officers' mess with David Raven, who was soon after released from National Service through the efforts of Edward Heath, then the government Chief Whip and a family friend of his from Broadstairs. My conversations with David in the mess bar and in our rooms were effectively tutorials, and when he resumed his research at Oxford and became Dean of Trinity College, I called on him later while I was at Cambridge. David was a sensitive soul who was never suited to the military life. He later committed suicide while teaching at the King's School, Canterbury, which, several decades later, was attended by my daughter Laura.

David told me that Heath had fallen in love with his sister Kay and they had been expected to marry. In the end, fed up with waiting, she had married someone else. Heath apparently kept a photograph of Kay Raven by his bedside until the day he died. In those days, of course, homosexuality was a crime and rarely talked about. David didn't say that Heath was gay; just that he wasn't 'the marrying kind'. He believed Heath had considered marrying Kay to assist his political career, dithered about it, then decided against it on the grounds that it would be a dishonest and ignoble thing to do to someone he really cared about.

In my first term at Selwyn, I was invited for a coffee in the rooms of a tall, rather tortured-looking student with a big nose and floppy black hair. He admitted afterwards that he had been attracted by my looks – he swung both ways, as they say – but had realised at our first meeting that I was as straight as an architect's ruler. Christopher Dixon and I became good friends, to the extent that Richard Harries, later the Bishop of Oxford, said of us: 'We used to watch in awe as Christopher and Donald walked round the quad deep in conversation, wondering what they were discussing. They were both much cleverer than the rest of us.'

That was certainly true of Dixon, who got a First in part one of the English Tripos, then a starred First in part two of the moral sciences

Tripos, a two-year course which he completed in a year. I couldn't have dreamt of getting a First without Dixon as my guru. At Oakham School and later as a subaltern in the Sherwood Foresters, he had amassed a formidable knowledge of literature and philosophy, which he took no pains to hide, often to his tutors' discomfort.

He once took me along for moral support to a lecture given by John Wisdom, the professor of philosophy, because he believed he had spotted a logical flaw in one of his books. When he put the point to Wisdom at the end of the lecture, he was invited to discuss the matter in his rooms at Trinity College. Again, I went with him for moral support.

As we climbed the unlit stone steps to his rooms and knocked on his door, there was no reply. We waited a while, then heard a heavy tread coming up the stairs and a voice coming out of the darkness asking us our business. When Christopher explained that we were there to visit Professor Wisdom, the voice boomed: 'I am Wisdom,' which was evidently a practised response that he enjoyed saying. I can't now remember the outcome of the philosophical debate, but I do remember noting with surprise that the venerable philosopher read the *Daily Express*.

One evening, Dixon decided to trace the concept in Shakespeare that beautiful women have a duty to bequeath their beauty – essentially the parable of the talents – and found a date when the bard had heard this theme in a sermon in London. He then produced a long sheet, the pages stuck together into a roll, tracing the theme through all the plays and sonnets from that date onwards. It was virtually a doctoral thesis produced in a single night.

He woke me at around 7 a.m. by throwing pebbles at my bedroom window and took me through his findings. He asked me to accompany him to visit James Winny at Selwyn. The English tutor, probably fed up with being disturbed so early, was unimpressed. He made a single laconic comment: 'The problem with you, Dixon, is that you've had too much Kant and too little c***.'

I was able to perform one single service in return for the many lessons Dixon had taught me. I enabled him to meet his future wife,

Christine, who worked as a staff nurse at Addenbrooke's Hospital. I used to smoke a bit in those days and lit up as we left the college hall after dinner. There was nowhere to dump the match, so I put it back in the Swan Vestas box. The next minute my right hand was on fire. Dixon, who loved a drama, summoned an ambulance and off we sped to Addenbrooke's, where Christine happened to be on duty.

He had actually met her before through a doctor he knew at the hospital, but hadn't built up the courage to ask her out. Later I met the doctor friend at a party and heard him say to someone: 'If you are ever in doubt on a question of taste or etiquette...' (the subject under discussion was whether coloured wine glasses were ever acceptable) '...just ask yourself this: would the Queen do it?'

Christine was a very attractive brunette with an extremely posh accent, so I was surprised to discover, when I attended their wedding in Leicester, that she came from the same kind of lower-middle-class family that I did. Christopher, using the pseudonym Matthew Vaughan, went on to write three novels, the first of which, *Chalky*, won the David Higham Prize for Fiction in 1975.

He was an inspirational teacher at a number of schools, including City of London, where he taught Julian Barnes, and Eton, where Charles Moore and Earl Spencer were among his pupils. After a spell in the United States, he became headmaster of Cobham Hall in Kent before ending up at Radley College, where he and his wife lived a hermetic existence. Later, Christopher died and Christine survived in what appears to have been a suicide pact.

● ● ●

I must be the last journalist ever to have got a job by simply walking down a street and seeing a sign in an office window saying: 'Reporter Wanted – Apply Upstairs.' I was in my last long vacation from Cambridge and wandering aimlessly around Coventry city centre when I saw the sign. I opened the door to a winding staircase and fetched up outside a door marked: 'Editor: Captain Edgar Letts.' This was only a decade or so after the war and many former officers hung on to their military ranks.

I straightened my tie, tidied my hair and knocked on the door. 'Come in,' cried a brisk, military voice. As I stood in front of his desk, I suppressed a sudden urge to salute him. 'Who are you?' he asked. When I told him who I was, careful to mention the RAF and Cambridge, he visibly relaxed.

After a few more questions, he barked: 'Right, you're on. Eight pounds a week.' I was rather startled by this and it must have shown on my face, for he went on, obviously thinking I was disappointed with the wages on offer: 'Did you, by any chance, hold the Queen's Commission?' When I said I had been a pilot officer, wondering what on earth this had to do with anything, he beamed and said: 'Well, in that case it will be ten quid a week.'

I went downstairs to meet the other few members of staff and confided to one: 'I didn't tell Captain Letts that I'm only on vacation from university and will have to leave in a couple of months.' The reporter replied: 'I shouldn't worry about that. Nobody here lasts that long anyway.' One who didn't last was a woman who wrote a jokey headline on a page proof above a picture of a church fete: 'Fete Worse Than Death.' She never intended it to go in the paper but, sadly for her, it did.

It was rumoured that the chief reporter, a racy Scotsman who covered theatre as well as several other subjects on the weekly paper, as we all did, had a habit of tempting actresses back to its Dickensian offices from the green room at the then newly opened Belgrade Theatre. He would write his review of the show, and especially her performance, while she hung around the otherwise empty newsroom.

Legend has it that he kept a blow-up mattress in a cupboard on which the actresses were invited to return the favour of a rave review. After writing the puff, he would take the mattress out of the cupboard and blow it up: whether he had any puff left for anything else is not recorded.

He left the paper suddenly in unexplained circumstances and I later heard that he had become a highly paid press officer with the United Nations in the Congo. I hoped he fared better in the Congo than a boy in my class at school who had gone out as a missionary and ended up dead and reportedly eaten.

The Scotsman's successor as chief reporter was sacked a few days later when the editor caught him with a bottle of port on his desk. That is how I became chief reporter after only three weeks on the paper. It was this that decided me to become a journalist: as Malcolm Muggeridge famously said, it was better than working. I wonder, though, how many journalists would have survived in Fleet Street, then or now, if they had had to pass a breath test after lunch (me included).

• • •

My life might have taken a completely different turn if I had succeeded with two job applications when I left Cambridge. One was to become a graduate trainee at the BBC. The interviewer was called Brian Batchelor and we seemed to get off on the wrong foot from the start. He asked me: 'Are you an optimist or a pessimist?', which struck me as a pretty pointless question.

So, I replied – cheekily, even arrogantly, as it might seem now – by saying: 'I'm not an optimist if that's the kind of question you want me to answer.' His face showed that he wasn't impressed with this young Oxbridge smartass. A friend told me afterwards that he would have replied differently: 'An optimist can be defined as the only man in the room who hasn't heard the bad news.'

The other interview was for a job with *The Guardian*, which had only just ceased to be called the *Manchester Guardian* and moved its head office to London. The interview took place in Cambridge with two genial and long-serving *Guardian* figures, Patrick Monkhouse and Harry Whewell, and I left with the strong impression that I had a good chance of securing one of the two traineeships on offer. When I mentioned that I had done some summer work on the *Coventry Standard*, they asked me to send them some cuttings.

This is where it all went wrong. I rang my mother, who got in touch with the *Standard* office and asked them to send her a collection of my articles, which she could then post on to Manchester. Unfortunately, they sent the clippings of somebody else; there were no bylines in the paper and my mother wouldn't have known who had written what. They belonged to the racy Scotsman, whose tabloid writing style clearly failed to commend itself to the *Guardian* talent scouts.

In due course, I received a long and rather puzzled letter from Harry Whewell saying that I had seemed just right for the paper when they met me, but that unfortunately another candidate had pipped me for the job. I only discovered the error over the clippings when they were sent back to my mother and I saw them while visiting her in Coventry. I decided not to tell her. As a result, I was to start my career in journalism on the other side of the Pennines.

• • •

At Cambridge, I had written for *Varsity*, mostly on sport ('Don Trelford reporting'), and told my tutor that I wanted to become a journalist. The tutor had evidently conveyed this to the University Appointments Board and the next thing I knew I had received a letter at my Cambridge digs from the Thomson Organisation, enclosing a railway voucher and inviting me for an interview in London about becoming a graduate trainee.

When I arrived at their Gray's Inn Road headquarters, I was asked to use the tradesman's entrance at the back rather than the swanky main reception area, so my expectations of the visit were not high. I was met there by a man called Wenbourne, who was evidently impressed enough by my flimsy credentials to show me in to see C. D. Hamilton, who was editorial director of Thomson's rapidly expanding group of regional papers at the time.

This was in 1961. Later that year, Hamilton was to become editor-in-chief of *The Times* and *Sunday Times*, two years after Roy (later Lord) Thomson had bought the newspaper group from Lord Kemsley, for whom Hamilton had been a sort of chief of staff since the end of the war. When I saw him for my interview, he was still running the regional papers.

He was a tall, dark, trim-looking figure with neatly combed hair, dressed in an immaculate double-breasted pin-striped suit, which I wouldn't have known where to buy even if I could have afforded one. He wore a military moustache that reminded one of his distinguished war career on Field Marshal Montgomery's staff as the youngest brigadier in the British Army.

It was a strange interview, in that Hamilton said virtually nothing throughout, just stared down at my application form on his desk, hardly looking at me. I learned later that that was his style, allowing the other party to the interview to babble away and thereby reveal oneself. After several long, embarrassing silences, he finally looked at a map of Britain on the office wall, on which all the Thomson regional offices were marked with a star. Finally, after looking several times between me and the map, he uttered the single word: 'Sheffield.'

This, I gathered, meant that, when I left Cambridge in the summer, I was to become a Thomson graduate trainee on the *Sheffield Morning Telegraph*. I worked there, learning the nuts and bolts of the newspaper business, for a couple of years. I arrived early for my first day and was met by Gordon (later Sir Gordon) Linacre, then editor of the *Star*, the evening paper, who asked me into his office.

When I told him my background, he replied: 'If you want to be a success in journalism you must forget everything – and I mean everything – you learned at Cambridge University.' I reflected afterwards that he was wrong about this. Some of the things I learned at Cambridge were to prove extremely useful: how to play cards, chat people up and hold my drink, for example.

I never thought of myself as ambitious, but it became clear that others did. Two incidents on the *Sheffield Telegraph* come to mind. One was when I accidentally overheard a conversation in the office canteen between the news editor, Michael Finley (later the editor), and Howard Green (father of Conservative minister Damian Green), who was a newspaper manager from Wales doing a stint as a journalist in Sheffield as part of his training.

I suddenly realised they were talking about me. Green said: 'Young Trelford is only twenty-three – just imagine where he'll be when he's thirty-three.' I was astonished to hear this, but in fact, as it turned out, I became deputy editor of *The Observer* at thirty-one.

The other conversation took place at the Royal Festival Hall in London, where I had gone from Sheffield with two colleagues to hear a concert by the Russian cellist, Rostropovich. The colleagues were Tony Tweedale, the paper's film critic, and Michael Ratcliffe, who went on to hold senior posts in the arts and books sections of *The Observer* and the *Sunday Times*.

In the drinks interval, one of them said I was bound to become a national newspaper editor, to which I replied: 'I'm not ambitious. I just like to have things done my way.' At this they laughed and said: 'You idiot! That's what ambition *is*.'

I was sitting at my desk at the Sheffield paper one day when Tweedale came into the office, very excited about a fire that had broken out at the cinema where he was due to attend a preview. Seeing the editor, Bill Lyth, in the newsroom, he approached him and spoke in a rather camp fashion: 'Mr Lyth, I think I may have one of those scoop things.' The editor politely listened to the story and told him to go away and write it. Then he turned to the news editor and said with a curled lip: 'Get that fat bastard out on the road.'

• • •

I spent some time as a leader writer, working in tandem with Peter Tinniswood, who went on to become a successful writer of comic books, like *Tales from a Long Room*, and television sit-coms such as *I Didn't Know You Cared*. I once had a hilarious dinner in Manchester with Peter and his friend and fellow script writer David Nobbs, creator of *The Fall and Rise of Reginald Perrin*. He also came to see me much later at *The Observer*, still smoking the filthy pipe that caused his early death.

The editor of the *Sheffield Telegraph* when I joined, the aforementioned Mr Lyth, prided himself on having once been art editor of the *Daily Sketch*. I was surprised to find him one evening counting up the toilet rolls in a cupboard in the gents' lavatory. By way of explanation, he said: 'We've got to find ways to cut back on editorial spending.'

He used to take great pride in mixing with the great and the good of the city in the Sheffield Club or at ceremonial dinners in the Cutlers' Hall. He would come back to the office in high spirits, having had a good dinner, usually with gravy stains on his waistcoat to prove it. Tinniswood and I used to take turns: one of us would be in the pub while the other hung around waiting for the editor's return.

On one particular night, it was my turn to wait in the office while Tinniswood went to the pub. The editor summoned me with an air of suppressed excitement. 'My friends and I', he said, pausing for me to take in just how important his friends were, 'have decided that the World's Fair shall come to Sheffield. It is your great good fortune, Trelford, to write a front-page editorial about this historic moment for tonight's paper. I'm going home now, but I look forward to reading it in the morning. I'll give you the headline: Sheffield – Centre of the Universe.'

I sat at my typewriter struggling with this bizarre assignment. In the end, I came up with something like: 'It is Sheffield steel that makes the tanks that fight wars for freedom around the globe … It is Sheffield steel…' etc, etc. As I sat there at my typewriter I made a silent vow that one day I too would become an editor and I too would return to the office from my club with gravy stains on my waistcoat and then go home after ordering some other poor blighter to write my editorials.

Mr Lyth was pleased with my offering and even more pleased when the *Yorkshire Post*, a great rival, wrote a front-page editorial mocking Sheffield's pretensions. He came by my desk, showed me the *Yorkshire Post* and said: 'Tonight, Trelford, you will write another front-page editorial. It will begin like this: "A Leeds-based newspaper has this to say about your great city…"'

The to-and-fro between the two cities went on for several days. At a party some years later, I was talking to Hugo Young, then deputy editor of the *Sunday Times,* later a columnist on *The Guardian* and eventually chairman of the Scott Trust that owned the paper. I recalled this amusing story about the enmity between Sheffield and Leeds, knowing that he came from a prominent Sheffield family and had worked on the *Yorkshire Post*.

He looked at me in astonishment and said: 'It was me writing those *Yorkshire Post* editorials. I've always wondered who was championing Sheffield. So, it was you!'

We had a talented group of graduate trainees on the Sheffield paper, including Michael Ratcliffe, John Barry, who was to be a key figure on Harold Evans's *Sunday Times*, and Jackie Gillott, later a novelist and TV presenter. Sadly, Jackie was to become the fourth of my early friends to take their own lives.

During my time there, the *Telegraph* and Lyth's successor as editor, David Hopkinson, picked up a number of national press awards for exposing what became known as 'the Sheffield rhino whip scandal'. CID officers were shown to have taken suspects into a dark alley outside the station and applied the said rhino whip in order to force confessions.

The hero of this campaign was Keith Graves, who went on to become a star foreign correspondent for the BBC. My humble role in the matter was writing editorials deploring the police conduct and demanding an inquiry. Hopkinson, a fine journalist from whom I learned a great deal, went on to become a long-serving executive at *The Times*.

● ● ●

Late one evening, after a visit to the pub, Tinniswood and I decided to break into the editor's empty office. As I recall, our object was to get hold of some bottles of wine and spirits and boxes of chocolates, which had been confiscated by the editor from the desk of the women's editor. He evidently thought she shouldn't accept what he considered to be bribes from the companies she wrote about.

Among the assorted papers we found on his desk – and read unashamedly – was a letter from the head office of the Thomson Organisation seeking candidates within the group to edit a newspaper they owned in Nyasaland. I seized the opportunity to apply for the job, which I might never have heard about if it hadn't been for this illicit nocturnal invasion.

CHAPTER 3

KAMUZU

I had barely heard of Nyasaland when I went out to edit the country's English-language newspaper. I was twenty-five and the youngest editor of a national newspaper in the world. I knew Nyasaland was somewhere in Central Africa, that it had some association with Dr Livingstone (I presumed) and a famous lake. I didn't even know if the country had electricity. As I was likely to be living there for several years, I decided to find out a little more. So, I rang up the Foreign and Commonwealth Office in London.

A gloomy official voice told me, after a worrying silence: 'I think you should read this morning's newspapers. The Prime Minister, Dr Banda, has some very unpleasant things to say about foreign journalists in Nyasaland – as a matter of fact, he wants them all to leave. If you still want to go, I'd be glad to tell you more about the situation. But I warn you: it isn't very nice.'

That was my first introduction to the problems of the press in Nyasaland. The gloomy voice on the telephone had been right: it wasn't very nice. That very day, Dr Banda had warned foreign journalists to 'keep their white noses' out of his country's affairs – a phrase I was to hear again, at close quarters, in the period ahead. He wanted to take Nyasaland out of Sir Roy Welensky's Central African Federation and make his country self-governing and independent.

When I applied for the post within the Thomson group, I was interviewed by Gordon (later Sir Gordon) Brunton, who was to be a recurring figure in my life. He told me that the main reason I was being appointed was that I was just about the only suitably qualified journalist they could find in the group who believed that Africans should run their own countries – not a universally popular idea in the England of the early 1960s.

He explained that the Thomson group owned a prosperous publishing business in Nyasaland, with bookshops and a magazine distribution network, but the newspaper's unpopularity with Dr Banda was putting the whole enterprise at risk. It was important that the newspaper change its character and win the approval of the new black government.

While I was with him, Lord (Roy) Thomson, the owner of the group, came into his office and Brunton introduced me. Thomson stood close to me, clutched my hand tightly, examined me through his thick pebble glasses and said: 'You make a dollar for me, boy, and I'll make a dollar for you.'

I had only been married for a few months, but my wife was enthusiastic about the prospect of an African adventure, however risky, as opposed to teaching in a tough Sheffield comprehensive school where all the pupils wanted to talk about was the Beatles.

● ● ●

The *Nyasaland Times* had started life in 1895 as the *Central African Planter*, providing news for the tea and tobacco settlers. It had later become the *Central African Times*, and was still popularly known by its initials as the *CAT*. When I got there, I found one banner headline that ran: 'Dr Banda Gets Really Nasty with the *CAT*. He Called Us Stupid Thirty-Five Times'. After reading a few back issues of the paper, I came to the conclusion that Dr Banda was probably right in the low view he held of the paper.

It was still defending the Central African Federation, run by whites in Salisbury, long after the cause had been abandoned in London and rejected by the Africans of Northern Rhodesia and Nyasaland; the blacks in Southern Rhodesia weren't even asked. The federation was dead, finished. It didn't need a constitutional genius to see that the country's only possible future was as an independent sovereign state under Banda's leadership. So, it seemed to me, one either got on with Banda, or one did not get on at all.

Before daring to approach him, however, I decided to make an impression in the way I knew best – through the newspaper – to demonstrate that my arrival really did represent a total change of out-look. I recruited the paper's first African reporters, and wrote the first leading article the paper had dared to carry for more than a year. I published it on the front page.

'The *CAT* has lived several different lives since it began in 1895, and the time has come to give it a new one,' I wrote. 'In the rapidly changing conditions, the newspaper has failed to adapt its outlook to the needs of the times.'

I deplored the absence of editorial opinions at such an historic moment in the new country's life and continued:

> We have decided to set off in a new direction, with a new name, and
> a policy more in line with the aspirations of the people … As the only
> independent newspaper in Nyasaland, we are conscious of our great re-
> sponsibility, and we propose to do our best to discharge our obligations
> to the concept of a fair, honest and responsible press.

To my surprise, this editorial was quoted widely throughout Africa and in British newspapers. I still have a copy of a front-page story in the *Daily Telegraph* about my changes to this obscure Nyasaland paper. I soon found I was being invited to official Malawi functions, and the paper was quoted approvingly by African MPs in Parliament – though, perhaps as a corollary, I was blackballed at the British club.

A South African magazine, *News Check*, wrote an article about the paper at this time entitled: '*CAT* on a Hot Tin Roof'. It reported:

'Trelford's editorship has been a saga of tenuous survival in a hostile and threatening environment.' Funny how that word 'survival', written more than fifty years ago, would continue to be mentioned as a key feature of my entire career as an editor. For 'Dr Banda' read 'Tiny Rowland', two decades later, when he became my boss at *The Observer* – another 'saga of tenuous survival in a hostile and threatening environment'. The magazine went on to say: 'For almost the first time, reading the *Nyasaland Times* openly has become a fashion among educated Africans.'

I decided that the time was now right to make my peace with Dr Banda. His waiting room in Zomba was lined with Morley's *Life of William Ewart Gladstone* in many volumes, as well as books on de Gaulle, Churchill and other Western heroes. He was calm and utterly courteous, dressed in a Savile Row suit with a waistcoat, and dark glasses. 'Your paper has changed,' he said, 'and I welcome that. But can the leopard really change its spots?'

I told him that, as an Englishman, I felt I was an historical anomaly in his country. I was a guest and guests had to meet certain standards of conduct if they were to remain welcome. All this sort of thing went down quite well, as you might expect. But then I said, trying to be helpful: 'I think it is wrong for a European to edit an African newspaper. I hope that by the time I leave I shall have trained an African to succeed me.' I meant it, and I thought he would be pleased.

Instead, he looked at me strangely for a long time, then said slowly: 'You must not insult my intelligence. No African in this country will be capable of running a newspaper in less than fifty years.' This remark has always intrigued me – not just because he was so manifestly wrong, and insulting the intelligence of his own people, but because it provided a clue to Banda's curious personality. He did not really regard himself as an African; he talked about Africans as another race and obviously saw himself, judging from his library alone, as part of a European tradition going back to Churchill and de Gaulle.

A story comes to mind that demonstrates the power – and the eccentricity – of Banda's personality. It was the opening of the University of Malawi (Nyasaland's new name after independence). It was a cold afternoon, and we sat in our thousands to hear Banda speak. He was dressed in the academic robes he had acquired at universities in Scotland and America and he spoke without notes for over two hours.

The assembled dignitaries could hardly believe their ears when he started to take them through the whole of an English language textbook (still without notes), starting at chapter one and going right through the parts of speech, transitive and intransitive verbs, proper nouns, common nouns, objects in sentences, and so on – even giving examples to illustrate every point. As my wife muttered afterwards, the only chapter he had plainly missed was the one on precis.

This grammatical tour de force was climaxed by a ringing declamation of the best of Churchill's wartime broadcasts, all by heart. The audience of invited academics, Western diplomats and illiterate Malawi peasants all looked at him with equal amazement.

Once I had established a working relationship with Banda, and set the paper on its new course, it became clear to me that I was living in a time of hope and great excitement. I had left England at the fag end of the Macmillan era, amid the Profumo scandal and a general air of decadence and demoralisation. Here, however, I was at the birth of a new nation, offering scope for youthful ideals.

I threw my paper wholeheartedly behind this new national mood, keeping up the flow of front-page editorials, and I gave African reporters increasing prominence in the paper. Three of them turned out to be outstandingly good. I don't know where they had learned their idea of how a journalist should look and behave – from Chicago films of the 1930s I should think, to judge by their snap-brim hats and their wise-cracking. They were characters straight out of Ben Hecht's *The Front Page*.

Austin M'Madi had worked on papers in Southern Rhodesia and was a fairly sophisticated operator by Malawi standards. I can remember interviewing him for the job and asking where his family came from. With immense pride, he told me: 'My mother is kachasu queen of Zingwangwa.' Kachasu is a lethal African gin and Zingwangwa is an African suburb of Blantyre-Limbe. In the social hierarchy of the time, she was a very important lady indeed.

Roy Manda was a highly intelligent sub-editor with excellent English who, with training, could have held down a job on any paper in the world. Levson Lifikilo was our ace football reporter, with an immense following, judging by the letters I received.

At the time, I had not realised what a dramatic innovation it would seem to give African reporters a chance to write in their own country. It was not a racial or political gesture on my part, however, but a professional decision: Africans knew what was going on in their country, they spoke the language, they had access to places that white reporters couldn't go.

The changes in the paper were again noted by the South African magazine *News Check*, which remarked: 'The change has picked up the *Times*'s ailing fortunes. With ruin and closure hanging over it a year ago, the paper is fattening once again. Since Trelford's dramatic editorial, circulation has gone up over 30 per cent and advertising has risen over 20 per cent.'

All this was true enough – or nearly true, as I found out a little later. I went on a circulation tour, using a small plane, to the remote parts of the country. In the very north, close to the border with Tanzania, was a small town on the lake. The main road – the only road – lay between two lines of houses, some of them Asian shops. It was covered in grass. I steered the plane down on the street between the houses, causing some excitement – not only to the spectators. I particularly wanted to visit this place because we seemed to be selling a remarkable number of papers there. So many, in fact, that the local African agent had qualified several times for the bicycle I was offering as a reward for enterprise.

I found this wizard salesman in his small hut by the lake, where he told me his secret. The retail price of the paper was three pence. As an agent, he got it wholesale for two pence, then separated the sheets of paper and sold each double-page spread for a penny to the local fishermen, who used them to wrap up their fish. It was the only source of paper in the area. With any bits that were left over, he cut out the pictures, especially pictures of Dr Banda or the Queen, and sold them to the villagers as decorations for their huts. He was making a fortune: and not a single copy of the paper, as far as I could see, was being read.

Now, every editor has to get used to the idea that his paper will wrap tomorrow's fish and chips – but not today's, and not before the paper has even been read. What could I do about this appalling situation? I decided to do nothing about it, and flew out the next day, leaving the agent secure with his secret monopoly. After all, he was happy enough, his customers were happy, and I was happy to be selling so many papers. The only people who would not be happy were the advertisers, who were paying good money on the assumption that the paper was actually being read. I decided that the truth might upset them, so I kept it to myself.

This was not the only way in which running a newspaper in Africa turned out to be different from what I was used to in Britain. It is the usual practice on newspapers in the UK, for example, to prepare for the death of famous men by having an obituary notice written in advance. I found there were none at the *Nyasaland Times*, so I had a biography of Dr Banda quickly prepared and sent out to the printing works for setting into type.

After a while, the head printer came to see me. 'You'd better go out and have a look,' he said. I went into the printing works and found that all the African workers had abandoned their jobs and were leaning over the machine of the operator who had been given this story to set. They were reading it with mounting amazement and muttering among themselves.

'What's the matter?' I said. Eventually one of them came up to me and explained. 'This article is about the death of Dr Banda. They think this is very bad magic. They think you must want him to die, and if he does die, they are afraid that they will be blamed.' On reflection, I decided that this was a healthy attitude – more healthy, perhaps, than our own.

• • •

I said that the paper had been founded in 1895. The printing works seemed to go back at least that far. The printing plant consisted entirely of museum pieces, and when one machine broke down one day, I wrote off to seek a spare part. Eventually, I got a reply from the manufacturers, explaining that that particular machine had ceased being made in Chicago in 1906.

In my final weeks in Sheffield, before setting out for Africa, I had been working the late shift in the composing room, which meant that there wasn't much for the printers to do as they hung around waiting until the early hours in case there was sensational news story that required changing the paper. I had taken in copies of my African paper for them to see. The type-faces were all broken from cracked wooden type, so they suggested an alternative that I should take with me to Africa. They cast the letters of the alphabet in Century Bold, down from seventy-two point to thirty-six point, then put them together in a chase (a page in a metal forme) and converted the metal into papier-mâché flongs, which were used as part of the printing process.

I took a dozen flongs with me in a suitcase to Nyasaland, where they were recast into metal and cut up into individual letters. It had a revivifying effect on the look of the paper. It occurs to me now that very few journalists in this digital age – certainly none under the age of forty – will have the slightest idea what I am talking about. But I'm sure that old hands like Harold Evans, Peter Preston and Paul Dacre would be impressed – as would my former managing editor, Jeremy Hunt, who qualified as a printer before becoming a journalist.

The wages paid in the printing works were shamefully low – some operators getting about £5 a month. With the rising expectations created by their new-found political consciousness, it was only a matter of time before we had wage demands and other industrial problems on the *Nyasaland Times*. The situation came to a head when one of the European supervisors was accused of racism. The Africans said he had insulted them, talking to them as if they were monkeys and asking them when they had 'come down from the trees'. They refused to work with him and insisted that he be sacked. I was summoned from my editorial office to help break the deadlock.

It was midday and very hot. We all trooped out into the yard – about 120 angry Africans and me. They fetched a stool for me to sit on, and crouched on the ground all around me. It was to be a traditional African *indaba*. One by one, they stood up to say their piece. The senior African printer did the translating, but I did not need the translation to judge their mood.

It went on for two hours in the hot sun. At the end, the senior man said I had heard their case: I must decide what to do. They would accept my decision, but tradition required me to give my judgement immediately, without consulting anyone else. I gave my judgement: the offender would leave, but only when arrangements had been made for his successor; meanwhile, they must work as normal. I would personally conduct an inquiry into their wage rates, with a view to correcting anomalies, but they must accept my verdict.

I also announced that they must throw away the old oil cans out of which they drank their tea, and the company would provide them with decent mugs. We would also supply them with a bag of maize for their lunch. These primitive proposals, like something out of Victorian England, were received with great applause. This was my first and last excursion into industrial relations in Africa. How unlike – how very unlike – the life I was to find in dear old Fleet Street.

● ● ●

The independence celebrations in July 1963 came and went in a mood of national euphoria. Prince Philip flew over, along with many heads

of state; I had a desultory conversation with a surprisingly shy Moshe
Dayan; there were fireworks and football matches; everything seemed
to be going perfectly. Then, suddenly, one month after independence,
it all changed.

In August 1964, the bulk of the Cabinet revolted against Dr Banda
because they thought he was too autocratic. They also claimed to be
ashamed, as African nationalists, that Banda insisted on trading with
South Africa and the Portuguese colony of Mozambique, arguing that,
as a landlocked country, he had no choice and would trade with the
devil if it helped to feed his people.

Banda, seeing that he had lost the confidence of his Cabinet ministers,
was inclined to resign, but the Governor, Sir Glyn Jones, urged him to test
his popularity by holding an emergency vote of confidence in Parliament
instead. This took place – a very dramatic day in the history of Malawi –
and the culmination was that he got an overwhelming vote of support.

I was present that day in the Malawi Parliament. The atmosphere
was electric. Banda himself arrived early, sat rigid in his seat all day,
and when his turn came to speak he turned on his enemies with such
violent vituperation that they physically cowered. It was a performance
of staggering personal power. He rounded on his critics one by one,
summoning up every insult he had ever heard about them, clearly hitting home with many of the barbs, as the MPs roared their approval all
around him. He won hands down. But the national mood was broken:
the slow descent into dictatorship had begun.

Banda had sacked the rebel ministers and won a vote of confidence.
But what would the ministers do next? They scattered to their home
districts, and the country waited to see if they would take up arms
against him. It was in this period of uncertainty that my newspaper
was to play its most important role. Even Banda didn't know what
was going on. The people certainly didn't. I asked my staff who they
thought would win a civil war: Banda or the rebels? My white reporters
and commercial staff all said the rebels would win: the black employees, down to the man who swept my office floor, all said Banda.

For further advice, I went to see the Governor. He played me a recording of the latest Cabinet meeting (in English because that was their only common language), from which it was clear that Banda was in fighting form and the rebels were in retreat. So I decided that the paper would support the side that was going to win – not so much out of principle as pragmatism, I have to admit.

The key man in the opposition to Banda was Henry Chipembere, the only one of the rebels with a national following. He was a powerful orator, and a highly educated man, having been to universities in South Africa and California. Banda was desperate to keep Chipembere on his side – so much so that he called me to his office one day and gave me a letter that Chipembere had sent to him only a few weeks before, in which the rebel minister had addressed Banda as 'my father' and professed his undying support for the leader. Banda wanted me to publish this letter as evidence of Chipembere's loyalty. I did publish it, but I retained some doubts as to whether Banda could count on that loyalty much longer.

Then we got word that Chipembere was to address a meeting of his followers in his home town of Fort Johnston, near Lake Nyasa, about 120 miles south of Blantyre. This raised a number of problems for me. For a start, Banda had issued some emergency laws, making it an offence (punishable by five years in jail) to publish any material 'likely to undermine public confidence in the government'. The next problem was that Chipembere spoke in a local dialect called Yao. Fortunately, Austin M'Madi spoke this dialect, and so did another African on the staff. I sent them off, with instructions to take down every word that Chipembere spoke, then report back to me.

They returned, covered in dust, with their notebooks overflowing. I made them sit down and translate the whole thing into English for me. It was plain that Chip was throwing down the gauntlet. He had attacked Banda, as the Americans would say, on the issues, but he had held back from personal abuse. I judged that Chipembere was staking out his ground very carefully. He had not broken completely with Banda, but the gap was widening fast. I decided to publish.

As it happened, Banda himself had made a major speech that day, so I thought it would be prudent to lead the paper on that, and, knowing his vanity, I also ran a big picture of him. Under the Banda story, I ran a short factual precis of the Chipembere speech. The paper went out on the streets and we waited to see what would happen. The paper sold out almost straight away. Africans were grabbing them and folding the front page over to read the Chipembere story at the bottom, then rushing off to show their friends. It was Chipembere, not Banda, they wanted to read about, teaching me an important lesson about journalism: news is what governments don't want people to read.

After a short while, the telephone rang in my office. The Prime Minister would see me immediately. I rang my wife and warned her that we might have to pack in a hurry. Banda was more agitated than I had ever seen him. He was angry that I had reported Chipembere's speech, and yet he wanted to know exactly what he had said. At one point, he poked my chest in rage: 'Keep out of my politics, white man!' He told me not to report rebel speeches.

I tried to reason with him, pointing out that his Malawi Congress Party controlled all the other media outlets, and they did not mention the rebels. Yet everyone wanted to know what Chipembere was saying: if I did not tell them, in a straightforward, factual, unsensational way, the Africans would hear things by word of mouth, in the form of rumours that might be untrue or exaggerated. By the skin of my teeth, I won the right to carry on. But it was a close-run thing. The last words he hurled at my back as I left his office were: 'Watch it, white man.'

I returned to my office feeling rather shaken, in time for the telephone to ring again. This time it was Chipembere. Every word of our conversation is clear in my memory.

'Is that Bwana Times? Chipembere here.' He was using the African word 'bwana', meaning 'master', ironically. He went on: 'I didn't like the report you gave of my speech today. I thought it deserved more prominence.'

'I already gave it more prominence than was good for me,' I replied.

'Yes, I would expect the powers that be to bring pressure to bear on you. But I wouldn't like you to think they're the only people who can bring pressure to bear.'

I asked rather nervously: 'What do you mean, Mr Chipembere?'

'I'm sure you wouldn't like me to lead a boycott of your paper among the Africans, or for anything to happen to your precious printing machinery.'

There followed a long pause while I swallowed hard.

'I'm sure you're above that sort of thing, Mr Chipembere.'

His turn for a long pause. Then: 'I wouldn't count on it, bwana editor.'

Banda's Malawi Congress Party ran its own newspaper, the *Malawi News*, which was just a propaganda sheet, and its English-language pages were full of unintended mistakes. The party's symbol was a black cockerel. One election day, to my everlasting delight, it ran a caption under a picture of the Great Leader that read: 'Dr Banda votes for his own black cock.'

The British press had turned up in force at the prospect of a revolution in the newly independent Malawi, for Banda was a well-known figure in Britain, having worked as a GP in north London for many years. It is hard now to recall how big Africa was treated as a story in British newspapers at the time. Africa correspondents were often the best reporters on the paper. Richard Beeston of the *Daily Telegraph*, Colin Legum of *The Observer*, Peter Younghusband of the *Daily Mail*, John Monks of the *Daily Express* – they were all legendary kings of the African jungle.

Younghusband and Monks maintained a fierce rivalry that kept us all amused. There was an occasion when Younghusband filed a story from the Congo that went something like this: 'I am writing this while sheltering behind a car as bullets whistle overhead.' Monks received a telegram from his office the next day, demanding: 'Younghusband shot at. Why not you?'

I remember being in a bar in Salisbury when Monks came in looking anxious and asked if anybody had seen Younghusband lately. Tongue in cheek, we said we had last seen him heading for the airport. Shocked that his rival might have a headstart on him, Monks raced off in pursuit. Actually, none of us knew where Younghusband was; in fact, he ambled into the bar a bit later on – and asked where Monks was. We said he had gone to the airport. Peter shot after him.

In Malawi, the correspondents all made a beeline for my little office to pick my brains as to what was going on. Their favourite eating place was Ku Chawe Inn on Zomba plateau above the capital, where Monks would set up a powerful camera on a stand in case any disturbances took place down below. One day we were accompanied on the mountain by Tom Stacey of the *Sunday Times*, an Etonian toff who was later sacked by the paper for making up an interview with the jailed Sultan of Kashmir. He was also an intrepid explorer, a novelist and a publisher. When I became editor of *The Observer*, we met at his club, White's, for a jolly lunch.

We all had our own cars and Stacey proposed a bet as to who would be first down the mountain. There was really only a single track, except at one of the many hairpin bends, where it was just possible to overtake. As we took off from the car park, all having partaken of drink, Stacey shot into the lead, with me behind. I knew the road best and thought I might catch him. But it soon struck me, after a few skirmishes at the corners, that he would rather die than lose the race and, on the whole, I didn't feel the same way… So he claimed the prize – and we all lived to drink another day.

● ● ●

British news desks had no real idea where the countries of Africa were, or how you could travel from one to another. As a result, while sitting in my office in Blantyre, I would receive requests for stories on the other side of the continent that could only be reached at that time by two days of air travel. Once, I remember, the *Daily Mail* said there had been reports of trouble in Nigeria: 'Please file 600 words by six o'clock.'

Reluctant to give up on any possible source of income, I rang my friend in the British High Commission, Ronnie Bloom, who was really MI6, though we kept up a pretence that he was just a diplomat. He checked with his colleagues in Lagos and sent me details of the situation in Nigeria, which I passed on, over my byline and date-lined Lagos, to an unsuspecting *Daily Mail*.

I had all these payments made into an account in London, from which, when I returned to England three years later, I was able to buy my first family home, a four-bedroomed house in Kew Gardens with a garden front and back and a lovely may tree at the front. I bought it for £6,000 in 1966 and sold it two years later for £7,500, thinking I had made a killing. It must now be worth £2 million.

• • •

When my wife and I arrived in Nyasaland, we had been put up in an apartment while we looked for a permanent home. We turned up just as the previous occupants, a young couple, were leaving. 'Good luck on 7 July,' the young man said slyly. 'Why's that?' I asked. 'Because that's the day after Malawi becomes independent and that's when you'll probably have your throats cut.' A woman less resilient than my wife would have taken fright at this typical expatriate horror story.

I soon met a rather eccentric doctor called Mowschenson, of vague European descent, who drove a beautiful vintage Rolls-Royce. He told me I should rent the house of 'Sanders of the River', the nickname for a Colonel Sanders, a long-time resident of Nyasaland who had recently died. Mowschenson said his widow was about to leave for the Cape in South Africa and was desperate to rent out the property before she left.

My wife and I went round and were overwhelmed by the house and garden in its sixty-eight acres of mostly wooded land. When Mrs Sanders said the rent would be only £40 a month, I must have stared with my mouth open, because she evidently misunderstood my reaction and promptly reduced the rent to £30 a month. We took it.

The house was built on the South African rondavel principle, with a square dining room at the centre and other rooms, including a living room, two bedrooms, study and kitchen, all filling out a circle in segments around it. Three servants came with the house – a cook, a gardener and a watchman to protect the trees from marauders. For a young couple brought up in working-class Coventry, it was a dream. There were two cottages in the grounds, which we did up and rented out (for £30 a month each) to an Israeli doctor and to the Reuters man, Jack Gillon, a Scot who turned up with a leggy, 'debbie' sort of girl in a large hat who, Gillon said, he had brought from a party in Chelsea.

There was a squash court in the garden with a bamboo top that let in the rain. I allowed a local club to use it and played there myself. My main partner was the Israeli ambassador, Gideon Shohat, a former air force colonel who mysteriously shot himself on a beach in Tel Aviv after returning home. He was an admirable man who had become a good friend.

I also played with Gillon. One day, while we were in mid-point, a snake fell into the court from the bamboo roof. I quickly picked it up on my racket, opened the door and threw it out, then stood ready to go on with the game. I found my opponent in a state of shock, white-faced, with his back to the wall of the court. When he saw what I had done with the snake, he said: 'You could do that to people!'

• • •

Malawi's short-lived civil war brought one piece of excitement my way, when Donald Wise, a well-known foreign correspondent of the *Daily Mirror* and a delightful companion, asked me to drive him into rebel-held territory. It was getting dark by the time we arrived at a village in the bush where a makeshift roadblock had been set up. We were ordered to wind down the car's front windows. Africans on both sides stuck guns at our heads, shining a torch into our faces. When they saw we were white men, they roared with laughter and passed us each a bottle of Coca Cola and we laughed too. At that age, we thought we were immortal.

• • •

Early in 1966, I received an invitation out of the blue to visit the Ivory Coast, all expenses paid. I leapt at the opportunity to see parts of Africa I had never seen before. At Nairobi airport, I teamed up with Richard Hall, who was on the same trip. He was editing a paper in Zambia, as I was doing in Malawi. We travelled on together through Addis Ababa, Khartoum and Accra, stopping off briefly on our way to Abidjan, crossing Africa from east to west. According to Dick's account of the trip in his book: 'We hit it off at once. Donald proved good company, quick and knowing, with a humour that was rather conspiratorial, making you feel you were sharing in his cache of light-hearted secrets.'

I have a letter I wrote to my parents about the trip. Even after fifty years the youthful excitement we felt at this great adventure comes through strongly. We missed our connection to Abidjan from Accra and had to suffer hours of bureaucratic bullying because we had no visa for Ghana. Eventually we were sent to a tenth-rate hotel with a carpet of cockroaches under the bed and African dance music that seemed to go on all night.

Getting out of Ghana was even harder than getting in, though we were keen to escape such a run-down and unwelcoming place, with banners everywhere reading 'GET OUT WHITES'. The pompous official who had harangued us for not having a visa on entry the night before had failed to stamp our passports, so we were now accused of entering Ghana illegally – and for journalists, a hated species, that was no joke; a German journalist had recently been jailed for forty years for entering the country without a visa.

Abidjan was completely different: very French, which was the country's official language, with little bistros next to the skyscrapers and people drinking coffee or beer under sun umbrellas in the pavement cafés. We were treated regally in a super-plush hotel with free meals and wine, driven around in a Mercedes, and entertained every night until the early hours. Dick and I, plus a couple of journalists from Tanzania and Uganda who were on the trip, managed to escape the official entertainment one night to visit a frisky nightclub called La Boule Noire in Trecheville, the city's red-light district. Oddly, I don't seem to have reported this excursion to my parents.

When the Ivory Coast visit ended, Dick and I decided not to go straight home, but to move along the coast to Lagos, which had recently been the scene of the Commonwealth Prime Ministers' conference. We stayed with a friend of Dick's, the Zambian High Commissioner to Nigeria, a man of the cloth called Isaac Munpansha. Like everyone in Lagos, we were woken in the middle of the night when the hum of the air conditioning suddenly stopped. The lights weren't working either, the power station having been taken over in a military coup which had resulted in the death of the country's main leaders.

We tried to file the story of the coup, but the post office was closed and no overseas telephone calls could get through. We decided to go to the Congo, which required another visa. At the Congolese embassy, a dirty office up some back stairs, a fat girl in hair curlers said we couldn't have a visa because there was a revolution going on and, besides, the ambassador was at a party. There were pictures of Tshombe on the walls; evidently, they hadn't been told that he had been overthrown three months before. We managed to bribe a cleaner with a nasty-looking bandage on her leg to 'borrow' the visa stamp from an office and stamped our own passports.

The Rev Munpansha nobly agreed to drive us to Lagos airport while we hid under a blanket to get through the police and army roadblocks on the way. We passed a long line of lorries and cars with people sleeping in the back, since no private transport was allowed through. When we reached the airport, a soldier put his head and his gun through the window of the Mercedes, but was reassured by our host's dog collar and diplomatic status.

When we got there, we found the place deserted apart from a handful of people in the bar: British and American diplomatic couriers taking out news of the coup and two diplomats – one Japanese, the other Liberian. A slightly drunken Nigerian pilot said he could fly us to Doula in Cameroon in a Fokker Friendship, but we discovered that our plane, miraculously, was still scheduled for take-off, presumably because no one had thought to stop it.

While we were on the runway, aware of living through a surreal episode in our lives, a green and white helicopter came down from the skies and disgorged Archbishop Makarios of Cyprus, in full Greek Orthodox regalia. He had gone up north after attending the Commonwealth conference in Lagos. We filled him in on the army coup.

Our plane pitched and tossed in a storm, and at one point Dick got on his knees to pray, while I took a map into the cockpit to make sure the pilot knew how to miss a small mountain close to Douala airport. There we were able to file some stories about the Nigerian coup and were interviewed about it by British and American correspondents. We went on to Togo and then to Leopoldville in the Congo, where we found that we had stamped our passports with the wrong date. We were left to stew in a huge hangar, where we stood by helplessly while aggressive officials shouted at us in Belgian and young boys went through our luggage. We had to fill out some forms in Belgian and though, apart from our names and passport numbers, we wrote gibberish, it was enough to get us through.

A local correspondent found us an empty house belonging to an absent Canadian journalist, with cockroaches all over the floor. I slept in a bed which had a gigantic pair of boots next to it. These, it turned out, belonged to a Belgian mercenary who also lived there. 'He won't be back tonight,' said our local host, 'but if by any chance he appears he will certainly shoot you for sleeping in his bed.' I didn't get much sleep that night.

We managed to talk a Congolese pilot into giving us a lift on a military flight to Elizabethville on a plane which had no pressurised cabin. We were met there by someone from the British consulate, who persuaded the Congolese police to let us through, even though our visas were out of date. We stayed in the shell of a beautiful hotel, the Leopold II, built in the days of colonial grandeur, but I couldn't get to sleep for the sound of rain crashing onto a tin roof. When I opened the curtains, I found there was no glass in the windows. The manager said they were smashed so often it wasn't worth repairing them.

There seemed to be no legal way to change money in the Congo; I managed to change some with a bunch of mercenaries I met in a bar. The British consulate said they couldn't help us with a visa to get out of the country and advised us to get hold of the Associated Press correspondent, a man called Lax who enjoyed signing all his press cables 'ex-Lax Elizabethville'. He ran a Chinese laundry in his spare time (when not helping the CIA) and we were asked to use a code for security reasons when asking for him: we were to ask to see 'the paintings.'

Lax told us to be in the main square at a quarter to midnight and we would be picked up by a white Mercedes taxi that would take us to the Zambian Copperbelt via an old diamond smuggler's route. The fare was £15 each. At Ndola, we had to empty our pockets and our luggage to show that we hadn't taken out any diamonds, but no visa was required. This was home for Dick. I took a plane to Salisbury and on to Malawi after one of the most colourful adventures of my young life.

Meanwhile, a much bigger African crisis had been boiling up as Ian Smith's right-wing government threatened to break its links with the British Queen and declare Rhodesia independent. When UDI (Unilateral Declaration of Independence) was finally declared on 11 November 1965, my journalists, white and black, crowded round a small radio in my office to hear Smith's historic broadcast.

I met my friend Ronnie Bloom for a drink that evening at Ryall's Hotel and told him I was planning to go to Salisbury the following week for a meeting of the Commonwealth Press Union's Central Africa

committee, of which I was a member. He showed great interest in
this and asked if I would be willing to carry out 'a few small tasks' for
him, since British diplomats would no longer be free to visit Southern
Rhodesia.

I had no doubt that the 'few small tasks' would be on behalf of MI6,
or Ronnie himself would not have been involved. I was to go on several
trips in the coming months, and each time I performed 'a few small
tasks', usually dropping a letter through a gap left in the window of
a parked car, or handing over letters addressed to named individuals
at different hotels. I had no qualms about doing this, because I was
strongly opposed to a right-wing coup in Salisbury designed to exclude
Africans from power – which is what UDI amounted to.

After each visit, I gave Ronnie Bloom a written account of what I
had seen in Salisbury and how I judged the public mood. By the time
of my third trip, he asked if I could use my journalist's nose to find out
more – or at least form a view – about the feelings that ordinary white
Rhodesians had about the revolutionary and illegal step being taken by
their rulers. I managed to do more than that. I blagged my way into the
Salisbury Club, using my out-of-date membership card for the RAF
Club in London, and there I struck gold.

I met a small group of aircrew, two of them pilots, from the Rhodesian Air Force. Over pints and gin and tonics, therefore, we were able
to compare experiences of flying training aircraft in Salisbury and the
UK. They were happy to meet someone with my RAF experience and
took me along with them to a military club for a few more drinks. They
knew I was a journalist and would be asking some questions about
the impending showdown with Britain, but the fact that I came from
neighbouring Malawi, not from London, blunted any suspicion. At the
next club we came across more military personnel and I was able to
gauge their attitude without asking too many leading questions.

I went back to Malawi and sent in a report on these conversations,
concluding that Southern Rhodesian forces would be very reluctant
indeed to fight British troops. I went way beyond my brief to suggest

that if British planes were to fly under the radar over Umtali from an aircraft carrier they kept off the coast at Beira and land paratroopers in Cecil Square in the centre of Salisbury, they would not be met by gunfire. If the action was swift and decisive, I felt sure it could and would succeed.

It was some time later that Ronnie Bloom told me that my paper had found its way, doubtless amended by going through the hands of MI6, to a Cabinet committee in London, presided over by the Foreign Secretary, Michael Stewart. It had failed to find favour, which didn't surprise me. It would have required a bold and risky decision of the kind Margaret Thatcher was to make over the Falklands seventeen years later.

I noted with irony that Harold Wilson and Stewart were to have no hesitation, a few years after this, in sending arms to help Nigeria crush the breakaway eastern state of Biafra, causing the loss of an estimated million lives. But those were black lives. Risking a few dozen white people, on the other hand, was something they couldn't possibly contemplate, even though it would have saved hundreds, possibly thousands of both white and black lives over the next decade and a half.

Wilson, who (unlike many members of his Cabinet, such as Roy Jenkins, Denis Healey, Anthony Crosland and Tony Benn) had never heard a shot fired in anger, was much too cautious to run the risk of killing what he called 'our kith and kin' (code for white people, many of whom still held British passports). What he ignored was the corollary that 'our kith and kin' would also be unwilling to kill British people. I doubt very much if an order to kill British troops would have been issued by Smith's rebel regime in 1965 or early 1966, with the prospect of being hanged for treason if it went wrong.

The British government at the time cannot have seriously believed that Smith and his men could be 'negotiated' out of their cast-iron conviction that Africans should never rule 'their' country – even when the negotiations were led by the formidable Lord Goodman. They succumbed eventually to the only argument they could accept: brute force – but it had to be applied by Africans, since whites could not be persuaded to take on whites.

I still believe that if Wilson had shown more guts in 1965, Smith's rebellion could have been snuffed out with minimal casualties and the country spared a vicious fifteen-year civil war that destroyed its previously booming economy, brutalised the next generation of African youth and brought a white-hating Marxist monster like Robert Mugabe to power.

• • •

Malawi's civil war soon fizzled out. A series of guerrilla raids were planned from Tanzania, but came to nothing. Ronnie Bloom asked me to go to the Tanzanian border to find out what was going on. I found myself escorting a frightened group of Frelimo guerrillas from Karonga in the north to Fort Johnston in the south and helping them set off by boat to Mozambique to conduct guerrilla operations.

Chipembere, exiled in California, was laid low with the diabetes from which he later died. With that, the opposition to Banda effectively died too. Internal opposition was put down ruthlessly. I was invited to the public hanging in Zomba prison of one of the captured rebel ministers. It came on a stiff white card with gilt edging like an invitation to a party at Government House to mark the Queen's birthday, with an RSVP at the bottom. The wording, however, was rather different: 'The Ngwazi Dr Hastings Kamuzu Banda, President of Malawi, invites your presence at a public execution...' I declined.

The country's prison camps were soon full to overflowing. Unknown to Banda, the administrative secretary of the Malawi Congress Party, Albert Muwalo, was found to have been organising the throwing of bodies over a cliff – an offence for which he was later hanged. Foreign pressmen were no longer allowed into the country.

Three of the people in his prisons were Austin M'Madi, son of the kachasu queen of Zingwangwa; Roy Manda, my bright sub-editor; and

Levson Lifikilo, ace sports reporter. They were held without trial for three and a half years. What eventually happened to them I was never able to discover, despite many efforts through the British High Commission and international journalist organisations. I also sought news of them, without success, on my only return visit to Malawi, in 1983.

Their offence was to publish a story about a report of an alleged border incident – which they had said was 'unconfirmed' – that turned out to be untrue. If the same rules applied in Britain, how many of our journalists would be in jail for publishing 'unconfirmed' stories that turned out to be untrue?

• • •

Looking back on my time in Africa, I have often wondered what good I achieved. An independent newspaper in a one-party state was always an anomaly and was bound to come to grief. My predecessor was forced to leave the country, and so were the two editors who succeeded me. *Their* African successors are in jail. Some years after I left the country, my paper was taken over by Dr Banda's private company.

I was very lucky: I managed to hang on long enough to leave of my own volition in 1966, when the country became a republic. I had seen it develop from a colony, through independence, into a republic that was well on the road to dictatorship. I was glad to leave in the end. The country's dreams had faded. The sense of expectation had given way across the land to the most primitive fear – that of the knock on the door in the night.

I derived more benefit from my time there than Malawi did. I learned some useful things about newspapers and about politics. And I trained a few journalists in the tricks of our trade, it is true – but look where that led them: to jail, without trial or hope of justice. Lord Thomson's publishing business survived, but I never got that dollar he had promised.

CHAPTER 4

DAVID

David Astor was a great editor because he was a great man.

That was the opening sentence of the address I gave at the memorial service for my former editor at St Bride's, the Fleet Street church, on 22 February 2002, fourteen months after his death at the age of eighty-nine.

We had first met in May 1966, when I flew from Africa for a job interview. Thinking back to that interview – for the relatively junior post of deputy news editor – I am sure we would both have found it utterly incredible that, thirty-five years on, I would be the person chosen by his widow, Bridget, to make that memorial speech, or indeed that I would take over his job less than a decade after that first meeting.

David would then have been fifty-four, having edited the newspaper for eighteen years – the same period that I was destined to sit in the editorial chair as his successor. I was twenty-eight and had arrived for the interview from Malawi, where, as the previous chapter described, I had spent three years editing a local newspaper and working as an occasional correspondent for *The Observer*, *The Times*, the *Daily Mail* and the BBC – and even more occasionally as a contact for MI6.

What I remember most about this initial meeting was David's apparent nervousness, bending down shyly from his great height, almost apologetically, but with a gentle courtesy, to examine with a shrewd and wary eye his short, unprepossessing and thoroughly unimportant visitor. The interview was conducted in what I was to learn was David's usual cryptic, allusive and elliptical style. When he asked me a direct question – which writer I particularly admired – I said George Orwell, which was an extraordinary piece of luck on my part that probably clinched the job. I didn't know then that Orwell was his great hero and friend.

The outcome of the meeting was that I was offered the job of assistant (not deputy) news editor – a subtle distinction that I took to indicate some reservation on David's part. I was made to understand afterwards that this wasn't personal: it was just that David cared deeply about who should be admitted to the *Observer* family and disliked taking a risk, especially with someone he had met only once.

I was naturally delighted to join the paper I had worshipped since my school days, even though Jan, my first wife, was plainly upset to be leaving Malawi, where she had been chairman of Save the Children Fund and also taught at a school for teenage African girls. She cried at the airport as we left. I was never quite sure if this was because she was giving up her work and a grander style of life than we had known before (or since, come to that); or because she had to have Fred, our golden retriever, put down; or because she was over seven months pregnant with our second child at the time of our departure. All of the above, perhaps.

•   •   •

I can still remember the moment I was advised by Ken Osborne, a fellow sixth-former at Bablake School, to read *The Observer*, mainly for its sports pages which, as I found out later when I got to know them both, had been revamped by Christopher Brasher and Michael Davie so that they had a style, inventiveness and literacy usually associated with books or arts pages.

Much of the freshness came from using non-journalists to write on sport, such as Clement Freud, the philosopher Sir Freddie Ayer, John Jones, later an Oxford professor of poetry, and an England footballer,

George Eastham, who would file copy from the telephone in the Arsenal dressing room after the match – the first time this had been done without a journalist intermediary, and it produced infinitely more urgent and lively copy than the ghosted columns we read today.

But it wasn't only the sports pages that excited me. Kenneth Tynan was attacking traditional theatre in sparkling prose that my friends and I used to read out to each other; Patrick O'Donovan and John Gale wrote delightful pieces of a kind that you couldn't find anywhere else.

Ian Jack shared this youthful enthusiasm for *The Observer*, writing recently: 'Throughout the 1950s it was the dominant quality Sunday paper, certainly in its cultural and political influence among the young.' Jack, a former editor of the *Independent on Sunday* and of *Granta* magazine, said the *Observer* of his teenage years was 'patrician, humane, cosmopolitan and inspiring'. That sums up my recollection exactly.

My own juvenile addiction to the paper was such that my friend, the novelist Susan Hill, has since written that, when asked what I planned to do with my life at the age of nineteen, I had announced: 'I'm going to be editor of *The Observer*.' That same ambition is confirmed by a former girlfriend at Cambridge, who used to joke that I would be lucky to become editor of the *Wigan Observer*. Michael Frayn, later a brilliant columnist on *The Observer*, evidently entertained the same ambition when he was at school.

I first met Susan Hill in Coventry when my sister brought her round to our house for tea after school; later she would visit me in Cambridge, where she was terrified to ride pillion on my Lambretta. Susan and I both worked in university vacations on the *Coventry Standard*, the old-fashioned weekly paper I described earlier. She was sacked and I became chief reporter inside three weeks, which must say something about the paper's editorial standards, though I'm not sure exactly what.

While still at school, Susan had sent some of her work to Pamela Hansford Johnson, the novelist wife of the writer, scientist and civil servant C. P. Snow (later Lord Snow), and had been greatly encouraged by her response. When I told her that I had devoured the whole of

C. P. Snow's novel series *Strangers and Brothers* while at Cambridge, sensing some kinship with our respective backgrounds – he from Leicester, me from Coventry – Susan said she would arrange for us to meet.

I had become so involved in the novels that when I wrote to my Cambridge friend, Christopher Dixon, he greeted me in our next telephone conversation with the words: 'Hello, Lewis,' identifying me with Lewis Eliot, the narrator of the Snow novels. Susan took me along to one of the Snow–Hansford literary soirees at their house in London and I exchanged a few words with the great man while he sat grandly in a winged armchair. Afterwards, I asked Susan what Snow had said about me. 'He said you were a very potential young man,' she told me.

Snow's lecture about 'The Two Cultures', in which he had said that it was as important for an educated person to know the Second Law of Thermodynamics as the plays of Shakespeare, had been headline news at that time and had famously raised the ire of F. R. Leavis, the Cambridge literary critic, in a hilarious public rant which I, among others, was privileged to hear.

When Leavis asked his young audience, unbelievingly, if any of us had ever read a Snow novel right through from the beginning to the end, several of us put our hands up. At this, Leavis gathered up his papers in a rage, scattering them all over the floor, and marched out muttering: 'I can't be expected to talk to people who take C. P. Snow seriously as a novelist.' And then he cycled off.

● ● ●

My first year as an *Observer* reader – 1956 – was the year of the Suez adventure, a crucial episode in the newspaper's fortunes. Astor had bravely condemned Anthony Eden's government for illegally colluding with France and Israel to invade Egypt on the pretence that it was 'saving' the Suez Canal as an international waterway from an attack by Israel – an attack that, in fact, the three countries had plotted together in secret beforehand.

In ringing tones that still echo down the decades, the paper said Britain and France had acted 'not as policemen but as gangsters ... we had not realised that our government was capable of such folly and such crookedness.' Words like 'gangsters' and 'crookedness' were a refreshing change from the fustian, stilted and overly respectful prose favoured by most editorial writers at that time. Such stirring language and shining moral certainty attracted idealistic young people like me and my friends, but alienated many of the paper's older readership, who regarded it (only a decade after the Second World War) as tantamount to treason to write such things while British forces were risking their lives.

More damagingly for *The Observer*, many major advertisers withdrew their support, especially Jewish-owned companies. The loss of Jewish readers was a particular source of regret to David and he made great efforts to win them back, most notably by sponsoring the Masada exhibition at the Royal Festival Hall at the end of 1966, soon after I had arrived at the paper. Masada was the site of the last stand of Jewish zealots who reportedly chose mass suicide rather than submit to Roman rule. The symbolism of Masada is central to Israeli consciousness.

The exhibition, which displayed recently discovered Dead Sea Scrolls recovered from the Qumran caves by the great soldier-archaeologist Yigael Yadin, had the desired effect of restoring relations between *The Observer* and leading Jewish families, such as the Sieffs and the Wolfsons. This was a great relief to David who, according to Cyril Dunn, an old hand at *The Observer* who had a look of George Orwell about him, had 'an indestructible respect for the brilliance of the Jewish mind'.

Not all brilliant Jewish minds reciprocated this respect, however. Isaiah Berlin, for example, described David Astor as 'a neurotic, muddled, complicated, politically irresponsible, unhappy adventurer, permanently resentful of somebody or something ... a typical poor little rich boy'. This only goes to show that very clever men can sometimes say very silly things.

Isaiah once invited me to his house in Hampstead for an evening in honour of Sir Georg Solti, the conductor. Yehudi Menuhin, the violinist, was among the guests and I remember his wife saying to me by way of introduction: 'Have you met the old fiddler?' I had arrived late and dashed into the house through a rainstorm, to be greeted by Isaiah as I folded up my umbrella with the words: 'Ah, here's the only man who can answer this crucial question.' I was wondering what insoluble philosophical riddle was about to be thrown at me in front of this gilded audience when he added: 'Do you know if Manchester United won the replay tonight?'

It has been said that the real damage that the Suez affair caused to *The Observer* was not so much commercial, though that was plainly severe, but the effect it had on David Astor's self-confidence. I can't make a reliable judgment on that because I never knew David in his editorial prime between 1948 and the early 1960s. By 1966, however, when I joined the paper, he certainly seemed weighed down by editorial uncertainty and by heavy commercial losses – caused by increased competition from the *Sunday Times* and the recently launched *Sunday Telegraph* and by the increasingly outrageous demands of the printing unions.

David had a highly developed sense of guilt and he was still clearly obsessed by the damage his Suez line had caused the paper. He asked Iain Macleod at an *Observer* lunch I attended in 1970, shortly before the Conservative Chancellor died, why the paper still suffered from the fallout of the Suez affair when it was now manifestly clear that *The Observer* had been right all along. Macleod replied: 'The trouble is, David, you can be wrong by being right too soon.'

Observer guest lunches in the late 1960s and early 1970s were lavish affairs, offering a taste of the opulence David had enjoyed at Cliveden, the stately home of his parents, Lord and Lady Astor. There would be a drink (two drinks usually) at the bar beforehand (whisky or gin and tonic), then white wine and red wine (both of top quality), even brandy and cigars, all served with a smooth and silent efficiency. The brandy and cigars were dropped by the mid-1970s, either for reasons of economy, because of changing tastes or, more likely, because David was no longer the editor. The guests were usually senior politicians of all parties, but sometimes there were figures from the arts or literature, occasionally even royalty, in attendance.

It may not have been just the Cliveden effect, for other newspapers also entertained lavishly at the time. Once, when I was invited by Denis Hamilton to a lunch at *The Times*, we were served on gold plates. At the *Daily Telegraph*, Lord Hartwell had a grass putting green on a balcony outside the dining room, looking over Fleet Street, where we were served by an ancient manservant who looked as though he had wandered in from *Downton Abbey*.

The nicest guest I can recall at an *Observer* lunch was John Betjeman, who charmed everyone, especially the serving and kitchen staff, making a point of thanking each one personally. The nastiest was Richard Crossman, the Labour Cabinet minister. I had been warned that he usually found someone round the table to bully and would wait for a stray thoughtless remark to seize on like a dog with a bone. In this case the victim was Nora Beloff, the paper's political correspondent, whom he tried to tear limb from limb, though she put up a characteristically feisty defence.

I invited Margaret Thatcher for lunch with senior executives and the political staff in 1976, a year after she had become Leader of the Opposition. Just as my secretary received a message from reception to say that her car was arriving and would I go down to meet her, I had to take an urgent call from Lord Goodman telling me that the trustees were almost certainly going to ask Rupert Murdoch to buy the paper. As a result, I was a bit late greeting her and also in a confused state of mind.

As we got into the lift I muttered something, by way of small talk, about the late-night sittings and narrow majorities that the Callaghan government was patching up with the Liberals. Unfortunately, I prefaced my remarks by saying: 'I see you've been having fun in the House of Commons.' It was a tiny lift and we pretty well filled it; suddenly it felt even smaller when Mrs T. puffed out her ample chest and bellowed: 'Fun, Mr Trelford? Fun?! Is that what *The Observer* thinks about our national politics?'

Having led with my chin, I had only myself to blame for getting it punched. She clearly didn't feel at home at *The Observer* and continued in a defensive/aggressive mood throughout the lunch, doubtless feeling trapped in a crypto-Marxist hideout.

I was reminded of this episode, some decades later, when Simon Hoggart entitled his book about Parliament *House of Fun*. I amused myself with the thought of the Iron Lady thundering from beyond the grave: 'Fun, Mr Hoggart? Fun?! Do you think Parliament is fun?' To which Simon would doubtless have replied: 'Well, yes, actually.'

A most productive lunch took place two years later when the guest was Dickie (later Lord) Attenborough. Our correspondent in South Africa, Donald Woods, editor of the *Daily Dispatch* in the Eastern Cape, had just made a dramatic escape across the border to avoid arrest for his robust reporting on the death of his friend Steve Biko. The young leader of the 'black consciousness' movement had been battered to death in custody by the South African security police.

Attenborough was so taken by the story that he eventually made a film about it, *Cry Freedom*, with Kevin Kline as Woods and Denzel Washington as Biko. It may have been made several years later but the seed had been planted at that *Observer* lunch.

The *most* productive *Observer* lunch, however, resulted in the launch of the London Marathon in 1981. It was the brainchild of Christopher Brasher, who had been sports editor of *The Observer* as well as taking part in the first four-minute mile with Roger Bannister, winning a gold medal in the steeplechase at the Melbourne Olympics in 1956, and being head of features at the BBC. In addition, he was a mountaineer, an environmental pioneer and an expert at fly-fishing – and as if that wasn't enough, he became a rich, racehorse-owning businessman when his running-shoe company was taken over by Reebok.

Chris was a determined man, used to getting his own way, and he was frustrated that the idea of a London Marathon, devised by himself and his old friend and fellow Olympic athlete John Disley, was being held up by bureaucratic objections from the police, the keepers of the royal parks and politicians from the London boroughs. He asked me to host a lunch at the newspaper, to which he would invite all the groups whose cooperation he needed.

I wasn't surprised that Chris had got people's backs up. He had a manic energy and bustling single-mindedness that brooked no opposition. Once, in a hot-tempered exchange at *The Observer*, I asked him: 'Are you so big-headed because you won an Olympic gold medal, or did you win an Olympic gold medal because you were so big-headed?' He looked chastened at this, a rare occurrence. He chewed on his filthy pipe and growled: 'Good question. I don't know the answer.'

Sir Horace Cutler, leader of the Greater London Council, gave us strong support at the lunch in banging the heads together of the Metropolitan and City of London Police and sweet-talking the bosses of the parks and the main London boroughs affected by the marathon route. He was scathing when they asked for the launch to be delayed for a year to give them more time to get their act together. Cutler was a keen sports fan, wore a goatee beard and was regarded as a bit of a showman.

Many years later, in 2003, I was surprised and flattered when several of Brasher's obituaries credited me with playing a key role in getting the London Marathon started. The truth is that Brasher and Disley were 99 per cent responsible for that; the contributions of Cutler and myself amounted to no more than 0.5 per cent each. Even so, it is something *The Observer* can be proud of.

When, some years later, Princess Margaret came to lunch to make a presentation to Dame Ninette de Valois, I suggested a loyal toast. The Princess Royal replied: 'Oh, well, if you like. Sorry, what I meant to say was, how very kind. I'm sure my sister would be pleased.' Then she added with a laugh: 'I don't suppose Andrew Neil would be doing this at the *Sunday Times*.'

• • •

I have now written articles for *The Observer* in seven different decades, a record that only Katharine Whitehorn could possibly match – though William Keegan, whom I recruited as an economic correspondent in 1977, can perhaps claim an even greater achievement in having now completed fifty years' continuous writing on the paper. I began writing, in a small way, for the sports pages while still an undergraduate at Cambridge. I covered some rugby matches from Coventry and Cambridge and wrote up the first Oxford–Cambridge tiddlywinks match.

I still have the letter dated 17 September 1959 from Geoffrey Nicholson, then deputy to Christopher Brasher on the sports desk, commissioning my first piece: 'You know the sort of thing, I imagine: an attempt to convey the atmosphere of the match and to combine comment with the blow-by-blow stuff.' I blush to recall that the first line of one of my early match reports was a quotation from Scott Fitzgerald's *The Great Gatsby*: 'Reserving judgments is a matter of infinite hope.'

When Geoff came to cover matches himself at Coventry or Cambridge, I would join him in the press box and act as his bag man, offering to telephone his copy through to *The Observer* for him while he caught his train back to London or to Wales. As we walked from the rugby ground to the railway station I would nag him for stories about my heroes on the paper.

He used to tell me tales about his early career in advertising, saying that his sole lasting contribution to the profession was one slogan: 'Hey fella, Fruitella.' He told me about a campaign from his own agency that used the line: 'Daks – the Trousers that Stand Out in Front.' He had spotted the innuendo, but decided not to point it out and the ad duly appeared in print.

About fifteen years after this, when I became editor of *The Observer*, I appointed Geoff Nicholson as my sports editor. He had recently returned to *The Observer* from the *Sunday Times*. As a man who smoked sixty Gauloises a day all his life – he even wrote a history of the cigarette called *Passing Clouds* – Geoff had not been happy with a prolonged fitness campaign in the *Sunday Times*, which was addressed not just to its readers but to its staff as well.

Geoff commented: 'What the *Sunday Times* could do with is a deep breath of foul air.' He found the boozy camaraderie of *The Observer* sports desk – described by sports editor Peter Corrigan as 'a pub-loving, carousing bunch of laid-back troubadours' – much more to his liking.

But he preferred writing, especially on Welsh rugby or cycling, to being a desk-bound executive and gave up the job after a couple of years to follow a wide range of sporting events, most famously the Tour de France, about which he wrote a classic book.

I took a train to Wales for his funeral, accompanied by Harry Enfield Sr and Richard Ingrams, then editor of *The Oldie*, for which Geoff's wife Mavis, the well-known television interviewer, wrote an agony column. He was buried in a hillside cemetery in a valley of bleak beauty at Llanrhaeadr-ym-Mochnant, where he and Mavis had lived.

● ● ●

My love affair with *The Observer* was undiminished during my time in Africa, where we would receive a beautiful airmail edition on thin and very white newsprint that was laid out, I discovered later, by the paper's veteran managing editor, Ken Obank ('KPO', as he was universally known), and won many design awards. My house in Blantyre was on the airport road, so I bribed the African van driver who collected all the overseas newspapers to stop off at my house to make his first delivery.

Eventually, even though it wasn't what she really wanted herself, my wife said to me one morning as I stood by the roadside waiting for the papers to arrive: 'If you're so desperate to know what is happening in England, maybe it's time you went home.'

And so I did, joining *The Observer* in July 1966, in the week that

England won the World Cup. Despite my wife's pregnancy, we had stopped off on our journey home in Nairobi, Cairo, Athens, Belgrade and Milan. In all these places I would seek out a television set, either in a hotel or a bar, to follow England's progress through the opening rounds.

Our son Tim was born three weeks after I joined the paper, conveniently on a Sunday morning, so that I could attend mother and son in hospital for a couple of days – a couple of days being deemed sufficient father care in those benighted times.

My arrival in the newsroom caused some confusion; I felt that I wasn't really expected. This was because I had been appointed as number two to John Thompson, but he had quit the news desk to take over the colour magazine in the period between my interview in May and my arrival in the office in July. William Millinship was now the news editor and he had never met me.

This might have made for a difficult relationship, but Bill and I hit it off from the start, though I bore some slight resentment over his habit, in the Blackfriars pub after work, of ordering a gin and dry martini (five shillings and sixpence) while I could only afford a half-pint of bitter (one shilling and threepence).

Bill had spent his entire journalistic life in the field and had never handled any reporter's copy except his own, so he welcomed my sub-editing experience. Bill was always a reporter at heart and when, in 1968, France was overcome by the student revolts and industrial strikes, he insisted on quitting the desk for a couple of weeks and going back on the beat.

He had been the paper's Paris correspondent for many years, covering the Algerian war, and was later our man in Moscow and Washington, where his meticulous reading of documents made him the most reliable reporter of the Watergate affair. He afterwards returned to London as my managing editor, looking after budgets and staffing problems. He was adept at both, careful with the paper's pennies and handling temperamental staff with what Neal Ascherson described as 'almost Buddhist patience'.

By the time I arrived, *The Observer* had recently left Tudor Street, in a warren of lanes behind Fleet Street, and moved to Queen Victoria Street, opposite the Mermaid Theatre and Blackfriars station, occupying one wing of the building that then housed *The Times*. On a Saturday, when *The Times* wasn't working, we took over their newsroom for the day. The production arrangements were not just pre-digital but pre-war, a throwback to the 1930s.

When a sub-editor had finished with a story and it had been passed by the chief sub, the typed copy was then placed on a pulley system, rather like those once used in department stores, and transported by overhead wire to the print room. Unfortunately, the copy quite frequently got lost in transit. I remember one panic over a lost 'splash' or lead story that was eventually traced to the gents' lavatory, where it had slipped off the pulley line into a urinal and made a different sort of splash.

My first Saturday on the paper was the day of the World Cup final. As the match reached extra time, I went down to the stone, where the paper was set into type by the printers, to find a big debate going on. KPO, who had a blind spot about sport, insisted that the first edition should go at its usual time in order to catch trains to Scotland and other places and flights abroad. The sports editor thought the paper should wait for the result; the head printer and the circulation manager stood impatiently waiting for a decision.

As I approached this stand-off, Ken surprisingly asked for my opinion, even though I was the newest kid on the block. I replied (in a way that sounds a bit pompous now): 'I'm sorry if it makes the paper late, but you can't possibly send out a copy of *The Observer* anywhere tomorrow without the result of a World Cup final played in London. We would be a laughing stock, especially if England win.'

To my amazement, this spirited intervention carried the day and we waited for our legendary sports writer, Hugh McIlvanney, who was to become a good friend over the next half-century, to complete his report by telephone straight to the stone, where it was copied down in biro onto a page proof by one of the printers.

After the first edition, the night editor would turn up and take over the paper. It was then a huge, bald Yorkshireman called Ronald Harker, who during the week ran the paper's foreign syndication service. It was his habit, when he arrived around 6 p.m., to roll the back of his hand across the proof of the front page of the first edition with a disdainful air, then take out his pen and cross out some headlines. He did this to set out his stall, to show he was the boss and that the rest of us might as well go home and leave him to it, as he clearly hoped we would.

My involvement with the World Cup, on this, my first production day at *The Observer*, was not over. On the front page of the first edition the only reference to this historic event was a brief paragraph containing the result and a cross-reference to the sports pages. When we got back upstairs to the news desk, I plucked up the courage to suggest to Millinship that there ought to be a story about it on the front page. He reported my view to KPO, who passed on the suggestion to Harker.

Eventually Harker's towering figure stood over me: 'I gather you think we should have a story about winning the World Cup. Since you've got so much to say for yourself, I suggest you write it – here's all the agency copy.' At this he dumped a pile of paper on my desk and said I had twenty minutes to write 500 words. The story duly appeared and there was even a front-page picture with it of Bobby Moore lifting the Jules Rimet trophy.

Two and a half years later, in the first week of January 1969, KPO invited me to do the night editor's job myself when Harker was on holiday. This, I knew, was a great compliment and I was nervously determined not to make a mess of it. It turned out to be an exceptional Saturday for late news. Just before 9 p.m. the wires were buzzing with a report of the Marden rail crash, when a passenger train ran through two danger signals in thick fog and crashed into the back of a parcels train in Kent. Four people were killed and eleven injured.

We had just remade the paper for the last edition with news and pictures across several pages, and were beginning to think about going home, when a reader rang up around 1.30 a.m. from close to Gatwick

airport and said she had seen a bright light through her kitchen window
and thought there might have been a crash. There was nothing on the
wires about this, so we started working the phones.

Arthur Gould, who worked for us on Saturdays and later became a
senior figure at *The Times*, established that the story was true. A Boeing
727 of Ariana Afghan Airways, flying from Kabul via Frankfurt, had
crashed in the enveloping fog, killing forty-eight passengers and two
people in a house east of the airport, a mile and a half short of the
runaway. The pilot, co-pilot and eleven passengers had surprisingly
survived.

I had to give the order to 'stop the presses' – something all journalists dream of doing – to ensure that there would be enough copies of
the paper left to print that would carry the latest news. There would
be no point producing an extra edition if the print run had already
finished and the machine room staff had all gone home for the night.

I couldn't help thinking of one of my great heroes in journalism,
Arthur Christiansen, the long-serving editor of the *Daily Express*, who
had made his name at the age of twenty-six, while working as night
editor, with his handling of the crash of the giant airship R101 in 1930.
In the dramatic fire and subsequent crash over France, forty-eight of
the fifty-four people on board were killed, including the Air Minister.

Christiansen's coverage of the R101 disaster became the stuff of
Fleet Street legend. I still have a well-thumbed copy of his book, *Headlines All My Life*, which was one of several newspaper memoirs that I
cherished – others were Hugh Cudlipp's *Publish and be Damned!: The
Astonishing Story of the Daily Mirror* and Tom Hopkinson's book, *In
the Fiery Continent*, about his time editing *Drum* magazine in South
Africa. I also absorbed every word and illustration of Allen Hutt's classic work on newspaper design.

It was after 4 a.m. by the time I took the final edition home under
my arm, feeling that we had a paper that any editor would be proud of.
Or so I thought. KPO was certainly delighted with my debut performance as night editor and asked Astor on the following Tuesday (our

first working day of the week on a Sunday paper) to congratulate me in person. When I went into his office, however, David seemed unusually subdued, as if suffering some inner torment. Finally, he said: 'KPO tells me you did a good job with the paper on Saturday.' Then, after a long silence, he blurted out: 'But you mustn't think this is what *The Observer* is about.'

I left the office feeling rather deflated, and when I got home that night I got out Christiansen's book to compare David's response with that of Lord Beaverbrook, who had telephoned Arthur to say: 'You have secured a wonderful feat of journalism. I am proud to be associated with a newspaper on which you work.' Yet I can understand now what David was trying to say: people don't buy *The Observer* to read about rail or air crashes; they buy it for stimulating opinions and brilliant writing.

That was one reason, I believe, why David never showed any serious interest in the paper's Saturday news operation: that wasn't what *The Observer* was 'about'. On a Saturday, he stayed in his office, rather than on the back bench with the paper's senior executives, and usually went home early before the first edition was out. He wasn't even interested in knowing what story the paper would be leading with, though he might sometimes be consulted by KPO if it was likely to be politically controversial or running a serious legal risk.

He would spend Saturday mornings working painstakingly on headlines for the leader and the leader page articles, usually with John Silverlight, a sprightly and delightful character, known as the paper's 'super-sub' who, unlike most sub-editors, was admired by reporters for clearly improving, rather than mangling, their precious words. He was immortalised as John Dyson in Michael Frayn's comic novel about newspapers, *Towards the End of the Morning*, published a year after I joined the paper. Although the rest of us could see that the gestures and attitudes struck by Dyson in the book were pure Silverlight, the man himself could never see the resemblance.

I can still see John in his shirtsleeves, spectacles gleaming, hair flopping, as he confronts a writer while clutching a sheaf of subbed copy or galley proofs, plus a dictionary or some other work of reference, crying out, as he often did to Frayn and to others: 'Pure gold!' Every week I would pass Silverlight's tiny office and see Frayn sitting patiently on the radiator until John finally turned and uttered the words: 'Michael, you write like an angel.'

Eventually I would take part myself in the leader page discussions with Astor and Silverlight and came to admire David's own unexpected skill as a headline writer and copy editor. He sought exactitude, even if it meant keeping the production line waiting. But the work David really cared about took place on a Friday evening, when he would sit alone in his office, long after his secretary had gone, often with a blanket or overcoat round his shoulders – not because the room wasn't heated but because of the lasting effects of a gunshot wound he had received in a German ambush after landing in the Ardennes with Special Operations Executive (SOE) in 1944. There he would wrestle for hours with the main leader or the profile, which were treated like Holy Writ.

When I showed him an article, he would take ages to read it and would then read it all over again, even more slowly, to make sure that he fully understood it. He often said how amazed he was that I could read something and express a view about it so quickly. I have since come to the conclusion that David was dyslexic – probably the only dyslexic editor in the history of Fleet Street. This would explain the problems he had with his studies at Eton and at Oxford, where his teachers were puzzled that someone of obviously high intelligence had such problems with written work such as essays and exams. I have sometimes wondered if David could ever have finished a book in his life.

From an early age David acquired his knowledge, not from books, but from listening to people talking. In his childhood, the talkers at his parents' dinner table would have been eminent politicians of the day or writers like George Bernard Shaw and H. G. Wells; Charlie Chaplin and Mahatma Gandhi were among the more exotic visitors to Cliveden and the Astors' London home in St James's Square. Later, David would listen to George Orwell and Brendan Behan, one of whom he tried unavailingly to save from TB and the other from alcoholism.

I believe it was because he enjoyed listening that he called so many editorial conferences. He hardly bothered with the day's newspapers; he relied on his *Observer* colleagues to keep him informed – and not just informed, since news as such didn't interest him very much. He wanted to know what it *meant* and enjoyed nothing so much as hearing discordant voices arguing over the rights and wrongs of an issue.

John Pringle, who had been deputy editor until five years before I joined the paper, wrote in a memoir:

> If Mao-Tse-tung invented the permanent revolution, David Astor invented the permanent conference ... he presided over this intellectual bear-garden with extraordinary patience and good temper ... listening attentively with a smile on his handsome, boyish face, occasionally brushing his hair off his forehead with a characteristic gesture, and sometimes intervening shyly but effectively.

None of this had changed very much by the time I arrived, though some of the personnel had moved on, especially David's post-war coterie of distinguished German and East European intellectuals such as Sebastian Haffner, Isaac Deutscher, E. F. Schumacher and Rix Lowenthal (a Foreign Office press officer once asked, tongue in cheek, what language *The Observer*'s conferences were conducted in). The conferences were still interminable and though the discussions were often brilliant, they used to drive production people frantic because of the difficulty of getting a decision.

It used to be joked around Fleet Street that after these four days of non-stop talk, from Tuesday to Friday, *The Observer* would then be produced on Saturdays by KPO and a few other professionals with little or no reference to what had been said before. Not entirely true, in my experience, but not entirely untrue either.

I was driven frantic myself, just a year after joining the news desk, when the Six-Day Arab–Israeli War broke out in the Middle East. Millinship and I were desperate to send out reporters to Jerusalem, Cairo, Amman and Damascus to cover this huge story. But we couldn't get access to David to authorise the expenditure because he was locked in his office all day – pretty well all week actually – with Colin Legum and Robert Stephens, the paper's foreign panjandrums, with occasional sharp interruptions from Nora Beloff, the political correspondent.

Legum, a South African, was a strong supporter of Israel, having once worked for David Ben-Gurion, the country's first Prime Minister. Stephens, who was diplomatic correspondent, was an Arabist who had worked in Palestine radio. The paper's Middle East policy was David's attempted compromise between their opposing views.

Legum had a habit of turning up late at the editorial conference, after the main decisions had been made, and then persuading us to change everything, much to KPO's frustration. He would open his remarks by saying pontifically: 'There are four points to be made about this.' We would all then have to sit in impatient silence while he ticked them off. He spoke with an authority that no one dared challenge. It was maddening, but he was often right.

For all Astor's belief in editorial democracy, the paper's policy on the Six-Day War was not made in conference, but behind closed doors. The news desk's attempt to get reporters out into the field to tell our readers what was actually happening was a much lower priority. The episode illustrated David's core belief that news wasn't what *The Observer* was about: what mattered was what the paper thought about it.

And what did it think? When the leader page was finally unveiled after days of anguished debate, the main headline read: 'Two Wronged Peoples'. An unarguable point, it has to be admitted, but I suspect the readers of the *Sunday Times* got more useful information about the war from their correspondents in the field.

•   •   •

My progress at *The Observer* was remarkably swift. After less than two years I had been made assistant managing editor to Ken Obank. The purpose of this new appointment was to give me more money to persuade me to stay with the paper. I had received two outside job offers. One was from Granada Television, then a hothouse of editorial talent that went on to occupy key jobs in British culture – people such as Jeremy Isaacs (head of Channel 4 and Covent Garden), John Birt (Director-General of the BBC), and Gus (later Lord) Macdonald, chairman of Scottish TV and a minister under Tony Blair.

I was approached by Jeremy Wallington, a talented TV journalist and editor, who wanted me to join a new investigative unit he was setting up. Its main outlet would have been *World in Action*. I suspected the hand of Leslie Woodhead behind this offer. Les was a brilliant, award-winning documentary film-maker for Granada and had produced and directed *World in Action* programmes.

He knew me well from the time we spent reading English together at Selwyn College, Cambridge. I will always remember with a rosy glow coming back to the pavilion after scoring a fifty for Selwyn, including two sixes, seeing Woodhead sitting with my then girlfriend, a pretty Jewish mathematician from Newnham with long black hair, and crying out: 'All this, Trelford, and a First as well!'

The other offer was from Gordon Brunton, who had been head of Thomson Publications, the part of the group that contained my Malawi newspaper. I had evidently impressed him on his visits to Africa. I remember him admiring some front pages we had framed about the assassination of President Kennedy at the end of 1963. By 1968, when all this was happening, Brunton had become chief executive of the whole of the Thomson group and wanted me to be his personal assistant, to act as liaison with the group's newspaper interests.

These interests included, most notably, *The Times* and *Sunday Times*, over which Denis (later Sir Denis) Hamilton – the man who had given me my first proper newspaper job in Sheffield – now reigned as editor-in-chief.

So I said to Brunton: 'Isn't Denis Hamilton your link to the newspapers?' He replied: 'I want my own man to report to me about the newspapers, not to have to go through Hamilton all the time.' That sounded like an uncomfortable position to be in, as Hamilton was an immensely powerful figure. The idea that I could act as a buffer between him and Brunton didn't seem entirely feasible. He would see me as Brunton's spy.

So I turned the offer down, though I sometimes wondered what would have happened to me if I had joined the Thomson group. I might have ended up running one of their oil rigs, since Brunton had expanded the group into the oil business in a big way. Or, perhaps a more likely scenario, I might have joined the *Sunday Times* and found myself working for Harold Evans in rivalry with *The Observer*.

I confided to Millinship in the pub that I had received these offers out of the blue; he immediately reported this to KPO, who felt he should warn Astor. David called me in and was highly flattering about my work at the paper and promised me that the next time a big promotion came up it would be mine. He said he hoped desperately that I would stay.

I was a print man at heart, so I had no problem turning down the Granada offer as well. I had never worked in television, had no idea how it worked and rarely watched it. Furthermore, the medium was much less influential in people's lives in the '60s than it became later. Again, I have sometimes wondered how a TV career might have worked out. It was only in the 1980s that I started presenting some programmes for the BBC and Channel 4.

• • •

You couldn't work for very long on Astor's *Observer* without learning that psychology was not a subject you made jokes about. Journalists on the women's pages bore the brunt of this obsession. One sometimes wondered why David employed any women at all, especially those who had children, since he believed so fervently that a mother's place was at home. He once accused Katharine Whitehorn of 'penis envy' when he disagreed with her line on some current gender issue.

The women's liberation movement of the 1960s caused him great confusion. He was delighted when Arianna Stassinopoulos (now Huffington) wrote a book, *The Female Woman*, challenging the main arguments of the women's liberation movement, and made us buy some extracts for serialisation.

I got to know Arianna later when we both appeared on *Any Questions?* She was what I called a great ball-carrier. When the chairman, David Jacobs, asked a tricky question, I would keep my head down in the hope that he wouldn't call on me first to answer it. Arianna, however, would stride straight in and give it both barrels. She and her then paramour Bernard Levin once invited me to see Jonathan Pryce's amazing *Hamlet* at the Royal Court in a party that included Prince and Princess Michael of Kent. When they came to the line in the play, 'Observed of all observers', the princess gave me a poke in the ribs.

David's obsession with the healing powers of psychotherapy stemmed from his own internal problems, which went back to his childhood. His lack of progress at school and university was usually put down to the struggle he had to cut himself off from Cliveden and the life of stupefying wealth in which had been brought up. His agonised letters home to his mother, the legendary Nancy Astor, from Eton and Balliol show how hard he found it to break with her overpowering influence, and also his determination, for the sake of his own sanity and individuality, to do so.

It was no surprise to learn later that he had had therapy sessions almost every day of his life; with Anna Freud until she died in 1982 and with others afterwards. He would do this every morning before going to the office. No wonder his chauffeur, Jack, was heard to say: 'For a rich man he doesn't seem to have a very good time.'

At David's memorial service in 2002, his son Richard explained the importance of psychotherapy in his father's life. He said that the mental problems rooted in his childhood had caused 'acute internal difficulties' in his youth. Richard believed it was no coincidence that his most celebrated years as an editor came after he began his daily sessions with Anna Freud.

> His formerly crippling self-doubt developed into constructive self-questioning, which led to unusually profound self-knowledge. Insights into his own mind gave him a clearer understanding of human nature, which sharpened his exceptionally good judgment of character and enhanced his ability to distinguish sense from nonsense in even the most controversial situations.

Richard's use of the word 'nonsense' reminded me of one of David's most frequent quotes from Orwell: '*The Observer* must be the enemy of nonsense.'

Richard concluded: 'He learned to use the emotional strength and the moral courage he had built up by overcoming his internal difficulties, combined with his inherited advantages, to fight and win brave battles on behalf of people suffering every kind of misfortune.'

David's philosophy, insofar as he had one, began with people and their suffering and how it should be removed. It grew out of his natural kindness and the conviction impressed on him by his father, Waldorf Astor, that those blessed with riches had a special duty to serve the community as best they could.

His great American friend Sam Beer, whom he had met at Oxford, said of him: 'I have never known anyone who cared so much about being kind, from rescuing a donkey from a bad master, to helping battered women, to financing anti-apartheid efforts.' As an *Observer* colleague pointed out, even his initials – F. D. L. A. – sounded like a freedom movement.

When he left Oxford in 1934, David had virtually run away from home, visiting his family only at Christmas. He was so obsessed with bridging the gap between his privileged life and those of 'ordinary people' that he took a job in a Glasgow factory, working on a machine, and later led a pantomime troupe in Whitby. It was clearly a happy time in his life.

It must have been during this period that he acquired some of his favourite slang phrases, such as 'chums', 'hols' and 'okey-dokey', which came oddly from the mouth of an aristocrat and an Eton and Balliol man. He had also acquired a remarkably powerful whistle, which he would use to call taxis. I was with him outside the Waldorf Astoria Hotel, once owned by his family, when he summoned a taxi with a whistle that not only brought the cab to his side immediately, but was marvelled at by anyone within hearing range. He told me that he had been taught to whistle by a shepherd on the Isle of Jura, where he spent his summer holidays.

The Astors owned much of the island and took their own cow on their holiday in a special railway carriage and then by steamer. On one occasion when David was on holiday, I was working on a Saturday evening on the news desk when I took a call from a Glasgow hotel. The Astor cortege had apparently missed their rail connection from Glasgow to London after their holiday in Jura and were trying to put up at the hotel. Unfortunately, like the Queen, Astor carried no money – nor, being an unworldly man, did he even have a credit card. The hotel manager wanted me to vouch for him.

And so it was that this grandson of two Durham coal miners had to reassure the hotelier that Mr Astor was one of the richest men in the country and he need not fear for his money. I admit to having had a brief, mischievous moment when I wondered what would happen if I'd said I'd never heard of him.

Even though he had joined his parents and other notable figures, including George Bernard Shaw, on a jaunt to Soviet Russia in the 1930s, he was never one of 'Stalin's useful idiots', as Communist apologists were labelled. Nor, having visited Germany himself in the 1930s and seen a Nuremburg rally at first hand, did he have any illusions about the nature of the Nazi regime. He distanced himself from friends and family who met at Cliveden and hoped to avert war by making peace with Hitler. He once defined the ethic of *The Observer* as 'doing the opposite of what Hitler would have done'.

Nevertheless, the Beaverbrook press, following the lead of Claud Cockburn and his *Private Eye*-style magazine *The Week* – which (it turned out later) was controlled by the Communist Party and funded from Moscow – used to brand David, along with all the Astors, as part of 'the Cliveden set', a phrase Cockburn had invented.

But a letter David wrote to his mother before the war shows how far this charge was wide of the mark in his case: 'I can't help smiling at our bird-watching, trout-fishing, good kind Mr Chamberlain in his woollen underwear dealing with this womanishly deceptive, hysterical, homicidal coward Adolf.' The letter also displays his gift for language, though he was always reluctant to write much himself in *The Observer*, possibly because he found it such hard labour.

• • •

I followed my opening line in that tribute to David at his memorial service – 'David Astor was a great editor because he was a great man' – like this:

> The two things do not always go together. There are highly successful editors who are not great men – and, if truth be told, are not very *good* men either. In David, the man and the journalist were of a piece. If *The Observer* stood for important values and convictions, these came from him – dug painfully out from his own mind, heart and conscience. If the paper was characterised by humour, idealism, a sense of justice and a wide-ranging curiosity about the world and the vagaries of human nature, which it was, those qualities had their source in David's own complex and elusive personality.

It is generally thought that a chief requirement in an editor is decisiveness, but as anyone who ever worked for David could testify, he often belied that belief – so much so that the phrase 'the editor's indecision is final' was actually coined about him by Katharine Whitehorn after a notably unproductive editorial conference.

This was not the case over major issues like Suez or apartheid, where he saw the truth with blazing moral clarity. But over lesser decisions he frequently tortured himself – and, it has to be said – tortured his subordinates too. I can still see KPO and the head printer, Dick Gale, wringing their hands in agony outside David's office as he wrestled with a final page proof. He was a restless worrier about the paper. I still have pages of notes he would send me, outlining apparently insoluble staff problems or urging more coverage of complex social or international issues.

David's habitual indecisiveness was caused by two things, I believe. A kind of perfectionism rare in newspapers: a determination to say the right thing – above all, to avoid saying the *wrong* thing – no matter how long it might take, because he believed that it matters what newspapers say and that they have a duty to be fair to people in public life. This was a result, I think, of the unkind way in which the press had sometimes treated his own family, especially his mother, but also his elder brother Bill, who inherited Cliveden and the title that went with it, and became embroiled in the Profumo scandal of the early 1960s.

It was also because David didn't like laying down the law. He operated in an oblique, rather feline way, prompting people towards a solution rather than imposing it on them. However, that habit of hesitation, that apparent diffidence, masked a steely determination. For all his deceptive air of befuddlement, he had a bold simplicity of mind. One of my senior colleagues remarked: 'In all the time I've known David, I've never once heard him raise his voice.' There are few, if any, other editors of whom that can be said – or people for that matter.

Neal Ascherson said that his *Observer* colleagues were like 'a brilliant dysfunctional family' led by a man whose 'enduring qualities were kindness and courage'. Neal went on: 'David fed them, and his feeding hand was sometimes sharply bitten. It was a frightfully emotional paper.'

David's *Observer* was also rare among newspapers in that it made no claim to omniscience. There were no thumping certitudes on every subject under the sun. I once heard him say: 'There are some problems in this life to which there are no answers. There are other problems to which there may be answers, but we don't happen to know what they are.' This attitude gave special authority to the paper's opinions when it did express them.

Astor was an exceptional talent-spotter, a prime function of any successful editor. Proof of this is shown by the sheer resonance of the writers and thinkers he gathered around him: George Orwell, Arthur Koestler, Alastair Buchan, Philip Toynbee, Kenneth Tynan, Edward Crankshaw, Patrick O'Donovan, Katharine Whitehorn, Gavin Young, Michael Frayn, Anthony Sampson, Andrew Shonfield, Sam Brittan, Hugh McIlvanney, Ascherson himself and many, many others. I was lucky to inherit about half of these writers from him.

None of these were orthodox journalists and David did not find them in an orthodox way. He recruited Nigel Gosling, an old school friend who became a distinguished art and ballet critic, at a bus stop. Terry Kilmartin, translator of Proust and widely acknowledged as a great literary editor, even though he never went to university, jumped with David into France with SOE during the war and is said to have applied a field dressing to the wound he received.

Clifford Makins, a brilliant though shambolic sports editor, was plucked from *The Eagle*, a children's comic paper. Michael Davie was offered the job of diplomatic correspondent while still an Oxford undergraduate, on the basis of some letters he had written about his holidays. Sadly for journalism, these things couldn't happen today.

David always insisted that nobody was too important, or too unimportant, to write for a newspaper. He was always suspicious of so-called professional journalists, whom he referred to as 'plumbers'. For him, a journalist was someone who had something to say or wanted something done in the world. A writer, he said, was more important than the sub-editor who marked up his copy for the printers.

In my early days on the paper I was suddenly asked by Silverlight as

I was giving him a late lift home: 'People can't make you out. Are you a plumber or a journalist?'

'What's the difference?' I asked.

'Well,' said Silverlight, 'are you here to help David save *The Observer* or to help him save the world?'

'A bit of both, I suppose,' I muttered unconvincingly.

It is hard to think of any other newspaper, with the possible exception of *The Guardian*, where such a conversation could have taken place.

David used to liken the running of a newspaper to being the conductor of an orchestra. Others have likened it to running a theatre – and of course David had done that at the seaside in the years before the war. John Heilpern, an *Observer* writer who went on to produce the definitive biography of John Osborne, said David's habit of throwing his overcoat round his shoulders like a cloak was the gesture of an actor-manager.

Pringle likened David's way of running *The Observer* to 'a Maoist commune'. Given some of the wild and eccentric characters he collected on the paper, it sometimes seemed to me that a more apt description might be circus master, with slow-moving elephants and a cage of naughty monkeys.

● ● ●

I owe a great deal in my life to David Astor. Before I ever knew him, I was educated by *The Observer* as a teenager in the 1950s, as were many people of my generation. The paper gave us a political and moral education that no school or university could match. Colin Legum introduced us to Africa; Cyril Dunn to India; Dennis Bloodworth to China; Edward Crankshaw to Russia; Patrick Seale to the Middle East; Anthony Sampson to the mysterious workings of the British establishment.

The Observer taught several post-war generations how to think and feel about the great issues affecting Britain and the wider world. It became part of our conscience. David was at the heart of this process, not because he had a political message to deliver – he didn't fit into any party mould – but because he puzzled things out for himself and, in so doing, helped others to think for themselves, unencumbered by class or ideology.

It was the war, of course, that forced him to do this. I think he saw the problems of this island with greater clarity because he was half-American. It also helped that, as a child at Cliveden, he had mixed with the leading figures of the day and was far from overawed by those set above us. I remember him putting Harold Wilson in his place when the Prime Minister tried to bully him into getting rid of the paper's terrier-like political correspondent, Nora Beloff.

On another occasion, when the paper wanted to reproduce a *New York Times* report that demonstrated how badly the British Foreign Secretary, George Brown, had behaved on the *Queen Mary*, Wilson harangued Astor on the phone about the damage it would cause to the country's interests. David listened patiently, then said, rather less patiently: 'Mr Wilson, there have been six Prime Ministers while I have been editing *The Observer* and I sincerely hope there will be another six before I go. Good afternoon.'

David taught me many things about editing, including the important principle that the paper should always be better than the editor. By this he meant that an editor who acted like a dictator and banned any opinions he didn't agree with, and removed staff he didn't agree with, could only produce a newspaper as good as himself. (Are the names of Andrew Neil and Paul Dacre going through readers' minds at this point, I wonder? You may think so; I couldn't possibly comment.)

David insisted that the paper should always be better than him. As a result, he took risks with writers and ideas he wasn't sure about, insisting only that they be 'authentic' – one of his favourite words. When I was writing an article to mark *The Observer*'s 200th anniversary, I asked David how he would describe himself. After a pause, he replied: 'Quixotic and seemingly diffident.'

Of the many things I owe him, apart from the main one of entrusting me with the continuation of his life's work on *The Observer*, was the conviction he passed on that the simple questions in life are the most important and the most difficult – and that the job of a newspaper is to go on asking them.

CHAPTER 5

MICHAEL

Astor made me deputy editor on April Fool's Day 1969. I remember the date well, for three things happened on that same day: I started my new job, a second son, Paul, came into the world, and we moved house to Wimbledon.

In promoting me, David honoured the promise he had made a year before when I turned down two outside job offers. Michael Davie, the incumbent, had disappeared from the office for weeks on end and nobody knew where he was. It turned out that he had gone to the United States and then to Australia because his office affair with Anne Chisholm, whom he went on to marry, had been discovered by his wife.

Anne Chisholm was then working on the Pendennis diary column, a job she shared at one point with a young Polly Toynbee. They occupied a tiny cubicle with no natural light, just outside the newsroom. One morning, Anne called me on the telephone, even though I was only a few yards away, and asked if I would go in and see her. She sounded distraught, which surprised me, as she was usually calm and controlled.

I found her clearing her desk and packing her files in a bag. She asked me if I would finish the diary column for that week as she had to go. I asked her where she was going in such a tearing hurry and she paused before replying, dramatically, in words I never forgot: 'I'm eloping with the deputy editor.' For a moment I thought we must both be characters in *Compact*, a popular BBC soap opera in the 1960s that was set in a magazine office. The mystery of Michael's disappearance was finally solved.

When I passed on the news about the elopement to KPO, he was amazed. Astor, it turned out, was not amazed, because he knew already. David and his wife Bridget were friends with Michael's Australian-born wife, Robin, and had been comforting her. Later, when Michael finally returned home to pack his things and clear out of the marital home, he asked a couple of colleagues to help him. They were Nora Beloff and Gavin Young, a roving foreign reporter: it would be hard to think of two people less suited to dealing with the emotional and practical fallout from a distressing marital break-up. It wasn't just that one of them was gay and the other an ageing spinster, but that they were temperamentally unfit for the task.

They were upset after seeing Michael at his home in Little Venice and, already fairly inebriated, took a taxi to David's splendid house in St John's Wood, close to Lord's and next door to Paul McCartney, turning up unannounced in the early evening. David was upstairs and appeared at the head of the staircase to find out what the noise was all about.

Beloff shouted up at him: 'You're a murderer.' David came down and asked what she meant.

'You've murdered Michael's marriage,' she cried, blaming David for all the personal problems suffered by *The Observer*'s staff. David, kind and courteous as ever, asked them to stay to supper.

According to Gavin, the dinner was a comic disaster, with Nora either too drunk or too upset, possibly both, to talk coherently, and David nodding tolerantly as to a naughty child. At one point, Nora was in full flow when she was suddenly overcome with a bout of nausea. Undeterred, she opened her handbag, vomited into it, snapped the handbag shut and resumed the conversation with hardly a pause.

Dinner at the Astors', usually a civilised though fairly sombre affair, with a sluggish flow of alcohol – I was rather alarmed on one occasion to see a half-bottle of wine produced at a dinner for six – was occasionally relieved by comic moments. The Astor children were fans of Kenneth Williams, star of the *Carry On* films, so David asked one of the paper's journalists, Edward Mace, who knew the actor, if he would invite him to tea with them. Mace said he was too much of a star to have tea with the children and suggested that David should invite him to dinner instead and introduce him to the junior Astors beforehand.

When the dinner took place, the conversation got on to serious topics, and the unusual guest of honour made a remark that sounded rather racist, certainly to liberal *Observer* ears. According to Mace, David started tearing the bread in his hands in anguish before quietly, but firmly, putting the actor in his place. This was followed by a few moments of stunned silence until Williams blurted out: 'OK, duckie, if you put your cock up my nose I'll put my cock up yours.' The silence that followed was even longer – until everyone burst out laughing.

● ● ●

The reason Astor chose me as his deputy, according to media commentator Roy Greenslade, was that I 'had all the management and technical skills that Astor and most of his senior staff lacked'. I was also, he wrote, 'a clever politician' with 'a good grasp of production, bags of tenacity and a helping of boyish charm'.

David's main problem in promoting someone so 'boyish' was persuading Colin Legum and Robert Stephens, his veteran foreign policy gurus, that I wouldn't tread on their toes in the creation of editorial policy. He offered them some reassurance by making them associate editors at the same time. When I asked David what associate editor actually meant, he just shrugged his shoulders and said: 'People prepared to associate with the editor, I suppose.'

It was assumed at the time that the managing editor, KPO, might have been put out by my promotion over him, but he told me afterwards: 'I was relieved, to tell the truth. I'd been afraid that you would take over *my* job.'

Michael Davie's shoes were very large ones to fill. He was one of the most important figures in *The Observer*'s post-war history. His problem, in a way, was that he had too much talent and couldn't decide how to use it best. A brilliant writer himself, he was forever torn between writing and editing. He was also torn about whether to live in Britain, the United States or Australia, all of which he loved and had spent some time living.

The US probably wouldn't have been his final choice because they didn't play much cricket there. Michael was one of the most obsessive cricket fans I have ever come across, and I have met many. Soon after I joined the paper, he telephoned me in the office and whispered conspiratorially: 'Sobers is batting at the Oval. Shall we head off?' We watched the great man score an elegant eighty-one. Modesty fails to forbid me mentioning a cricket match in which Michael and I contributed ninety-nine runs to the total *Observer* score of 109.

I spent three years on the MCC Committee, which ended when I led the so-called David Gower campaign, protesting against his omission from an England tour of India. After the meetings, I used to give the doyen of cricket writers, E. W. Swanton, a lift from Lord's to Baker Street station. Once, when Mike Gatting, the England captain, had been forced to quit after tabloid exposure of an alleged liaison with a barmaid, an episode that was generally condemned as a lowering of standards in cricketers' conduct, I asked him if that sort of thing hadn't always gone on but had been hushed up. He thought for a moment, then said: 'What this incident illustrates is the decline in the standards of the English barmaid.'

While on the subject of cricket, it may be worth mentioning Michael Davie's only published comment on me, which he contributed to a book of tributes on my fiftieth birthday, collected by my then wife Kate: 'My favourite Donald anecdote,' he wrote, 'combining as it does cricket and politics, comes from Barbados.'

Having gone to the USA ostensibly to interview the President, or for some other trifling purpose, he then took off on the serious part of the trip, which was to watch a West Indies *v.* England Test match in Barbados. He was sitting in the Press Box (and therefore surrounded by wholly trustworthy witnesses) when someone came into the box and said that the Prime Minister wanted to see him. 'Which Prime Minister?' said Donald.

Michael, for all his brilliance, was congenitally indecisive, which made his quandaries all the harder to resolve. At various times, he had been an excellent news editor, sports editor and the launch editor of the colour magazine, where he could control his own editorial space, but as deputy editor he seemed to find it hard to function. This may have been because he didn't control any particular area of the paper. He also saw the role as doing David's bidding, while it wasn't always clear what David wanted or that Michael agreed with it anyway. He was full of exciting feature ideas, but he was hesitant about making other people do what he wanted.

Bill Millinship and I would sometimes ask for his advice on a problem that was perplexing us on the news desk and would find him oddly unable or unwilling to help. Once, I recall, we sent him the cuttings of two female candidates for medical correspondent because we couldn't decide between them. His scrawled comment, 'Choose the one with the biggest tits', wasn't very helpful – nor, it has to be said in fairness, was the vulgarity at all typical of him. I once sent him an article for his comments and he sent it back with a cryptic note on the top: 'Not boring enough.'

Although he was attracted to the US and Australia, Michael was a quintessential Englishman at heart. With his matinee idol good looks and faultless public-school manner and accent, he would have looked completely at home at a 1930s country house party in an episode of Agatha Christie's *Poirot*. It may be no accident that he was drawn to edit Evelyn Waugh's long-lost diaries, which were supplied by a literary

agent in barely decipherable longhand – probably because Waugh had
penned most of the entries in his study late at night while drunk. The
diaries, peppered with deliciously malevolent comments, about his
friends as well as his enemies, were a huge success, both as a newspaper serial and as a book.

Michael also wanted to write a biography of P. G. Wodehouse. Once,
when he was in the US, he looked up the exiled author's address in the
telephone directory, then turned up on his doorstep on Long Island.
When he introduced himself by saying he had been to school at Haileybury, that was enough to gain him admittance to the great man's
home. Wodehouse proceeded to demonstrate how he had scored a try
for Dulwich College against Haileybury in 1899.

• • •

Another person who fascinated him was Lord Beaverbrook, owner
of the Express titles and the *Evening Standard*. They met in curious
circumstances towards the end of 1956, around the time of the Suez
affair. One Saturday afternoon, shortly before the paper was due to go
to press, *The Observer*'s news desk belatedly realised that, alone among
Fleet Street papers, it had failed to send a reporter to cover the arrival
of Marilyn Monroe and Arthur Miller, the newly-weds of the decade,
who had been greeted with an hysterical reception at Heathrow airport.

Michael, then a reporter, was handed a pile of Press Association
copy and told to knock out a 600-word story for the front page. This he
did, making the point that few intellectuals in history could ever have
been so widely envied as Mr Miller. A week later, Michael received
a message inviting him to fly out to Beaverbrook's villa in the South
of France. The old man had evidently been greatly impressed by the
article and, on the strength of it, was ready to offer Michael the job of
New York correspondent on one of his papers.

A bewildered Davie arrived at La Capponcina to have dinner with
Beaverbrook and his house guests, an assortment of ancient aristocrats

whose conversation was mainly about Churchill, Lloyd George and gossip about old sexual and financial scandals. Michael eventually turned the job offer down, but wrote a long and delightfully amusing account of the visit.

These contemporary notes were to form, thirty-six years later, the introduction to a full-scale biography of Beaverbrook, which he and Anne Chisholm wrote together. The biography was highly praised, one reviewer saying it was better than the authorised version by A. J. P. Taylor.

●　●　●

As David's deputy, I took to sitting beside him at conference. Soon, however, he asked me to move back to my former position half-way down the table. When I asked him why, he said: 'You have a very expressive face and I can tell what you think when people put forward ideas just by glancing at you, especially if you don't like them. If you sit next to me, I can't look at you without turning around.'

Although the seemingly endless editorial conferences could be frustrating, especially for those of us with things to do outside the leader pages, I began to understand why David valued them. It was partly, of course, because he preferred listening to reading, but also because it was a way of getting to know his staff better – not being the sort of editor who buys large rounds of drinks in the pub. He seemed to see conferences as a form of staff therapy, giving writers a chance to get ideas off their chest.

Some senior colleagues, especially busy departmental editors, used to beg me to try to persuade David to cut these conferences short. But I had begun to see the point of them if it meant that the office specialists simply talked their ideas out at length, then retired to their desks satisfied that they had had their say, rather than inflicting them on the paper's readers. This was, of course, a luxury that only a weekly paper could afford to indulge.

After the frustrations that Bill Millinship and I had suffered over the Six-Day War, I was determined to use my new position to ensure that this could never happen again. It always struck me as ludicrous for the paper to have a single news editor who covered both home and foreign affairs. The custom was a throwback to the days of eight-page papers, caused by newsprint rationing which lasted beyond the war until the mid-'50s. As I wrote in a forceful memo I sent to David – and which I still have – this was no longer an appropriate arrangement for papers that had grown to sixty-four pages.

'One man', I pointed out,

> is responsible for the ordering of all stories on all the news pages (some-times as many as ten or eleven), for supervising closely the work of a large staff at home and abroad, plus foreign and local stringers, and all administrative chores attached to this work (such as reporters' expens-es and the paper work involved in sending people abroad), answering up to a hundred telephone calls a day, attending endless conferences, lunches and other meetings, as well as personally handling and often rewriting all the news copy (as much as 40,000 words) that comes into the office on a Friday and Saturday.

I got my way eventually, with KPO's strong support, but also, I think, because David had little real interest in news anyway and was disin-clined to make a big issue out of it.

• • •

Running the paper while David was away on holiday could be fraught with difficulties. Michael Davie had learned the hard way to steer well clear of any of David's pet subjects. John Pringle had once fallen foul of David for running a profile in his absence of Roy Thomson when he bought Times Newspapers. Pringle put this down to the fact that David cared so passionately about the paper that he couldn't bear the thought that policy decisions were being made without him.

While there was some truth in this, I would have been inclined myself to play safe and call David, even on holiday, about a profile of a rival newspaper owner. David was fond of quoting a remark Beaverbrook had once made to fellow proprietors at some media crisis in the past: 'Gentlemen, we must not bomb each other's headquarters.'

With one significant exception, I found deputising for David a more rewarding experience. For some weeks in 1970, soon after I became his number two, he was stricken by a mysterious illness, so I was thrown straight into the hot seat. I recently found a letter he wrote to me in June of that year that said:

> Just a word to say that I thought the last issue of the paper was excellent. Naturally, this makes me very confident of your ability to cope without me … I watch your activities with enjoyment and congratulate you on being able to assume the 'father' role in the office with such apparent ease.

Jeremy Lewis's excellent biography of Astor quotes a letter he wrote to his friend Mary Benson around this time saying: 'I am enormously helped by having at last a really good deputy in the form of Donald Trelford. He runs the paper much better than I do when I'm away.' David said of me later:

> In my experience, Donald always used his own head, although he never made a show of his independence. He also had the supreme merit of usually being right, particularly in resolving clashes of will, where the whole repertoire of diplomacy is of less use than the right hunch about timing.

But I was to fall out with David over something that appeared in the paper while he was away – our only serious disagreement in the six and half years I served as his deputy. It was during the Vietnam War. Gavin Young was in Hue for the paper and filed a long and brilliant piece which I put on the right-hand leader page – sacred territory for David. But I couldn't understand why he was so upset when he returned to the office. The subject was top of the news agenda and we were lucky to have one of our best men on the spot.

David said his objection was to the introduction to the article, in which I had described Gavin as 'International Reporter of the Year', a title he had won that week in the British Press Awards. I thought it was reasonable to mention this in the intro to the article, but David argued that it gave Gavin's piece a spurious authority which it didn't need.

On reflection, I decided there were really three separate strands to David's rather puzzling objection: one was that he hated anyone else deciding things in his absence, as Pringle had found, especially on the leader page; another was that he despised press awards as meaningless baubles; but deep down I think he objected to the anti-American tone of Gavin's article, in which he depicted the US troops as incompetent and heartless.

David, being half-American himself through his mother, had an abiding belief in the essential goodness of United States intentions and believed that only they, working with Soviet Russia, could force peace upon the world. Many of us had doubts about this policy – I couldn't see Russia being able to influence China, for example – but it was part of the fundamental Astor creed. The Vietnam War brought out some serious office divisions over David's generally benign attitude towards Americans.

I had a different attitude from Michael about the role of the deputy editor and became much more interventionist. David was really concerned with the leader pages, with the main article on the front of the Review section, with the so-called women's pages if they were covering feminist issues, and in the colour magazine if it was majoring on a subject that interested him. But he didn't even read some sections of the paper.

I felt it was my job to assume that role. At first, I sensed that section heads naturally nursed some resentment at my intrusions, since they were used to being left alone. Gradually, however, eased by some frank and friendly sessions in the pub, usually the Blackfriars or the Cockpit, they got used to my involvement in their fiefdoms, which generally took the form of writing comments on galley or page proofs. Some, such as Terry Kilmartin, the distinguished literary editor, actually welcomed a second opinion, especially if it was offered gently over a gin and tonic. This was a surprise, for Terry had a reputation for guarding his territory fiercely.

I didn't always succeed in persuading him to do what I wanted. He was resistant at first to my argument that John le Carré, for example, deserved to be reviewed as a serious novelist, rather than as a thriller writer. When I tried to get him to give my old friend Susan Hill more serious coverage, he viewed this as log-rolling on my part. I tried to persuade him to publish a bestseller list – this was some years before the *Sunday Times* carried one – but he argued that most bestsellers were either rubbish or spin-offs from TV shows.

One area where it was soon made clear that my intervention was not welcome was the women's pages. Reading my set of galley proofs one day, I decided that Shirley Conran's article, though very good, was much too long for a column and suggested some cuts. The next thing I knew, David had summoned me to his office and said I had caused grave offence to the editor of the section, George Seddon, and he advised me to leave that department to its own devices. 'George understands these matters better than you and I do,' he said by way of explanation.

I forbore to point out that Seddon, while a highly skilled editor and a thoroughly genial soul, was not actually a woman. He had 'come out' after joining *The Observer*, wearing pastel shades rather than the pin-striped suit and bowler hat he had previously worn at *The Guardian*. After a token protest at this limit imposed on my powers, I gave in gracefully, aware that Seddon really did know his job and was adept at keeping a disparate team of women writers happy.

I remember once, when Seddon was away, his place was taken by the redoubtable Mary Stocks, long-time women's editor at *The Guardian*.

As I entered the room with a set of marked galley proofs, Mary turned her forbidding spectacles in my direction as if to say: what is this *man* doing here. She listened to my comments patiently, as to a child's suggestions, and made no changes at all. I left abashed and never dared to return while she was around.

When I became editor and abolished such 'no-go zones', I found the women's pages caused me more problems than any other department. The oddest women's editor I had was Ann Barr, who had been a star at *Harper's Bazaar* but found it difficult to adjust to the very different context of a newspaper. Talking to her was sometimes disconcerting, because she carried marks on her neck inflicted by a pet parrot she kept at home. She became so eccentric that I decided to part company with her, provoking a protest campaign from her admirers, who included people like Germaine Greer and Julian Barnes.

Miriam Gross, who was brilliant at running books pages but less so at running women's pages, claims in her memoir that she resigned because I asked her to make the pages 'more raunchy' and that in a dispute I took the side of a fashion editor because 'she was a blonde with large breasts'. Reading these sexist insults, I reflected that a man who accused a female executive of basing her editorial decisions on a man's attractiveness, let alone the size of his private parts, would be hung, drawn and quartered – and rightly so. For a woman to say that about a man, however, is apparently all right, even if the claims are preposterous and wholly untrue.

Observer readers didn't want 'raunchy' pages and neither did I – and I never used such an ugly phrase. But we did want something on those pages of greater appeal to women than an article about a male Marxist art critic, which was actually the cause of our falling out. Miriam had the honesty to admit afterwards that the article 'was totally unsuitable for women's pages'. So was she, I'm sorry to say, though I was pleased when she went on to be a such a success on her return to running literary pages at the *Sunday Telegraph*.

Not all editors of women's pages were so critical of me. It was comforting to read a flattering account by a former women's editor, Suzanne Lowry. 'Among the many and various editors for whom I have worked,' she wrote,

> Donald Trelford was by far the most sympathique – mainly, I suspect, because he was the only one who actually *liked* women, in general as well as in particular.
>
> This is not to suggest that we did not have ferocious arguments and major disagreements. We did, and they were sometimes painful, but Donald at least always had the argument, always listened, and handed down what I now see to have been fair judgements.

• • •

David Astor and I fell out over Eric Newby, the paper's intrepid travel writer. He had arrived through one of David's unorthodox methods of recruitment, hiring him while he was a fashion buyer for John Lewis. In this role Newby had got to know Katharine Whitehorn at the Paris fashion shows and she recommended him to *The Observer* on the basis of some books he had written, notably *The Great Grain Race* and *A Short Walk in the Hindu Kush*.

Newby had won a Military Cross while serving with the Special Boat Squadron in Italy, where he had been captured and made a prisoner of war. He escaped with a broken leg and was hidden from the Germans by a Slovenian family who had moved to Italy and hated all fascists. Wanda, the teenage daughter of the family, used to take Newby food while he lay hidden in a hay loft. He went back after the war to find her and they married in Florence in 1946.

In the early 1970s, I was living in Wimbledon, as the Newbys did, and we became good friends. I remember lively dinner parties at their exquisite little house, at one of which I remember meeting their neighbour Jane Gardam, the novelist. Eric would become so excited and red in the face that we feared he might burst a blood vessel.

Newby's genius was in writing great travel epics, but what the paper required – or, rather, what the advertisement department demanded – was puffs about places where readers could take their holidays, against which they could sell adverts to the travel trade.

For Eric, of course, this was anathema. Peter Crookston, then editor of the colour magazine, had a splendid idea for a series on 'Hidden Europe'. When I called Eric to my office to try to enthuse him with the idea, he was horrified at the thought of exposing some of his favourite places to the vulgar gaze of *Observer* readers. So, there was some point to Astor's opposition, and I lost the battle to keep Newby on the paper. Later, when he appeared on *This Is Your Life*, Eric kindly paid tribute to me for trying to save him.

I sensed some personal animosity in Astor's attitude towards him. Eric had a rather posh accent on which David, as an aristocrat, would have looked down as a middle-class affectation. Really posh people, it seems, do not talk posh. David was not a snob, but I caught occasional glimpses of him seeking reassurance about someone's background.

He had accepted me for what I was – a grammar-school boy from Coventry who had become an officer in the RAF, taken a good degree at Cambridge and edited a paper in Africa. But one day it came up in conversation that a former *Observer* contributor, Professor Robert McKenzie of LSE, the leading psephologist of the day, whose swingo-meter became one of the best-known props on TV at general elections, was a distant relative of mine and that Trelford was actually his middle name. David seemed to take comfort in the discovery that he could 'place' me and that I wasn't just a man from nowhere.

●　　●　　●

Book serials had always been a major part of the *Sunday Times*'s success, so I made it my business to try to compete in this area as well – an impossible task, as it turned out, since our budget was a fraction of theirs. This meant talking, mostly over agreeable lunches, to agents and publishers. We bought some good circulation-boosters, such as the memoirs of Rose Kennedy, mother of the assassinated brothers John and Bobby Kennedy; and Piers Paul Read's book, *Alive*, about the South American football team that survived a mountain air crash by eating parts of their dead teammates.

When Mrs Kennedy came to London to publicise her book, I was invited by the publisher, Sir William Collins, to join them for lunch at his office. She wasn't an easy woman to talk to. In fact, it became clear that the lunch itself was what interested her most. While she was silently munching, her nose never far from the plate, I asked her about Gerald Ford, who had just succeeded Richard Nixon as President.

'Do you know Mr Ford, Mrs Kennedy?'

'You mean the man who makes the motor cars?'

'I meant the President, Mrs Kennedy.'

'No, he's a mid-westerner. I wouldn't know a man like that.'

At that, her attention switched rapidly back to the plate in front of her. I got the point: her mouth had much better things to do than answer my tomfool questions.

I am reminded of a conversation David Astor once had with President Lyndon Johnson in Washington. Patrick O'Donovan, who was present, told me that David asked a long, hard-to-follow question about the Vietnam War, including several sub-clauses, to which LBJ replied: 'You mean to say you came all the way across the Atlantic to ask me a chicken-shit question like that?'

● ● ●

A succession of sports editors had to get used to my intrusions, which resulted in good working friendships, usually fostered in the pub, with people like Clifford Makins, Hugh McIlvanney, Peter Corrigan and my old chum Geoffrey Nicholson. I got to know McIlvanney better when he strayed from the sports pages to cover some major sporting event that appeared on the Review Front, which was my territory.

Once, while he was abroad, I shifted around some paragraphs in his report. This was a daring thing to do, for nobody messed with McIlvanney's prose. When he returned to the office, however, he saw the point of my modifications and I sensed that our relationship changed for good once he accepted that I had a genuine feel for words.

McIlvanney has been described as 'the best writer ever to apply words to newsprint'. That high praise came from David Randall, a highly skilled newspaper technician who made himself an indispensable backbench operator on *The Observer* and later on the *Independent on Sunday*. In his book, *The Great Reporters*, he quotes some examples of McIlvanney's striking way with words.

On Lester Piggott: 'A volcano trapped in an iceberg.' George Best: 'Feet as sensitive as a pickpocket's hands.' Boxer Joe Bugner: 'The physique of a Greek statue but fewer moves.' Or on the skinny build of snooker champion Stephen Hendry: 'Never has a wearer of dinner suits been so urgently in need of dinners.' Or this, on the comeback of the sportsman he understood better than anyone: 'We should have known that Muhammad Ali would not settle for any old resurrection. He had to have an additional flourish. So, having rolled away the rock, he hit George Foreman on the head with it.'

By the early 1970s, Hugh was generally regarded as the best writer on the paper, even on one that prided itself on brilliant writers. It was inevitable that other papers would try to tempt him away from us, especially as the salaries we paid were not competitive. On a number of occasions, around six o'clock in the evening, he would put his head round my door and ask if he could have a word. I would ring my then wife and say I was going out with Hugh McIlvanney. After a pause, she would reply: 'I'll see you tomorrow then.'

We would head off into the night, often to Soho, where (insofar as I have any reliable recall of our well-fuelled jaunts) we would end up in the early hours in some seedy club where we would engage in a friendly bout of arm wrestling and Hugh would swear his undying love for *The Observer*. Another crisis over his potential defection had been averted. Recently, when I was staying at the Garrick Club, one of the old waiters said to me: 'I thought you'd be interested to know that the record you and Mr McIlvanney set for the longest lunch in the club, finishing at 7.25 p.m., has now been beaten.'

It was a surprise, not to mention an editorial and commercial calamity for *The Observer*, when he accepted an offer to join the *Daily Express*, presumably for a much higher salary. I warned him that the *Express*, for all its promises, would really value him for his adjectival brilliance and would not allow him, after a honeymoon period, to enjoy the space to which he had become accustomed on *The Observer*. This was something, however, he had to find out for himself.

Meanwhile, I had to find his successor as chief sports reporter. After meeting a number of Fleet Street's sporting heavies, I settled on Peter Corrigan, then writing on a variety of sports in the *Daily Mail*. The big problem came when, as one might have predicted, Hugh became disenchanted with the *Express* and asked to come back.

We met a number of times in secret, trying to work out a way in which I could manage his return to *The Observer* without putting Corrigan's or anyone else's nose out of joint. He had critics on the paper, notably KPO and some people in management, who objected to the size and lateness of his expenses and the length and lateness of his copy.

I was lucky in that the two people whose opinion would carry most weight – Astor and Corrigan – were not opposed to his return. Had they been hostile, it would have been impossible to secure the restoration of our star writer. Corrigan, in particular, was completely grown-up in his attitude and eventually became sports editor for a decade in which the pages won many awards. Peter was a fine man and exuded a natural authority, partly though his size but also as a result of his engaging personality.

● ● ●

Had David Astor retired in the mid-1960s, as he might well have done, to sort out the paper's complex financial affairs, which were inextricably mixed with those of his family, Michael Davie would have been the obvious successor as editor. A decade later, however, when David finally retired, he wasn't a candidate, having made it clear that he didn't want to be considered.

He seemed happy enough with his return to writing and showed no resentment, at least to me, that I had taken his job. He was given a back-page column of his own in which he explored any subject that took his fancy. This quickly became one of the most popular parts of the paper. He won a Granada press award for some investigative columns about the secret workings of Cabinet committees.

He left later to edit *The Age* in Melbourne, where he was adjudged to be a big success, adding an investigative edge to the paper and bringing in some excellent writers. He returned in 1981 and wrote for *The Observer* until he retired to write books full time in 1988.

David's retirement, when it came in 1975, followed a long, drawn-out battle with the printers, who were told that the paper would have to close unless staffing costs could be cut by a third. The printers insisted that journalist numbers should be included in the cull.

I handled the negotiations with the *Observer* chapel of the National Union of Journalists (NUJ) – in some discomfort, as I recall, hobbling around on a pair of crutches after snapping an Achilles tendon on the squash court. David, against all advice, agreed to allow a BBC documentary team to wander round the office while all this was going on. They even sat in on some of my meetings with the NUJ. The printers refused to talk to them.

In the end, a deal was struck in which about 25 per cent of the paper's massively inflated payroll costs were reduced. The *Observer* management insisted that all printers accepting redundancy would have to appear in person in the managing director's office to receive their compensation package from the safe.

As a result, many of them never appeared to collect their redundancy money – people with names like Mickey Mouse, for example, who were listed on the union's schedule of *Observer* Saturday workers, but were never required to work. A number of employees had been paid several times under different names.

At the conclusion of this crisis, David announced that he would be leaving at the end of 1975 and asked the paper's trustees to find his successor. The concept of workers' control, much favoured by Tony Benn, then a minister in Harold Wilson's government, was in the ascendant at the time. At *The Guardian*, when Alistair Hetherington retired earlier that year, the journalists organised a kind of beauty contest in which all the staff had a vote.

The two main contenders were Peter Preston and John Cole. When Preston was shown to be the more popular choice, Cole was persuaded to join *The Observer*. Cole, who became my deputy, told me later that it had been made clear to him when he joined that, whatever selection procedures were adopted by the NUJ, or indeed by the paper's trustees, I would be the next editor and he would be my number two.

This has led some people to conclude that the whole selection process was a farce, since the result was pre-ordained in my favour. This view underrates, in my opinion, the quality and independence of the *Observer* trustees and the determination of the NUJ chapel to see a fair fight.

Although more than half a dozen senior Fleet Street figures put their names forward, it soon became clear that the contest was between me and Anthony Sampson, who had worked on the paper before I joined and had afterwards written some successful books.

David Watt, political editor of the *Financial Times*, made a favourable impression on Goodman, but he was thought to lack the all-round experience that an editor, especially one running a Sunday newspaper, would need. Watt was sadly electrocuted a decade or so later by a live power line he picked up, thinking it was a branch from a tree, at his Oxfordshire home after the storm of 1987.

Other candidates included Joe Rogaly, a talented columnist on the *FT*; Geoffrey Cannon, a former editor of *Radio Times*, who went on to write some bestsellers on dieting; and Dennis Hackett, who had worked on a variety of Fleet Street papers.

Hackett later became editor of *Today* and was then rather foisted on me by Lonrho, who owned *Today*, when they sold the paper. I made him editor of the *Observer* magazine. Dennis was an engaging character and one of the most skilled operators in the business, but even a friend described him as 'blunt, forthright and combative'.

When I told him I didn't like the direction in which he was taking the magazine and objected to the fact that he never consulted me, he replied defiantly: 'And what is the penalty for displeasing Donald Trelford – ex-fenestration?' I told him to pack his bags and leave that afternoon with an abruptness that was unusual for me – provoked by his tone and possibly by well-sourced rumours that he was after my job.

Sampson had his supporters among older *Observer* journalists who had worked with him in the past when he ran the Pendennis column. He was also much admired for his editorship of *Drum*, the South African magazine, which had used black writers and photographers during the worst period of apartheid. He became a friend of Nelson Mandela (whose biography he wrote many years later) and advised him on the speech he gave at his treason trial. He was also the author of bestselling non-fiction books such as *The Anatomy of Britain* and its several sequels as well as exposures of the oil, banking and aviation worlds.

He was clearly a powerful contender. What I had in my favour was that I was fifteen years younger and had effectively been running the paper for some time. After six and half years as David's deputy, the journalists were used to working with me. I suppose I was the continuity candidate, whereas Sampson offered unpredictable change, which might have made some journalists uneasy about their own futures. Some might also have wondered if he could give total commitment to *The Observer* if he was still engaged in writing books.

• • •

The NUJ chapel, in its wisdom, chose two staff members to sound out the views of individual journalists as to who should become their new editor. One, Michael Davie, was chosen because he was known to support his old friend Sampson; the other (Robert Chesshyre, the head of the NUJ chapel himself) because he was thought to favour me. Both were sworn to eternal silence on the exact result of their soundings and who had supported whom. All the chapel members were told was that there was strong support for both Sampson and for me and little for the other candidates.

After this exhaustive consultation process, the NUJ told the *Observer* trustees that it would object to neither of us as editor, but would oppose anyone else. In his biography of Astor, Jeremy Lewis says I won the support of the journalists 'by a fairly large margin', an assessment supported by Lord Goodman in his memoirs, in which he said I had been 'overwhelmingly the winner'.

Although it is true that this was the result that Astor, as the effective owner of the paper, always wanted, I would not have become editor if a substantial proportion of the journalists had been opposed. Having this degree of support from the paper's journalists gave me an authority as editor that I would not have had if I had been simply appointed on Astor's personal say-so. I was quoted in the press as saying that the protracted selection process, which lasted several weeks, was 'gruelling but worthwhile'.

I was particularly pleased to learn that I had the firm support of Terry Kilmartin, which must have influenced other journalists in my favour. Two of *The Observer*'s distinguished foreign correspondents, Gavin Young and Mark Frankland, called in at my office to say that they had supported Sampson out of loyalty to an old friend, but promised me their full support – a promise they both scrupulously honoured.

I had first met Gavin in 1964 in Malawi, where he had been sent by *The Observer* to cover the civil war that broke out after independence. He was quite unlike most of the Fleet Street correspondents who turned out to cover the story. Tall, handsome, impeccably dressed in keeping with the style of a former Guards officer, he commandeered a large car, a driver and an interpreter and acted more like a High Commissioner than a hack. His father had been a colonel in the Welsh Guards and his mother was the daughter of a baronet.

Many years later, I was having lunch at the Garrick Club when a man in owlish glasses, whom I knew to be Sir Maurice Oldfield, head of MI6, padded up to my table and whispered: 'Any news of Gavin? We heard he was swept overboard in a storm off Celebes. If you get any news, you'll know where to find me.' Then he sidled off.

I could only assume that by 'we' he meant the Secret Intelligence Service and that Gavin belonged to it, or was at least well enough known to it for 'C' to care about his whereabouts. By this stage in his career, when he was combining reporting with book-writing, Gavin had licence to roam pretty well anywhere he wanted. We wouldn't hear from him for weeks and would then receive reams of wonderful copy from one of the remote corners of the world. So I wasn't unduly worried about him.

When I returned to the office, I asked the news desk secretaries if they had heard from him and, as it happened, they had just received a message (by Telex in those days) saying he had been shipwrecked but was OK. I duly passed on the message to what I had to assume was his other employer that 'our' man was apparently safe.

CHAPTER 6

ARNOLD

When Lord Goodman summoned me to the *Observer* boardroom, his chubby hands were clasped in front of him on the table and he had put on his grave face, like a country solicitor preparing to read out a will that would bring disappointment to those with expectations. The news he brought me, however, was not in the least disappointing, though it carried a gloomy coda. He announced in his rotund way that the paper's trustees had decided to offer me the editorship, the job for which I had yearned since my teenage years, and had been greatly encouraged in this decision by the support I had received from the paper's journalists.

'However,' he went on,

> I must urge you to consider very carefully whether you should accept the offer. Speaking confidentially, I have to tell you that I cannot guarantee that *The Observer* will still be in existence in six months' time. You are a young man [I was thirty-seven] and you should therefore take account of the effect this could have on your future career.

I told him I would take my chances, though I had been shocked by his pessimism over the paper's immediate prospects. At this time, Goodman and I hardly knew each other. In fact, Robert Chesshyre says that when he was told formally that I was to be appointed editor, Goodman had said: 'It's going to be a man called Treffle.' Although we had met a few times at the dinners that followed trustee meetings, my name had clearly failed to register on the great man's radar.

Goodman had chaired an important board meeting about *The Observer*'s future which David had invited me to attend, even though I was still his deputy and not yet a director. My chief recollection is of Jakie Astor, David's younger brother, saying: 'If this was a racing stud, I know what I'd be doing now. I'd be drawing up a list of likely buyers on the back of an envelope and finding out who's interested.'

So, Goodman's warning to me about the paper's uncertain future had not come as a complete surprise, though I had been led to believe that the savings we had just achieved in the long and bitter cost-cutting exercise with the printers, said to be 25 per cent of the wage bill, had bought us some time.

I asked Roger Harrison, who was taking over from Tristan Jones as the paper's manager, whether the paper I was about to edit was in such troubled waters as Goodman had told me. He said the trustees were so hamstrung by intractable legal problems about using Astor family money to benefit *The Observer* – a problem which lawyers had been unable to resolve for over a year – that he wouldn't be at all surprised if they sold *The Observer* to anyone prepared to take on its debts.

My encounter with Goodman over the editorship was followed by another surprise when I met Tristan Jones, who said to me bluntly: 'I suppose you will expect a salary. All I can say is that there is no budget for one. David hasn't drawn a salary for twenty-seven years and in the current situation I don't know where the money would come from.'

I refused to be made to feel unreasonable for being paid a salary and replied: 'Well, Tristan, you know I have a family to support and that, unlike David, I don't have a private income. I suggest you just add an appropriate amount to my present salary and let me take it out of the editorial budget.' As I had been handling the editorial budget myself, I didn't see any problem with this and couldn't understand why he had to make such a pantomime about it.

It was probably Tristan's last act as the paper's manager, for David, with whom he had been friends since Oxford, insisted that he should quit the paper at the same time as himself. Tristan's father, Tom Jones (both father and son were known as TJ), had been a senior civil servant, rising to Deputy Cabinet Secretary, who worked very closely with Lloyd George and had been described as 'a man of a thousand secrets' and 'one of the six most important men in Europe'. He had been a regular visitor to Cliveden from the 1930s onwards and acted as a sort of consigliere to the Astor family.

Kenneth Harris, a veteran *Observer* writer, told me that when Tom Jones was on his death bed in 1955, he had whispered to David: 'Look after Tristan for me.' Tristan had been a Communist and a bit of a wild card in his youth. David brought him onto *The Observer* in several jobs, finally appointing him general manager of *The Observer*, a role for which he was wholly unqualified, which always struck me as an over-generous way of honouring the death-bed promise he had made to Tristan's father.

But then David didn't really understand the function of a newspaper management; he seemed to think they were like the retainers who ran a family estate, people you could trust with the money and to do what they were told. When Roy Thomson brought in a set of whizz-kid professional managers to beef up the marketing and classified advertisement departments of the *Sunday Times*, we were left looking like the amateurs we truly were.

Charles Vidler, the man in charge of *The Observer*'s general office, responsible for the post, messenger services and general repairs and supplies, was a former footman at Cliveden who had been sacked after being found in Lord Astor's bed with a maid who became his future wife. I once had a frivolous thought about a job swap between Vidler and Tristan Jones.

The building occupied by the paper when I joined, across the road from Blackfriars station in Queen Victoria Street, had a staircase that you could see from the road. I happened to look up one day and saw Tristan going down the stairs just as Charles was going up. It suddenly occurred to me that if Charles went on up to the sixth floor and Tristan carried on down to the first, they could have done each other's job at least as well, or as badly, as it was being done already – and TJ might have been a happier man.

In the late 1960s, before *The Observer* had an NUJ chapel, it was part of my job to go to Tristan with a list of journalists who had been recommended by their head of department for a pay rise. There was no such thing in those days as a general increase based on the cost of living. I would hand over the list and wait while Tristan perused it with a sceptical look on his face and his glasses on the end of his nose.

He would look down the list with a scowl, making comments on the individuals – 'I'm not giving him a rise,' for example, 'he was quite rude to me in the lift the other day – he refused to answer when I wished him good morning.' A female name got the response: 'I don't see why we should give her any more money; her husband must be loaded.' And so on.

On one of these occasions, the office central heating system had broken down and we all sat around in sweaters and overcoats – all except Tristan. He opened his shirt and showed me proudly that he was wearing a curved hot water bottle – a Victorian relic – that exactly fitted his protruding belly. He was an avid collector and used to spend Friday mornings, while the rest of us were putting a newspaper together, at Bermondsey Market.

It wasn't really surprising that the staff soon demanded a more formal method of representation in wage negotiations through the NUJ, though David was very concerned about what he called 'the unionisation of journalists'. Neal Ascherson, who had just returned from covering Germany, where he had been reporting on the revolutionary activities of student leaders like Rudi Dutschke, persuaded me on an evening's pub crawl – a rare event for him – that David had to allow more democracy in the office.

Tristan once invited me to his splendid house in Kent, where he had an amazing collection of ancient royal coaches and every kind of historic political artefact. He had met his charming Polish wife while he was sitting on a tank and she was walking on the road with a column of homeless refugees. When Anthony Sampson asked me afterwards what I thought of Tristan's home and collection, I replied in my pidgin French: 'C'est magnifique, mais ce n'est pas journalism.'

• • •

A man of enormous girth and standing over six feet tall, Arnold Goodman had crinkly hair and extravagantly bushy eyebrows over a rumpled face that no one, not even his own doting mother, could honestly have described as attractive. He must have been well over twenty stone in weight.

These gigantic physical attributes gave him an imposing, even threatening presence, which he doubtless used to good effect in handling industrial disputes, international negotiations and the many other official and unofficial tasks he undertook for two British Prime Ministers, sundry powerful clients and several members of the royal family.

A man who had been on the receiving end of some clever Goodman manoeuvres in the property world once said to me: 'That man uses his brain like a bludgeon.' Judging by the times I saw Goodman in action, I would say there was some truth in that, though it fails to make allowance for the subtlety and humour he also brought to the table and which often swung the argument his way.

I marvelled at the skill with which he could reconcile apparently warring points of view. Having listened to both sides of a question, he would work out exactly where the compromise solution could be found, and would then patiently push both parties in that direction. It was a great feat of intellect and imagination, seeing before anyone else in the room how an apparently intractable problem could be resolved.

He was greatly assisted by his ability to make people laugh – a gift he had evidently developed at school to deflect bullies who set out to mock his size and unprepossessing appearance. Once, when *The Observer* was offered a fortuitous property deal that was to save the paper for several years, a director with much City experience argued that they could strike a better deal than the one Goodman was proposing.

'Arnold,' he said in some exasperation, 'can we not just forget for a moment that this is a newspaper and discuss it as we would a normal property deal?'

Goodman replied: 'Very well, go ahead, let us imagine that my mother was a number eleven bus.'

The resulting laughter – caused in part by the implicit joking reference to his size, prompting the thought that his mother might well have been as big as a London bus – closed off any further argument.

For nearly two decades after 1975, I came to know Goodman fairly well (insofar as he allowed anyone to know him well), not just at *Observer* board meetings or through the labyrinthine moves and counter-moves surrounding changes of ownership, but at relaxed dinners at his Portland Place apartment in London or at his college in Oxford, usually on Sunday evenings.

Although I saw him regularly throughout the late 1970s and the early 1980s, it was only in the second half of the '80s, when, with Thatcher in her prime, he had a less prominent role to play in public affairs, that we became close enough for him to reminisce openly about his great days. I think it was these conversations, in which he mostly talked and I mostly listened, that gave him the confidence to allow me to interview him later for a two-part television series on BBC Two.

By then he had lost the patronage he enjoyed in Downing Street and no longer ran the Arts Council or the Housing Corporation; he had ceased to be Master of University College, Oxford, and his connections with the property world, the film industry, the Royal Shakespeare Company and the Royal Opera House had all gradually petered out. His work had been his whole life. Without it I sensed that he had become lonely and rather lost, since he had never had a family or private life, and therefore welcomed the company of old friends who would remind him of his days at the forefront of British public life.

I couldn't help reflecting on these occasions, as we relaxed as best we could among some charming paintings by Henry Moore and some rather disturbing ones by Francis Bacon (doubtless in lieu of payment by former clients), how very different things had been when 'the Blessed Arnold', as he was jokingly known, had been the country's supreme 'fixer', the miracle-worker, its *éminence grise*, its Lord High Everything Else (to use a phrase from the journalist Frank Johnson).

•   •   •

Goodman became a close confidant of Harold Wilson during his first period as Prime Minister and was used as a reliable sounding board on a whole variety of issues, thereby incurring the jealousy of Marcia Williams, later Lady Falkender, who saw that as her own role. Goodman complained to me once that Harold kept him hanging around in Downing Street for so long that he often missed his dinner, giving the lie, at least on those nights, to *Private Eye*'s nickname for him: 'Two Dinners Goodman'.

He was so busy in his nominal role as a founding partner in the firm of solicitors, Goodman Derrick, and so easily sidetracked by other demands on his time, that he was notoriously late for all his appointments. His memoirs bore the appropriate title, *Tell Them I'm On My Way*.

Every day would start with meetings in his Portland Place apartment. Goodman would emerge from his bedroom (already late after a hectic round of telephone calls in bed) in a bright-red dressing gown, looking like some grand court vizier, to find about a dozen well-known people – businessmen, solicitors, theatre owners and the like – seeking his advice, all sitting around like patients in a dentist's waiting room.

As the supplicants were ushered in one at a time, his housekeeper would serve him an enormous breakfast, which he was constantly prevented from eating by calls on the telephone he kept on a small table by his side. He would then be late for all his meetings for the rest of the day.

On one occasion, when I went to see him as my chairman for advice on some pressing issue, I found him ill in his giant bed, lying fatly in his outsize pyjamas, with the ubiquitous telephone close to hand. We were interrupted by his housekeeper, who pointed to the wardrobe and made the rather startling announcement: 'Mrs Fleming would like her black dress.' Mrs Fleming, I assumed, was the divorced wife of the second Lord Rothermere and the widow of Ian Fleming. I was left wondering in what circumstances the dress had been taken off.

I discovered later that Mrs Fleming often stayed over at Goodman's flat after acting as his hostess for an evening of theatre and dinner. They were inseparable and he adored her, even though (perhaps because) she had a famously barbed tongue. She evidently indicated to him once that an amorous approach would not be unwelcome, but he courteously declined. His friends were surprised by the tears he openly shed when she died in 1981.

Goodman's sexual nature, like that of Edward Heath, was a subject of constant speculation. He had a succession of hostesses, most famously Clarissa Eden, widow of Sir Anthony, the Prime Minister brought down by the Suez adventure, and earlier Jennie Lee, widow of Aneurin Bevan, with whom (as chairman of the Arts Council while she was Arts Minister) he helped to create the Open University.

Others included Hilde Himmelweit, a distinguished social psychologist from the LSE who had published important research on the impact of television on children. The one I knew best was Gael Elton Mayo, whom I first met at Goodman's flat in 1986. Through her late third husband, she was the Comtesse de Chamberet, and, like Goodman's other hostesses, she was a strong, intelligent and attractive woman. She was also multi-talented: in turns a model, a novelist, a painter, songwriter and a photographer who had worked at Magnum in Paris.

Having been born in Australia as the daughter of an American professor, Gael was a genuinely cosmopolitan figure who had lived an adventurous life in Paris, New York, London and Beirut, and had had one Russian husband and two French. She had escaped the invading

Nazis on a French train to the border while pregnant at the age of seventeen. She had an invincible beauty that survived a long and ultimately losing battle against facial cancer, which she described defiantly in a book, *Battling with Beelzebub*. Goodman said of her: 'She had no hates and many loves.'

She told me she was sure that Arnold had no sexual life. She also told me that at a New Year's Eve party, as the guests in his apartment were looking at the heavens for a fireworks display in nearby Regent's Park, she asked him if he believed in God. His answer was: 'It can't be an accident.'

It was in 1992, after a party in Gael's memory at an art gallery close to the Tate, surrounded by her colourful landscapes on the walls, that Goodman gave me one of my best stories. He had asked me at the memorial meeting if I was free to join him afterwards for supper at the Savoy. When Lord Goodman invited one to dinner, one was always free, especially if you were a newspaper editor.

Not only did Goodman have his own table at the Savoy Grill, he had his own, specially adapted, entrance for his wheelchair. During dinner, we talked about the royal family, who were in the news at the time over their various marital discords. When I mentioned Prince Charles and wondered how he could cope with being King if it meant he had to mute his strong opinions on so many aspects of life, Goodman suddenly said: 'He doesn't really want to be King.'

'Good heavens,' I said, 'are you sure about that?'

Goodman replied: 'I saw him only this morning.'

This, of course, was five years before the death of Princess Diana, and long before he could have any public relationship with the love of his life, Camilla Parker Bowles. When Goodman came out with this bombshell, it was one of those moments when an experienced journalist knows not to say too much, or indeed anything at all, in case it provokes a response like: 'Of course, you won't be publishing any of this, will you?' So I kept my mouth firmly shut.

Back at the office, I told one or two senior editors what I had heard and they agreed it was an excellent story. But we couldn't see any way to check it out or follow it up without inviting a crushing Palace denial or a demand by Goodman not to publish it. Since I couldn't reveal my source to anyone, it was hard for the news desk to know how to judge it. I said I would publish on my sole responsibility.

The story led the front page with the headline: 'Charles: I Don't Want to be King.' No other paper could pick it up because the Palace, as I had expected, steered them away from it. A Palace press secretary asked to see me on the following Tuesday and we had lunch at the Garrick Club. After going round and round for a while, with me unable to tell him my source, I said: 'I assume you would like us to publish your official denial?'

To which he made a careful reply that astonished me: 'I am not at liberty to comment on whether the story is true or not. That is not why I am here. I am here to complain that the headline suggests that Prince Charles provided you with the story himself. We would like you to make it clear that he didn't.'

So we published a correction to make that point clear, and that was that.

• • •

David Astor and Lord Goodman became best friends around the time I joined *The Observer* in 1966. A couple of years later, David was persuaded by the outgoing chairman of *The Observer*'s trustees, Ifor Evans, to pick Goodman as his successor. In return, Goodman persuaded Harold Wilson to make Evans a life peer. In 1970, Astor pushed for Goodman to be chairman of the Newspaper Publishers' Association (NPA), in which role he spent six laborious years trying (and mostly failing) to talk sense into the printing unions.

He had a low opinion both of the print union leaders and of the newspaper owners he represented. He described the NPA as 'the most impossible body of men that could have been assembled outside the League of Nations' and once said to me: 'If I was to choose a cricket team of the most unreliable villains I've ever come across in my life, some of the newspaper owners would be on there. Max Aitken would be opening batsman.'

Aitken was the war hero son of Lord Beaverbrook. Like his father, he was an indefatigable womaniser, but unlike his father a hopeless newspaper man and, according to Goodman, 'absolutely impossible, quarrelsome and boorish' when drunk, which he was quite often. The only time I met Aitken he advised me to print *The Observer* in one large unit rather than in separate sections – advice which I did not regard as sensible.

His most stupid decision had been to deny the editorship of the *Daily Express* to David English in favour of one of his drinking chums, Derek Marks. English immediately left to join the opposition Daily Mail group, which he turned into such a powerful rival that it overtook the *Express* and never looked back. The Express group went into serious decline and Goodman arranged for it to be sold off in 1977.

Once, in a time of industrial crisis, the head of the print union NAT-SOPA (the National Society of Operative Printers and Assistants), Lord Briginshaw, was away on holiday, but said he would meet Goodman if the chairman would be willing to travel to his holiday address. Goodman replied: 'Please tell Lord Briginshaw that nothing would please me more than to meet him on a high cliff-top overlooking the sea.'

Arnold and David spoke every day, often several times a day, mostly about politics or newspapers but also about good causes for which Goodman sought Astor's support. David really believed that Goodman was a cross between a saint and a genius and Goodman probably thought the same about him, saying he was 'as big-hearted and liberal a man as can be found on this earth'. They both had a touch of genius in their different ways, but Astor was the more saintly of the two.

Much has been made, notably by *Private Eye*, of the attempts by Lord Badman, as they called him, to bully newspapers out of carrying stories that might embarrass his commercial clients or Harold Wilson and the Labour government. Goodman denied strongly to me that he was ever 'trigger-happy' over libel and argued that he invariably advised clients against suing newspapers. Instead, he frequently extracted apologies and damages without going to trial. The 'fear of Arnold', as it became known in newspaper offices, was often enough to make editors back off.

He once persuaded David Astor to remove from *The Observer* an article about a drunken George Brown, then Deputy Prime Minister, who had allegedly asked the wife of the French ambassador to sleep with him. When she declined, he protested that she had surely accepted such invitations in the past. She is said to have replied: 'Yes, but not before the soup.'

In my time as editor he never asked me to spike any story, but I have to confess that his Saturday telephone calls still set me on edge. He would sometimes ring up on a fishing expedition to find out if we were planning to write about someone he knew – never in a menacing way, but one always sensed that menace might have been just been around the corner if I had refused to tell him or had warned him that we were about to insult or even criticise a client of his.

I used to take the opportunity these occasions afforded to sound out his views on some current political issue and frequently found his comments helpful, especially when he quoted what government ministers had told him, though in considering his views one had to remember which of many public or private bodies he was currently engaged to represent and lobby for.

He had a rather contradictory attitude to press publicity. He liked being famous but he heartily disliked being written about. On the issue of press freedom, I concluded, Goodman was a firm believer – but not so firmly, perhaps, when he himself, his friends or his clients were involved.

I got the feeling at our Sunday evening soirees, especially towards the end of his life, that Goodman had doubts about some early legal victories he had won and which had damaged his relations with the press. He certainly seemed to wish to defend his conduct in these cases and significantly titled a chapter in his memoirs, 'Professional Misgivings'.

One case that clearly still worried him was against *The Spectator*.

Although it took place long before I knew him, two of my deputy editors, John Cole and Anthony Howard, had covered the case and both had remained heavily critical of Goodman's role. He had been acting on behalf of three senior Labour luminaries – Aneurin Bevan, Richard Crossman and Morgan Phillips, the party secretary – who were accused by the magazine of being drunk at a conference in Venice.

Even though Phillips, in particular, was shown to have been extremely drunk, the Labour figures won the case and were awarded damages, chiefly because the judge, Lord Goddard, had a grudge against *The Spectator* and shamelessly intervened on the politicians' behalf.

It wasn't surprising, of course, that Goodman should have been invited to help Labour Party figures, but I could never understand why he had played such a central role in exonerating the prominent Tory, Lord Boothby, from charges brought by the Labour-supporting *Sunday Mirror*. The paper had accused an unnamed Tory peer of being involved with the Kray twins and of attending sex parties with the gangsters. Boothby was widely supposed to be the peer in question.

Goodman helped him draft a letter to *The Times* denying that he was homosexual and that he barely knew the Krays. He then demanded damages of £40,000, a record for the time, and the *Mirror* climbed down and paid it, even though they had incriminating photographs in their possession that would have justified their story. They didn't produce these photographs because they also implicated a leading Labour figure, Tom Driberg, a promiscuous homosexual.

It was established later that the story was not only true, but that Reggie Kray regularly procured young boys for sex for himself and for Boothby. Why, then, had Goodman become involved at all in such a sordid affair – and did he not know that his client was guilty as charged?

Murky waters, indeed, in which Goodman later regretted having dirtied his feet. I heard him describe Boothby as 'the most corrupt man in London'. The harsh truth could not be evaded, however, as I suspect Goodman himself saw in later life, that in both these cases he had helped guilty men to evade justice.

Jeremy Thorpe was Goodman's client when he was accused of con-spiring to kill a former lover, Norman Scott, to prevent him exposing their brief homosexual affair. Did Goodman know Thorpe was gay even as he drafted public denials for his client? It is hard to believe that he didn't know, but then he could be very naïve in matters of sex and was generally inclined to accept the word of important people.

Eventually he was able to hand over the case before the trial of Thorpe and his alleged co-conspirators to Sir David Napley, on the grounds that he had greater experience of criminal law. I sensed that this was a great relief for Goodman and that he wished he could have washed his hands of the whole affair much sooner, when he discov-ered that Thorpe and some of his unscrupulous friends, such as Peter Bessell and David Holmes, were taking steps to silence Scott without letting him know. Goodman and Napley were so obsessed with keep-ing their communications secret from the prying eyes of the press that they invented false names for themselves: one was 'Gooseberry' and the other 'Loganberry.'

In the event, the prosecution case was torn to shreds by George Carman, Thorpe's QC, in the first of his famous cases, with the un-disguised support of the judge, Mr Justice Cantley. When the news of the acquittal was received in the *Observer* office, I heard Alan Watkins, the political columnist, mutter in disgust: 'Class justice.' Good-man himself always believed, or claimed to believe, that Thorpe was wholly innocent.

The end of the trial, however, did not end press speculation about Thorpe's role in the affair. I became involved when I was persuad-ed by my friend Tom Rosenthal, the publisher, to buy what became known as 'the Pencourt Papers', written by journalists Barrie Penrose and Roger Courtier. They had been working on a BBC documentary about Thorpe, but Goodman persuaded the BBC to drop it. They had continued on Thorpe's trail as freelances when they received a surprise invitation to meet Wilson, in his final period as Prime Minister, at his house in Lord North Street.

It was clearly a bizarre occasion and the thought occurs now that Wilson might have been in the early stages of the Alzheimer's disease that eventually overwhelmed him. Not long after this I heard Wilson make an embarrassing and wholly inappropriate speech at a dinner given by Lord Weidenfeld in honour of a visiting Israeli political figure. Wilson went on about the two British sergeants who had been murdered by Jewish terrorists in a wood in Palestine in 1947 until he had to be interrupted and taken to sit down.

Wilson was mysterious with Penrose and Courtier, describing himself as 'the big fat spider' who would keep supplying them evidence about the sinister role played in British affairs by agents of the South African secret police, with which he had become obsessed. He claimed that they were working against him and against Thorpe and wanted to help the Liberal leader. He supplied very little, if any, further information about this supposed South African plot, which seems to have been a figment of his imagination.

It seems strange that he didn't call in his own security services to help him find out more. The reason he didn't, of course, was that he suspected that they too were also working against him – a suspicion which turned out, after the *Spycatcher* case, not to be the paranoid delusion it might have seemed, but the simple truth.

I published some Pencourt stories about Thorpe and also Wilson's fears about MI5, but we held back on some of their more sensational allegations (most of which, it has to be admitted, turned out to be true). Goodman's biographer, Brian Brivati, claims that the paper 'threw away a series of scoops' because I had been 'got at' by my chairman.

The more prosaic truth is that we didn't publish them because my news desk, led at the time by Robin Lustig, was troubled about the lack of convincing evidence, and I had to establish a basic principle in handling Pencourt material that no more of their stories should be published unless we had stood them up with our own research.

I never discussed the Thorpe case with Goodman until many years later. I sensed then that he wished he had never become involved. The case had brought out two of his less exalted qualities – his naivety about people's sexual lives and his compelling need to be on the public stage.

•   •   •

Wilson's resignation came as a complete shock to everyone, provoking speculation, much of it unfounded, as to why he had decided to go. We now know that it was his fear of the onset of Alzheimer's disease and a promise he had made to his wife Mary that he would not remain as Prime Minister for more than two years after his surprise victory in 1974.

On the Friday evening before Wilson's announcement, Roger Harrison, the paper's managing director, came into the office straight from a dinner party at Goodman's apartment. He told me and John Cole, then my deputy, that Goodman had hinted strongly at the dinner that Wilson would be resigning in the coming week.

John hit the phone to all his Cabinet contacts, but he could get no confirmation. It turned out later that Wilson had confided in only a few members of his Cabinet and that John's contacts didn't happen to be among them. It was a great story, handed to us on a plate, and we missed it. I tried to ring Goodman, but he had gone to Oxford for the weekend and didn't return my calls (or didn't get the messages). For once I would have dearly welcomed his call. The 'fear of Arnold' would no longer have applied.

CHAPTER 7

LAJOS

Looking back, I can see that there was always a touch of Stasiland about him. Eastern Europe was his subject and the place where he came from. In those dog days of the Cold War, three decades after the end of the real one, Lajos Lederer carried into the *Observer* office the exotic atmosphere of intrigue, espionage and faintly hidden menace that will always be associated with that period in the minds of the people who lived through it – not quite saying what he meant, not quite meaning what he said, communicating through an arcane code of nods and winks and whispered hints.

Not that there was anything the least threatening about Lajos himself, who always presented a sunny demeanour to the world. Nevertheless, he had that unmistakable air of a man who knew things, and had seen things, both of which he would rather not talk about. Had Orson Welles met him (which wouldn't surprise me, actually, since Lajos seemed to know everyone), he would surely have cast him as one of those quirky Viennese characters in *The Third Man* who won't, or daren't, reveal the secrets trapped behind their wary eyes.

It is difficult now, at a time when airlines offer cheap holidays to all parts of what President Reagan called the 'evil empire', to remember the grip the Iron Curtain countries had on their people in those four sinister decades after 1945. The restrictions on travel and other freedoms; the secret police; the informers; the show trials; the torture; the propaganda; the covert operations – like the one in which a Bulgarian exile was stabbed to death with a poisoned umbrella in a London street; the problems for Western governments and for the media in finding out what was actually happening within those closed societies. It was the day of the spy – and of journalists like Lajos Lederer.

Come to think of it, there was a touch of espionage about our first serious encounter after I became editor in the mid-1970s. Until then, I had seen Lajos merely as the benign and rather handsome white-haired old man who had a bizarre habit of handing out sweets to the staff. On this occasion, when he popped his head into my office, he found me looking preoccupied. 'What's the matter?' he asked. I hesitated before replying because Lajos had a reputation as an office gossip. Then, for no reason I can think of, except perhaps the look of genuine concern on his face, I decided to confide in him. It turned out to be one of the best editorial decisions I ever made.

Lajos immediately saw my predicament when I told him of my concern about an unexplained management meeting upstairs, and offered to help. 'Leave it to me,' he said, and disappeared for a while. He reappeared in my office with a reassuring smile.

'You don't have to worry. They're not talking about you, or about editorial matters at all. They are worried about the printers, who have threatened to go on strike.'

'How on earth did you find out?' I asked.

'These,' he replied, waving the depleted bag of boiled sweets in the air. He had simply entered the boardroom without knocking and proceeded to offer a sweet to everyone present, all the while noting their conversation. They were all too startled to refuse. Besides, old Lajos was part of the furniture.

There was plainly more to the ritual of the sweets than met the eye. But then, there was more to Lajos Lederer than met the eye, too; much more. From that time on, and for the rest of his life, he came to perform an undefined but indispensable role for me – a mixture of guru, cheerleader and house detective.

Lajos got on well with everybody. He was trusted and liked and acted like a father confessor to some of the journalists. The point of the sweets, he once explained, was that they gave him an easy introduction to anybody he wanted to meet – and that was pretty well anybody he came in contact with, no matter how high or low their position on the paper, or even in the street or on the bus for that matter.

Lajos had an insatiable interest in people and was equally at home dining with the rich and famous, of which he knew many, or eating lunch on a tray with secretaries and printers in the office canteen. Monty Berzinski, head of *The Observer*'s machine room, put his finger on the clue to his popularity: 'The thing about Lajos', he said, 'is that he makes you feel good about yourself.'

The *Observer* journalists would have been amazed if they had known that Lajos, for over a decade, was my chief guide and mentor, a sort of angelic Rasputin in the newspaper's byzantine internal politics. Maybe it was his upbringing in central Europe's tortuous history that had given him such an aptitude for conspiracy and an instinctive understanding of how to deal with complicated situations.

He also knew how to handle rich men. Among many other services, Lajos made it his business to introduce me to his high-ranking friends, such as Denis Healey, Harold Lever, Keith Joseph, Randolph Churchill's son Winston, Lord Shackleton, son of the Antarctic explorer, and to various branches of the Rothschild, Sieff and Wolfson families.

The contacts were extremely useful and produced some good stories. Dinner with Sir Marcus (later Lord) Sieff, chairman of Marks & Spencer, at his house in Chester Square produced a charming story about Margaret Thatcher. When she came to dinner with him she had said, rather mischievously: 'I hear you're a bit of a ladies' man, Sir Marcus.' He replied: 'Well, let's see your legs, then.' At which point she rose and did a coquettish twirl round the table.

Lajos was a good friend of Harold (later Lord) Lever, and we went to his luxurious Eaton Square apartment, complete with marbled hall and Louis XIV staircase, to hear his views on the economy and to pick up any gossip around Harold Wilson's government. But the great financial guru, then

Chancellor of the Duchy of Lancaster, had obviously forgotten about our appointment, for he came downstairs late, still wearing his nightclothes. As he droned on about the exchange rate mechanism and other economic mysteries, I was wholly distracted by the sight of the male member of the Member for Manchester East peeping out from his pyjamas.

Many of these influential figures were prepared to talk openly with me because I was a friend of Lajos, which broke down the usual inhibitions between journalists and politicians. After one lunch, Sir Keith Joseph wrote to Lajos: 'I very much enjoyed meeting Donald Trelford and came away even more awed by the range of responsibilities – from industrial to philosophical – that an editor must cover. I found the discussion stimulating.'

Once, at a dinner party given by *The Observer*'s managing director, he said to me suddenly: 'Donald, your surname is very unusual. Tell me, was your father an unusually short man?' When I said he was barely five feet tall, Sir Keith went on: 'I remember him. He was very brave at Monte Cassino. We should have given him a medal. Perhaps we did.'

When I raised this conversation with my father, I got the usual blank response to any questions about the war, plus a muttered comment about Joseph: 'Mad Tory, isn't he? What are you doing with people like that?'

• • •

One of the most interesting people Lajos introduced me to was his old friend Sir Robert Mayer, a tiny figure then aged ninety-nine, who had been a great patron of music, having started Concerts for Children before the Second World War and Youth and Music after it. He invited me to dinner at the Athenaeum, along with Robert Armstrong, later Sir and then a Lord, who became Cabinet Secretary in the Thatcher years.

The dinner was given by a club whose proceedings, by convention, were never reported, and its dinners therefore attracted guest speakers of an unusually high calibre, presumably because they felt safe from the dreaded media. The speaker that night was Prince Philip, who made some remarks about the dangers of uncontrolled immigration which struck me as uncontentious, but would doubtless be regarded these days as politically incorrect and provoke screaming headlines in the papers.

After the dinner, Prince Philip moved around the room talking to the guests. By this time, he had had a fair amount to drink and kept saying, in response to virtually anything anyone said: 'Nothing wrong with that, nothing wrong with that.' Later I sat on a body he chaired called the British Sports Trust. We got on so well that he sometimes sent notes round to my home address that he hoped I might use in my sports column in the *Daily Telegraph*.

I asked Sir Robert: 'You know so much about music you must be able to say who was the greatest composer – one of the three great Bs or the great M?' He replied: 'Well, I'd have to say Brahms, wouldn't I?' I was surprised and asked him why. His reply was disconcerting: 'Because he was the only one I ever met.' He explained: 'I was studying music at the Mannheim Conservatoire. The winner of the student piano competition played for Brahms and the runner-up sat next to him. I didn't win,' he said defensively, 'because I was so short my feet couldn't reach the pedals, but I did sit next to him.' Later I checked the dates: Brahms died in 1897, when Mayer would have been eighteen.

Rather dazed by this, I turned to the topic of the evening, immigration. 'You must have been an immigrant yourself, Sir Robert. When did you first come to this country?' '1899,' he said, which silenced me for a while until I countered with a slightly jokey follow-up: 'So which side did you fight on in the First World War – Germany or Britain?' 'First World War, old boy?' he replied in a puzzled tone. 'Much too old to fight in the First World War.'

There I was, sitting in a London club, talking to a man who went back a century. I said to him: 'You must have been remarkably fit all your life, to be still running around and dining out at your age.' 'Oh, no,' he said. 'I've never been well. I had two heart attacks in my sixties. That was my crisis. Everybody has a crisis at some time in their life: if you conquer it, they seem to forget about you. Have you had your crisis yet?'

The following year he sent me an autobiographical pamphlet entitled *My First Hundred Years*. I used to have lunch with him occasionally after that at his luxurious flat near Portland Place, where I noticed
that the first entry in his visitors' book was the composer Bela Bartok,
dated 1922. Because of his great age and apparent frailty, I didn't like to
stay long at these lunches, assuming he needed a nap in the afternoons.
I needn't have worried about him. Once, as I stood waiting at the lift,
I heard him bustling up behind me, on his way to the Metal Exchange
in the City, where he had made his fortune and tried to visit every day.
He married again at the age of 101 and lived to be 105.

• • •

One reason Lajos and I got on so well is that his clandestine manner
seemed to suit my beleaguered situation on the paper. He was the
perfect ally: cunning, loyal and discreet. He operated like an East
German spy, reporting directly to his chief on the words and conduct
of those above or below me in the office. I felt a bit like a character in a
John le Carré spy thriller – not quite knowing what the owners or the
management were plotting behind my back, or what the journalists
were saying – and I needed an extra pair of eyes and ears to find out.

Most of my time on *The Observer* seemed a bit like that. When I was
editing the paper in Malawi, a magazine had once said I was operating
in 'a hostile and threatening environment'. At *The Observer*, I found
myself in another one, where I never knew who was plotting against
me, whether the paper was being sold, or whether I was safe in the
editor's electric chair. Three senior Fleet Street figures told me later
that they had been sounded out for my job, and there may well have
been others. Lederer, a veteran of Communist politicking, was an ideal
guide to this duplicitous world.

There was some jealousy between Lajos and Kenneth Harris, another office courtier who cultivated the rich and famous. Both had

a wide circle of social and political contacts and attended the same sort of grand parties. Lajos told me rather sourly once that Harris had edged him out of the affections of one of the Sieffs by flattering an old widow and taking her out to casinos. She would give him money for gambling. If he won, he would keep the proceeds; if he lost, it went on her bill. When she died she left him a Vuillard painting.

Lord Barnetson, a dour Scot who was chairman of Reuters and later of *The Observer*, once nudged me at a reception when he saw Harris and Lederer deep in conversation together and muttered: 'Rival head waiters.'

The journalists called Lajos 'Uncle Bulgaria' after the cartoon character in *The Wombles*. Every time he walked past the sports desk, Clifford Makins would mutter: 'Here comes Trouble in the Balkans.' A former *Observer* colleague, John Pringle, referred in his memoirs to Lederer's 'romantic and startling history'.

His elegant good looks and mysterious background made this entirely credible. There were tales – and, according to the news desk secretaries, actual photographs – of Lajos with the present Queen when she was a girl, as her riding companion in Windsor Great Park.

I once overheard a debate among the secretaries as to who was the most handsome man in the office. Even though he must have been well into his sixties at the time, Lajos was the unanimous choice (as I recall, Neal Ascherson, Terry Kilmartin and Gavin Young were the other finalists; to my chagrin, I didn't rate a mention, which probably serves me right for eavesdropping).

●   ●   ●

When Lajos wasn't spying for me, he was the paper's East European correspondent. His strength was in working his charm on individuals to dig out the facts – or if facts proved too hard to come by, then gossip would do instead. He met the Soviet leader Nikita Khrushchev

in the Romanian capital of Bucharest and the two men got on so well
that they engaged in cheerful public banter at a cocktail party, with the
other guests, including Kremlin luminaries like Gromyko, Bulgarin
and Mikoyan, looking on in disbelief.

He was an expert on Yugoslavia and developed a close relationship
with Marshal Tito that provided *The Observer* with a number of scoops in
the post-war years. Tito, born Josip Broz, led his country's underground
resistance against the Germans in the Second World War and was the
country's Prime Minister and then President from 1948 to 1980. He exercised an iron control over regions like Serbia, Croatia and Bosnia, which
were to collapse into anarchy and civil war after his death.

Tito had a lively relationship with the Kremlin, which admired his
control over the country but hoped for greater subservience. Lajos's
first scoop about Yugoslavia – which was relayed around the world
– was to forecast Tito's break with Moscow in 1948, when he declared
a new foreign policy of 'positive neutralism'. Lajos had not met Tito
at that time and put the story together from snippets of information
provided by contacts in East European capitals.

Tito was intrigued as to how he had uncovered the story and invited
him to Belgrade. 'I was met by Tito's secretary at the airport and treated
like a VIP,' Lajos wrote afterwards, 'which meant there was no need to
show a passport or go through the usual boring immigration procedures in a Communist country.' He continued:

> I was taken by car to Tito's villa at 15 Užice Street in the Dedinje district
> on the hilly side of the city. He was an imposing presence, a huge bear-
> like figure in his Marshal's uniform covered with medals. He spoke to
> me in German. After some awkward preliminaries, he poured us both
> a glass of Slivovitz and we began to relax. He asked me about my up-
> bringing in Hungary and what life was like there today. He asked me
> about Romania and other East European places I had visited. Then we
> got round to the story I had published about his break with Moscow. I
> explained that I couldn't give him the sources of my information, for

professional reasons. He accepted that with a nod, but I had the feeling
he liked me and that we would be having more dealings in the future.
In fact, as I left, he said: 'I hope we will soon meet again, Dr Lederer.'
Then he lowered his voice, gave me a card and added: 'Don't go through
official channels if you want to talk to me. Just phone my office and they
will fix a date.'

They had many meetings over the next thirty years, sometimes at Tito's
fifteenth-century hunting lodge near Bled, which looked like part
of an Alpine skiing resort, and always over glasses of Slivovitz. They
became so close that, at the end of his life, when Tito hosted a meeting
of the International Monetary Fund in Belgrade, the assembled international journalists were startled to hear the 87-year-old leader open
a press conference with the booming demand: 'Lederer, what are you
doing here?'

Lajos paid court to Tito's wife Jovanka, a former Serbian partisan
thirty years younger than her husband, who had caught the leader's eye
by mining a bridge singlehandedly to halt a German advance. Lajos
sent her flowers on every birthday. He was rewarded when she gave
him the exclusive inside story as to why Tito had sacked his oldest
comrade, Aleksandar Ranković, head of the security services. 'Ranko',
as she always called him, 'has been bugging our bedroom,' she told
Lajos, plainly outraged.

This was another world scoop for Lederer and *The Observer*. Later,
when she and Tito split up, Lajos was able to write the best-informed
account of their troubled marriage. Although the world's press had
failed to find her, Lajos managed to track her down, after a tip-off, in a
crowded Belgrade street market, armed with eighty red roses.

In those days of recondite Kremlinology, when no one knew what
was really going on in the Communist world, every word or turn of
phrase was scrutinised for a hidden political meaning. Lederer was
greatly assisted in this task of interpretation by his good friend Edward
Crankshaw, the paper's Moscow expert and a skilled biographer of the

Austro-Hungarian Empire, who would sift out any gold nuggets from his interviews or tip-offs and convert them into a significant story.

The problem was that often no one could tell if Lajos's stories were true or not, since they couldn't be easily checked, resting as they often did on a single, anonymous and interested foreign source. Sometimes the news desk would be nervous and relegate what looked like a spectacular revelation – a thaw in Sino-Russian relations, a power shift in Moscow or Beijing, a new purge of Soviet Jews, or a secret plan to reunite Germany – to a few paragraphs on an inside page. Years later, when his story was finally vindicated, Lajos would produce a yellowing cutting from his wallet and parade it to his colleagues in retrospective triumph.

●　●　●

Lajos had always claimed to have known the actress sisters Zsa Zsa and Eva Gabor from his Hungarian childhood. When Zsa Zsa came to London to perform in a West End play, the news editor called his bluff and asked if he could get the paper an exclusive interview with the star, half-expecting it would come to nothing.

The reporter given the assignment, Robert Chesshyre, was astonished to see Lajos ushered into her dressing room and greeted with hugs and kisses like a long-lost friend, as indeed he was. Lajos even persuaded her to come into the *Observer* office, draped in mink, after the show on Saturday night to see the newspaper being printed. The looks on the printers' faces were a revelation. Somehow the subject of face-lifts came up. Zsa Zsa drawled: 'Dahlinks, I've had so many face-lifts I'll soon have a moustache.' He also took Miss Yugoslavia on a tour of the office when she was chosen as Miss World.

●　●　●

Perhaps as a consequence of arriving in this country as an immigrant who knew no one, he cultivated every contact he made and usually converted them into friends. He did this in a way that might shock a modern journalist. For every Yugoslav national day, every birthday of Tito or his wife, a small gift or flowers would arrive from him at the London embassy. Each would be punctiliously acknowledged by the ambassador on Tito's behalf.

He went through the same performance with other embassies, especially Israel. An appearance on television by any prominent figure he knew would invariably be followed by a handwritten note of congratulations. But then he was just the same with his friends, always remembering birthdays and anniversaries and the birth of children, sending flowers or a bottle of Tokaji.

It didn't matter how elevated a person was – a switchboard operator at *The Observer* was just as likely to receive a bunch of flowers as the Queen or a foreign head of state. It was part of an old-world code that made him such an attractive figure on the London social scene, like a character from some romance about the mythical kingdom of Ruritania.

After the war, the Lederers entertained liberally at their small house in Gordon Place, south Kensington, becoming popular hosts to an unusually wide group of friends. The Canadian High Commissioner wrote to his wife Jean: 'I think you and Lajos give the best parties in London.'

A regular guest was Denis (later Lord) Healey, who became Defence Minister and then Chancellor of the Exchequer in the Labour government. Lajos had met Healey when he was head of the International Department at Transport House and Lajos was urging the Labour Party not to recognise the post-war Hungarian government as fellow Socialists.

His inside knowledge of Hungary and other parts of Eastern Europe brought him into contact with many senior members of the Labour Party, including the post-war Prime Minister Clement Attlee, Sir Stafford Cripps and Herbert Morrison – the man who, as Home Secretary, had interned him during the war.

• • •

To a modern journalist, working for a security service is total anathema, the betrayal of an honourable profession. But this is a relatively recent attitude, dating back to the demonisation of the CIA at the time of America's war in Vietnam. To the generation of Lederer, and indeed of David Astor, who had survived two world wars, working for your country was not a betrayal but a patriotic duty.

Besides, Lajos could easily reconcile passing on messages between political leaders with his journalism, since it gave him access to information and contacts not otherwise available. Some of these messages were from Tito to pass to other leaders in Eastern Europe, especially in Bucharest, where Lajos also had high-level contacts and which he tended to visit on his way home from Belgrade. I suspect he also kept the Israeli Foreign Office or their embassy in London closely informed about everything he found out, especially about changing Soviet attitudes to the Middle East.

Did that make Lajos a spy? If so, he would not have been alone on David Astor's *Observer*. David himself had been in the SOE during the war and had been wounded while being dropped into occupied France. Some of the staff he recruited to the newspaper at the end of the war came from SOE or other intelligence backgrounds.

Several foreign correspondents – Gavin Young, Mark Frankland and John de St Jorre – admitted to me in later years that they had been recruited by MI6 but hadn't seen it through. Then, of course, there was Kim Philby, *The Observer*'s Middle East correspondent, who, it turned out, had been working for both MI6 and the KGB at the same time. Philby's deputy for *The Observer* in Beirut, Patrick Seale, was widely assumed, rightly or wrongly, to be engaged in intelligence, but it was never clear who he might have been working for.

Lajos was certainly accused of being a spy. Among his papers is a document, mainly about one of his Hungarian contacts, Ferenc Kiss, which says that 'Dr Lajos Lederer is in the Secret Service of a foreign

Great Power' (it doesn't specify which). The document, which appears to be an English translation of a Hungarian Communist report, adds: 'Through Lederer, Kiss also kept General de Gaulle informed about the situation in Hungary.'

He was once interviewed by the Israeli newspaper *Ma'ariv*, which described the encounter thus:

> He is tall, with a sportsman-like appearance and a somewhat dancing walk. He took me immediately to the corner of the hotel, so that no one could eavesdrop on our conversation. Most of what he told me was about a secret mission which he had fulfilled and which could not be disclosed generally. He always added: 'Please, this is for your information only. The matter is still top secret.' He is always remarkably up-to-date about the Eastern bloc and creates an aura of mystery around himself.

The last bit was certainly true.

Frankland, an *Observer* correspondent in Moscow, described Lajos as 'essentially a central European gossip who enjoyed confounding the experts and getting them in a tizzy'.

●　　●　　●

Lajos was regarded as Israel's unofficial ambassador at *The Observer*. He had been converted to Zionism in the late 1920s at a dinner at the home of Israel (later Lord) and Rebecca Sieff, where he met Chaim Weizmann, who two decades later became the first President of an independent Israel. Although he was never a practising Jew, Lajos was well connected to many of Israel's leading politicians and to the senior figures in British Jewry.

Lajos was Jewish when it suited him. To say that is not to impugn his sincerity. He had been born Jewish, but his family did not practise religious observance in Hungary and he married outside the faith. But because many of his friends were Jews, he showed respect for their

religion and often spoke at meetings in London synagogues or to
Jewish MPs at the House of Commons about Israel, the plight of Soviet
Jews and developments within the Communist world. He was a guest
speaker, for example, at a memorial meeting in London for the victims
of the Warsaw Ghetto.

Teddy Kollek once wrote to Lajos: 'Jerusalem and its Mayor have no
better friend than you.' Lajos accompanied me on two visits to Israel
and opened doors for me with many of the country's notables, from
the Prime Minister and Kollek downwards.

• • •

Despite his long association with *The Observer*, Lajos was never a
member of the permanent staff. He hung on narrowly to his meagre
retainer through several budgetary purges as the paper's financial
situation deteriorated in the 1970s. Given the level of entertaining at
Gordon Place, I sometimes wondered how he managed for money.

He may have received legacies from the first Lord Rothermere, for
whom he worked in the 1930s, and from one of the Rothschilds, and
at one time there was a monthly allowance from Israel Sieff. He also
provided useful commercial intelligence about the Communist world
for his rich friends and they seem to have found ways of repaying him
– either through assistance with school fees (Anthony Rothschild) or
through paid consultancies (the Sieffs and Wolfsons).

For all his expertise on Yugoslavia, Lajos was in fact a Hungarian,
born in 1904 at Lőcse (now Levoča) in the Carpathian Mountains,
where his father was the mayor and editor of the local newspaper. His
family were among the 3.5 million Hungarians uprooted by the Treaty
of Trianon, part of the Versailles peace conference that ended the First
World War, when his home town became part of the newly created
Czechoslovakia.

Apart from his post-war scoops about Tito's Yugoslavia, his best
journalism was published at the time of the Hungarian Revolution in

1956. He went into the country with the young student idealists – with the help of old friends who were now generals, professors or liberal politicians – and shared their high hopes for the outcome of the uprising.

He stayed on to see these hopes shattered and the democratic dreams for his homeland crushed by Soviet tanks. The tragic fate of his country had a profound effect on him and it took him some time to recover his normal high spirits, though he went on to speak on a number of British platforms to protest at the plight of his countrymen and the purge of Jews from senior posts.

Sadly, he was to die four years before Hungary was liberated by the collapse of Communism and the end of the Cold War he had spent his life reporting.

'My father refused to swear an oath of allegiance to the new country,' he said, 'and he had his house burned down for his pains. In 1921, we were all – that is, my father, my mother, my grandmother and my two brothers – hustled into carts, taking whatever household chattels we could carry.' They were driven into exile in what remained of Hungary after its dismemberment. For months, he said, they survived mainly through his grandmother selling off pieces of family silver. Lajos was in his late teens.

They settled finally in Budapest, where his father went back into politics – 'he could have been Prime Minister if he had lived in different times,' Lajos claimed. He himself took a doctorate in law at the University of Budapest. The family album of this period shows a handsome, well-dressed middle-class family in large gardens, playing with toys and dressing up for amateur theatricals, or out on the ski slopes. His father is shown in a uniform that looks like something out of a comic opera by Gilbert and Sullivan.

Francis Lederer, a cousin with whom Lajos shared a family resemblance, became a matinee idol in Hollywood and appeared in such films as *Confessions of a Nazi Spy* and *The Bridge of San Luis Rey*. He did not appear in *The Prisoner of Zenda*, but there was something of the dashing Rupert of Hentzau about both Hungarian cousins.

Lederer came to London in 1926, at the age of twenty-one, to pursue a postgraduate course in international law. He evidently arrived armed with social introductions, for he was soon to be found in the drawing rooms of London's leading families. Friendly letters from Lord and Lady Astor, half a dozen Rothschilds, the Duke of Kent, the Earl of Athlone, Lord Camrose (owner of the *Daily Telegraph*), Randolph Churchill, Sir Simon Marks and several Sieffs survive among his papers.

While in Budapest in 1935, he had shown the visiting Lord and Lady Astor around the capital. Nancy Astor, the first woman MP to take a seat in the House of Commons and a strong personality used to getting her own way, was entranced by the rich tapestries and glass in the old Hungarian palaces and churches and instructed Lajos to help her acquire them for their stately home at Cliveden.

He was horrified at the idea of ransacking his country's national treasures and finally persuaded her to allow him to have copies made instead. This was duly done, at vast expense, and the artefacts, including a gigantic candelabra modelled on one in the Alexander Palace, were transported to England.

After the war, the Astors used to entertain the whole *Observer* staff at an annual party at Cliveden. At one of these outings, many years after their successful shopping spree in Budapest, Lajos was surprised and rather hurt when he heard Nancy say to her son, Lajos's editor: 'David, surely you're not still employing this old Jew.' David, a gentle liberal, was deeply embarrassed. Lady Astor had a habit of saying shocking things like that, believing them to be light-hearted banter, without realising that they were likely to cause offence.

• • •

Back in the salons of 1930s London, Lajos made good use of his contacts with Hungarian and other foreign exiles to assist his upward social mobility. Names like Count Esterházy, Count Apponyi, Baron von Ullmann, Baron Lang, Mrs Philip de László and Ferdinand Goldschmidt-Rothschild appear in his address book of the period.

One can visualise the dinner-jacketed, moustachioed men with their gold cigarette cases, the coiffured women sparkling in their haute couture dresses, the crystal glasses, the grand pianos, the Art Deco drawing rooms, like something out of a Hercule Poirot television series. In this setting, Lajos played the perfect boulevardier.

By far the most useful of his contacts was Zsigmond Strobl, the fashionable Hungarian sculptor who received A-list commissions in the 1930s from the British social elite, including the royal family. Strobl appears to have been a family friend from Budapest. The arrangement worked to both men's advantage. Lederer would meet society ladies and persuade them to let their husbands, daughters or themselves sit for Strobl. The sculptor would get a financially rewarding commission and Lederer, helped by his charm, his single status and his patrician demeanour, would become a welcome guest in the salons of yet more of London's society hostesses.

The Duke of Kent, the Earl of Athlone, Lord Camrose, General Allenby and George Bernard Shaw were among Strobl's subjects. Lajos would court these exalted figures by attending the studio sessions and get himself invited to some of their homes.

The real coup, however – the jewel in the crown you might say – was the young Princess Elizabeth, then aged ten, who sat for Strobl in 1936 and 1937 after Lajos had met her mother, then the Duchess of York, at a party and persuaded her to visit Strobl's studio. She was impressed and agreed to commission a likeness of her daughter.

There were many handwritten letters to and fro between Lajos and various ladies-in-waiting at Buckingham Palace and Balmoral about the details of the arrangement – from Ladies Helen Graham, Katharine Seymour, Cynthia Spencer, Lettice Bowlby and Victoria Wemyss, sometimes asking him to call at the Privy Purse Door at Buckingham Palace.

There were also some friendly personal notes from more than one of these ladies from private addresses, thanking him for flowers, suggesting that the dashing young bachelor had worked his exotic charms on them too. His success with the royal courtiers is perhaps not surprising, given that he was a consummate courtier himself.

Once the Duchess of York's commission of Strobl was settled, Marion Crawford, governmess to the princess, became a key figure. Lajos became good friends with the legendary 'Crawfie', who was still writing him chatty letters about her holidays after the war and giving him snippets of information about her charges that a modern newspaper diarist would die for. She obviously took to Lajos and trusted him to sit in the studio with the little princess to keep her amused.

Fortunately, he kept detailed notes of these sittings. They provide a fascinating insight into the personality of Princess Elizabeth at the historic moment when, through the abdication of her uncle, King Edward VIII, she became heir to the throne. They also illustrate how far the skilful deployment of charm and other social graces could elevate a penniless young Hungarian immigrant, even in the stratified society of pre-war England.

He recalled that the princess burst into Strobl's Kensington studio wearing a homespun woollen jersey, a tartan skirt and wrinkled socks in buttoned shoes. 'What am I supposed to do?' she asked brightly. When she caught sight of other busts Strobl had made, she exclaimed: 'Why, there's Uncle George,' pointing at a clay figure of the Duke of Kent, 'and there's Great-uncle Athlone. And isn't that Mr Bernard Shaw?' Then, pointing at Ramsay MacDonald: 'Wasn't he the Prime Minister?'

A bust of Herbert Morrison, however, defeated her. When told he was leader of London County Council, she said: 'Oh, is that important?' Reassured that it was, she asked: 'But is he a nice man?' (By all accounts, he wasn't. There is a story that when Ernest Bevin heard someone say: 'Morrison is his own worst enemy,' the Labour Foreign Secretary replied: 'Not while I'm alive he isn't.')

The princess gave Strobl eighteen sittings over two years for two works – one a head, which is now in Clarence House, and the other of her as an equestrian figure sitting on her favourite pony, Snowball, a gift from King George V. Lajos made conversation with her throughout these sessions, which each lasted over an hour. He was impressed by her knowledge of history and geography, especially about countries in the British Empire. 'I am reading *The Times*,' she said proudly at one point.

But it was her knowledge of horses that really amazed him. She had been an accomplished rider since the age of six and had read books on thoroughbred breeding. When he told her he was Hungarian, she said the best thoroughbred horse would be a mixture of Arab and Hungarian. She added that she had some Hungarian blood too. This surprised him, but it turned out that her grandmother Queen Mary's own grandmother had been the Hungarian Countess Rhédey.

The princess said she much preferred receiving toy animals, such as horses, dogs, cattle or sheep, to dolls as Christmas presents. She loved games, riddles and puzzles and asked Lajos: 'Why is the sea so strong?' When he was stumped, she clapped her hands delightedly and explained: 'Because it's full of mussels!'

She told him she used to have a secret arrangement with her grandfather, King George V, after his afternoon nap. She would look through binoculars and wave from the bedroom of her parents' home at 145 Piccadilly and he would wave back to her from the balcony of Buckingham Palace.

George V had died in January 1936 and been succeeded by the Duke of Windsor, her father's elder brother, who became King Edward VIII. She knew him as Uncle David. Then came the constitutional crisis which led to his abdication in December of that year over his refusal to give up Mrs Simpson, his mistress, whom he chose to marry and thereby renounce his claim to the throne. Around this time, Lajos was in a car with the princess and Crawfie when they saw newspaper placards about the growing crisis. The young Princess Elizabeth turned to them and asked: 'Is Uncle David in trouble?'

She continued with her visits to the studio after her father became

King George VI, but Lajos noticed some differences. She was now the heir presumptive. She was more subdued and there was less spontaneous merriment. She no longer chattered on. She didn't rush into the studio, but arrived with a detective, and there was a policeman placed outside the door.

But she seemed happy enough about her new status. Six days after her father was proclaimed King, she brought Lajos an autographed photograph of herself, torn from a book. As she handed it to him, she said solemnly: 'This is the first time I have signed my name since I became heir to the throne.' Lajos kept a number of photographs of these sessions with the future Queen.

Many years later, when Lajos and I were introduced to the Queen Mother at the opening of new premises for the Press Club in London, she remembered the Strobl episode fondly.

• • •

Lajos had persuaded the Hungarian daily, *Pesti Hírlap*, to take him on as a London correspondent in 1926. It was a liberal newspaper, dedicated to democratic ideals, opposed to the rise of fascism and committed under its campaigning editor, Dr Otto Legrady, to the return of the territories lost by Hungary in the Treaty of Trianon – a cause close to Lajos's heart. The country had lost 70 per cent of its territory, 58 per cent of its population and 32 per cent of ethnic Hungarians, like the Lederer family.

This cause was also close to the heart of Harold, the first Lord Rothermere, owner of the *Daily Mail*, Northcliffe's younger brother and a fascist who admired Adolf Hitler and met him in Berlin. Northcliffe was a newspaper genius, owning *The Times*, *The Observer* and sundry magazines; Harold was a financial genius, taking over and expanding his brother's newspaper interests when he died, becoming, it was claimed, the second richest man in England.

Lederer, as a young correspondent for a Budapest newspaper, was desperate to interview the powerful English lord who had used his *Daily Mail* to campaign for the return of Hungary's lost territories. What prompted Lajos to approach him was a front-page editorial under Rothermere's byline entitled: 'Hungary's Place in the Sun'.

Overnight, Rothermere became a hero in Hungary. His interest in the country had been quickened, it is said, by a romance with a Hungarian beauty, Stephanie von Hohenlohe, who had become a princess through marriage. When his many requests for an interview were declined, Lajos found out that Rothermere was living in a suite of rooms at the Savoy Hotel. So, he went round there in his best suit and stood around in the foyer trying to look as though he lived there too.

Eventually he dodged into a lift and asked the bellboy, casually: 'What room is Lord Rothermere in?' Overhearing the question was a well-dressed old gentleman at the back of the lift: 'I am Lord Rothermere,' he announced. 'And who the devil are you, young man? You had better come with me…'

The resulting interview, in which Rothermere said that Hungary's frontier would once again be the Carpathian Mountains, caused an even bigger sensation in Hungary. Thousands of letters and telegrams flooded into Rothermere's office – so much so that Lajos had to go to work there to look after the lord's Hungarian affairs.

Once established in Rothermere's office, Lajos's main worry was how to keep up Rothermere's interest in Hungary, for he had a reputation for taking up causes and dropping them when he became bored, just as he did with women. Then Lajos had an idea. Hungary was a kingdom without a king. Why not make Rothermere King of Hungary?

He tried out the idea rather diffidently on his editor, Legrady, who was enthusiastic and sounded out his political friends in Budapest. They too were enthusiastic, as were the country's aristocrats, and for the next three years delegation after delegation came to London to plead with Rothermere to become King of Hungary.

Although this bizarre proposal didn't finally come off – Rothermere withdrew when the British Foreign Office expressed opposition – it maintained his interest in Hungary for the rest of his life. He even bought land there in case England was invaded. When, after the Munich agreement of 1938, Hungary recovered territories from Czechoslovakia, he was invited to Budapest for the celebrations and received a ticker-tape welcome in the streets – like the king he never was. A memorial to Rothermere still stands in Budapest.

As a royal gesture to the Hungarian people, Rothermere had sent his entire collection of Old Masters on long loan to the Budapest Gallery of Fine Arts. They included priceless works by Botticelli, Bellini, Holbein, Rubens and Rembrandt. Then two things happened to complicate this arrangement: the Second World War was declared in 1939, Hungary joining the Axis powers and coming under Nazi control; and Rothermere's own death in Bermuda in 1940.

Even though Rothermere had many sources of wealth, the absence of the Old Masters made it impossible to finalise his will – a situation which the family and their lawyers had no option but to accept until the end of hostilities in 1945. Then Lajos received a call from Edmund, Rothermere's son, asking him to report to Coutts Bank in the City of London, who were trustees of the old man's will.

He was offered a sum of £5,000, a fortune in those days, to go to Hungary and discover what had happened to the paintings and, if they had survived, to see what formalities would be required to get them back to Britain. It was a rather naive request – requiring a James Bond to fulfil such a daunting assignment – since Hungary, a defeated enemy country, was now in the hands of the Red Army.

Lajos was determined to go, however, for family reasons, for he had heard nothing since 1940, when he had last visited Budapest, from his mother and two older brothers and didn't know if they had survived the war. To get there he required permission from the Four-Power Allied Control Council, which he obtained by becoming an accredited correspondent of *The Observer*.

He arrived in the shattered city on a bleak October day in 1945. There he found his eldest brother, Aladar, who told him that their mother had died in May and that their other brother, Zoltan, had been shot dead on the Russian front while serving in a labour battalion.

He went to the Gallery of Fine Arts, which was surrounded by Soviet tanks and Red Army patrols. He found the place bare. The head of the gallery was an old friend, who told him that the paintings, along with sculptures and priceless antiques, had been seized by Hungarian Young Nazis in April, a day or two before the Russians reached the outskirts of Budapest.

Their orders were to take them to the Nazi 'Gold Train', which already contained Hungary's gold reserves and the thousand-year-old St Stephen's Crown and was waiting at a station ready to go west, away from the advancing Red Army. The Hungarian Young Nazis went along as guards, with instructions to meet the American troops advancing on Vienna.

But once they were over the Austrian border some of the guards had left the train, taking treasures with them, including the Rothermere paintings. They found sanctuary with local villagers, with the result that the paintings were now scattered over the mountainous borderland between Hungary and Austria. Finding them would be a formidable, if not impossible, task.

Astonishingly, however, Lajos did trace them, after weeks of risky adventure that I always thought would make a good film. He was helped by getting a letter of authority from another old friend, Zoltán Tildy, who was now Hungary's Prime Minister, and by dispensing loads of the Coutts cash to agents who went looking in mountain villages. Eventually, with their help, he was able to compile a list of where the paintings were being held.

In Munich, he persuaded the American Third Army commander to provide him with a Jeep, two military policemen and a secret service agent to go in search of them in the homes of peasant villagers. They found paintings in attics, under beds and on open carts, some rolled up and some still in frames, including a Tintoretto and an El Greco.

But they then discovered that most of the Rothermere paintings had

been discovered earlier by an American search party and returned to
the Fine Art Gallery in Budapest. This would have been the MFAA
(Monuments, Fine Arts and Archive) unit set up by the American
army under General Eisenhower and celebrated in the 2014 film *The
Monuments Men*, starring and directed by George Clooney.

This was a serious setback, since getting the paintings out of Austria
was a much easier task than getting them out of Budapest, which was
under Russian control. Somehow Lajos persuaded the generals who
headed the British political and military missions in Budapest, part
of the Allied Control Commissions, to send a plane from Vienna into
the Russian zone under cover of darkness and take the paintings back.

Meanwhile, he arranged for the paintings to be packed in crates,
which he took by van – using a circuitous route to defeat the Red Army
roadblocks – to a military airfield and waited for the plane to land. He
helped to load them onto the plane, which took them to Vienna and
into the hands of the British section of the MFAA. From there, Rothermere's precious paintings were transported to London.

Lt Col Humphrey Brooke, who later became Secretary of the Royal
Academy, wrote to Lajos:

> Having seen the pictures which were recovered by your initiative, I
> would like to congratulate you on the amazing feat of saving these val-
> uable British treasures. When one considers the condition of Hungary
> today, it is nothing short of a miracle that these works of art should have
> been brought back intact.

● ● ●

Lajos was the sort of person you never forget. He adored the company of
women and was an accomplished flirt. He talked about sex a great deal,
but never pruriently. I never heard him tell a dirty joke, for example, or
brag about his early conquests, though these were evidently numerous.
He referred to attractive women as 'yum-yum' and sex as 'jiggy-jiggy'.

Although uxorious himself, he always assumed that powerful men needed mistresses and his tolerance brought him many confidences.

He told me once that the wife of one of his rich and famous friends had consulted him about her husband's notorious affairs and asked for his advice. Lajos had said to her: 'When he comes home to change before going out to dinner, are you always ready?' 'Oh yes,' she replied, 'he insists that I should always be ready.' Lajos advised her: 'Well, I suggest that you should be not quite so ready. Maybe you should still be in the bath or in your lingerie. That might make him a bit less inclined to flirt with other women when you go out.'

There is an intriguing and unresolved mystery about Lajos's relationship with Violette de Talleyrand, a great society beauty between the wars. Daughter of the Duke and Duchess of Talleyrand, she lived in one of the most palatial mansions in Paris, a pink marble replica of the Trianon at Versailles. Among Lajos's papers is a cutting from the *Continental Daily Mail* of 1934, showing her in a glamorous photograph, reporting her engagement to Comte James de Pourtalès.

Superimposed onto the newspaper cutting, however, is the photocopy of another engagement announcement, dated October 1933, from a Hungarian newspaper – of the same Violette de Talleyrand to a certain Dr Lederer, London correspondent of *Pesti Hírlap*.

The engagement to Lajos had evidently been broken off. But why? The mystery does not end there, however. Many years later, long after Lajos's death in 1985, a man knocked at the door of his son Randolph's house in Greenwich and announced that he believed they were related. At first, Randolph thought he must be a crank, then looked closer, saw a family resemblance, and invited him in.

The man said he was the grandson of a maid of Violette de Talleyrand and that his grandmother had had a daughter by Lajos before the war. The grandmother was still alive at the time of the grandson's visit, a very old lady living in the Austrian Alps. She had kept the birth secret because Lajos was Jewish and it was fraught with danger to be thought to be harbouring anyone of Jewish descent in Austria before and during the war.

Many questions remain. Was it really the maid's own child – or is it possible that she was looking after it to shield Violette de Talleyrand from scandal? Or was the affair with the maid the reason for ending the engagement to Violette? The story in the *Continental Daily Mail* says Violette had been suffering from 'ill-health' that winter. Could she have been having a secret baby at that time? Did Lajos ever know he had fathered a love child? If so, did he tell Jean, whom he married in 1940 and to whom he remained faithful for nearly forty years? The news certainly came as a shock to his children. I couldn't help noticing that Violette de Talleyrand's name still appears in the address book Lajos was using at the end of his life.

●　●　●

Lajos had met Jean, a Cornish doctor's daughter, in typically exotic circumstances on one of the last trains out of Europe before the Second World War. He recounted the tale of their meeting:

> I was London correspondent of a Hungarian newspaper, holidaying in Austria in 1938, when Anthony Eden resigned from the Foreign Office. My editor ordered me back to London. I was a contented bachelor, with no thought of marriage. I believed all British girls to be unfriendly, frigid, and insular. Travelling through Switzerland at midnight, an English girl entered my dimly lit compartment at Basle. In what I thought was strong language, she demanded fresh air. Next morning in the dining car I thought she would like frivolous reading and passed her the *Daily Mirror*. But what she wanted was my copy of *The Times*. She is beautiful and fifteen years younger, and two years later we were married. Then she told me that she had swapped her second-class ticket and paid her last five shillings so that she could join me in first-class.

Jean's calm temperament was the perfect foil for his exuberance. As he had noticed at their first meeting, she had a strong, cultured voice – inherited

by their daughter Vanessa – and firm views that brooked no nonsense.
One might have expected Jean, with her down-to-earth Englishness,
to bridle occasionally at Lajos's flamboyant and excitable manner. But I
never saw anything of the kind. He adored her and she seemed constantly
to marvel at the exotic and unpredictable creature she had married.

Their newly married life was soon disrupted, however, not just by
the war itself, but by the fact that Lajos was suddenly arrested and interned with a group of other Hungarians at the beginning of December
1941. He was transported to the Isle of Man, where he became prisoner
number 95228. The Home Office refused to give any reason for his de-
tention. Jean began an intensive campaign for his release, calling upon
the help of the many eminent friends he had collected in Britain.

A key figure in this campaign was Randolph Churchill, the Prime
Minister's son, who wrote to the Home Office:

> I have known Lederer for many years and have had many political dis-
> cussions with him dating back to at least five years before the war. He
> was always a firm advocate of resistance to Hitler and a fervent advocate
> of a Grand Alliance to frustrate German expansion. He has an extensive
> knowledge of central European politics and I should have thought that
> he could have been made use of at this time … from my experience of
> him I should judge him to have been a consistent and passionate enemy
> of Hitler's.

Similar pleas were sent on his behalf to the Home Secretary, Herbert
Morrison, from the Astors, a number of MPs, and from Hungarian
exile groups. The official handling these appeals, Captain Osbert
Peake, must have been amazed at the number and eminence of Lederer's advocates.

Lajos was finally released – and, according to the release order, supplied with a ration book – on 14 March 1942. The Home Office then
banned him from working as a freelance journalist, but the ban was
later revoked after another campaign by eminent friends on his behalf,

including a strongly worded letter from Randolph Churchill to Morrison. He spent the rest of the war working for Rothermere's Associated Newspapers, mainly monitoring broadcasts from Hungary.

Lajos remained devoted to Randolph for the rest of his life, naming one of his sons after him and speaking for Randolph's son, Winston Jr, in a general election campaign in his Manchester constituency. He would never allow it to be said in his company that Randolph was a drunken old boor. Friendship always mattered more to Lajos than party politics, which is why he also felt able to support another friend, Harold Lever, a Labour candidate in another part of Manchester, in the same general election in which he supported the Tory Churchill.

●   ●   ●

Like Scott Fitzgerald's Jay Gatsby, Lajos Lederer had a 'gift for hope' and a 'romantic readiness' for the promises of life. He was a man who always looked for the best in people and brought out the best in them. Even when he was in his late seventies and early eighties, he retained his unquenchable curiosity about other people. He kept coming to the *Observer* office to the last day of his life and was always first to seize a copy of the paper from the presses on a Saturday night.

He was still the life and soul of the party, telling his many amazing stories as he squired a series of attractive ladies around London after Jean's early death. I once left the *Observer* office close to midnight on a Saturday and dashed through heavy rain to pick up my car. As I did so, I was astonished to see Lajos and an attractive woman, who must have been half his age, emerge laughing from a darkened shop doorway like a young courting couple. He introduced her as a Countess.

Since he must have been close to eighty at the time, I had to assume they were just sheltering from the rain. With a man like Lajos Lederer, however, you could never be sure.

CHAPTER 8

RUPERT

Three of the most powerful figures in *The Observer*'s hierarchy – Lord Goodman, chairman of the paper's trustees; David Astor, the former editor and effective proprietor; and Roger Harrison, the managing director – all had a high opinion of Rupert Murdoch's abilities. Even so, it came as a surprise to everyone, including Rupert himself, that they should choose a man once described as owning a 'bordello' of tabloids as the most suitable person to buy the high-minded liberal newspaper over which they presided.

At that time, in 1976, Murdoch owned only two British newspapers, the salacious *News of the World* and *The Sun*, which he had revived as the country's sleaziest tabloid, with topless pin-ups on page three. These were papers, one may reasonably assume, his three admirers had rarely, if ever, read.

When Murdoch had bought the *News of the World* in 1969, his first venture into British publishing, Goodman's firm of solicitors had its offices in the same building in Bouverie Street, and they had done a good deal of legal work for the previous owners, the Carr family. As a result, Goodman had got to know the young Murdoch and began to act for him, soon coming to admire his business drive and acumen.

Astor and Harrison were on the board of London Weekend Television, representing *The Observer*'s minority shareholding, and had seen Murdoch turn the ailing company round with the injection of cash and management expertise. When Harrison suggested that they should

approach Murdoch to buy *The Observer*, other potential avenues having
turned out to be cul-de-sacs, Goodman demurred, thinking Murdoch
wouldn't be interested. When, finally, he was persuaded to make an
approach, he was surprised at the Australian's positive response.

• • •

The other avenues explored by *The Observer* trustees through the
course of 1976 had included the *Financial Times*, United Newspapers
(publishers of the *Yorkshire Post* and other regional papers) and the
Mirror group, none of which had shown any interest in acquiring a
loss-maker, no matter how prestigious.

Astor and Goodman held high hopes of a scheme for newspapers
like the one that had been used in the docks, in which the government
would provide loans to buy out the printers and install new technology.
Although the idea found favour with a Royal Commission on the Press
that was currently sitting, chaired by Lord McGregor, it foundered on
lack of support from many newspapers because it smacked of a government subsidy for the press.

I went with Goodman and Astor to see Edmund Dell, the Trade
Minister in the Callaghan government, but he was dismissive of the
whole idea. When Astor said it would at least save the paper from
being bought by sources in Libya or Saudi Arabia – both of which had
been mooted – Dell replied coolly: 'It seems to me that *The Observer* is
in no position to refuse help from anyone.' Astor muttered on the way
out: 'I don't think he would care if the Kremlin bought the paper.'

This was the gloomy context in which *The Observer* trustees had
decided to offer the paper to Murdoch. He came to London from New
York to talk the matter over with Goodman and Astor. He made it clear
that he would bring in his own editorial team. Astor was dismayed by
this, but Goodman felt the trustees had an overriding obligation to the
jobs of all the paper's employees. Besides, any other possible options
had apparently been exhausted.

Not being a trustee of the newspaper, I knew nothing about the Murdoch talks until David unexpectedly called me into the *Observer* office on Monday 4 October, my day off. He urged me to go to New York to meet him before anything was finally settled. I later discovered that Murdoch had strongly opposed meeting me, as a mere editor, but Astor had insisted.

I was naturally startled and asked David if he really thought Murdoch was the answer to *The Observer*'s prayers. David shook his head uneasily, saying: 'Well, he owns *The Australian*, which is a respectable, upmarket paper. We can only hope that he handles *The Observer* in the same way. Better an efficient Visigoth than nobody at all.'

Then he told me that Murdoch proposed bringing over the editor-in-chief of *The Australian*, Bruce Rothwell, to play the same role at *The Observer*, with Anthony Shrimsley, political editor of *The Sun*, as editor. I was to be editorial director, sandwiched somewhere between the two. I had little doubt that the sandwich would be devoured as soon as Astor and Goodman left the premises.

Rothwell himself was undoubtedly a serious journalist, having been a war correspondent for an Australian paper, then worked in Berlin for the *News Chronicle* and in New York for the *Daily Mail*. He rose to be the *Mail*'s deputy editor until he and the editor, Arthur Brittenden, were ousted by David English in a palace revolution in 1971.

Rothwell was then hired by Murdoch to edit the Sunday edition of *The Australian*, where he wreaked havoc, causing staff unrest by unseating the popular editor of the daily, Adrian Deamer, and giving the paper an unwelcome and hotly contested lurch to the right. For all that he had a respectable CV, two things troubled me about Rothwell before I had even met him. One was that he was such a divisive figure wherever he went, and also very right-wing. This made him an odd choice for *The Observer* if it was to maintain its liberal character.

I knew nothing about Shrimsley except that he was the younger brother of Bernard Shrimsley, then editing Murdoch's *News of the World*, and part of a talented family of journalists. Anthony's son

Robert became managing director of the *Financial Times* website. Anthony himself went on to be political editor at the *Evening Standard* and the *Daily Mail* and was editor of Sir James Goldsmith's short-lived news magazine, *Now*. He also wrote some books about politics.

He was clearly a considerable journalist and, for all I know, might have made a good editor of *The Observer*. But the paper already had an editor and, having gone through the unwieldy Papal-like process of consultation about selecting me only a year before, the *Observer* journalists seemed unlikely to welcome a writer from *The Sun* being thrust upon them.

I flew to New York without telling anyone and had two meetings with Murdoch in his office. He was easy to get on with, oozing what Harold Evans described as his 'dangerous charm'. We talked about *The Observer* and I showed him some campaigns we had run. His interest quickened when we got down to looking at headlines and newspaper design and exchanging the latest Fleet Street gossip.

At dinner with an American journalist friend between my meetings with Murdoch, I heard a rumour that he might be on the verge of buying the *New York Post*, a much bigger deal for him than *The Observer*. When I asked him about this the next day, he looked surprised that I knew about it and muttered evasively, clearly resenting my intrusion: 'Dorothy Schiff has asked me to take a look at it, that's all.'

I see from the notes I wrote down on the plane home that I had allowed a faint hope to rise in my mind that if Murdoch bought the *Post* he wouldn't want *The Observer*. But I was clutching at straws. The prospect was gloomy. If he was bringing in Rothwell as my boss, that would mean shifting the paper to the right and abandoning all that Astor had represented over the previous three decades. I wondered whether David really understood this, or was in a haze of denial about it, worn down by the paper's financial woes and carried along by Goodman's conviction that this was the only possible salvation.

I urged Murdoch not to come into *The Observer* swinging an axe but to leave the senior staff in place until he could judge their performance.

I said it was important that I should meet Rothwell to hear about his plans for the paper. Only in this way, I argued, could I make a fully informed recommendation to Astor and Goodman, and ultimately to the journalists, that the new arrangements would be in the paper's best interests.

Murdoch, I'm sure, thought this was so much tosh, but he was amiable enough about it and arranged to see me again in London the following week. We met in the *News of the World*'s oak-panelled offices in Bouverie Street, which looked like a relic of the 1930s. As we walked down one of the gloomy corridors, he said laughingly: 'When I came here most of the offices contained Oxbridge characters, usually wearing their Vincent's or Hawks Club ties.' My first thought was that I was glad I hadn't chosen to wear a Cambridge tie that day. Then it struck me that, whether he liked it or not, he and I were both 'Oxbridge characters' ourselves.

He agreed to set up the meeting with Rothwell, assuring me I would find his ideas exciting. Rothwell and I met for lunch at the Garrick Club, where he was a member and I was on the long waiting list, proposed by Harry Evans, my rival at the *Sunday Times*, and by Tom Rosenthal, the publisher.

As soon as I met Rothwell, I could tell that Murdoch had failed to pass on my suggestion that the present editorial hierarchy should remain in place until he could get to know them. Rothwell, a burly, bespectacled, unsmiling figure, was scathing about what he called *The Observer*'s 'wishy-washy liberalism' and clearly couldn't wait to get his hands on the paper and bend it to his will.

He urged me to read the American right-wing magazine *Commentary* and especially the ideas of Irving Kristol, the founding father of the budding neo-conservative movement. He enjoyed quoting Kristol's definition of a neo-con: 'A liberal who has been mugged by reality.'

I argued that moving *The Observer* to the right would be a suicidal strategy. Not only would readers be disaffected, but it would make no commercial sense, since the *Sunday Telegraph* and the *Sunday Times* (for all Evans's attempts to liberalise its attitudes) were already serving that end of the market. He didn't appear to be listening, his bright eyes shining through his glasses with the fervour of a religious convert.

I left the lunch with the firm conviction that *The Observer* was about to be mugged, not just by Rothwell's crude conservatism, but by the inevitable drift down-market that was part of Murdoch's DNA, no matter how hard he pretended otherwise. He was proposing to bring in a journalist from *The Sun* to replace me, without the slightest apparent awareness of how this would look to *The Observer*'s staff and readers. Neither man had uttered a single good word about *The Observer* or anyone who worked on it.

I then had a call from Bert Hardy, the senior management figure at Murdoch's British newspapers, asking to meet me at Ye Olde Cheshire Cheese, an historic pub down a dark alley just off Fleet Street, where Dr Johnson, Charles Dickens and P. G. Wodehouse used to be regulars. (It occurs to me that Tom Stoppard could have written an amusing script of the conversation if they had all been there at the same time, clutching their pints.)

Hardy was a shrewd and experienced newspaper manager. He plunged straight in, saying he had a feeling that I wasn't happy with the projected sale to Murdoch.

'Why do you say that?' I asked.

'Well, Rupert says he can't make you out and Rothwell didn't think you liked him and wasn't sure you would get on. That's why they asked me to talk to you. You look a bit jumpy about it to me. You're worried about your precious baby, aren't you?' he added, not unkindly. 'But your baby is in intensive care and is in urgent need of treatment. We can provide that and I hear that nobody else is interested in keeping it alive.'

Hardy was a big man, founder of a dining group called The Fat Boys' Club, where he conferred with other media figures of similar stature – in all senses. Behind his office desk he kept a gun in a glass case, presumably a relic from the Second World War, which added to his general aura of menace. He had a cast in one eye that made it difficult to look him squarely in the face.

He told me that I was too close to the journalists and that the editor at *The Observer* had too much authority and independence in the organisation. He explained: 'This goes back to Astor, who was both editor and proprietor. You are not the proprietor, yet you talk as though you have the same power as Astor. In our organisation editors know their place, which means they are answerable to Rupert and the management.'

I left the meeting unsure about what to do next. I was certain that the Murdoch/Rothwell takeover would be the end of *The Observer* I loved and whose character I had committed myself to maintain. At the same time, I was fully aware of the financial peril that the paper would face if Murdoch backed out. I decided it was time to tell my senior lieutenants and seek their advice.

As we were leaving the office after putting the paper to bed on Saturday night, I invited John Cole and Adam Raphael, the political correspondent, to supper at my house in Wimbledon on the following Monday evening and told them to come alone. They looked at me sharply, hoping for enlightenment, but I told them that all would be revealed, and that meanwhile they should tell no one about our meeting. They looked suitably intrigued and rather nervous.

When I revealed the Murdoch plan they were both depressed and outraged at the same time. John was angry with Goodman for suggesting it and said he would talk to his contacts in the Labour Cabinet who, he was sure, would be appalled. Adam said he failed to understand how David could invite a gangster like Murdoch to destroy his life's work. I urged them to keep quiet until we could see a way forward and we agreed to meet again after giving the matter further thought.

We were pre-empted, however, by the front-page headline in the *Evening Standard* on 21 October saying that Murdoch had bought *The Observer*. There was a picture of me, that and the article reported I had seen Murdoch in New York and that my job was now at risk. There was a general assumption that I had leaked the story, but in fact I was as surprised as anyone else. A Fleet Street source told me later that the tip had, in fact, come from New York.

I was immediately assailed by my horrified *Observer* journalists, who naturally wanted to know what was going on. I rang Goodman and suggested that he should talk to a meeting of the journalists. He was reluctant but, after consulting Astor – and probably Murdoch too – agreed that such a meeting was unavoidable.

It took place in *The Observer*'s conference room, with Goodman and myself seated in front of a roomful of bristling journalists. Goodman gave a short introduction, outlining the paper's serious financial problems and the trustees' consequent dilemma, explaining that the approach to Murdoch was a last resort, though he expressed his high opinion of the Australian's abilities.

When I was asked directly when I had known about the Murdoch deal, I reported on my meetings in New York and London and said I hadn't finally decided what attitude to take to the deal when the news broke in the papers. Asked if I was now recommending the deal to the staff, I hesitated a long time, during which Goodman turned to me with a puzzled frown, and said I would like to hear the views of my editorial colleagues before answering that question. Alan Watkins, the paper's political columnist and a good friend, told me afterwards that 'the look of abject misery on your face said it all'.

Clive James, the paper's TV critic, said people like Murdoch were the main reason why he and people like him had left Australia in the first place. Selling *The Observer* to Murdoch was 'like giving your virgin daughter to a gorilla'. There was much comment in a similar vein. No journalist expressed any support for Murdoch, though some printers, who had joined the room to eavesdrop at the back, told me after the meeting that they weren't going to allow the 'bloody journalists' to decide their future. The production unions were apparently all in favour.

These exchanges, especially the more quotable ones, appeared verbatim in the next morning's papers, after which Murdoch issued a statement in New York saying he was withdrawing from the deal – 'in view of the deliberate orchestrated attempts to build this into a controversy'. Fingers were pointed at me by several papers as the likely conductor of the dissenting orchestra, even though I had not uttered a single word in public against the deal.

Goodman told me bluntly that he regarded my 'unenthusiastic' attitude at the journalists' meeting as 'unhelpful and somewhat disloyal', but went on to say that he had spoken to Murdoch and that his statement of withdrawal was not necessarily his final word. He might still be interested in *The Observer* if the offer was renewed. Goodman then added: 'All he did actually was grunt, which I took to be a peculiarly Antipodean form of affirmative.'

Goodman must have known that the hostility he had encountered among the journalists made it impossible for the Murdoch deal to be revived. I reflected afterwards that it was Rupert's own candour that had been his undoing: he didn't have to say in advance that he would be ejecting me as editor, introducing two of his own candidates to run the paper and moving it politically to the right. Had he refused to see me at all, which was his first instinct, I would have had no ammunition to lead what Goodman later called a *révolution de palais*.

A few years later, reflecting on his failure to buy *The Observer* at a lunch with *Times* executives, Murdoch said to Suzanne Lowry, a former *Observer* women's editor who was sitting next to him:

I should have had *The Observer*. My mistake was to underestimate Donald Trelford. It was all agreed. Astor and Goodman had agreed. Then they said: 'You must meet the editor.' We shook hands and he was very polite and charming. Then he went off and organised the opposition. And that was that.

Author and journalist Henry Porter, after referring to my 'deft political skills and quiet opportunism', commented on Murdoch's remark: 'It is the highest compliment that Murdoch, a man who is rarely outwitted by editors, let alone editors of liberal-minded newspapers palpably on the brink of crisis, could pay. It is also an accurate account of events.'

The Observer was now big news, and speculation about the paper's future filled many newspaper columns. Questions were asked in Parliament. The publicity mobilised a contingent of interested bidders. From having nowhere to go except to Murdoch, the paper was suddenly offered a variety of possible homes.

The front runner was Associated Newspapers, publishers of the *Daily Mail*, which had prospered under the editorship of David English and outstripped its historic rival, the *Daily Express*. English gave an impressive editorial presentation to the trustees, and Lord Rothermere, the chairman, gave a characteristically languid and credible account of his relationship with English, saying that he allowed his editor a free hand in journalistic matters and kept a light touch on the tiller.

The chief drawback to Associated's ownership, a key factor for Astor, was that it was an overtly right-wing publishing group and had even been blatantly fascist under Rothermere's grandfather, supporting Oswald Mosley's Blackshirts and admiring Adolf Hitler in the 1930s. I sensed no warmth in Astor or Goodman towards the *Mail* and that neither of them thought it was a natural bedfellow for *The Observer*.

•   •   •

Looking back now, I can see a pattern in all this that wasn't clear to me at the time. English's mind was moving towards a Sunday version of the *Daily Mail*, which actually emerged less than six years later in the form of the *Mail on Sunday*. I think English would have made *The Observer* into a mid-market partner of the *Daily Mail*, saving the group the bother and expense of launching a new paper from scratch.

They must also have been concerned about the future of their floundering *Evening News*, which was losing a fortune (and which they closed in 1980), and knew they might need a Sunday partner for their presses and to cover the group's overheads. The *Mail*'s interest was such that they made another unsuccessful bid for *The Observer* five years later, in 1981, just a year before the *Mail on Sunday*'s launch.

I suspect that Murdoch had a similar idea for *The Observer*, though this only occurred to me afterwards. Both he and English were two of the most far-sighted players in the British newspaper market and they must have seen an attractive mid-market opportunity in the decline of the *Sunday Express*.

Murdoch virtually admitted this to me when we happened to meet on the day after the *Mail on Sunday*'s launch in May 1982, which had the good fortune to lead its first issue with the fall of Port Stanley in the Falklands War. He was speaking to a body called the Milton Keynes Forum, of which I was a patron. Since I was one of the few people he knew at this gathering, he made a beeline towards me to talk about this dramatic new development in Fleet Street's affairs.

He was clearly excited and asked me what I thought of the first issue. I said I didn't think it was very good. The sport, in particular, was a joke, leading the back page with the story of the world roller-skating championships. He brushed these comments aside impatiently and said: 'English will soon sort that out. Believe me, it's going to be a big success.'

And, of course, he was right. After six weeks, English did sort it out, sending in his storm-troopers from the daily, launching a comic and a colour magazine and beefing up the news, features and design. The paper did become a big success, as Murdoch had forecast, soon overtaking the sales of its historic rival, the *Sunday Express*.

He had been extremely cordial with me, as though we had no past history to worry about, then looked at me rather meaningfully and said: 'I could have produced the same sort of paper years ago if a certain person hadn't stopped me.' In reply, I pointed out that, had he succeeded in taking over *The Observer*, he would have been prevented from acquiring the *Sunday Times* and *The Times*, which he had bought from the Thomson group just a year before. He nodded in acquiescence, belatedly recognising perhaps that I had done him a favour after all.

• • •

Two footnotes to the Murdoch episode are worth recalling. When I eventually became a member of the Garrick, I went into the club and read the notice board containing the list of new members. A man standing next to me turned as he saw the club secretary approaching and said: 'Will you point out Donald Trelford to me if he comes into the club?' The secretary replied: 'Mr Trelford is standing next to you.'

At this, the man introduced himself as Ian Hamilton, a former editor of *The Spectator*. When I invited him up to the bar for a drink, he said he couldn't stay long as he was being inducted into the Roman Catholic church that afternoon. Then he explained why he wanted to meet me. 'I thought I should tell you that I wrote a letter to the club committee asking them to blackball you.'

'Why on earth did you do that?' I said. 'You don't even know me.'

'No, I'm sorry about that,' he replied rather sheepishly. 'I had a letter from a man called Rothwell saying he was trying to get you blackballed and asked me to join his campaign. Luckily for you, the committee don't seem to have taken any notice.'

The other incident also related to the Garrick. I was late for a lunch at the club and urged my office driver, Jimmy Rennie, to take a short-cut through the narrow streets in Covent Garden. We swung around a corner where the Boulestin restaurant used to be sited just as a man stepped off the pavement into our path. As Jimmy slammed on the brakes, just in time, the man's arms were spread-eagled across the bonnet, his frightened eyes scanning the windscreen. I looked up in disbelief to see that, of all people, it was Bruce Rothwell – and we had nearly run him over.

I was in the back, so I don't think he saw me as he shuffled off. Rothwell had gone on to edit the *New York Post* under Murdoch and died in 1984 – as, by coincidence, did Anthony Shrimsley, my intended replacement as editor of *The Observer*.

I said to Jimmy: 'What if we had killed him? Nobody would have believed it was an accident after the battle we've been through to stop him getting his hands on *The Observer*.'

'Not to worry,' said Jimmy. 'I'd have just popped him into the boot and taken him down to the docks, where my mates would know how to get rid of 'im.'

I *think* he was joking.

I got to meet some of Jimmy's 'mates' a few years later when his son asked me to speak at his funeral in the East End. Jimmy was a lovely man, one of the most popular and best-informed characters in the office. A short, perpetually cheerful figure, he relished the excitements of newspaper life and was equally at home in the company of printers, journalists or commercial staff. He talked of *The Observer* as 'a family'.

As chauffeur to the editor and managing director, he knew many company secrets, which he handled with great tact, especially at times when the newspaper was involved in a takeover or industrial crisis. It was once said that if Jimmy Rennie had kept notes of all the conversations in the back of his car, he could have written an explosive bestseller.

When I turned up for his funeral, I could see that these friends of his, dressed smartly in black suits and white shirts and wearing Mafia sunglasses, were wondering a bit suspiciously what this toff (in their eyes anyway) was going to say. I started by saying: 'It would be sad for Jimmy to die at any time, but this weekend was especially tragic. It was the time when his beloved Charlton beat my beloved Coventry City 3–2 in the third round of the FA Cup. How Jimmy would have enjoyed lording it over me.'

I could see the audience visibly relax. It was one of many occasions in my life when sport has come to the rescue as the *lingua franca* between all classes, generations and nationalities. Once, as I was going into the *Observer* building with one of the managing directors, I was met by several jocular shouts from the messengers at the reception desk. The managing director said: 'Why do they talk to you, Donald, and not to me?' I replied: 'It's sport – the universal language; I speak it and you don't.'

• • •

While in Coventry as a young man, I had got to know a reporter on the *Evening Telegraph* called Robert Warren, a rather posh character who had been to school at Lancing and had been a naval officer on his National Service. Bob was eagerly pursuing a young woman called Margot, but every lunchtime, after his latest date, he would shake his head ruefully and report: 'No-go Margot.'

Bob moved on to the *News of the World*, becoming its news editor for twenty years, and was the man behind many notable scoops. In all he served forty-five years on the paper, ending up as the highly valued executive editor. He worked under sixteen different editors from Stafford Somerfield (whom he couldn't stand) to Andy Coulson (whom he liked very much).

Rebekah Wade, who had been his editor, described him to me many years later as 'the paper's rock, the coolest head in the office'. When I joked that 'we used to chase the same barmaids,' she joked back: 'He still is, though now it's the drink he's after.' Although his sudden death in 2009 was a shock at the time, it now seems to be a blessing that he never knew about the phone-hacking scandal that resulted in the paper's closure and the jailing of his friend Coulson.

When I joined the *Observer* news desk in London in the mid-'60s, Bob and I resumed the friendship we had formed in Coventry and used to share stories about our respective papers. This was an unusual alliance, not just because the papers were so different, but because *The Observer* rather snootily turned its back on Fleet Street, mentally as well as physically, and had little to do with other papers.

We used to lunch in a Fleet Street basement restaurant, close to the *Daily Express*'s 'Lubianka' building, which used to charge five shillings and sixpence for a three-course meal. In those days, the *News of the World* carried just as many salacious stories as it did later, but with more subdued presentation and in a text-size format.

Furthermore, as Bob described to me with some amusement,

everyone took the job very seriously. At the editorial conference, the executives were all dressed in dark suits with white shirts, sober ties and black shoes (suede shoes forbidden). As they went down the list of smutty stories, nobody ever laughed. Occasionally someone would shake his head sadly at the revelation of human weakness or another would be angry about a miscreant, say, spying on naked women taking a shower through a peep-hole in a caravan park.

Somerfield edited the paper throughout the 1960s, maintaining and even increasing the sex-and-scandal quotient of a paper that reached a world-record sale of 10 million copies. In 1968, he fought off the embrace of Robert Maxwell in crypto-racist language, insisting that the paper was 'as English as roast beef and Yorkshire pudding'.

But he failed to resist the embrace of Rupert Murdoch the following year, when the Carr family sold the paper to the 38-year-old Australian. It was Murdoch's first newspaper acquisition in Britain, followed closely by *The Sun*. It is hard to believe that the self-righteous internal culture of Somerfield's reign lasted long under Murdoch's ownership. Somerfield himself certainly didn't last, being sacked a year later by Murdoch, who was quoted as saying: 'He was too nasty even for me.'

• • •

Along with Associated Newspapers, another serious suitor for *The Observer*'s hand was Sir James Goldsmith, the eccentric billionaire businessman. Goldsmith had left Eton after winning thousands of pounds in a bet and then eloped with a Bolivian tin heiress, who subsequently died in childbirth. He had remained in the newspaper headlines ever since.

He was known to be interested in buying a newspaper to purvey his political ideas and had often been linked with the *Daily Express*. He later launched a news magazine, *Now*, which was an excellent product, but failed to engage the British public in the way that such magazines did at the time in France and the United States, and it died in its infancy.

He invited me to bring some senior editorial executives for supper at his luxurious house in The Boltons in Kensington. After pre-dinner drinks, we were all sat at a table in the basement, attended by his butler, who brought in a succession of marvellous dishes, while Goldsmith himself wandered around the room like a benevolent maître d', assuring us that under his proprietorship there would be many evenings like this. Each individual place setting had a bottle of high-class claret alongside. This struck my friend Alan Watkins as a rather convenient arrangement, but insulted more sensitive colleagues, who thought he was assuming that all journalists were drunks.

John Cole, who was sitting next to me, whispered: 'Isn't it marvellous being a journalist – and to think we're getting paid for this.' His written recollection of this occasion is worth recording:

I arrived late in the pre-dinner drinks period. When I asked Sir James what kind of paper he would like *The Observer* to be, were he to become its proprietor, I was rewarded with the thought that – subject, of course, to the views of senior staff, not least myself – he would, on the whole, and other things being equal, rather think that it ought to be somewhat left of centre.

Michael Davie confided to me afterwards that when he had asked a similar question before my arrival, Sir James had seemed to think *The Observer* ought to be somewhat right of centre. He was patently a man of decent flexibility. Sir James had clearly done his homework, not only on political attitudes, but on the lifestyle of Lunchtime O'Booze.

The discussion flowed merrily on, we trying to pin the great man down on specifics, he taking what might charitably be called a minimalist proprietorial stance. What would he see as his role at *The Observer*, we asked nervously? Well, he replied, assuming that we were finding the evening agreeable, he rather thought his proprietorship might be conducted principally at a series of such dinners, where he and senior staff would toss around ideas of what the paper ought to be doing. It all sounded extremely agreeable, not a touch of menace in sight, not a whiff of sulphur.

Donald, driving me back to Waterloo afterwards, gave me an old-fashioned look. 'You do realise, don't you, John, that there has just been spread before us the prospect of an ideal future. We are intended to go home with the thought that if we will only give him support to take over our paper, life will be an endless vista of agreeable feasts, with a priceless bottle of claret placed in front of each of us, never having to share?'

John's recollection of the evening concluded: 'We drank, but we did not bite.' More importantly, the *Observer* trustees did not bite either, especially Goodman, who clearly had no time for Goldsmith. His bid was contingent on using the presses of the Express group, which would have involved another prolonged round of redundancy negotiations with *The Observer*'s printers, with all the perils of industrial action. 'It would end up', Goodman warned, 'with the closure of *The Observer* – and very possibly Beaverbrook Newspapers as well.'

The one good thing to result from Goldsmith's approach was that he dropped a libel action against *The Observer*, in which the paper had claimed that one of his company's most famous food brands was bad for babies. I had made this a pre-condition of meeting him.

The next suitor for *The Observer*'s hand was a Hong Kong businesswoman called Sally Aw Sian, whose Sing Tao group's profits were based on massive sales of Tiger Balm, a patent medicine. She also published five dailies and three magazines in Hong Kong, with overseas editions for Chinese readers in San Francisco, Vancouver, New York and London. In 1971, she had been the first female president of the International Press Institute.

I received a blast from the past when Ronnie Bloom, my MI6 contact in Malawi, rang me to ask if I would like to meet Ms Aw at the hotel where she was staying in Jermyn Street. He said he was now working for her, among other things. She had already made a formal approach to *The Observer*'s trustees but wanted to meet the editor as well.

When I turned up I found she had another unusual figure in her

entourage: Norman Barrymaine, an Australian journalist who had
been captured while covering the Korean War in the 1950s and released
some years later after having been apparently 'brainwashed' by the
Chinese. For some time, he was suspected of being a Chinese agent,
but wrote a book about his experiences that appeared to clear him of
these suspicions.

We had a pleasant chat about *The Observer*. But I got the impression
that Sally still needed to convince her financial backers in Hong Kong
that the paper was a good investment. That was doubtless why she kept
asking me if *The Observer*'s building, owned by the Astors, would be
part of the deal. I said I wasn't the person to ask about this.

She then flew back to Hong Kong and issued a statement saying that
Sing Tao newspapers were 'not interested' in buying *The Observer*. This
announcement, it appeared, was to protect the company's share price
on the Hong Kong stock exchange. Although it was generally assumed
that this meant she was out of the race for *The Observer*, in fact she
had always intended to buy the paper with her personal fortune, and
negotiations continued in secret.

The man chosen to conduct this secret mission was David Astor's
nephew, also called David Astor, son of his younger brother Michael.
He was running a bookshop in Burford at the time. As he set off for
Hong Kong with Barrymaine, Goodman joked: 'Tell the lady that the
chairman's hand in marriage goes with the offer.'

For no obvious reason, except that he was playing a cloak-and-
dagger role, Astor travelled under the name of Attenborough. This
caused him problems at both ends of his journey. At Heathrow, he
found it difficult to shake off the attentions of an airline PR man who
kept asking for details of his next wildlife TV assignment.

At the Mandarin Hotel in Hong Kong, where he had booked in
under the name of St John, he had to explain to the police, who were
hunting a gang of hijackers, why he had called himself Attenborough
and St John when the name in his passport was Astor. In any event, his
journey was in vain, since Ms Aw's financial advisers were opposed to

the deal unless some security, such as *The Observer*'s building, could be thrown in.

Meanwhile, other bidders had made themselves known. One was Robert Maxwell, whom Goodman rejected out of hand. When Tiny Rowland threw his hat in the ring, Roger Harrison was dispatched to his office in Cheapside to explain that his company, recently described by Edward Heath as 'the ugly and unacceptable face of capitalism', was not considered by *The Observer*'s trustees as a suitable owner.

Then there was an approach from Olga Deterding, the rich daughter of the founder of Royal Dutch Shell, who had worked as a nurse with Dr Albert Schweitzer at the Lambaréné hospital in Gabon. I went to see this rather eccentric lady in her plush apartment in Grosvenor Square and couldn't help noticing a strange smell around her person, which I (perhaps charitably) put down to her choice of perfume. When I asked her what she would like see in *The Observer*, she said she would like it to be 'more whimsical'. Her offer was politely rejected because, like Goldsmith, she would have printed the paper on the presses of the *Daily Express*.

Patrick Seale, *The Observer*'s Middle East correspondent, came bearing a courteous letter from Colonel Gaddafi offering Libya's financial help to save a paper he regarded as constructive and fair on the problems of the region. Woodrow Wyatt called me to his house next to Lord's cricket ground and, puffing on his habitual cigar, said he had a wealthy client who would be willing to invest several million pounds in *The Observer*. When I pressed him for a name, he reluctantly divulged that it was the kingdom of Saudi Arabia. Both offers were politely declined.

Callaghan, who had asked to be kept in the picture, grew exasperated with Goodman when he heard that all these approaches were being turned down: 'For God's sake, Arnold, what does it matter which of them you choose?' Goodman replied with an air of reproof: 'There are degrees, Prime Minister, even in the nether regions.'

On 21 November, I took part in a gloomy trustees' meeting in

Goodman's apartment in Portland Place, where the various offers were reviewed and finally seen as impossible. There was an air of doom. The hunt for an alternative to Murdoch had taken six weeks and we were all exhausted. Advertisement bookings were down because people didn't know what kind of paper *The Observer* might become. The journalists were restless. The printers were making threats. We knew we couldn't delay any longer. We were worried we might be left with nothing.

It seemed that we had no choice but to go back to Murdoch. It was a Friday morning and we agreed to meet on the following Monday to work out a way of presenting this solution to the staff. As we trooped out to the lift, David said: 'I feel I'm attending a funeral.' I said: 'I feel as though I'm in the middle of *Macbeth*.'

What neither of us knew was that, before we could meet again on the Monday, salvation was riding towards us in a most surprising form.

CHAPTER 9

KENNETH

By the end of 1976, when the Murdoch crisis erupted, Kenneth Harris was enjoying a comfortable, semi-detached role on *The Observer*. He worked from home but shared an office on the management floor, from which he organised the annual debating tournament for the *Observer* Mace. He also wrote one or two leisurely interviews a year with famous people and made political programmes for the BBC; David Astor thought the BBC had missed a trick in not making him the successor to Richard Dimbleby.

Harris was an elegant, well-groomed man with carefully brushed black hair and a suave, eloquent, rather old-fashioned style that disguised the faint remnants of a Welsh accent. His *Observer* colleagues regarded him as pompous and nicknamed him 'the bishop'. It was said of him at the BBC that 'he could have patronised Winston Churchill'.

Debating had shaped his life. He took part in the first Oxford Union debating society tour of the United States in 1947, along with Tony Benn and Edward Boyle, who became Labour and Conservative ministers. He wrote a book about the tour and about post-war America that caught the paper's attention and Astor – in one of the extraordinary gambles he took on young journalists in the early 1950s – sent him to cover Washington for the paper after he had worked for two years on the *Sheffield Telegraph* (my own training ground, as it happens, a decade later).

On his return to Britain he covered trade union affairs, then a major subject in newspapers, making friends with the Labour Prime Minister Clement Attlee. He wrote a biography of Attlee, amounting to more words than any publisher could reasonably accommodate. The book was saved by Alan Bullock, who had taught him history at Oxford – and was later an *Observer* director – who revised it and cut the manuscript by half.

So, there was Harris, a 57-year-old widower, enjoying his prestigious but undemanding assignments for *The Observer* and the BBC, working in a leisurely fashion on his books, lunching on expenses with well-known people at his club and enjoying bets on the races and on the gaming tables at night, when his life was changed by a single telephone call inviting him out to dinner.

The call was from Douglass Cater, a former White House correspondent who was working for the Aspen Institute in Colorado, a high-minded think tank and convenor of conferences on major global issues. He had arrived alone in London on a Saturday and was looking for someone to have dinner with. He had made several unproductive calls, including one to Harold Evans, the editor of the *Sunday Times*, before finding that Harris, an old Washington friend, was free to join him at Rules, a restaurant famous for its game, in Covent Garden.

Their meeting saved *The Observer*. Cater was shocked when he heard that Rupert Murdoch might take over what he regarded as one of the world's great newspapers. He rang his boss in Aspen, Joe Slater, to seek his advice. Slater said the only man who could decide whether or not to become involved with *The Observer* was Robert O. Anderson, the chairman of Arco (Atlantic Richfield), the oil giant that was a major funder of the Aspen Institute.

Slater agreed to call Anderson at his ranch in New Mexico. Although none of us had ever heard of him, Anderson turned out to own more land than any other private citizen in the United States. There then followed a flurry of telephone calls – none of them, I have to add, to a mere editor like me. Slater rang Cater, Cater rang Anderson, Harris spoke to Anderson then to Lord Goodman, Goodman rang Astor, and eventually the main bout of the evening came on with Anderson and Goodman talking serious business after midnight London time.

They discussed the outlines of a deal, in which Arco would buy *The Observer* for a nominal £1, take on its debts and pay a discounted rent to the Observer Trust (meaning the Astors) for use of the building and the printing works. Astor rang me joyfully on the Sunday morning to share the good news, describing the proposed sale as 'a godsend'. He, Goodman and Roger Harrison would be heading off to Arco-land in Los Angeles the following day to seal the deal. Meanwhile, it was to be kept a secret.

It was indeed a 'godsend', not just for *The Observer*, which would have an infinitely less intimidating new owner than Rupert Murdoch, but for the Astors, who would shed their debts at a stroke and retain a building on a prime site on the edge of the City of London.

Harris has been credited with achieving this happy outcome, though he later resented the idea that he had 'found a fiver in the gutter'. My own view is that Cater, as a former journalist of some reputation, played a more crucial role in convincing Anderson that *The Observer* was a distinguished newspaper that Arco should be proud to be associated with. Anderson had probably never heard of the paper before that night. I suppose tribute should also be paid to Murdoch, for it was his dark shadow looming over the paper that persuaded Arco to move so swiftly to save it from the clutches of Beelzebub, the Prince of the Philistines.

When I asked Thornton Bradshaw, Arco's chief executive, why the company had bought *The Observer*, he replied: 'Frankly, we thought we were doing a good deed in a dirty world that was bound to reflect well on Arco in the long run.' A highly cultivated man who went on to be president of two other major American corporations, NBC and RCA, Bradshaw seemed more like an academic than an oil tycoon. In fact, he had spent a decade teaching at Harvard Business School before putting his business philosophy into practice.

He was described by the *New York Times* as 'a slightly rumpled man

whose face seemed to be always on the brink of a smile'. He pioneered
the concept in company thinking of social responsibility towards the
communities they served and once wrote: 'The new dimension for
business is social approval.' Arco's high reputation as a socially responsible corporation, a sponsor of the arts and funder of community
education projects owed more to him than to Anderson, who was basically a tough old oil prospector and deal-maker.

Anderson was more likely to have been persuaded by the consid-
eration that acquiring a strong presence in Britain by owning one of
its leading newspapers would improve Arco's chances of securing lucrative North Sea oil and gas licences, which were then coming onto
the market. That is certainly how he sold the deal to his fellow Arco
directors.

The paper's journalists were delighted when the takeover was
announced. Few had even heard of Atlantic Richfield, but the oil company had one persuasive advantage as owners: they were not Rupert
Murdoch. It was also reassuring to the staff that Goodman and Astor
would remain on the board and that I would continue as editor.

Anderson himself, wearing his habitual cowboy hat, appeared with
Goodman, Astor and myself at a press conference, where we all oozed
with contentment at the new arrangement. He said to a group of us
afterwards: 'I guess advertising is important to your business.' Assured
that it was indeed very important, he went on: 'I'd like you to invite the
chairmen of all the advertising agencies to meet me for a drink at the
Savoy Hotel at 6.30 p.m. on Thursday. If the chairman himself can't
make it, tell them not to bother.'

As I recall, seventeen out of twenty-one agency chairmen turned up
to meet him. Anderson was again wearing his cowboy hat and cowboy
boots and put both on the table while saying something along these
lines: 'I want you all to know that The Observer is a great paper and
will become even greater in our hands. We are a rich company and
we will spare no expense to achieve that. Good to meet y'all.'

When we announced on the front page that Atlantic Richfield had

With Margaret Thatcher: 'Do you think politics is fun, Mr Trelford?'

In the composing room at the *Times of Malawi*, 1964.

A rare joke with Edward Heath; his lost love was Kay Raven.

Discussing layout with KPO, 1969.

ABOVE LEFT
The happy day I was appointed editor, 1975.

ABOVE RIGHT
Presenting David Astor with a printing press on his eightieth birthday, 1992.

LEFT
In Zimbabwe with Godwin Matatu, who later caused an *Observer* crisis, 1983.

Receiving the Newspaper of the Year award from Lord Devlin, 1983.

In Baku with Garry Kasparov, his mother Klara and manager Andrew Page, 1986.

In Aspen with Kenneth Harris and Danny Kaye: 'I can tell you're English by your hat.'

Meeting Richard Nixon. Lord Longford is on the right.

With *Observer* award winners, 1984: Alexander Frater, David Leigh, Sue Arnold, Hugh McIlvanney, Alan Watkins, Martin Amis.

Prince Charles and Princess Diana on a visit to *The Observer*. Talking to the princess with me is Terry Robinson of Lonrho.

ABOVE LEFT
In a party mood with friend Sir Robin Day.

ABOVE RIGHT
With actors Clare Higgins, Zoe Wanamaker, Brenda Blethyn and Juliet Stevenson at the Olivier awards, sponsored by *The Observer*.

LEFT
With Pamella Bordes, the picture that haunted me.

With Prince Philip. He used to send me notes.

With Prince Charles. We differed over Zimbabwe.

On Adnan Khashoggi's plane with Imelda Marcos: 'I don't seek power: I seek love.'

ABOVE
Me as co-pilot of an RAF
Tornado, 1988.

LEFT
At an *Observer* event with
Neil Kinnock, 1991.

LEFT
With Joanna Lumley
at *The Observer*'s 200th
anniversary party at
Covent Garden, 1992.

With Shimon Peres, the Prime Minister of Israel and later President.

With Gaddafi in the Libyan desert: 'An unmistakable aroma began to fill the tent.'

bought the paper, I was surprised that I couldn't hear the rumble of the presses starting up in the basement. I rang the machine room manager to find out why. He said the NATSOPA night machine room chapel had held a meeting and the father of the chapel, Bert Hand, wanted a word with me.

I had always got on well with the printers. Having had a good apprenticeship in Sheffield, where I often worked a shift late into the night in the composing room, I was well versed in their techniques. By the time I reached *The Observer*, having also run a print room in Africa, I was comfortable talking shop down there and some of the printers became friends.

When he was put on the telephone, Hand said:

Donald, we've seen the story on the front page about the paper being taken over. We wanna be sure this is OK for you. We trust you because we know you've got the paper's best interests at heart. We don't like Yanks and it's all a bit of a surprise after expecting Murdoch to take over. But if you say it'll be all right that's good enough for us.

When I assured him that everything would be fine, but not if they failed to print the paper, he agreed to let the presses roll. I was rather touched by the episode.

That same weekend, Goodman, who had just become Master of University College, Oxford, threw a celebration party there for 150 people, who included five Cabinet ministers and six other newspaper owners. Among the guests was Rupert Murdoch, who mixed easily – with no obvious sign of resentment – with Anderson, Bradshaw, Astor and myself, even though we had effectively joined forces to defeat him.

For his part, Anderson wanted an even bigger party to celebrate Atlantic Richfield's acquisition of *The Observer* and arranged for Harris to organise a massive banquet at Lincoln's Inn, to be attended by the great and the good and addressed by giant political celebrities such as Harold Macmillan and Henry Kissinger.

Harris was in clover: it was the role his whole life had prepared him for. He had an impressive contacts book, partly from his time in Washington, but also among Labour Party and trade union figures and the eminent people he invited as participants or judges in *The Observer*'s debating competitions. The guest list on the programme still looks stellar, even after four decades.

There were four of these annual feasts, called the Astor–Goodman dinners, until *The Observer* – for reasons we shall come to – fell out of favour with Arco, which saw no reason to go on celebrating the connection. While they lasted, however, these occasions were quite splendid and doubtless did much to burnish *The Observer*'s reputation, as well as to give Atlantic Richfield an identity in Britain.

● ● ●

At the first board meeting since the Arco takeover, Anderson brought along some new directors he had appointed, all of whom were seen as welcome additions by the old *Observer* contingent. They included Bradshaw, Frank Stanton, a former leading light at CBS in the States, and Lord Bullock, whom they knew as a regular at Aspen meetings. Cater and Harris, the paper's saviours, were rewarded with places on the board.

Harris had already begun to get close to Anderson, escorting him around town and introducing him to his A-list friends. The two men were also seen in glamorous company at fashionable nightspots such as Annabel's. Anderson accepted Harris's offer to write his biography, an assignment that guaranteed they would be spending a good deal of time together, both in Britain and in the United States.

What the board lacked, however, was a British-based chairman who would carry conviction in the London newspaper world. While the new ownership was getting the paper a good press and also settling any fears that it might disappear, the arrangement lacked commercial credibility. Roger Harrison and I approached Lord Barnetson, chairman of the United Newspapers group of regional papers and also chairman of Reuters.

He was a short, cigar-smoking Scotsman with a bristly moustache, a waistcoat and a gold fob watch, respected for his canny shrewdness and liked for his jokey style. He had a look of the late Duff Cooper, but I suspect he was less of a ladies' man. Goodman was not impressed with our choice, muttering dismissively: 'He's gone a long way for a man of his ability.'

Anderson and Bradshaw – impressed, I suspect, by the fact that he was a lord – fell in more readily with our choice and went so far as to provide him with a luxurious apartment in Hill Street, Mayfair. Barnetson's chief recreation was said to be playing the drums to big band swing records in the basement of his house: I doubt if that would have gone down too well in Mayfair.

Soon after his appointment I went with Barnetson to see Anderson in his suite at Claridge's. As they shook hands, I almost choked as the former said to the latter: 'Saw the Queen last night, Bob. She was asking about you.' I made it my business to check this story out, as far as I could. I established that Barnetson had indeed been at a reception the night before which had been attended by the Queen. But they could hardly have exchanged more than a few words if or when His Lordship was introduced to the monarch. I suppose it's *possible* that the recent sale of *The Observer* was mentioned and that Anderson's name *might* have come up in that conversation…

Barnetson's first decisions were to reinforce the commercial and editorial management of the paper. He brought in Brian Nicholson, a greatly respected advertising executive with experience on the *Sunday Times* and the Express group, making him joint managing director with Harrison. How Harrison felt about that I never knew. He would know of Nicholson's high reputation in Fleet Street and the value he could bring to the paper, especially in areas such as advertising and marketing, of which he had no direct experience himself. But I suspect that he didn't take kindly to having to share his power with anyone.

In the event, the two men got on well together, covering different areas of responsibility. I received a long, handwritten letter from Jocelyn Stevens, then head of the Express group, begging us not to take Nicholson away from him, fearing that it might cause fatal damage to the group. In the event, the Express papers were sold the same year.

Unlike Harrison, who was seen as rather buttoned-up, Nicholson was popular with journalists and enjoyed nothing more than exchanging Fleet Street gossip with them. One of my colleagues once said: 'Brian actually likes journalists and gives them the impression that they are the most interesting and important people on a paper; Roger gives the impression that editorial is just a loss-making department that spends too much money.'

Nicholson then brought in an able young advertising executive, Nicholas Morrell, who went on to become advertisement director and eventually managing director, first of *The Observer* and later of Lonrho after the company bought the paper from Arco four years later. It was a shrewd and far-reaching piece of recruitment, giving *The Observer* a more cutting professional edge. Like Nicholson, Morrell enjoyed the company of journalists and liked nothing more than drinking with the sports department on a Friday evening in their favourite haunt, the Cockpit.

On the editorial side, Barnetson brought in Iain Lindsay Smith, deputy editor of the *Yorkshire Post*, one of his regional papers, and a former editor of the *Glasgow Herald*. He was given the title of executive editor and an office close to mine. The assumption in the newsroom was that Lindsay Smith was earmarked to take over my job.

Alan Watkins echoes this in his memoirs:

He [Barnetson] intrigued against Trelford by importing another engaging Scotsman, Iain Lindsay Smith, into the paper with the intention of providing a rival, a possible successor. Trelford – the Rocky Marciano of newspaper politics – saw the punch coming and defended himself by giving Lindsay Smith a commodious office, a full set of daily newspapers,

which remained neatly displayed on a side table, and nothing to do all
day long.

I think Alan was wrong about Barnetson intriguing against me. In fact,
he was to give me vital support when my position came under fire. Had
Iain really been out to get my job, he made little visible effort to do so.
He hardly ever spoke in editorial conferences and I never got wind of
any plotting. It is true that I didn't give him any specific departmental
duties, but he never seemed to want any.

I was told that his friend Jack Crossley, whom he brought in as news
editor, used to rail against him for failing to unseat me. But Iain was a
gentle soul, lacking the stiletto quality needed for stabbing rivals in the
back. He played the bagpipes at office parties wearing a kilt. Iain always
seemed a bit uncomfortable on *The Observer* and I suspect he was glad
enough to leave a few years later when Brian Nicholson found him a
good job as managing director of Lloyds List.

I had always got on well enough with Harris personally and lunched
with him from time to time. He recounted some excellent gossip,
though I sometimes wondered why he didn't feel a need to see it published in the paper. He kept his friendships in good repair, as they say,
staying in regular touch, mostly at *The Observer*'s or the BBC's expense, with a wide variety of well-known people. These days he would
be called a networker. He once introduced me at a party to Harold
Wilson, then the Prime Minister, soon after I had become editor. He
told me afterwards that Wilson had said of me: 'He's my sort of chap.'

Harris's interviews with the rich and famous were not a popular
form of journalism at the time, at least with other journalists. This was
mainly because he allowed the person interviewed to have the final say
on what would appear in print. In fact, this worked out very well as a
method, because it allowed the subjects to say many unguarded things
in the course of the interview, confessing their innermost thoughts,
private family moments and dragging up half-forgotten memories
from childhood.

Kenneth took no notes, relying on his prodigious memory, which also encouraged people to speak more freely. A big part of his skill was his silky charm in flattering his subjects that these private confessions reflected well on them and would improve their public image. Even today some of these interviews, which he reproduced in book form, still read well – on senior figures like Presidents Nixon and Reagan, Prince Philip and Lord Mountbatten. Sir Gordon Richards admitted, for example, that he would have preferred to be a singer rather than a jockey.

I had no problem with Harris before he helped to bring about the Arco takeover. In fact, I had more time for him and his old-fashioned style of journalism than most of *The Observer*'s staff. But I had never once seen him attend a single editorial conference in the decade I had worked on the paper. He took no part whatsoever in the creation of policy or the stimulation of ideas that were at the heart of the newspaper's activities.

It came as a bit of a shock, therefore, when he and Cater set up a joint office at *The Observer* and started pouring out comments and criticism about the paper, mostly in memos to me but also to individuals on and off the paper. News of these opinions usually reached me by one route or another. It was unsettling for me and confusing for the staff.

I also learned that they had set up a series of meetings, without bothering to inform me, with senior figures in the media world to obtain their views about *The Observer* and how it could be improved. These involved people like Robert Kee, David Attenborough, Keith Kyle and Andrew Knight, the former editor of *The Economist*, who had caught Cater's attention with the financial dexterity he had displayed in saving the RAC Club. Because I or my senior staff knew all these people, rather better in fact than Cater did, we quickly learned what was going on behind our backs.

In the end I rebelled, sending a sharp note to Cater and Harris that said their editorial thoughts should be directed to me or through me as the editor. I warned that I would not tolerate them trying to establish their own channels of communication to the journalists or organising meetings about the editorial content of *The Observer* without my prior knowledge. Arco's acquisition of *The Observer*, I said, would be seen as a test of American ownership of media in the UK and it would not look good if they abused their power by diminishing the role of the editor.

I got no immediate response from Cater and Harris, but I learned from the management that I had stirred up quite a storm. They evidently wanted their own roles to be defined and formalised. Their plea to Anderson was redirected to Barnetson as the paper's chairman. Astor and Goodman became involved. These discussions were going on way above my head but I knew that my own future as editor was part of these discussions. Being only dimly aware of what was going on was not good for my peace of mind.

David Astor took me to lunch at Boodles and gave me some idea of the way things were heading. He told me that Harris had been to see Goodman, evidently encouraged by his new friend Anderson, to seek support for his own appointment to a more senior role on the paper – apparently as editor-in-chief or in some similar controlling position. In any event Goodman had sent Harris away with a flea in his ear.

The words Goodman actually used, according to Astor, were:

Kenneth, we are as other people see us, and the way we are seen depends on the way we have lived our life. I know, for example, that I would make a splendid prima ballerina, but alas the world will never see me in that role. Likewise, Kenneth, people will never see you as editor or editor-in-chief of *The Observer*. It is not just that you lack the technical qualifications: you would have no credibility.

The ballerina analogy, coming from a man of over twenty stone, was especially wounding. Harris, not a man lacking in vanity, was gravely offended.

Astor added that Barnetson, an experienced operator who knew how newspapers worked in the real world, had no time for Harris and little more for Cater. So I had nothing really to fear from them, except as a nuisance. He let me see a confidential memo that the chairman had sent to Anderson and Bradshaw, saying that the company would be hard-pressed to find another editor who could combine my alleged 'first-class brain' with my 'technical expertise and editorial know-how'. He said he 'certainly couldn't think of anyone better suited to edit *The Observer*'.

However, David warned me that the owners were thinking of creating an editorial board containing well-known intellectuals like Isaiah Berlin and Alan Bullock to help the paper meet their Aspen-type aspirations. They were also considering the appointment of an editor-in-chief who would be in charge of policy and would leave the running of the paper to me. The editor-in-chief might or might not work in tandem with an editorial board – that would be up to him.

What was essential, he said, was a buffer between the owners and the editor. He then came to the main point of the lunch: that he would like to put forward the name of Conor Cruise O'Brien as the editor-in-chief – but only if I approved. At that stage, he had no idea if Conor would be interested, but he had recently heard him speak at a meeting of the British-Irish Association and immediately thought he could be the ideal figure the paper needed – someone whose intellectual credentials would satisfy Arco and who would not seek (nor had the necessary experience) to run the paper on a day-to-day basis.

As it happened, Conor was one of my heroes. Collections of his essays on political and literary themes had always had pride of place on my bookshelves alongside those of George Orwell, and still do. They seemed to me to combine good sense and good style in a way that reflected my own beliefs and convictions more closely than anyone else I had read. Long before I met him, I had hero-worshipped him as an intellectual action man.

So, when David told me in 1978 that he was thinking of proposing O'Brien as my editor-in-chief, I was surprised and delighted, even though the arrival of such a strong-minded figure was likely to impinge on my own editorial freedom of action. I went to Dublin to see him, armed with a letter from Barnetson (which I naturally opened beforehand) offering him a salary about three times my own. In the taxi from the airport, I asked the driver if he knew Dr Conor Cruise O'Brien and what he thought of him. 'There are two views of Conor Cruise O'Brien,' he said. 'I'm of the other view myself.'

We met at the Gresham Hotel and immediately hit it off. He already knew my deputy John Cole and shared his approach to the Irish question. He also knew Terry Kilmartin, the literary editor, from writing book reviews for the paper. He knew Colin Legum, the paper's Africa guru, who had strongly supported the stand he took in the Congo as the UN's special representative in Katanga. The backing of these senior figures smoothed Conor's entry to the paper.

Mary Holland, our Irish correspondent, caused a few tremors, however, by reminding the staff that Conor had censored media coverage of the IRA when he was Minister of Telecommunications in the Dublin government. The tension between these two strong-minded Irish figures, Holland and O'Brien, would eventually lead to a major confrontation.

The Americans had been greatly impressed with Conor when they met him – 'to the point of infatuation,' as Goodman put it – though Anderson was heard to say to Bradshaw afterwards that he could be 'a difficult man to deal with'. Bradshaw replied that if he wasn't a bit difficult to deal with he wouldn't be the kind of person they needed.

His arrival had the desired effect of putting the noses of Cater and Harris seriously out of joint. Cater, however, after showing initial hostility to Conor's appointment, soon fell graciously into line and, after a heart by-pass operation, limited himself to attending board meetings and introducing famous American visitors to the paper, such as Lady Bird Johnson, the former President's widow, when they were in London.

Harris was a harder nut to crack. He was never reconciled to Conor's appointment, whose job he doubtless thought should have gone to him, and did all he could to undermine his authority. In his memoir,

Conor said Harris's objections to him were 'formidable, deep-laid and dangerous' and described him as 'a poisonous presence in my professional life'. They had two meetings over dinner. At the first, according to O'Brien, Harris 'was faintly menacing. At the second he was openly bullying, or tried to be, and then there were no more dinners.'

The truth of the matter is that, because Harris and Cater had saved the paper, there was never a clear line of command between *The Observer* and Arco. They always got in the way. There should have been a straightforward management link between *The Observer* and the executives who ran Arco's business in Los Angeles.

We planned to use *The Observer*'s name to broaden the company's operating base into related activities – perhaps a publisher, a provincial newspaper (*The Guardian*'s link to the *Manchester Evening News* had saved the paper at a crucial time) or a mail-order firm. Although several projects were proposed, they all foundered on Arco's refusal to see *The Observer* as anything but a charitable investment that might pay dividends in North Sea licences.

But life under Arco wasn't all conflict and plotting. In the summer of 1977, the whole board and their families travelled on an Arco jet to Aspen. As we stood on the tarmac at Stansted airport, David Astor nudged me and pointed at Barnetson, who was dressed in a summer suit with a big cravat and a straw hat. 'I haven't seen anything like that since the 1930s,' he whispered.

On the journey, the children found some videos scattered across the floor and put them on. They were porn films, left behind by Arco oilmen on their way home from the drilling fields in Alaska. There was a bit of a fuss among the adults until Barnetson spoke up: 'Leave them alone,' he advised. 'They'll soon get bored.' As indeed they did, or at least pretended to.

The annual outings to Aspen suited me perfectly. I was quite good at that type of high-minded Aspen-speak and prepared a paper for the board each time on my plans for *The Observer*'s future that seemed to go down well. Even Harris was heard to mutter: 'Excellent delivery.'

I took part in a Greek play, wearing a toga, and enjoyed a concert given by the Juilliard Quartet, who were resident at Aspen. One day I arranged for the board to go white water rafting on the Colorado River. Another time I stayed with my three older children in a condominium in Aspen and they had the time of their young lives.

When our annual visit coincided with the Fourth of July, the board was invited to join a big Independence Day party in a forest just out-side Aspen. I found myself sharing a picnic basket under the shade of a tree with Danny Kaye and the actress Jill St. John, a rather upmarket former Bond girl. When I was introduced, Danny pointed to the Stet-son I had bought myself in Denver and said: 'I can tell you're English by your hat!'

One year, after a formal dinner at Aspen, I couldn't find my way back to my guest-house in pouring rain. My situation wasn't helped by the fact that my luggage had failed to arrive from Denver and I had to turn out in the casual gear I was wearing to travel on the plane, covered by an old raincoat.

I tried to take a shortcut to what looked like the right house when two men stepped out of the bushes with loaded guns and grabbed me. It turned out, after I had been closely questioned under armed guard, that they were FBI agents protecting Henry Kissinger, the grounds of whose guest-house I had unfortunately stumbled upon in the rain.

• • •

I had some forebodings when Bob Anderson rang me out of the blue and asked me to meet him in Los Angeles. It was my first visit to Arco's palatial and highly tasteful headquarters. It turned out that I had nothing to worry about. Anderson said he had arranged for me to have breakfast at the California Club in LA with Helmut Schmidt, the former West German Chancellor.

Newspaper editors don't spend all their time on jaunts like this, I'm sorry to say. Most of one's time is spent in the office taking news, features and leader conferences, arguing with the management about editorial space, talking to individual journalists and departmental heads, meeting the NUJ chapel, responding to legal issues, taking endless telephone calls from publishers and literary agents trying to sell me a serial, not to mention family matters.

One entry from my journal from that time is worth repeating:

Any Questions? in Cambridge with Arianna Stassinopoulos, Michael Winner and Paul Ostreicher, preceded by dinner at Downing College. In car on way back Ostreicher tells me that the wife of Runcie, the new Archbishop of Canterbury, had had a row with Margaret Thatcher at a Downing Street function over poverty in Britain. She had also been heard to say: 'Too much religion makes me go off pop.' Mention this in the office and say that Runcie seems a bit of a wimp. Patrick O'Donovan shuts me up by saying quietly: 'I was with him in the Irish Guards. He won an MC for saving people from a burning tank.'

Winner good company, though political views simplistic. Invites me to glossy party at his house after the first night of his remake of *The Big Sleep*. Watched Robert Mitchum reach into ice bucket with huge hand, fill his mouth with ice, then pour a bottle of vodka over it.

When I first appeared on *Any Questions?*, John Cole gave me some advice: 'Two gin and tonics at dinner; not one, not none.' When I got there, however, rather late because of the Friday-night traffic out of London, I found Roy Jenkins and Lord Hailsham way beyond Cole's proposed alcoholic intake.

Jenkins's so-called Balliol 'r', I decided, was not a speech impediment but a drink impediment. As I came in he was saying: 'I say, is there any more of that claret? It's rather good.' Hailsham had had so much to drink that when he took his seat for the broadcast he was waving his stick around his head and nearly fell off the stage.

The other member of the panel was Glenda Jackson, the actress and then Labour MP. As we took our places she said to me waspishly:

'You're far too young to be editor of anything, never mind *The Observer*.' It was on the tip of my tongue to reply: 'And you're too ugly to be Glenda Jackson,' but I was too gentlemanly, or too scared, to say so. She kept up a running left-wing commentary, in an angry whisper, about everything the other panellists had to say.

• • •

Before Conor came on the scene as my Lord Protector, I had to endure board meetings where the directors would weigh in against writers or parts of the paper they didn't like. I remember Lord Bullock complaining that the colour magazine was much inferior in quality to the newspaper. He was backed by Frank Stanton, who said ours was third out of three among the Sunday magazines. Bullock proposed that the magazine editor and the design director should attend the next board meeting to hear the directors' views.

Barnetson, a bully at heart – but a cautious one, who would wait to see which way the wind was blowing before acting – was suddenly emboldened enough to declare: 'The editor has abdicated his responsibility for the magazine.' He went on to maintain that I had 'resisted the talents' of Iain Lindsay Smith and Jack Crossley.

Sensing that I was about to explode, David Astor intervened gently to remind Bullock that board members should not talk directly to the paper's journalists but only through the editor. I was tempted to quote the comment of Arthur Mann, the great pre-war editor of the *Yorkshire Post* (under whom Astor had some training): 'Gentlemen, as directors you may dismiss me if you wish but you will not tell me how to do my job.'

Bullock then backed off, saying he was happy to leave the matters he had raised in my hands. Astor whispered to me: 'Well done. In your place I would have made a fool of myself.' Barnetson's face was like thunder. This was the sort of thing I had to deal with at every board meeting, even from well-meaning directors, because everybody thinks they are an expert on newspapers.

What really annoyed me, however, was that it was easy for them to pick out faults in the newspaper, but they did absolutely nothing about the overwhelming problem that was bringing *The Observer*, like many other papers, to its knees: the over-manning and so-called Spanish practices of the printing unions, who held the paper to ransom almost every week.

The American directors would come over once a month for the weekend, usually with their wives, stay at Claridge's, shop in the West End, attend the board meeting on a Monday morning, then fly back home later in the day. It was all very cosy but did nothing to address the paper's fundamental problems, which were several floors below the editorial department. Arco's ownership may have been benevolent (Harris's disruptive influence excepted) but the paper was effectively coasting along and avoiding tough realities.

This became a crucial issue when the management of *The Times* and the *Sunday Times*, then owned by the Thomson group, shut the papers down for eleven months in a showdown with their printers. *The Observer* and the *Sunday Telegraph*, seizing their opportunity, upped their production to over a million copies each. This was difficult and expensive for us, because we had to introduce mid-week shifts to get some sections printed in advance, because we couldn't cope with the much larger papers in one run on our presses. The extra cost was covered by the massive increase in advertising.

When the strike ended in failure and the papers resumed printing, *The Observer* had a dilemma. Should we go on with mid-week printing to produce a million copies and aim to retain the *Sunday Times* readers we had 'borrowed' over the strike? Or should we accept that demand for the paper would return to its pre-strike level and therefore abandon the expensive mid-week printing schedule and reduce the number of pages, knowing that many advertisers would return to the *ST*?

The cost of taking the fight to the *ST* would, admittedly, have been horrific. But simply abandoning those extra readers seemed to me to be a terrible wasted opportunity for the paper to make the breakthrough it had always sought. What were Arco's billions for, I thought, if not to take on a challenge like this? It would have been a bold and expensive gamble, and it might not have worked, but we didn't even try. In fact, it was hardly considered for a moment, even though it meant turning away thousands of pounds of advertising we hadn't room to accommodate.

This was happening in 1979, some years before Eddie Shah and Rupert Murdoch made the breakthrough that finally put paid to the power of the printing unions. For *The Observer* to have led this revolution would, perhaps, have been over-ambitious, even foolhardy. The print unions might have put us out of business rather than agree to new arrangements that would have knock-on effects on the rest of the industry.

I can see all that, but it was a critical moment in the paper's history and there should at least have been a strategic review of the options. Arco's casual, passing-through approach to *The Observer*, saluting the flag while spending weekends at Claridge's, did not allow for the kind of concentrated management planning they brought to their oil business.

Besides, Arco was already becoming disillusioned with owning *The Observer* – for reasons we shall come to – and was in no mood to lead a Fleet Street revolution that would cost a fortune and involve them in battle they wouldn't have known how to fight anyway.

• • •

Conor had decided to rule by memo, rather than by taking editorial conferences himself, which made my life easier by not confusing the journalists as to who was their boss. He sent out some memos that were amusing and beautifully written. I sometimes wish I had kept them: *The Collected Memos of Conor Cruise O'Brien*. The subject of his first one was 'muzziness', which he described as *The Observer*'s abiding sin.

It became a bit muzzy, at least to me, what weight should be attached to Conor's views on specific topical issues: were they edicts that he expected the paper to follow, or just random ideas we could take or leave as it suited us? It was David Astor again who solved the problem. He said to me over lunch one day at the Garrick when I raised this matter: 'Why don't you use him as a columnist? All he wants is to get his thoughts into the paper.'

This turned out to be a brilliant idea, one of the most admired features in the paper, and won him two Granada awards as Columnist of the Year. In this way, he could express his own views without imposing them on other parts of the paper. I created a page containing the *Observer* profile, illustrated by a Marc drawing, with Conor's column alongside it at the top, with Alan Watkins's political column spread across the bottom of the page. I was pleased to see this once described in *The Spectator* as 'the best page in Sunday journalism', but I was not best pleased to see the idea credited to Anthony Howard, who hadn't even joined the paper at the time it was introduced.

●　　●　　●

One day my secretary, Monica Craig, whom I had inherited from Astor, came to find me in the newsroom and said there was a telephone call for me that sounded important. 'It's somebody called Bellow,' she said. Monica had many virtues, but knowledge of Nobel Prize-winning novelists wasn't one of them. A couple of years before I had carried long passages from a Jerusalem diary written by Saul Bellow. He had rung me at the time to thank me for running the extracts and for the way they had been presented. He said he would like to meet me and we agreed that he would call when he was next in London.

I took him and his wife to dinner in a private room at the Garrick Club, along with some members of the paper's literary department, the publisher Tom Rosenthal, and Conor and his wife Maire. I sat at one end of the table and Bellow was at the other, surrounded by the O'Briens. From where I sat, everybody seemed to be having a good time. But when, the next day, I said that to Rosenthal, he replied: 'You were at the wrong end of the table, Donald. It was actually a disaster. Maire O'Brien kept complaining to Bellow, saying things like: "You New York Jews are always moaning about your lot. You should lighten up.'"

Since Bellow was actually born in Quebec, two years after his Jewish parents arrived from Lithuania, and had spent nearly all his life in Chicago, he was not pleased at being depicted as some Woody Allen figure by someone with literary pretensions, but who clearly knew nothing about him and hadn't read his books. He was furious and needed restraining by Tom from walking out. I had missed this little drama completely.

• • •

One of Barnetson's innovations had been a weekly management meeting, chaired by himself and attended by the two managing directors, the finance director and the editor. It was his tactful way of exerting his influence on the paper. I suggested that Conor should be included. The benefit to me was that he had such a presence and reputation that the others had to listen to him. I would brief him carefully in advance about the paper's editorial requirements – perhaps more space for news or a bigger budget for buying book serials or hiring a new specialist writer – and he would put the case with much greater authority than I had been able to muster in the past.

He managed to make every request sound like a matter of principle that couldn't be denied, helped by the fact that Barnetson was rather in awe of him. In the past, operating on my own in a room full of managers, I would be fobbed off with comments like: 'Nice idea, Donald, but we can't afford it.'

On one occasion, however, when I needed Conor to put forward the editorial case on a very important matter, he failed to turn up, even though I had briefed him about the meeting earlier in the day. An hour went by with no sign of him, then another, until he finally arrived at five minutes to five, just as we were thinking of breaking up. For some time he said nothing at all, just sitting there with a blank look on his face. Finally, when asked a direct question, he answered coherently with his usual perfect sentence structure, but in a high-pitched squeak that diminished the authority of what he had to say. I failed to get the decision I needed.

Afterwards I tackled Conor about his absence and he muttered rather shamefacedly: 'It was all the fault of my fellow Irishman, the picture editor, who led me astray over lunch.' I went down to the editorial floor in a bit of a rage and confronted the picture editor, Tony McGrath. 'Tony,' I said, 'will you please not get the editor-in-chief drunk when I need him at a management meeting.'

McGrath replied in his gentle Irish accent: 'It wasn't my fault, Donald. It was Conor. We went to a Greek restaurant and he had three bottles of Greek wine, followed by several starboard lights (green chartreuse liqueurs). I couldn't get him to come back to the office.'

After that I detailed Iain Lindsay Smith to be Conor's accredited drinking companion – a suitable choice since he was famed for his 'hollow legs', never seeming to get drunk no matter how much alcohol he had taken aboard. Conor could be a joy in the pub, amusing everyone in earshot with his sharp repartee and delightful anecdotes, his rosy face lit up with enjoyment at the camaraderie. But a point would come, not very far into the evening's drinking, when his head would fall to one side and he would start giggling and talking gibberish.

While in London, he lived on a houseboat at Chelsea Reach and had to get aboard by walking across a narrow plank. Fortunately, he had an office driver to see him home or he might have ended up in the Thames by missing his footing and landing in the mud. In the end it was the driver (who couldn't read and so was unable to use a map), not Conor, who eventually had a heart attack.

Conor had a closer relationship with John Cole than he had with me. They would spend hours wrangling about Ireland or British politics. I suppose I could have joined them if I had been more interested in the inner struggles of the Labour Party as it clung on to power at the tail-end of the 1970s. When they talked about the paper's policy on Ireland, I was sometimes made to feel like an English intruder.

The only serious falling-out I had with Conor was over Mary

Holland. She was plainly republican in her sympathies, and even had a child by a well-known republican supporter, but she made no secret of this and she was one of the best-informed people about both parts of Ireland. I thought her political assessments were shrewd and as objective as she could make them.

None of us who were there will ever forget the powerful contribution she made to an editorial conference in 1968, when she held the room in thrall as she outlined the many forms of injustice and discrimination suffered by Northern Irish Catholics. In the silence that followed her passionate speech, David Astor said quietly: 'Go away, Mary, and write it.' Her double-page spread, entitled 'John Bull's Other Island', foreshadowed the troubles that started the following year. What was so surprising about this was that Mary was then the paper's fashion editor. She used to be seen in the office wearing a fur coat.

Mary based herself in Dublin and produced some of the most authoritative and best-researched articles on the conflict. She incurred Conor's serious displeasure, however, by writing a magazine article about the so-called blanket women, the wives and mothers of IRA prisoners who organised protests about their treatment, that seemed to Conor to be overly sympathetic towards them and to mislead readers about the real situation in the North. So he decided to sack her.

This is his description of the episode in his memoirs:

> I wrote to her about this and we had a somewhat acrimonious correspondence. She stuck to her guns and I told Donald Trelford that I had no confidence in the objectivity of her coverage of Northern Ireland. John Cole agreed. Donald Trelford acquiesced, for the moment, as he generally did if the opposition appeared adequately motivated. Mary Holland was out of *The Observer* as long as I was still there, but after I had retired as editor-in-chief Donald quietly restored her. This did not at all surprise me.

A bigger issue than Northern Ireland was looming in 1979 with the coming general election. Which way would *The Observer* advise its readers to vote? For an exhausted and divided Labour Party that had just about held on to power with the help of Liberal votes in Parliament? Or for a Tory government led by Margaret Thatcher that would be more right-wing than the one led by Edward Heath? For a paper like *The Observer*, this was a genuine dilemma. It was to determine the paper's ownership.

John Cole, the strongest political voice on the paper, was firmly for sticking with Labour. I was in favour of supporting no party, just setting out the choices for readers to decide for themselves, pointing out the strengths and weaknesses of both sides. Newspapers don't vote, I said: people do. Our job is to help them make up their minds, not dictate to them. To me Labour seemed to have run out of steam and was short of ideas and Thatcher seemed too extreme and untested for a paper with liberal values.

Even though he said in his memoirs that he would personally have voted for Thatcher, Conor never said this when the election was discussed in the office. In fact, I found his account of this episode in his memoirs, written twenty years after the events, either disingenuous or the product of faulty memory.

Conor had sat as a Labour MP throughout his political career in Dublin, and during the 1979 election campaign he went to Belfast to address a meeting of the Northern Ireland Labour Party. According to agency reports, he had assured them that *The Observer* would be supporting Labour in the general election, an announcement greeted with loud applause by his audience – and with some surprise by me, since we hadn't discussed it. He wrote to Thornton Bradshaw saying the same thing and received a horrified response. Arco clearly wanted *The Observer* to back Thatcher.

I suspect that Conor, as an Irishman, didn't really care much about the election either way, but he wanted to test the Americans' claims of non-interference with the paper by doing the opposite of what they wanted. It was a dangerous ploy that resulted in Arco offloading the paper as soon as they decently could.

He virtually admits this in his memoirs in an explanation that still leaves me baffled: 'I thought that, in the logic of the Astorian tradition I should defer to John Cole … I also thought that to be guided by John Cole on this issue might lead to a showdown with the owners.' How did the 'Astorian tradition', as he called it, lead him to defer to the opinion of the deputy editor rather than that of the editor?

Barnetson was so concerned about the effect that the general election leader would have on Atlantic Richfield that he asked me, as a special favour, if he could read it before publication. I took a proof round to his swanky Mayfair apartment on a Friday evening and agreed, after some debate, to make a few minor alterations to the wording. I knew what he was up to: he wanted to be able to tell Arco that he had toned the leader down a bit.

The chairman was so grateful for my cooperation that he gave me a bottle of 1964 Chateau Latour Premier Grand Cru to take home, even though I hadn't changed very much. When I got home that night, however, rather annoyed that I had allowed the chairman to interfere at all in an editorial matter, I said to my wife: 'We'll drink that when Barnetson dies.' Sadly, he died only a year or so later and I felt bad for having said that, especially as I rather liked him. In the end, I couldn't bring myself to drink his bottle of claret and gave it away to an auction at my daughter's school.

After *The Observer* had thrown its support behind Labour's losing cause, relations with Arco were never the same again. It was only a matter of time before the paper would be sold. Conor's own position as editor-in-chief was also doomed. He knew that and didn't really care, though he was keen to keep his column. He was missing his family in Dublin; he was frustrated that he couldn't persuade *The Observer* to change its policy in crucial areas, such as the Middle East; and he had well-paid offers to do other things, over which he would have total control, such as write books, travel and give lectures. He didn't need the hassle any more.

• • •

After the failure of the long stoppage at *The Times* and *Sunday Times*, the Thomson Organisation put the two papers up for sale. Although the matter was never discussed with me or *The Observer*'s management, I discovered from Harold Evans that Arco were interested in joining a consortium he was putting together to buy *The Times*.

I discovered this at a crowded party I gave at a tiny house I then had in Canonbury, where I found Evans in deep conversation with Thornton Bradshaw. Harry said he had fixed a meeting with Bradshaw for the following day to brief him on his business plan. The benefit to *The Observer*, he said, was that *The Times* could be printed on the Sunday paper's empty presses during the week.

Evidently Arco had proposed merging *The Observer* and the *Sunday Times*. According to Evans, that idea had been gaining ground and had found some favour with Gordon Brunton, who was handling negotiations for the Thomson group. Needless to say, this had never been mentioned to me. The *Daily Mirror* got hold of the story and said Anderson was in town 'to decide between J.R. and Bobby Ewing – that is, between Harold Evans and Donald Trelford'.

Despite our professional rivalry, Harry and I had always got on well, partly perhaps we were both from working-class families in the provinces. We were both very short and were sometimes mistaken for each other. On a train from Sheffield to London one day I was approached by Tony Benn, who thought I was Evans and took some persuading that I wasn't.

All these schemes came to nothing because the Thomson Organisation, effectively Brunton and Sir Denis Hamilton, decided that the two papers should be sold together, not separately, and that they favoured Rupert Murdoch as an already established international publisher who had the clout to deal with the print unions and the experience to run a big newspaper operation.

Harry was the leading editor of my generation and we certainly missed him in the debates over press freedom and regulation in the decades that followed his emigration to the US. His mistake was to allow Murdoch to tempt him away from his unassailable position at the *Sunday Times* into the uncharted, shark-infested waters at *The Times*. As the son of a railway driver, he probably couldn't resist the opportunity to edit the so-called top people's paper.

Their failure to secure *The Times* was an added reason that Arco were ready to sell *The Observer*. After Barnetson's death and Bradshaw's move to NBC, there were no voices raised to keep the paper.

•   •   •

Conor Cruise O'Brien had an exaggerated idea of my skills as an office politician. He once said to Alan Watkins: 'Donald used to be a scrum-half, you know. I bet he could reach touch on both sides of the field by kicking the ball with both feet at the same time.' I certainly needed all the political skills I could muster when we reached the end-game with Arco. The confusion and chaos of that time are caught in some (barely legible) handwritten notes I made at the time. Here is a lightly edited summary of them.

WEDNESDAY 18 FEBRUARY 1981

Full of cold, but came in to sneeze through a lunch with Michael Foot. Bob Anderson [ROA] was in town. RH [Roger Harrison] obviously puzzled that he hasn't been in touch – 'I've no idea what Bob's up to,' he says, a bit fed up that Kenneth Harris [KH] obviously does.

Office rumour that Associated are buying *The Observer*. Continuing concern over who will be vice-chairman, since we all fear KH will use this position to lord it over everyone, as he would be senior *Ob* exec in London.

THURSDAY 19 FEBRUARY 1981

Savoy lunch to launch of new *Grove Dictionary of Music*. Meet Goodman [Lord G] in gents. Says he's seen ROA and wants to talk, but he's quickly surrounded at pre-lunch drinks. At lunch he sits next to George Melly, an unlikely couple.

Walk back along Embankment, risking my cold, and find KH (in Stetson) waiting for lift at the office. Happen to know he was due to lunch with ROA because RH had told me, so I leave him to mention it and tell him where I've been lunching. He doesn't mention his lunch. I press him a bit, saying I'd heard that ROA might drop in on our management meeting that afternoon. He replies in his grand cryptic way: 'Nothing Bob does would surprise me.'

I'm puzzled about this – the fact that he won't mention that he has seen ROA – so I tell Conor and Lajos, who also think it's odd. 'Fishy,' says Lajos. 'Up to no good,' says Conor. John Cole says he has seen KH and ROA lunching at Athenaeum. He and Jimmy Cox, the production manager, had actually pinched the table they had booked.

ROA wanders in at about 5 p.m. into our management committee meeting. After general chat, he said he had decided to take over the chairmanship himself – 'You guys have got a fight on your hands and I wouldn't want to miss it' (meaning the competition with Murdoch's *Sunday Times*).

We all welcome this – genuinely, because we were glad to have as chairman the man with the real power. We said there had been rumours of a bid by Associated Newspapers. He admitted Vere Harmsworth had offered to buy the paper, but he'd turned him down.

Went to Israeli Ambassador's house for musical evening. Among the guests were Lady Avon, Sir Isaiah Berlin, Lady Melchett, Peregrine Worsthorne, Max Beloff – and (a late arrival as usual) Lord G.

After supper Lord G took me aside. Had I heard that ROA planned to be chairman? I said I had – I thought it was good news. Did I know who he planned to make vice-chairman and his resident representative here? Not KH, surely? He feared so. Caesar was making his horse a consul. It had to be stopped. KH was an implausible figure who would make *The Observer* look foolish. He couldn't understand the curious relationship ROA had formed with him, his peculiar dependence on him. KH had had a poisonous influence. He said he would ring ROA before the board meeting to make sure he wouldn't propose KH as vice-chairman.

I sat next to the glamorous Lady Melchett, who asked about KH (I had first visited her house with him). She said he was typical of men who formed too close an attachment to their mother. On the way out Lady Avon said she had 'almost' started taking *The Observer* again – for the first time since Suez: 'It's so much better than the *Sunday Times.*'

FRIDAY 20 FEBRUARY 1981

Board meeting today. Lajos rang early to ask what was going on. He said he smelled trouble. I told him what Lord G had said about KH. 'You'd better warn the others', he said, 'in case it comes up.' In the office, I saw John Cole and Iain Lindsay Smith and told them about the Harris possibility. 'You'd better warn Conor,' they said. I knew of Conor's contempt for KH, so I said to him: 'You're the bravest among us and you've got the least to lose. If the subject comes up, you must ask for KH to leave the room. Once he's out of the room I'm sure he'll get no support.' Conor said he'd ask for that if the matter came up. He likened KH to Shakespeare's Malvolio.

I told RH, who said he was sure ROA wouldn't bring the matter up. Conor mustn't provoke anything. (RH always nervous about offending Arco.) I then went along the corridor to Brian Nicholson's office and was half-way through a discussion when Frank Stanton, one of our American directors, came in. I learned afterwards that Frank had gone to warn Brian that ROA intended to sell the paper. Brian, having heard Bob deny the Rothermere bid, didn't think he meant immediately.

It was now a few minutes before the board meeting. I found Alan Bullock taking off his coat. He asked me for the latest news. I said ROA was planning to make himself chairman – and KH his vice-chairman. 'You'll want to stop that, I fancy,' he said in his broad Yorkshire accent. 'And you'll be right to. But you can't count on me. I owe Bob too much for a start. And I taught Kenneth. Let's hope it doesn't come up.'

ROA took his place at the head of the boardroom table. KH sat in his usual place at the other end. Anderson started in his low drawl. He'd decided to take the chair himself, he said, since Bradshaw had left the company. We had a tough fight on our hands, but he was confident that we had the right people to tackle it. 'Brian, Roger… Conor – Conor's going back to Ireland and I think that's the right place for him.' (I looked across the table at Conor, who was looking straight down, not catching my eye – had Bob said something to him before the meeting?) Anderson went on quietly: 'Conor was due to go in March, but with the fight we're in I think Donald should be given the reins now, so from today Donald assumes all Conor's responsibilities. Off you go, Don, pick up the reins.'

I was rather amazed – was I now editor-in-chief as well as editor, or what? I looked across at Conor again: he had taken it like a lamb. Bob must have spoken to him – but when? I'd been with Conor until shortly before the meeting started and he hadn't said a word.

Then came the crunch. I think we all saw it coming. Everyone was silent, concentrating on every word. 'My friend Kenneth Harris', he began 'has been a great help to me from the moment we took over this paper. He is going to be very important to me if I'm to be your chairman. I would like him to be my vice-chairman and my main line of communication with the paper. But first, gentlemen, I think you should elect me to your board.' (He had never previously bothered to be a director.) We elected him with some mild humour. Then he said: 'Gentlemen, I'd now like you to propose myself as chairman and Kenneth Harris as vice-chairman.'

There was an uncomfortable silence for what seemed a very long time. Finally, Lord G, looking very unhappy, and sitting next to Harris, spoke up.

'I beg you, Mr Chairman, not to proceed any further with that motion. If you do, I regret to say this but I would have to break my twenty-year association with *The Observer*. I urge you most strongly to allow me to speak to you privately before going any further.'

ROA looked down, saying nothing. We all waited. He started talking again about his need for KH if he was to do this job. He didn't see him as a main line executive, but a channel of communication. Would he press the matter to a vote, linking his own appointment and Kenneth's together?

Then Conor spoke. 'I should like to add my support to Lord Good-man. None of us would be happy to see this motion go forward. Could I suggest that we discuss this matter in the absence of Mr Harris?' Goodman started objecting to this for some reason; there was a series of disconnected remarks around the table; then Anderson spoke: 'OK, Ken, on your hoss.' KH, who had sat impassive throughout, collected his papers and left the room.

The discussion went on for about half an hour, very tense. Everyone stressed our debt to ROA – 'You have given us so much and you ask for so little, yet we must deny you on this.' ROA insisted that he didn't see KH's role as that of a 'main-line executive', so what were we worried about? Stanton, RH and Astor said nothing; I said the heart of the matter was whether Harris as vice-chairman would be senior in commercial matters to Roger and Brian, and in editorial matters to me. If it was clear that he wasn't, the title wouldn't matter so much. But at present he was a member of the editorial staff and the staff would want to know if he had editorial authority over me. Bob looked a bit impatient at this.

Brian Nicholson said: 'It would be an insult to Roger Harrison and myself to be answerable to Kenneth Harris.' Finally, Bob spoke after an-other long silence: 'I guess we won't be proceeding with the choice of a vice-chairman at this meeting. I'd better tell Kenneth.' He then left to go to Harris's room.

There was a sense of release from high drama. RH turned to Stanton: 'I hope we persuaded you, Frank.' To which he replied: 'I didn't need any persuading. It was Bob you needed to persuade, and I think you have persuaded him. I've sat on many boards with Bob Anderson and never before have I seen him told by a board that he couldn't do something. You gentlemen have just done that.'

ROA and KH returned, KH smoking a cigar and muttering: 'Well, well...', but not looking too put out. The rest of the meeting was an-ti-climax. When it finished, Brian took my arm and muttered: 'Congratulations.'

As we gathered for pre-lunch drinks at the bar, I took KH aside. 'That was a very gruelling experience for you,' I said, probing for his reaction. He waved an arm expansively.

'I've lived a long life, Donald. I'm sixty-one. This isn't the worst thing that has happened to me, not by a long chalk (by which I took him to mean his wife's suicide). I only hope Bob will take it as well as I am. My only interest is *The Observer*. As long as everyone understands that. I've stopped Bob Anderson doing some things in the last twenty-four hours that wouldn't have been right for *The Observer* – now I get this for my pains.'

'Did he mean Rothermere?' I asked. 'I'd better say no more,' he replied. 'I've said too much.' ROA and KH left together. They weren't lunching with us. I was never to see ROA again.

There was a euphoric mood at the board lunch, which are usually boring affairs, a feeling that history was being made. How would ROA react? Would the rebuff over KH make him disenchanted with the paper and hasten Arco's departure? Astor was especially concerned about this. RH said everything depended on our commercial performance this year – we were on target for a reasonable year, and the *Guardian* printing contract might be very profitable. Why not a closer association with *The Guardian*, I asked? 'Wrong image for advertisers,' said Brian. We all agreed to keep mum about the Harris drama. 'It'll get out,' said someone. 'These things always do.'

After the lunch Conor took me to his room. 'This is the last time you'll see me as editor-in-chief. I'm going to Rome now. When I return it will be as a columnist, not editor-in-chief.' I asked if ROA had seen him before the meeting. 'Yes, he came in for five minutes and told me I should leave you to it. Since the editorial side of the paper is in good hands, I saw no point in disagreeing.' I said the status of the editor was now much higher in the organisation than it had been before, chiefly thanks to him. I meant it.

SATURDAY 21 FEBRUARY 1981

Brian Nicholson came in for a chat. He said ROA and KH had gone to Brighton for the night and were staying at the Metropole. What for,

I asked? Brian's eyes looked at the ceiling: 'Why else do people go to Brighton hotels?' Surely not, I said, remembering that Brian had seen them with two girls at Annabel's on Bob's last visit. We both laughed at the improbable thought. I asked Brian if he thought the chances had risen of the paper being disposed of. 'I think the likelihood of our being sold this year is very high – almost certain,' he said.

Sunday 22 February 1981

Family lunch at Adam Raphael's. At home, there was a message from David Astor on the answering machine: 'Nothing urgent, but give me a ring. It's good news, by the way.' When I rang he said he'd met ROA at Claridge's for coffee before he flew back to the States. The KH question didn't seem to be troubling him. He spoke in a very reassuring way about the paper and especially about me. He thought I ought to know, because he [David] had been worried about ROA's reaction to the Friday meeting. But all was well.

Monday 23 February 1981

Radio 4 programme about the great Fleet Street proprietors, back to Northcliffe and Beaverbrook. I was quoted and William Rees-Mogg described me as 'a highly successful editor'.

Wednesday 25 February 1981

Various routine meetings – features with Trevor Grove, magazine with Peter Crookston, miscellaneous admin items with Nigel Lloyd – when KH comes on from LA about 6 p.m. 'He says it's very urgent,' says my secretary, so out goes Nigel while I take the call.

He reads a statement to be issued at eight o'clock London time by ROA. I start to write it down, then freeze in mid-sentence when I hear the news. Arco have sold *The Observer* to Lonrho in exchange for 40 per cent of Lonrho's Scottish subsidiary, George Outram & Co., which publishes the *Glasgow Herald*. ROA to remain chairman of *The Observer*. 'Well, well,' I say, rather stunned. 'What does it mean, Kenneth? Is it good for *The Observer*?' 'Oh yes,' he says. 'It's much the best solution for *The Observer*.'

Ring my wife to warn her I might be late for dinner – we have guests due to arrive at eight. 'Heavens,' she says when I tell her the news. I warn Cole and Lindsay Smith there's something afoot and ask them to call the staff together. I take John aside and tell him in confidence – 'We've been sold to Lonrho' – and rush upstairs to see if the management have more information. RH just putting down the phone on a similar call from Los Angeles. He laughs and waves his arms up and down helplessly. What can one do? 'We've been through so much, you and I, over the years, one can hardly care anymore.'

He knew no more than I did, so I went downstairs to tell the staff – or the twenty or thirty who were still around.

'I've just been told that *The Observer* has been sold to Lonrho. As part of the same deal, Arco have taken 40 per cent of George Outram, who publish the *Glasgow Herald*. I know no more than that. But I thought I should tell you myself rather than let you learn it from watching TV tonight. I'll let you know more tomorrow when I know more myself.'

As *The Guardian* said later, it was 'the classic B-movie scene – editor tells staff their paper's been sold.'

The phone had started ringing, with every paper in Fleet Street wanting a comment. I pretended to be out. But one of the calls was from John Crawford, managing director of Outram's, who wanted a chat. I decided I'd better see him and took Iain Lindsay Smith with me to the Stafford Hotel, since he had worked for Crawford in Glasgow and knew him well.

We found Crawford in the bar – a neat, hard-looking Glaswegian. He wanted to know the reaction of the staff. 'Shock,' I said. What would it be like when the shock wore off? 'Hard to say.' What's your own reaction? 'Shock.' That all? 'Perhaps a feeling of inevitability – the Arco connection had begun to look unreal.' What will the staff do? 'That depends partly on my reaction. I think I should see Tiny Rowland to find out what he wants to do with the paper.' He doubted if that would be possible – 'He hardly sees anyone.' 'I'm afraid he'll have to if he wants my support. I can't convince the journalists that they should go along with this until I'm convinced myself.' He said he'd see what he could do.

Home late to the dinner party to find everybody high on the news and pre-dinner drinks. We watch the nine o'clock news – paper sold without knowledge of editor (picture of self on screen). Tiny Rowland shown as amiable: has he confidence in present editorship of *The Observer*? 'I've never met the editor, but if he was acceptable to Atlantic Richfield I'm sure he'll be acceptable to me.' On *Newsnight*, which we all watch, David Astor says he feels betrayed and fears for the paper's future.

Thinking things over that night, I couldn't help noting the irony that, while it was Harris who had saved *The Observer* from Murdoch, it was also Harris who had caused *The Observer* to be sold to Lonrho. But he wasn't the only person responsible. What if Conor Cruise O'Brien hadn't forced *The Observer* to vote Labour in the 1979 general election (against his own instincts, or so he claimed, and certainly against mine) and thereby caused Arco's disillusionment with the paper?

O'Brien and Harris: two men caught up in a classic personal feud. Two men who hated each other. The more I thought about it, the image came to mind of Sherlock Holmes and Professor Moriarty, his arch enemy, wrestling their way down the Reichenbach Falls. Meanwhile, the paper they were fighting about had landed in the hands of Lonrho. As my then wife said on hearing the paper had been sold: 'Heavens, Tiny Rowland and Tiny Trelford!'

CHAPTER 10

TINY

When the news broke about the sale of *The Observer* to Lonrho, dominating that morning's front pages, I emerged from the lift at Lonrho's Cheapside head office to find Tiny Rowland waiting with his arm outstretched. 'Mr Trelford, I recognise you,' he said, with a punctiliousness that reminded me suddenly of David Astor – both tall, fair, rich, handsome men of German extraction, and of a similar age.

I introduced *The Observer*'s two managing directors, Roger Harrison and Brian Nicholson. We were still in a state of shock, wandering around like men on laughing gas, not sure what to do next, not sure if we still had a job. Rowland introduced us to his two colleagues, Paul Spicer and Alan Ball. I had recently had a shouting match with Spicer on the telephone over a Lonrho story in *The Observer*, but we both decided not to remember this. Ball had a gloomy, almost funereal air. I gathered later that this was nothing to do with us; it was his habitual hangdog expression.

Our mood hadn't been helped by a statement from Glasgow by Sir George Bolton, the eighty-year-old deputy chairman of Lonrho and chairman of George Outram & Co., which had been quoted on the front page of *The Times* that morning. He had said *The Observer* would be run from Glasgow and that the editor of the *Glasgow Herald* would have as much say as anyone else in the running of the paper. He joked: 'I suppose there may be some editorial people at *The Observer* who are having kittens tonight,' and added: 'We have always wanted a paper so that we could really express the views of Africa and the Third World.'

Before we could start our meeting, Rowland was called away from the Lonrho boardroom to take a telephone call. While he was out, Spicer surprised me by asking what school I had been to. When I told him about my modest Midlands grammar school, he asked: 'Did you get any O Levels?' I recounted this bizarre conversation later to Conor Cruise O'Brien, who explained: 'I don't think he was trying to insult you, Donald. He wanted you to ask him the same question, so that he could tell you he had been to Eton and that *he* had some O Levels.'

Harrison was annoyed that his coup in securing a £500,000-a-year printing contract with *The Guardian* had been scuppered by the sale. Rowland agreed to ring *The Guardian* to say that Lonrho would honour the contract, but his lawyer later rang the newspaper back to withdraw the commitment. So *The Guardian*, quite reasonably, walked away. Anderson hadn't known about the printing contract. It was another example of Atlantic Richfield's lack of interest in *The Observer*'s attempts to become self-supporting.

When we complained about Bolton's overnight comments on the paper, Rowland dismissed them with a wave of his hand. 'Editorial control of *The Observer*', he said, 'will remain in London,' then adding, after a pause, 'by the people who control it now.' I asked him if I could define editorial control as I understood it and drew from my pocket a scrap of paper (which I still have) on which I had jotted down a few points: the editor would control the content of the newspaper and the recruitment and dismissal of journalists, subject only to an agreed budget; he would have final say on editorial policy; and he would be free to comment on Lonrho's affairs, including criticising the company if necessary, subject to hearing the company's point of view.

Rowland said blandly that he accepted all that. I thought this was rather too easy, so I asked him if he would repeat those pledges of editorial freedom to the journalists. He said he would. Why he ever agreed to meet the full body of journalists I never knew. It was a major tactical error and got the new arrangement off on the wrong foot. He could just as easily have said to me: 'Why don't you bring a representative group of the paper's journalists to my office?' That way he could have controlled the occasion, dispensing hospitality and charming a small group in the way he knew best.

The Observer's shabby basement canteen, with about seventy journalists slouching around on plastic chairs or sitting on the edge of chipped Formica tables, was hardly an encouraging environment for *The Observer*'s curious and slightly apprehensive journalists to meet their new employer. The meeting started badly and got worse. The first person Tiny confronted was John Davis, the City editor, who had described Lonrho's bid for House of Fraser as 'downright cheeky'.

But the case for the prosecution was put most forcefully by veteran Africa correspondent Colin Legum, who said it would be impossible for Lonrho to allow the newspaper to report objectively in places where its business relied on Rowland's personal friendship with the country's leader. Tiny was angry, bristling at the way Legum seemed to be claiming a superior knowledge of Africa, and hit back strongly. They talked about Kenya, the Sudan, Angola and other countries in a way that was over the head of most of the journalists present, who were only concerned about their jobs.

At one point, Rowland asked if the paper would support the removal of Cubans from Angola in return for the removal of South Africans from Namibia, a plan of his that had been approved by the American State Department. Legum said *The Observer* would take account of the benefits to the people of the countries concerned – not, by implication, the interests of Lonrho shareholders. When Rowland asked: 'Could I have counted on *The Observer*'s support when Lonrho's assets were seized in Tanzania?' Adam Raphael, the political correspondent, responded: 'Editorial freedom surely means that the owner can't count on anything.'

By this time Rowland had had enough. He had gone puce and was clearly raging inside – a rage that didn't subside on the car journey back to Cheapside, according to chauffeur Jimmy Rennie. After he had left, the NUJ chapel passed a motion approving the sale to Lonrho, subject to editorial safeguards. The journalists had obviously been impressed by Richard Hall's testimony at the meeting that Lonrho had never interfered with his paper in Zambia.

I was so worried by the angry confrontation that I went to see Rowland again on the following day. This time we had a civilised conversation, the first time we had met on our own. I had actually been introduced to him briefly at a Queen's birthday reception at Government House in Zomba seventeen years before, but he clearly had no recollection of this. He was interested, though, that I had worked in Malawi and travelled throughout the continent. The fact that Tiny and I could talk in shorthand about African politics was one reason why we were able to forge a good working relationship over the coming years. He felt comfortable talking to me.

Tiny was in a talkative mood, clearly hoping to dispel the unpleasant atmosphere of the day before. He gave me some interesting background on the sale of *The Observer*. He had been introduced to Anderson about eighteen months before, at the California Club in Los Angeles, by D. K. Ludwig, who owned much of the Brazilian rainforest and was said to be the second richest man in the world. He and Anderson had been doing oil business together in Brazil and Mexico. Rowland and Ludwig were partners in the Caribbean-based Princess Hotels group, which Lonrho eventually took over.

Tiny had said to Anderson: 'If you ever think of selling *The Observer*, will you give me first refusal?' He had been surprised by the American's reply: 'I doubt if we'll be long-term holders. I don't like their policy, and if I decide to sell I'll let you know.' This meeting would have been in the second half of 1979, after the British general election, reinforcing my view that *The Observer*'s support for Labour had been pivotal in Arco's decision to sell.

True to his word, Anderson had tried to get in touch with Rowland on Thursday 20 February 1981, the day before the board was to fall out with him over Kenneth Harris's role at the paper. So, Anderson was already preparing to sell the paper before that crucial showdown with the board. Tiny was abroad, so the two men met for lunch at Claridge's on the Saturday.

There Anderson had complained that Arco had no say in the commercial or political policies of the paper and that he had come to the end of the road. At the coffee stage, Anderson said: 'Tiny, do you want the paper?' Tiny had replied cheerfully: 'If you're making an unconditional offer, I'm making an unconditional acceptance, and that in law is a contract.' They shook hands and Anderson said: 'The paper's yours.'

'Why do you want *The Observer*?' I asked Tiny. '*The Observer* is a peach for Lonrho,' he said. 'It's the best-known British paper among African leaders, because many of them were exiled in London while fighting for independence and they remember that *The Observer* supported them. OK, it's losing money, but not much. Besides, it owns several thousand Reuters shares of significant value.'

He said Anderson had made it a condition that there must be no announcement of the sale until he and Kenneth Harris were airborne on the Sunday evening on their way to California. Any leak and the deal was off. Anderson was particularly concerned that Goodman and Astor should hear nothing until he had left the country. Even allowing for the requirements of commercial secrecy, this was all a bit rich. Anderson had brazenly lied to people to whom he owed some respect and gratitude.

I heard later that the board of Atlantic Richfield had actually stood up and cheered when Anderson told them he had sold *The Observer*. He said Arco and Lonrho were looking at joint oil projects in Angola and Mexico. This was more obviously comfortable news for the Arco directors to hear than the travails of a loss-making, left-leaning British Sunday newspaper.

Rowland confided in me a couple of special points about the sale. Anderson had made it a condition that Lonrho should 'look after Kenneth' and he said he would find a role for him within the company.

That's fine with me, I said, as long as he kept him away from *The Observer*. Harris was eventually made chairman of George Outram & Co., in succession to Sir George Bolton, the garrulous octogenarian.

The other point was more problematic. He had promised Anderson that he would get rid of Conor Cruise O'Brien, doubtless prompted by Harris. I said Conor was an important part of the paper and I didn't want to lose his column. He shrugged and said: 'He has been pretty insulting to me. I guess there's no immediate hurry, but I gave my word, so he will have to go sometime soon, especially if Bob raises the matter again.'

It seemed certain that Lonrho's ownership of its Scottish newspapers would automatically trigger an inquiry by the Monopolies and Mergers Commission (MMC, now the Competition Commission). That would delay the sale by at least three months and the MMC might decide it would be against the public interest. This official inquiry would be our main line of defence against Lonrho, giving me and *The Observer*'s journalists a chance to express our objections in the hope that their bid would be rejected.

Rowland said his offer for *The Observer* was conditional on the takeover not being referred to the MMC and pointed out that Rupert Murdoch had managed to acquire *The Times* and *Sunday Times* only the year before without any reference. He was right about Murdoch, but that was a politically loaded decision based on the fact that Margaret Thatcher wanted Murdoch to own *The Times* and *Sunday Times* for the political support that would guarantee her new government.

The papers escaped a reference on the spurious grounds that they might go out of business if the sale was delayed for three months – at a time when the *Sunday Times* was making an estimated profit of a million pounds a week. This ruling had caused such a storm of protest that the Secretary for Trade and Industry, John Biffen, was under strong pressure from MPs and the media not to allow the next newspaper merger to go through unchecked.

And so it came to pass. Rowland made a late bid to halt the reference by saying he would buy the paper himself, but that was quickly ruled

out on legal grounds. So *The Observer*'s heavyweights – Lord Goodman, David Astor, Conor Cruise O'Brien – joined me and the senior
staff in seeking to have Lonrho's bid overturned.

In my evidence to the MMC I cast doubt on Rowland's 'honesty and
reliability' and pointed out the obvious conflicts of interest that could
arise in Africa under Lonrho's ownership. Rowland, I said, was

> a man of powerful personality and immense resource – some would
> say ruthlessness – in the pursuit of his company's interests. The devel-
> opment of Lonrho may have required those characteristics, but *The*
> *Observer* carries influence in the very places where his interests are most
> extensive and most at risk. *The Observer* has the power to help Lonrho
> or to hurt it in those places. For Rowland to grant *The Observer* edito-
> rial independence would be to give one of his companies *carte blanche*
> to damage the whole business to which he has devoted his life. It is as
> illogical as it is unbelievable.

In sticking my neck out in this way, I was taking a risk. If Rowland succeeded in obtaining *The Observer* and ever read my evidence, he might
find it impossible to work with me. Copies of my submission were kept
under lock and key by my ultra-loyal secretary, Barbara Rieck, who
was ready to defend them with her life. It was an unexploded bomb.

I also appeared before the Commission to answer their questions.
I have to say I was not impressed with the chairman, Sir Godfray Le
Quesne, who didn't seem awfully interested in the proceedings, espe-
cially after lunch. Lord Goodman didn't think he was much of a lawyer.
David Astor sensed that editorial freedom did not rate highly among
the Commission's interests and feared the worst. At the same time,
Lonrho were going through a parallel inquiry into their bid for House
of Fraser.

John Cole, my deputy, added to our concerns when he escorted
Commission members on a site visit to the paper on a Saturday night.
He was infuriated and depressed to hear one member, Alastair Burnet,

the ITN news reader, say loudly: 'The Observer is lucky that anybody wants to buy it.' Later I wrote a profile of ITN for The Listener and was surprised to be invited by Burnet to join him in a large whisky, not long before he was due to go on air.

Cole brought further gloomy news after meeting the former Prime Minister, James Callaghan, at a party at the House of Commons. Callaghan had always shown an interest in The Observer. 'What I'm hearing, John,' he said, 'is that the government has decided that Lonrho can have one, but not both of their objectives. If they turn Rowland down on House of Fraser, which I gather they are minded to do, they will let him have The Observer.'

And so it turned out. I remember the day the decision was announced as one of the most depressing of my life. My wife was out that evening and I just sat in an armchair brooding in the dark. I told David Astor that until then I had always believed, perhaps naively, in the basic integrity of British institutions.

In preparing our case against Lonrho I had set several reporters onto the task of discovering all we could about Rowland's eventful life. The main investigator was a tigerish though twitchy reporter called Jack Lundin, who would drop his latest research through my letterbox at home in the dead of night. He insisted that no one should know about his involvement – possibly, I could only surmise, because he might have been concerned that some of his methods of research could be described as, well, unorthodox.

We didn't find anything incriminating in Tiny's family background, though it was unusual – father German, mother born in England of a Dutch father and a British mother. He was their third child, named William Roland Fuhrhop, and was born in a British internment camp in India (giving him British nationality) in 1917. The camp was in an unhealthy malarial district called Belgaum in the western Indian state of Karnataka.

The family were glad to return to their apartment in Calcutta when the war ended a year later and Tiny's father started to rebuild his business. He had been an importer of locomotives and heavy machinery from Europe, which he sold throughout India and Burma. While he was interned, his entire stock had been seized without compensation and his offices and stores around the country had been looted.

Thanks to the efficiency of the British-trained Indian civil service, we were able to find out the names of every family in their apartment block. One other family was called Roland, which might have been the original source of his name. He was called Tiny by his ayah because he was an unusually large baby.

In fact, I was to learn more about his past from Tiny himself than I did from the paper's somewhat illicit research. Over the next few years he would drop a personal anecdote into our weekly conversations on the telephone, or over lunches at Cheapside, or occasionally at a family Sunday lunch at Hedsor Wharf, his estate at Taplow in Berkshire, situated on a bend of the Thames, and next door, as it happens, to the Astor estate at Cliveden. I could tell that his children had never heard these personal stories before and were fascinated by them.

Around the time *The Observer* was sold in 1993, Rowland became much exercised by extracts published in the *Daily Telegraph* from a biography written by Tom Bower. He said he didn't recognise the person written about and described the book as 'smearing and distorting everything that belongs to me and giving me a character of his own choosing'. Neither I nor Tiny had talked to Bower and the author seemed to have relied heavily on sources with a grudge against the paper, some of them people I had sacked.

Bower impugns my motives and my integrity throughout the book, putting the worst possible gloss on any situation involving me, and makes numerous false allegations. The *Telegraph* presented the extracts with a picture of a face that was half Tiny's and half mine, implying absurdly that our personalities had become intertwined.

The tone of the book was unremittingly hostile – a formula that worked with Bower's biography of Robert Maxwell, a brave book that was written under extreme intimidation. But Maxwell was a monster. Tiny Rowland was an altogether more complex, subtle and many-sided character. Bower's unrelenting case for the prosecution created a portrait of Rowland that I simply couldn't recognise after getting to know him pretty well over a dozen years.

I couldn't challenge Bower on the history of Lonrho's business (though I'm sure Tiny could have done) but what he wrote about me and *The Observer* was seriously skewed. He had been misled by his sources into describing situations that never happened and quoting verbatim from conversations that never took place.

I told Tiny that he could expect to be misrepresented if he kept the details of his early life and business career secret, and I offered to publish anything he decided to write. I expected him to say no, but I was amazed when, just a few days later, an article of about 4,000 words landed on my desk. It appeared in the last issue of *The Observer* that I edited in May 1993, but it doesn't seem to have attracted much attention in the hullabaloo surrounding *The Observer*'s sale.

•   •   •

In the early 1920s, Fuhrhop had moved his family from India to Hamburg, where Tiny enjoyed a pleasant childhood by the Alster Lake. From an early age, he showed all the signs of being an entrepreneur, buying and selling all sorts of playground necessities and making money. In his teens, he travelled with an uncle to Romania, Poland, Norway and Denmark.

At school, he became the Hitler Youth Troop leader (*Scharfuhrer*) of about 150 boys, alarming his father, who was already concerned about the rising power of the Nazis. He swiftly despatched Tiny to England, where he became a boarder at Churcher's School, Petersfield, excelling at sport. After leaving school he spent a short time in the City of London before his uncle employed him in the family shipping business. He was soon travelling all over Europe, obtaining shipping contracts in Czechoslovakia, Romania, Germany and Austria.

He became involved in helping Jewish families to get their assets – or the small proportion of these allowed by the authorities – out of Germany. His family was well equipped for this role because it had extensive warehousing and customs facilities in London and several European countries, and a firm belonging to his mother's family, Ryley & Company, had a number of postal depots around Britain.

On the brink of war in 1939, he said he had been arrested by the Gestapo in Berlin, suspected of being part of a ring that helped Jewish families to take more assets out of Germany than the authorities allowed. He was held in total silence and darkness for long periods in Moabit jail, expecting to be taken out and shot. Eventually his family's protests that he was a British subject secured his release and he was dumped across the Dutch border. He returned to England and changed his name by deed poll. His father had refused to do that, making his life in war-time England more complicated than it needed to be.

• • •

After several months of enquiries, he found that his father had been interned on the Isle of Man, along with thousands of other German nationals, and had been appointed camp leader of 4,000 declared anti-Nazi detainees. Fuhrhop had been interned in both world wars and in both he had seen his business destroyed. Tiny himself had been drafted to a non-combat field ambulance unit in Hertfordshire, which was later transferred to Scotland. Because his father was German and his elder brother had been recruited into the *Wehrmacht* (where he later took part in the retreat from Moscow), Tiny couldn't join a British combat unit.

When he was refused compassionate leave to visit his father on the Isle of Man, he went anyway and was punished on his return with twenty-seven days in Barlinnie prison in Glasgow, one of the toughest in Britain. On his first day, an NCO (non-commissioned officer) slashed him across the face with a whip. His mother became ill and was sent, as the wife of a German (even though she was British), to Holloway prison, where the doctors missed her cancer and accused her of malingering.

In Edinburgh, Tiny had been befriended by his commanding officer, Colonel Malcolm McKinnon, even though he was the man who had sentenced him to his term at Barlinnie. He invited Rowland to his home for a supper. Allegations have sometimes been made that Tiny expressed pro-German, even pro-Nazi, sympathies at this time. His friendly treatment by his commanding officer surely argues against that.

Tiny is known to have applied to join MI6 and been turned down. A senior War Office figure interviewed him at Edinburgh Castle and said: 'Rowland, what are we going to do with you now? You could be of great use to us, but it's all very difficult. For instance, we are now allies of the Russians. Let me ask you, who is worse to you, Stalin or Hitler?'

Tiny replied: 'They are both equally evil.'

The officer then told Tiny that, because of this response, he was being placed under close arrest and would be charged under Section 18B, which referred to 'British-born persons with leanings towards fascism'. Tiny says they knew he wasn't a fascist, but it was the only regulation under which he could be detained, since its interpretation was elastic. He spent several weeks at Saughton prison in Edinburgh before being shipped to the Isle of Man to join his parents in internment.

By this time his mother's condition had worsened. She was sent for treatment in Liverpool, where Tiny was taken under armed escort to Walton prison to visit her there. Tiny finally watched in anguish as she died in British custody at Peel on the Isle of Man. It is easy to see why Tiny was so bitter about his mother's treatment and was to retain a profound hatred of the British establishment. She was British; her only offence was to have married a German forty years before. She was a sick woman in her sixties and clearly no threat to national security. Why she had to be moved around the country in her weak condition is hard to understand and can only explained by the bureaucratic chaos of war.

• • •

It is hard now, after more than seventy years, to understand what it must have been like to be a German in Britain at a time of war. Britain's propaganda efforts were aimed at demonising anyone and anything German. I remember seeing a sign outside an empty cinema where the name of the film would normally appear. The sign read: 'THE ONLY GOOD HUN IS A DEAD ONE'. In such a hate-filled atmosphere, reason often went out of the window.

Tiny may not have helped himself with his public-school accent, parading his money and his many visiting girlfriends in front of uneducated private soldiers, who would be only too ready to label him a Nazi. Knowing his tendency to cause mischief and the emotional turmoil he must have been going through, it wouldn't surprise me in the least if he sometimes played up to the image of an unreconstructed Hun.

He remained in internment until almost the end of the war, even though others were released earlier, prompting the suggestion in some quarters that this showed the authorities still doubted his loyalty to Britain. I have another theory about that, based on a hint he once gave me about serving British intelligence while he was interned. Even though he was turned down for MI6, the intelligence service would have known him and could see that such a strong character, speaking perfect German and English, could be useful to them in watching German prisoners or Oswald Mosley's detained British fascists.

I have also wondered about the excessively brutal treatment he received, serving in at least four British prisons during the war as well as one in Berlin – in Barlinnie, Saughton, Walton and Peel on the Isle of Man. Is it possible that this was a cover to give him 'street cred' as a British spy in the internment camp? An unproven thesis, I agree, but at least as plausible as some of the pro-Nazi stories published about him.

After being released from the Isle of Man, Tiny was briefly sent to work as a porter at Paddington station, where he concentrated on the first-class carriages because they gave bigger tips. Later he became what would then have been called a 'spiv', moving around shops in the luxury-starved West End selling fridges and nylon stockings. He told me that he wore a British Warm overcoat with plenty of inside pockets to carry the old white five-pound notes. Sometimes, at the end of the day, he said he could hardly walk for the weight of the money he was carrying.

Eventually he realised that there was even more money to be made from owning the factories that produced the products in short supply. As a result he got to know an engineer called Lionel Taylor, who was brilliant at mending old machines. One day Taylor called on Tiny at the Mayfair apartment he was now rich enough to live in, but said he couldn't stay because his baby daughter was in the car. Tiny went down with him to say goodbye and to meet the child. The baby's name was Josie, and twenty-four years later, dear reader, Tiny married her.

• • •

Lonrho was the creation of a powerful City businessman, Harley Drayton, and it was he who brought Rowland, Alan Ball and Angus Ogilvy together to run the re-activated company, holding the reins while keeping out of the limelight himself. He was a major formative influence on Tiny before his early death in 1966.

Ogilvy and his wife, Princess Alexandra, became close friends with the Rowlands, living in adjacent apartments for a time in Park Lane. It was a severe blow to Tiny personally when Ogilvy eventually resigned from the Lonrho board. Tiny always believed that Prince Philip had insisted on Ogilvy quitting.

It was interesting, therefore, when *The Observer*'s futuristic new building on Chelsea Bridge was opened, that Tiny should have invit-ed the Princess to perform the opening ceremony – presumably with a substantial gift attached – and interesting that she accepted. When I met her on this occasion, she asked in a conspiratorial tone: 'How do you find Mr Rowland?' In reply, I said: 'He's rather charming.' She looked at me for a moment and whispered: 'I'd watch that charm if I were you.'

Lonrho's rapid expansion throughout Africa, and Tiny's friendships with African leaders, must have brought him to the attention of MI6, if only to discover if his activities were serving British interests. In the early 1990s, both the security and the intelligence services began to open themselves up, revealing publicly for the first time the names of the heads of the two services. Editors were invited to meet them at their headquarters.

When I met Sir Colin McColl, who was 'C', Tiny's name came up in the conversation very quickly. Everyone round the table laughed when one of them said: 'Tiny knows more about Africa than we do. He's a hard man to keep up with.' Another man said: 'He has been useful to the service in the past.' He gave no particulars, and it didn't seem polite to ask.

I had lunch at MI5 with Dame Stella Rimington, and soon afterwards came across her at a drinks party in Islington. As we were leaving I said to my then wife: 'Do you see that tall woman over there?'

'Do you mean the one in the houswifey floral dress?' she replied. 'What about her?'

'She's the director-general of MI5.'

Her astonished silence at this news lasted all the way home.

I had a special interest in the opening up of the security services, for some years before I had been invited to address a joint meeting of MI5 and MI6 somewhere in the Home Counties. My name was the only one used that evening; I was introduced to people called 'Northern Ireland' or 'Counter-Terrorism'. I had been asked to advise them on their public image and so I told them that they had a choice: to be more open about their work voluntarily or to be overcome by a democratic tide like the one that was then engulfing the CIA in America.

While the spooks analysed my speech and prepared to cross-examine me about it, I was taken off for a drink by the then head of MI5, Sir John Jones. This was too good a chance for a journalist to miss. I asked him about the sudden resignation of Harold Wilson as Prime Minister. There had been rumours that he had got close to the Russians while president of the Board of Trade in the post-war Labour government. A Soviet defector, Anatoliy Golitsyn, had said Wilson was targeted by the KGB at that time, but had no evidence that he had actually been recruited.

'M' was dismissive about this. 'We have no reason to suspect Wilson of espionage. I don't know why he resigned. It may have been a private matter.' He hesitated, then added:

> Marcia Williams [later Lady Falkender, Wilson's powerful political secretary] – now that's a different matter. We have nothing against her, except that she is close to some people we know who do dubious business in Eastern Europe. I'm sure she knows nothing about that, but she may be introducing these people to Wilson, which troubles us a bit.

Later he got on to a subject that seemed to be obsessing him – Communist skulduggery on the factory floor. It struck me that if he really believed this posed a threat to Britain's security he must have placed some spies inside the factories and within the trade unions. When the spooks returned, they tore my thesis to shreds. It amused me to know that some years later events had obliged them to follow my unwelcome advice.

●   ●   ●

I got to know Lady Forkbender, as *Private Eye* called her, when she wrote some articles for *The Observer* about her time with Wilson in Downing Street. She was very difficult to get to, but on Lord Barnetson's advice I had turned up on her doorstep bearing a huge bunch of red roses, and that did the trick.

I once asked her to explain her powerful hold over Wilson if she hadn't been, as some papers slyly hinted, his mistress. She replied:

It was because, throughout his career and at all levels and among many conflicting voices, he had heard one voice telling him, not necessarily what was best for Britain or even for the Labour Party, but what was best for Harold Wilson. He learned to trust that voice and that voice belonged to me.

• • •

Although we had failed to persuade the MMC to ban Lonrho's ownership of *The Observer*, enough doubts had been raised about potential conflicts of interest, especially in Africa, that we were able to press for tough editorial safeguards. We were helped by the sole voice against Lonrho on the MMC, a trade unionist called Robert Marshall, who had worked in Africa. He said safeguards would be useless against Tiny Rowland and that he shouldn't be allowed to have the paper. I decided to seek the toughest safeguards for editorial independence that any newspaper had hitherto achieved.

As a blueprint, I chose the wording of the safeguards imposed on Rupert Murdoch when he was allowed to take over *The Times* and *Sunday Times* without a reference to the MMC. On paper, they gave *The Observer*'s editor and journalists all the protection they could possibly need. I chose existing wording, rather than inventing some new formula, because I thought the Department of Trade and Industry (DTI) could hardly object if they had approved the same wording before. I sent a stream of letters to civil servants at the DTI demanding the same protection as Murdoch had been forced to give.

Looking back, I think that achieving these written safeguards, to be incorporated into the company's articles of association, was the greatest service I gave to *The Observer* at that time, managing to keep Tiny at arm's length without a confrontation. In addition to giving me total control over content, policy and staffing, it was stipulated that the editor could not be dismissed without the approval of a majority of five independent directors; nor could a new editor be appointed without their approval.

Dick Hall, often a harsh critic of my relationship with Rowland, was forced to admit in his book: 'The last convulsive phase of Rowland's takeover saw Trelford at his most brilliant, showing all those characteristics which made Harold Evans call him a "master politician". He referred to my love of snooker, about which I was to write a book, saying: 'He delights in the soft, artful shot, leaving his opponent in a hopeless quandary. Trelford's intention was to get Rowland well and truly snookered.'

When these safeguards were made public, I was amused to hear Derek Jameson, a former editor of the *Daily Express* and the *News of the World*, say on his radio programme: 'It's well known that Tiny Rowland can't go to the lavatory without Donald Trelford's permission.'

Even so, I knew that the safeguards alone would not offer adequate protection unless they were properly policed. A year later, Murdoch was able to ride roughshod over the editorial safeguards at *The Times* by dismissing Harold Evans, not because the safeguards were weakly worded, but because the national directors charged with enforcing them were not up to the job. The journalists on Times Newspapers had had no say in their appointment, since the directors were a carry-over from the Thomson regime and had been appointed in different circumstances. Murdoch was able to ignore them with impunity.

I was determined that this would not happen at *The Observer* and prepared a list of suitably tough independent directors who could be relied upon to stand up to Rowland if it came to a fight. The setting for the negotiations was the gloomy premises of the DTI in Victoria Street, where Lonrho's case was presented by the formidable lawyer Lord Shawcross, who applied the same forensic skills he had employed when prosecuting the Nazi leaders at Nuremburg, the acid bath murderer John George Haigh, and the atom spy Klaus Fuchs. Shawcross later joined the *Observer* board and was a constant pain in my side.

Against him that evening stood John Cole and myself, armed with no legal skills but a determination to see that the paper's independence would be protected. Rowland himself, looking as always like a million dollars in a dark suit and tie and immaculate white shirt with gold cufflinks, looked down at us with what felt like disdain. Shawcross read out his list of six candidates and we began debating their merits while Tiny looked visibly bored as the DTI clock moved on.

Eventually John and I said we were happy to accept two of the names on the list – Lord Windlesham, a decent man who had worked in television and been a junior minister under Edward Heath, and Sir Geoffrey Cox, a former war correspondent who had been the first editor of ITN and was widely admired in the media world. There was a palpable sigh of relief from the other side, shared by the late-working civil servants, that we finally appeared to be making some progress.

Shawcross said Lonrho would now choose two more directors from their list. There was general surprise when I objected to this, saying that the next two independent directors should be chosen from *our* list. I thought I was on thin ground over this and doubted if I could win, since as journalists we would be effectively appointing directors they hadn't chosen to the board of a Lonrho company, which they might have regarded as a bit of a cheek. Shawcross asked what right the journalists had to propose such appointments.

Eventually Rowland asked for an adjournment so that he could talk to me in private. As we walked down a dark DTI corridor, I was surprised when he took my hand in the African way. After a while he said: 'You're not making this very easy for me, Mr Trelford.' After another pause I replied: 'Well, Mr Rowland, how would you feel if somebody had taken over your company without your say-so?' He looked at me and said: 'I'd be fighting it just like you,' then, after another pause: 'I think we'll get on.'

After that everything went through on the nod. Two further independent directors were chosen: David Chipp, former editor-in-chief of the Press Association, and William Clark, a former *Observer* journalist who had resigned as Anthony Eden's press secretary over the

Suez adventure, and later became a senior figure at the World Bank in Washington. The civil servants suggested that the four chosen directors should choose the fifth, subject to agreement on both sides. This turned out to be Sir Derek Mitchell, a former Treasury mandarin who had worked with Harold Wilson in Downing Street.

I had achieved everything I had sought in the way of editorial safeguards and strong independent directors. Even so, I still had some apprehensions: in a crisis, Rowland might very well tear up paper safeguards, and a newspaper that was losing money could never be truly safe. The fact was that Rowland had an editor he didn't want and I had an owner I didn't want. Somehow, for *The Observer*'s sake, we had to find a way of getting on.

The early signs were not encouraging. There was a lunch at the Savoy Hotel for the Lonrho directors to meet the *Observer* directors. Tiny appeared clutching a copy of the previous Sunday's *Observer*, folded over at the leader page, on which Colin Legum had written an article about the Sudan that was highly critical of Tiny's favourite rebel, the southern breakaway leader Jonas Savimbi.

Tiny was apoplectic about it and couldn't talk about anything else, which put a serious damper on the occasion. He brooded throughout the lunch and left early. I tried to smooth things over by suggesting an interview with Savimbi, which Tiny agreed to arrange, but with bad grace.

Lord Duncan-Sandys, the chairman of Lonrho, invited me to his house in Vincent Square, Westminster, where we were served tea and cakes by his delightfully chatty Chilean wife. Securing Duncan-Sandys, a former Defence and Commonwealth Secretary and Churchill's ex-son-in-law, had been quite a coup for Rowland, though the secret payments he received through the Cayman Islands were to be described memorably by Edward Heath in the House of Commons as 'the unpleasant and unacceptable face of capitalism', a phrase that attached itself to Rowland for the rest of his life – rather unfairly, I think, given the massive illicit payments made by many other corporations.

As we looked out on the cricket square in front of his French windows, I remembered playing there a number of times against the Old Westminsters for the Adastrians, a club of past and present RAF officers. When I mentioned this to Duncan-Sandys, he pressed me to tell him more. So I told him that I was an opening batsman and had previously been out for forty-four and forty-six at the ground. The next year I was standing on forty-nine and was determined to reach my half-century.

Unfortunately, I was batting with an old flight lieutenant who had a permanent leg wound and hated running, especially for someone else's runs. Eventually, after he had declined some easy singles, I just set off for the other end. My partner was unperturbed, resting on his bat handle, refusing to move. So I had to scamper back, where I was run out diving for the crease, covering my whites in grass stains.

When I got to the pavilion, thinking there was nobody else in the dressing room, I hurled my bat, pads and gloves on the floor, along with various bitter imprecations. I hadn't noticed that a very tall Air Vice-Marshal, a former head of RAF cricket, was watching my childish antics with some amusement. I told him what had happened. I'll never forget his reply: 'You'll get over it. The Japs tried to cut my balls off in the war. I got over that. You'll get over this.' I have to say that I remember this little story whenever life's petty frustrations begin to get on top of me.

Duncan-Sandys was highly amused by the tale. He ended our meeting by saying: 'I'm the chairman and you're welcome to come and see me whenever you want. But Tiny Rowland calls all the shots.' This advice was echoed by another Lonrho director, Sir Peter Youens, whom I had known in Malawi when he worked closely with Dr Banda as a colonial civil servant. After sharing some memories about our time in Africa, he took me firmly by the arm and said: 'Tiny Rowland is the boss here and heaven help anyone who doesn't remember that.'

Relations with Rowland fell eventually into a settled routine. He would ring me on a Saturday wherever he was in the world and discuss the latest news. Sometimes he would confide a secret deal he was about to pull off in Africa. I used to write down some of his comments on a scrap of paper and put them on a spike on my desk for my secretary to file later. I found one just recently that said: 'Today the future of the Sudan lies in the palm of my hand.'

He had a habit of calling me, then saying: 'I have a friend here who would like a word with you,' and I would find myself talking, or, rather, stumbling for something to say, to President Moi of Kenya or the deputy head of Mossad. Tiny had an impish sense of humour, as anyone who has read his stream of pamphlets about Mohamed Fayed or the Sultan of Brunei could readily confirm.

I can never remember without laughing an occasion when Tiny and I went to meet an Indian guru, called the Mamadji, who claimed to have useful information for the paper. He insisted on blessing us, so Tiny and I had to kneel down next to each other while benedictions were poured over our heads in a language neither of us could understand. We dared not look at each other for fear of laughing out loud – which we did with some gusto after the guru had left.

I was told about another occasion when a legal conference in the Lonrho boardroom, attended by several prominent QCs, was interrupted by the arrival of India's most famous Swami, standing about 6 ft 9 in. in height and weighing over twenty stone, wrapped in a white garment. Tiny startled the assembled lawyers by prostrating himself at the Swami's feet.

On one occasion, I went on a day trip to Delhi, arriving in the morning on the Lonrho jet and interviewing two people before flying back to London on a scheduled British Airways flight in the evening. One was the Prime Minister, Narisimao Rao (who later went to jail); the other the same Swami before whom Tiny had prostrated himself, a man who counted Richard Nixon, the Sultan of Brunei and Elizabeth Taylor among his disciples. I interviewed him while he was working out his gigantic frame on an exercise bike. The Swami also ended up in jail.

• • •

Rowland's main value to *The Observer* – apart from his company's financial support, especially in funding a properly staffed business section and investing in the conversion to new technology – was securing interviews for the paper with people who were otherwise hard to pin down. He arranged for me to see Colonel Gaddafi twice, as recorded elsewhere, to visit Iran and to meet a number of global celebrities.

Tiny had some hold over Adnan Khashoggi, the famous Saudi arms trader, and used to impound his private plane at Gatwick airport from time to time. He would then arrange for Khashoggi to help *The Observer* with some interview or information for a story in return for releasing his plane.

On one occasion, Tiny asked me to fly on Concorde to meet Khashoggi at his apartment in New York, just off Fifth Avenue, close to St Patrick's Cathedral. The apartment, which was so high it was surrounded by clouds while I was there, was crammed with Old Masters, or what looked like Old Masters to my untutored eye. When we went out to dinner with some of his friends, we were required to tell a dirty joke. I funked it because I can never remember any. But one of the women – a sultry, dark-haired Iranian beauty nursing a tiny dog – told a story that was positively cloacal.

Later, one of the guests called on me at my office in London and gave *The Observer* a scoop about the collapse of a major Arab bank. I asked him about the mystery woman at Khashoggi's party in Manhattan. 'Haven't you heard?' he replied. 'Khashoggi has just married her.' I can only assume he must have enjoyed her sense of humour.

The point of my New York trip had been to fly in Khashoggi's plane from New York to Dallas, where he was attending a party given by Barbara Hutton, the Woolworth heiress. I wasn't invited to the gathering myself, but he said I could interview Imelda Marcos, who was one of the guests, on the way there.

The widow of the Philippines dictator was much bigger than I expected. When she saw me glancing at her feet, she burst out: 'I know I had a lot of shoes, but they were all given to me by the makers. Most of them were too small for me anyway.' When I asked if she was seeking political power, as the papers were suggesting, she replied rather girlishly: 'Mr Donald, I do not seek power. I seek love.' If the *Observer* photographer hadn't been sitting next to me, and grinning, I might have been more nervous.

Once, Tiny took me to meet Khashoggi at the Hyde Park Hotel, where he was getting ready for a party that night in Beirut. He was in a dressing gown and sitting in front of a mirror, surrounded by a hairdresser and a make-up team. Tiny stood talking to him in the doorway while I waited next door. Then Tiny silently summoned me to peep into the next room. The tired old man I had met earlier had been miraculously transformed into a handsome playboy of the Eastern world.

Tiny also once took me to Mexico on the Lonrho private jet. No interview had been set up, so I wasn't sure what the purpose of the visit was. We settled for the overnight flight on comfortable beds on either side of the aisle. In the morning, I felt his hand on my shoulder to wake me up.

'Do you know what day it is today?' he demanded.

'No, Tiny, what day is it?'

'It's my birthday. I'm sixty-six today. And do you know what that means?'

'No, Tiny, what does it mean?'

'It means I don't give a damn any more, about anything.'

Thinking this was just routine banter, I countered: 'Well, Tiny, I'm forty-six and I don't give a damn either.'

At this he gave me a hard look and seized my arm tightly. 'But you do. You do care about things. And that's why I'm bound to beat you in the end.'

This was all happening at 50,000 feet and I felt like James Bond facing Goldfinger or Scaramanga, fearing that I might be hurled out of the plane at any moment into Mexico's golden dawn.

I never knew where that moment of malice came from. Friends

suggested that it was because Tiny could never get used to the idea that there was someone on his payroll over whom he had no control, who could oppose him or disobey him, and he couldn't do a damned thing about it.

The rest of the trip was perfectly friendly. In Acapulco, I stayed in amazing luxury in the Lonrho-owned Princess Hotel while he and Josie stayed at their house. On the terrace, there was a telescope trained on another house. Josie said it was the first one they had bought in Acapulco. For the sake of something to say, I asked: 'When did you sell it?'

That brought on one of Tiny's tirades.

'Sell it? Sell it?! Why would I sell it? I don't need the money. I never sell anything. I still have the first Rolls-Royce I bought in 1954, and all the others since. I still have all my Mercedes. I never sell anything.'

'Would you ever sell *The Observer*?' I asked mischievously.

'Never,' he replied firmly, then added with a glint: 'As long as you behave yourself.'

I went along when Tiny had a meeting with his local managers in Mexico. At one point, when they were discussing how to approach a particular problem, I made a modest suggestion. Tiny turned to me and said sharply: 'I'm not allowed to interfere in *The Observer*, so you keep your nose out of Lonrho's business.' Fair enough, I thought.

• • •

D. K. Ludwig, the man who had brought Rowland and Anderson to-gether, fascinated Tiny. He told me of an occasion when he had been in New York and rang to see if Ludwig was free for dinner. Ludwig said he was entertaining a young man at the 21 Club who wanted him to invest in a project. 'Why don't you come along too, Tiny, and tell me what you think of his idea?'

When the young man left the table to take a telephone call, Ludwig asked: 'What do you think?' Tiny said he was very impressed and would be happy to take a share in the project himself. 'Wait,' said Ludwig sternly, 'just wait. We haven't finished yet.' When the young man returned, the pudding trolley came round and he ordered two of the desserts. Soon after that he left, Ludwig having declined to commit himself to the project. He thumped the table and said: 'Did you see that, Tiny? Two puddings. No discipline. No deal.'

I remembered that story towards the end of a dinner at the Berkeley Hotel, Tiny's favourite. It was attended by most of the Lonrho board, known to me by then (though out of their hearing) as the Crazy Gang, plus *The Observer*'s two managing directors and myself. When the table was asked about a pudding, Tiny firmly refused. Roger Harrison said: 'Thank you, Tiny, that looks delicious.' Brian Nicholson said: 'Sorry, Tiny, I'm trying to lose some weight.' Then, to a man, the Lonrho directors all declined dessert. I assumed they had all heard the Ludwig story, probably more than once. I was last to be asked and, despite Roger's imploring look, I also declined, leaving him struggling to finish his plate in lone embarrassment.

●   ●   ●

In 1983, I asked my eldest daughter, Sally, what she wanted for her eighteenth birthday. She said she would like to see where she was born. She had left Malawi soon after her first birthday. We flew first to Harare, where we were greeted at the airport, much to my surprise, by Godwin Matatu, an African journalist from Zimbabwe, who was acting on this occasion as Tiny's messenger. He said Tiny had made a Lonrho plane available to us for the onward flight to Malawi and that he would escort us to ensure that the arrangements all went smoothly, which they did. Matatu, an intelligent and witty companion when he was sober, had a reputation as a bit of a surly drunk. On this occasion he behaved, but he was later to bring me a whole heap of trouble.

Sally and I made a radio broadcast for the BBC after her trip, using tape recordings we had made in African villages. When we went to

Broadcasting House in London to record the programme, I told Sally not to worry if she made any gaffes; the BBC studio technicians would be very understanding. I added reassuringly that I had made dozens of these recordings myself. In the event Sally made no gaffes at all, but her smug father made plenty.

• • •

At one of Tiny's Sunday lunches at Hedsor, the chief guest was Joshua Nkomo. One couldn't help noticing that he had grown so fat that he needed two chairs to sit on at lunch, one for each buttock. There was clearly a great deal of affection between the two men. Tiny had backed Nkomo and his ZAPU (Zimbabwe African People's Union) party for many years, when they looked certain to form the first government in an independent Zimbabwe. The fifteen-year civil war to oust Ian Smith's rebel regime had resulted, however, in a power shift in Zimbabwe's African politics. The Shona tribe, led by Robert Mugabe, had played a prominent part in the terror campaign and they had more voters than the Ndebele people, who were mostly located around Bulawayo in Matabeleland.

So, Mugabe had won the first election after independence and Nkomo had failed to come to terms with the country's new leader. There had been sporadic rioting in Matabeleland, which had been put down ruthlessly. Mugabe lashed out at Nkomo at a rally, declaring: 'ZAPU and its leader, Dr Joshua Nkomo, are like a cobra in a house. The only way to deal effectively with a snake is to strike and destroy its head.'

I once asked Tiny why he hadn't backed both horses in Zimbabwe, which had been his practice elsewhere. He said he had. He had paid £40,000 to Mugabe's man in London some years before, but he later discovered that the man had used the money to buy a house in Hampstead and it had never reached Zimbabwe.

• • •

Lonrho's position now was hazardous. Its huge investment in Zimbabwe was at risk. Mugabe saw Rowland's hand everywhere and suspected him of being behind the troubles that had broken out in Matabeleland. What Tiny desperately needed was access to Mugabe, just as he had access to African leaders elsewhere. But the door was firmly closed on Lonrho, not just by Mugabe but by his senior ministers as well. Tiny was in urgent need of a friend at the court of King Robert.

He was finally saved by Godwin Matatu, last seen helping my daughter and me in Malawi. His uncle was Edson Zvobgo, Justice Minister in Mugabe's government. Although he too was wary of Rowland, his attitude changed when his wife Julie, a nurse, began to work for a Lonrho company.

Although he was an intelligent and witty talker, a law graduate from Chicago University and a published poet, Zvobgo still came across as a bit of a thug. But he was willing to be Rowland's thug – at a price. The price included a loan to buy a farm, financial help with some hotels he owned in Zimbabwe – and a promise to find some work for Matatu on *The Observer*.

Zvobgo was invited to London by Lonrho and Tiny asked me to lay on a lunch at *The Observer*. The aim was to show Zvobgo that he could have some influence with the British press by talking to the editors at one of its leading newspapers. Zvobgo then seemed to think he could have lunch at *The Observer* on all his visits to London. I didn't mind this too much, since he was entertaining company and gave us some useful information about African countries, including his own.

Before one of these lunches, Pat Ferguson, from the foreign desk, showed me an article about Zvobgo becoming involved in a road rage incident in Harare. A white woman driver who had failed to give way to his Mercedes had been struck by Zvobgo's bodyguard. At the lunch, the minister made great play about the progress for women's rights in Zimbabwe. Ferguson and I could barely suppress our laughter.

The Zimbabwe minister was not so welcome when he turned up in my office at *The Observer* on a Saturday morning demanding £500, which he said Tiny Rowland had authorised, Lonrho's Cheapside office being closed for the weekend. I was cross about the interruption because I was busy getting the paper out. I rang Terry Robinson at home and asked him what I should do. 'Pay him,' he said immediately.

At this I blew up, saying: 'Terry, it's not my job to pay Lonrho bribes to corrupt African politicians. You should do your dirty work yourself.' Terry said it wasn't a bribe; the minister was simply short of cash in London, and the loan would be repaid. He arranged for *The Observer*'s accounts department, which worked on Saturdays to pay the printers, to supply the money.

Wherever Zvobgo went, Matatu went too, always drinking more than he ate. He had disgraced himself at Tiny's home by turning up late and drunk for dinner, rejecting the food on offer, eating an apple and slugging more wine. He started hanging around my office, and the ways I used to avoid talking to him became an office joke. There was a jauntiness about him that made me suspect that something was going on that I wouldn't like. I was right.

By this time Colin Legum had retired as Commonwealth correspondent, mainly to avoid a fight with Rowland. He wrote a long farewell article for the *London Review of Books* in which he expressed his fears for *The Observer* under Lonrho's ownership. But he included a generous reference to me, saying *The Observer*'s only chance of keeping its integrity was if I remained editor.

Thinking about his successor, I had a brainwave, appointing Richard Hall, who had lived in Africa for many years, was a close friend of President Kaunda of Zambia, and had been the lone *Observer* voice supporting Tiny Rowland's ownership. I assumed Lonrho would be grateful to him for the evidence he gave to the MMC, saying Rowland had never interfered with the editorial content of his paper in Zambia when they owned it. I thought he could build on the good relationship he had with Rowland and would be able to deflect him from a particular story if he didn't think it right for the paper, without causing a row or lasting offence.

On reflection, I think Hall's evidence was probably crucial in tipping the MMC's decision Lonrho's way. Although Astor, O'Brien and myself had given severe warnings about the conflicts of interest that would arise over Africa, our objections were hypothetical fears about a possible future, whereas Dick was providing direct evidence from a real past.

My appointment of Dick Hall as Commonwealth correspondent of *The Observer* may have seemed like a brainwave, but it turned out to be a disaster. He had been so irritated by jibes from *Observer* colleagues that he was Tiny's stooge that he set out to distance himself from Lonrho and refused to talk to them about Africa or anything else. In a curious *volte face*, the lone voice supporting Lonrho had become the champion of those who opposed the slightest interference from Lonrho, whether real or imagined.

But then Dick Hall had always been an excitable, volatile figure who liked to be at the heart of any drama. The next development in this saga suggested, however, that he might have been right to suspect Lonrho's motives – even though he had told the MMC that he believed them to be above suspicion.

That was when Edson Zvobgo told him that Godwin Matatu had replaced him as *The Observer*'s Africa correspondent. Dick had gone to Zimbabwe and arranged to meet Zvobgo, who took him on a trip to Heroes' Acre, outside Harare, where the country honoured its nationalist pioneers. As they drove along in the car, Zvobgo had said to Dick (according to Dick): 'What are you doing here? You are the Commonwealth correspondent and you should be in Canada or the Caribbean. Godwin Matatu is now *The Observer*'s Africa correspondent.'

Dick was naturally dumbfounded to hear this, as I was when he reported the conversation back to me. Unfortunately, Dick didn't just tell me. He told the whole office in his excitable way and stirred everyone up. Before long a motion was being proposed that the NUJ chapel should take the matter to the independent directors as a breach of the safeguards Lonrho had agreed to at the time of the takeover. Instead of leaving it to me to sort out the situation in my diplomatic way, he had turned a muddle into a crisis.

We only have Dick Hall's word that Zvobgo described Matatu's job as *The Observer*'s Africa correspondent, and we don't know exactly what, if anything, Tiny had promised Zvobgo about the job his nephew would do on *The Observer*. Tiny never raised the subject with me, except to say from time to time that he hoped Godwin could supply the odd story for the paper. Tiny never asked me to make him Africa correspondent, let alone 'ordered' me to do it, as some reports suggested. For by now Hall had got the whole of Fleet Street excited too.

Having been the diarist on the *Financial Times*, Dick knew all the gossip columnists and kept them informed about every twist and turn in the Matatu story. Alan Rusbridger, later *The Guardian*'s editor, was writing the paper's diary at this time and latched on to the story with some relish. He also started leaking my evidence to the MMC, having found, so it was claimed, an A4 manila envelope containing all 10,000 words of my submission on his desk. Who sent it became a matter of some interest and concern to me, since my unflattering description of Rowland could have an explosive effect.

The obvious suspect was Hall himself, though he strongly denied it. The only way he could have got hold of a copy would be if Colin Legum, whose office he took over, had left one in his files. Tony Howard had easy access to my secretary's office, which was next to his. He had also inherited John Cole's files, which might have contained a copy of my submission. If Tony was the culprit, he was too canny to have supplied the copy direct to Rusbridger; he would have used one of his cronies, either Simon Hoggart or Peter Hillmore, who had both worked for *The Guardian*.

At the time I couldn't believe that Tony would seek to undermine me in this way; now I'm not so sure. I remembered what Alan Watkins had said when I asked him if I should make Howard my deputy: 'He'll be after your job.' I'm not saying Tony did it, for I have no proof, but that he was capable of doing it. As the police might say, he had means, motive and opportunity.

The Matatu affair, or rather non-affair, rumbled on. The NUJ chapel wrote asking what I planned to do about this evident breach of *The Observer*'s editorial safeguards and insisted that if Matatu was to write for the paper he should be on the editorial staff, not paid for by Lonrho. I wrote back saying Tiny Rowland had neither asked nor ordered me to make such an appointment, and it wasn't going to happen, so there had been no breach of the paper's editorial safeguards. Dick Hall accused me of using 'some dazzling gamesmanship'.

I couldn't resist adding in my reply to the NUJ that I found it strange that journalists on a liberal newspaper like *The Observer* should be so opposed to a black African writing about Africa. My irony did not go down well. The last thing I wanted was Matatu's salary and drinks bill on my editorial budget.

It was all a storm in a tea cup, or perhaps a wine glass. Whatever he might or might not have said to Zvobgo, Tiny had never asked me to appoint Matatu, and I think I knew why. He was as aware as I was, perhaps more so, that Matatu simply couldn't do the job, or any job for that matter, because he was a helpless alcoholic and incapable of staying sober for more than a few hours in a day. The whole storm had been created by Dick Hall's heightened sense of drama. He was a Walter Mitty character who had to be seen at the centre of things.

Dick told me he was writing a book about Tiny, so I said he would have to leave the paper to do that. Matatu did have some pieces published in *The Observer*, but he was never described as the paper's Africa correspondent. When he drank himself to death a few years later, I spoke at his memorial service at the Africa Centre in Covent Garden.

• • •

My first and only really serious row with Lonrho took place at Easter 1984 when I went out to Harare to interview Mugabe on his fourth anniversary in office. The interview was set up by a TV production company to be broadcast on Channel 4. I had already presented a number of programmes for the company in Brussels, Paris and Moscow, and later I was to present two series of sports programmes on the same channel, called *Running Late*. It is important for the origins of the Mugabe interview to be properly understood. It was not true, as stated confidently in a number of places, that Rowland set up the interview.

My friend Robert Edwards, who had been editor of the *Daily Express* and the *Sunday Mirror*, said that if he had 'pissed on a parade organised by Lord Beaverbrook', he would have expected to be sacked. When I told him that Rowland had not been involved in setting up the Mugabe interview, and it wasn't, therefore, his parade, he changed his mind.

It was a spectacular row. The story began in the parched earth of Matabeleland, among the cactus and the baobab trees, and ended over lunch in a Park Lane casino owned by Lonrho, served by long-legged girls in fishnet tights. For two hectic weeks, the battle was monitored in every news bulletin, causing anguished debates about press freedom in Parliament and the media – and almost led to *The Observer* being sold to Robert Maxwell.

The row between Rowland and me became a Fleet Street soap opera that overshadowed the tragic human story that provoked it – the suffering of the minority Ndebele people at the hands of the North Korean-trained Fifth Brigade of the Zimbabwe Army. Although my travel and hotel expenses were not paid by *The Observer*, I had always planned to write an article for the paper. I told Rowland about the interview as a courtesy a few days before I travelled to Harare.

That was a mistake, since it gave Rowland an opportunity to ingratiate himself with Mugabe ('I have arranged for my editor to publish an interview in *The Observer*') and repair relations that had been seriously damaged by his long support for Joshua Nkomo. When I arrived in Harare, I was unpleasantly surprised to be met by Matatu, who whisked me off for lunch at Lonrho's office, where I discovered that Tiny had arrived ahead of me.

I had arranged to meet Neal Ascherson, who had been covering the drought and famine in southern Africa for the paper, and took him along to the lunch. I think he must have been amazed at the deference shown to Rowland by his lickspittle local board. Tiny said my interview had been delayed, but he had been in touch with Mugabe's office to reschedule it for a day later. The interview was clearly to be a Lonrho production, with Rowland himself as the producer and Matatu cast as my minder.

Rowland even turned up at Mugabe's heavily protected office, though thankfully he didn't sit in on the interview. It turned out to be disastrously dull, unusable for Channel 4, though parts of it were later used by PBS in the States and the text appeared in a specialist African magazine. Mugabe was mostly monosyllabic. He only came to life when I raised the subject of Matabeleland, where a curfew had been in force for ten weeks.

When I asked him if he would consider a political rather than a military solution in Matabeleland, he replied bluntly: 'The solution is a military one. Their grievances are unfounded. The verdict of the voters was cast in 1980. They should have accepted defeat then.' He added chillingly: 'The situation in Matabeleland is one that requires a change. The people must be reoriented.'

My interest in Matabeleland had been quickened by Mugabe's comments, and I told Ascherson this afterwards. He said he had a good contact who knew what was going on there and gave me his telephone number. When I returned to Meikles Hotel with the camera crew after the interview, I was met in the lobby by a small group of Africans, who asked if they could speak to me. One of them took me aside conspiratorially: 'You should go to Matabeleland to see what is happening to our people there. There are terrible things. Stay at the Holiday Inn in Bulawayo.' He hurried away, as if afraid to be overheard.

No media had been allowed inside the curfew area, but there had been rumours about brutal treatment of the population by Mugabe's troops, ostensibly searching for 'dissidents' from across the Botswana border. I said to Matatu: 'Let's go to Bulawayo in the morning.'

We found little sign there of military activity, just the odd 'hippo' armoured personnel carrier trundling along a dirt road with mounted guns, or a truck-load of troops with rocket-propelled grenades on their AK-47 rifles. Rain had made the Lowveld roads almost unpassable. Schoolgirls were marching quietly in green check dresses or lying in the shade; old men were scratching with hoes; cattle stood in the dry river beds; goats, donkeys, marmosets, even a kudu bull, dashed across the road.

The sight of the kudu bull took me back twenty years to a time when one of them had almost killed me and my whole family as we drove towards Bulawayo on the edge of the Wankie Game Reserve (now the Hwange National Park). It had emerged from the bush at the side of the road and seemed certain to crash into the car – until it suddenly took off, rising majestically over the vehicle, its hoof just touching the roof a few inches above the windscreen, then dashed off into the bush on the other side. A few inches lower and the windscreen would have been shattered, almost certainly forcing us into one of the many trees lining the road. The memory seemed like a bad omen.

We knew we weren't allowed officially into the curfew area, but asked our driver to brave the roadblocks anyway. We passed three without bother, all manned cheerily by policemen in brown boots, then Matatu did some name-dropping to persuade a tough-looking soldier to let us through. We were able to drive through the no-go areas, past Kezi, Antelope Mine, Bhalagwe Camp – all names, I learned later, that filled the Ndebele with dread. We saw nothing unusual and returned to our hotel.

Around 10 p.m., there was a call from the hotel reception to say that a man wanted to deliver a letter. An African tapped on the door and handed it over. It read simply: 'Please accompany this friend.' Moving quietly to avoid disturbing Matatu next door, I followed the man to the car park, where a headlight beamed in recognition. I had no idea where I was going, or who with; and nobody knew where I'd gone. I knew instinctively that I couldn't take Matatu with me. Apart from the Lonrho connection, he was a Shona and close to the government and his presence would have deterred people from speaking honestly.

I climbed nervously into the van and was taken in silence for several miles out of town into the curfew area. There – after a semi-comic interlude in which we gave a lift to a policeman – we stopped at a remote house, pipped the horn for ages, and finally changed cars with another man. He took us for another long ride to a Roman Catholic mission where, for much of the night, I was given a series of eyewitness accounts and signed statements from victims of the Matabeleland atrocities. These were graphic, horrific and profoundly moving.

One name kept recurring, as in a nightmare. Brigadier Shiri, known as Black Jesus, was head of the Fifth Brigade. And there was one recurring story, about a major who held up a dead baby and told villagers: 'This is what will happen to your babies if you help dissidents.' He then dropped the tiny corpse in the dust.

Back in the car again, I was taken to another Catholic mission, where I met a man from Esigodini village who had been beaten close to death by agents of the Central Intelligence Organisation (CIO) in front of his family. They were warned they would be shot if they uttered a sound. 'They began beating us with sticks and guns,' he said, 'bayoneting us, burning plastic against our skin while our hands and mouths were covered. They tore curtains, put cushions into our mouths. We were tortured for about four hours.'

A man called Jason was brought to the mission. He had been chopping trees at Welonke when two soldiers turned up with fixed bayonets and whips on their belts. They asked if he and his wife had seen any dissidents and grew increasingly angry when they said they hadn't. They beat his wife and grandmother and took him away. Neighbours were collected and they all marched on, their progress broken by periodic beatings and a fight they were forced to stage for the soldiers' entertainment. At the village school, the soldiers shot two children who had tried to run away. Eventually nine of them were forced to dig a hole to a depth of two or three feet and ordered to jump into it.

Jason told me: 'The commander leaned against a tree, opened his radio cassette and shot five men. On the grave, we put branches. I also saw a big grave which had stones in it. There are sixteen buried in this grave.'

Earlier I had come across Peter Godwin, of the *Sunday Times*, who said bodies had been thrown down a nearby mineshaft owned by Lonrho. (Later Roy Hattersley was sued by Rowland for making this claim in a speech – what Rowland never knew was that I had helped to draft Hattersley's speech.)

Godwin had already got some atrocity stories into print, but he was inhibited by the fact that he couldn't betray his presence in the curfew area for fear of being expelled or, as a white Zimbabwean himself who had been conscripted to Ian Smith's rebel army and fought against the Africans, suffering even worse retribution. Once he understood that I hadn't been sent by Rowland to put a Mugabe spin on the situation, we exchanged useful information.

I returned to the hotel at dawn, checked out without waking Matatu, then flew to London via Harare, leaving on Friday evening and arriving on Saturday morning with my story written. While waiting for my plane in Harare I had two meetings. One was with a military attaché at the British High Commission, who wasn't at all surprised by the news from Matabeleland.

The other was with a South African director of Lonrho, Nick Kruger, who wasn't surprised either. 'What you have discovered, Donald,' he said in a guttural Afrikaner accent, 'is the eternal truth of Africa. Stuff them, then they stuff you. For centuries, we stuffed the blacks; now it's their turn to stuff us. The Ndebele stuffed the Shona; now it's the Shonas' turn.'

My dilemma on returning – should I publish an anodyne interview with Mugabe or tell the truth about Matabeleland, thereby damaging the commercial interests of my proprietor? – has since been written up as a classic case by the Institute of Global Ethics. For me, there was no choice.

I wrote the story in longhand on the plane and typed it up when I arrived at an empty *Observer* office, too early for any other editorial staff to have appeared. I made two copies, one for Magnus Linklater, the executive editor in charge of news, and one for Pat Ferguson on the foreign desk. I told Tony Howard about the story and asked him to keep quiet about it, but didn't show it to him. I didn't want to risk word of the story somehow reaching Lonrho through office gossip. I planned to ring Tiny around 5 p.m. on Saturday afternoon, too late for him to do anything to stop publication.

Things didn't turn out as neatly as that. Terry Robinson rang Tony Howard to hear what was going in the paper, and Tony told him about my Matabeleland article, even though I had expressly asked him not to tell anyone. Within minutes I had an angry Tiny on the phone, asking what I had written. So I told him.

There was a few minutes' silence while he digested this. Then he made the point that brutalities of this kind could not be understood in isolation. It was the fifteen-year civil war started by Ian Smith's UDI that had distorted Zimbabwe's history and created a pattern of violence that was now playing itself out. There had been violence on all sides. I thought this was a fair point and said I would include it in the article, which I did.

He was not mollified, however. Far from it. I could tell he was choking with rage and unable to find the right words to express it. Finally he said: 'You are deliberately trying to destroy my business. You must expect me to defend myself.'

'I am only doing my job,' I replied. 'This is a story that has to be published.'

'And I have to do my job,' he said menacingly, and threatened to close the paper down if I went ahead with the article. I said I was not prepared to talk in those terms. He slammed down the phone.

Next morning, I turned on the BBC radio news to hear my story condemned as lies in an official statement by Mugabe, supported by a letter of apology from Rowland: 'I take full responsibility for what in my view was discourteous, disingenuous and wrong in the editor of a serious newspaper widely read in Africa.' He described me as 'an incompetent reporter' and announced that I would be dismissed.

MR ROWLAND

Observer editor could be sacked

LONDON.
MR ROLAND "Tiny"
Rowland, head of the
Lonrho Trading Company
and owner of the
Observer, yesterday
threatened to sell the
paper or sack the editor
after a row over its
coverage of Zimbabwe.
Mr Rowland has
strongly criticised a
report by editor Mr
Donald Trelford last
Sunday which alleged the
Zimbabwe National Army
was committing
atrocities in
Matabeleland.
Mr Rowland said in an
interview with the
Observer: "My
alternatives are: firstly,
to close down the paper,
retaining the title.
Secondly, to sell the
paper — and nobody's
going to tell me whom I
should sell it to. Thirdly,
to remove Mr Trelford as
editor."
Earlier last week he
accused Mr Trelford of
writing a sensational
story based on
unsubstantiated material.
Mr Trelford denied
this, saying that his
story was based on
interviews with some of
the alleged victims.
In the interview Mr
Rowland repeated an
earlier call for Mr
Trelford to return to
Zimbabwe with a team
of reporters for a further
investigation in
Matabeleland. — Ziana-
Reuter.

Nevertheless, I went ahead with a planned holiday to Guernsey and spent most of the Sunday morning hunting for a favourite doll that my daughter Laura, aged three, had lost on the ferry. I found it and went to the house of my then parents-in-law, where we were staying. Reporters from the BBC and ITN were waiting for me. When Lord Goodman saw my interviews on the midday TV news, he rang me to say that I should return to my office right away. 'You must be seen on the bridge of your ship. If people see you at the seaside they will assume you have given up already.'

The story was front-page news for a fort-night – 'the most entertaining hullabaloo', as one writer put it, 'since Harry Evans fell out with Rupert Murdoch.' Rowland wrote me an open letter, which he distributed to all papers before I could see it, saying Lonrho would not go on supporting a failing editor who showed no concern for their commercial interests. I replied in kind, pointing out that the circu-lation had actually gone up by 22 per cent in the eight years I had been editor. The *Daily Mail* published both letters in full under the headlines 'Dear Donald' and 'Dear Tiny'.

Rowland insisted that I should go back to Zimbabwe for a longer investigation. I refused, on the grounds that I had already established the truth of my story and that to do so would endanger the lives of my sourc-es. I received dozens of letters of support from *Observer* readers, who said they would give up the paper if I was sacked. The shortest letter came from Martin Amis, saying simply: 'Snooker him.'

The Zimbabwe Three. This Guardian *cartoon infuriated Tiny Rowland.*

The Foreign Office, more concerned about relations with Mugabe than with human rights – and doubtless sensitive that Britain had provided some training for the Fifth Brigade – was briefing against me. I learned this from Prince Charles, with whom I happened to have lunch around this time. 'The Foreign Office tell me your story about Matabeleland was greatly exaggerated,' he said airily. I ate my soup in silence.

At the pre-lunch drinks I had talked to Princess Diana, while Peter Preston, then editor of *The Guardian*, had spoken to Prince Charles. The princess and I talked about babies. I asked her, rather cheekily, if they would have any more children after Princes William and Harry. Her reply was chilling: 'We'll have to – because of the IRA, you see.'

I got to know the Princess better later. I attended a briefing for editors at Buckingham Palace, at which we were asked to go easy on her as a newcomer to the royal family. After the briefing, we were joined by the Queen and by Prince Charles and Princess Diana herself. When we met she said: 'I can see your halo, Mr Trelford. Your paper doesn't have to write all this ridiculous stuff about me.'

This was the famous occasion when the Queen reprimanded the editor of the *News of the World*, Barry Askew, in front of his fellow editors, for suggesting that Princess Diana should send a servant to buy her sweets, rather than go to the shop herself and run the risk of paparazzi. Her response – 'Oh, what a pompous man you are' – prompted Rupert Murdoch to sack him. I had known Askew on the *Sheffield Telegraph* many years before; he never recovered from this career setback and became an alcoholic.

Because *The Observer* sponsored the Olivier Awards, I got to meet the winning actors and actresses and had my picture taken with them all. When the Princess attended a theatre evening for the presentation of the awards, I got to sit next to the guest of honour. She arrived wearing headphones playing loud rock music by Wham!, but politely took them off for a chat.

I had to present the paper's Kenneth Tynan Award to a Russian troupe, the leader of which wouldn't stop talking. I could see the TV producer slitting his throat in a gesture meant to make me shut him up, because the show was going out as live, but there was nothing I could do about it. When I got back to my seat, I found the Princess rolling around in fits of laughter at my discomfiture.

● ● ●

Not all the papers were on my side about the Matabeleland story. Paul Johnson said editors had no business trying to be reporters. John Junor wrote: 'If Mr Trelford truly feels that way about Mr Rowland, wouldn't it be more honourable for him to stop accepting Mr Rowland's money?' *The Times* suggested I had forced a showdown deliberately. The *Daily*

Telegraph said: 'Those who pay the piper must be expected to demand some influence over the choice of tunes he plays.'

The Guardian said the paper should 'find its salvation where the people who write the cheques and the people who write the words can work together'. This proved difficult at *The Observer* when Lonrho announced it was withdrawing financial support. Provoked by a ruling from *The Observer*'s independent directors that Rowland had inter-fered improperly, it put a hard-faced accountant in the office to stop me spending money.

This brought questions in Parliament. When Peter Shore, for Labour, asked Norman Tebbit what he planned to do to protect the editorial independence of the editor of *The Observer*, the Secretary for Trade and Industry clearly enjoyed saying: 'Nothing.' This was soon after the paper's revelations about Mark Thatcher's business connections with Oman.

•   •   •

The Observer's journalists were highly supportive of their editor – until Rowland let it be known he was planning to sell the paper to Robert Maxwell. A breakfast meeting at Claridge's was announced for the next day and they were pictured laughing together. I had once asked Row-land what language he and Maxwell conversed in. 'German,' he said. I knew Rowland would never sell to Maxwell and this was just a bluff to frighten the journalists. If so, it certainly appeared to be working.

I was interested to hear an interview with Maxwell about *The Ob-server* on my car radio. He 'greatly admired' me, he said, and would retain me as editor (which I very much doubted – he was a good friend of Tony Howard, who would surely enter into his inheritance on a Maxwell-owned *Observer*). Then, asked what he would have done about the Mark Thatcher stories, he paused and replied in his deepest tones: 'I'd have stamped on him.' I assumed he meant stamping on me, not Mr Thatcher.

By now I felt the paper was being damaged and something had to be done to break the deadlock. Nick Morrell had told me that advertisement bookings were drying up. So I rang Robinson and asked to see him, but not at *The Observer* or at Cheapside. We met in a dingy workmen's café near St Paul's Cathedral. I gave him a letter to hand to Rowland. In this I said: 'I could not allow the paper's future and the prospects of its staff to be jeopardised by my personal position, which sadly seems to be all that stands in the way of the paper's development.' Tiny seized the olive branch, replying: 'I support your editorship and refuse to accept your resignation.'

We made up over an edgy lunch in the incongruous ambience of one of Lonrho's London casinos. Undeterred by the pop music and scantily dressed females, we concocted a priceless statement that we shared an affection for three things: for Africa, for *The Observer* and for each other. Tiny described our disagreement as 'a lovers' tiff', providing material for cartoonists.

"*Worked out well, Donald. Putting on quite a bit of circulation.*"

This Punch *cartoon strikes an upbeat tone between Tiny and me,
but this was misleading.*

For us and for the paper, that was the end of the episode. For the people of Matabeleland, however, it provided only brief illumination before the darkness came again.

•   •   •

Tiny was deeply wounded by the Matabeleland row and it took several months before we could resume anything like a normal relationship. He had been stung by the independent directors' attack on him and threatened to cut their directors' fees, describing them as 'plastic pygmies'. He had come over to the public as a hard-hearted capitalist who cared more about his company's profits than the welfare of the Africans he professed to love. Above all, as Neal Ascherson put it: 'He had been stunned to find an honest man on his payroll who refused to bend to his will. This had never happened to him before.' And an employee, moreover, against whom he was forbidden to take any action.

His pent-up rage boiled over at an *Observer* board meeting. He didn't always attend the paper's monthly meetings, but it was clear that he had come to make as much noise and trouble as he could. I was his main target and he lashed out at me, calling me a lousy editor who was losing readers and that Lonrho could not sustain the paper's losses indefinitely if the company got nothing in return. I hit back by pointing out that the losses were chiefly caused by Lonrho's failure to get to grips with the printing unions. The independent directors were shocked at the fierceness of our altercation. In an odd way, though, this argument seemed to calm things down between us.

Why had I stuck my neck out so far? I sometimes asked myself the same question. It would be hard to think of a story more damaging to my owner's commercial interests. Somebody wrote that 'perhaps Trelford just wanted to do some serious reporting'. That was true, but it ignored the nature of the story. My prime motivation was what I had told Rowland in our angry telephone discussion: it was a story that had to be published. If one emotion was uppermost in my mind, it was pity.

I owed it to the people of Matabeleland who had risked their lives to ensure that their voices were heard.

Dick Hall, hardly my greatest fan, wrote in his book:

> Trelford was now virtually a national hero – the brave little editor who had stood up for the truth and outfaced the wicked giant of capitalism. Politicians of all parties had come to his support. Soon he was in demand as a speaker on press freedom. His television performances acquired a new prestige. His name was put forward for international awards. Such a feat would surely have been applauded by Houdini himself.

The Houdini theme was picked up in an article by Peter McKay, who wrote: 'Donald Trelford is regarded by friend and foe as the Harry Houdini of journalism. Bound, gagged and tied to the rails and within seconds of the locomotive wheels, Trelford wriggles free from each succeeding crisis. There has scarcely been a dull month in all his years as editor.'

The award mentioned by Dick Hall was a commendation as International Editor of the Year from the *World Press Review* in New York 'for courage, enterprise and leadership at an international level in defending human rights and fostering journalistic excellence'.

By this time, as Hall put it,

> the granite-faced Andrew Neil had taken over at the *Sunday Times* ... and the effects were calamitous. Neil was the authentic voice of the New Right, someone Murdoch could trust to finally obliterate the liberalism which the paper had become imbued with in the Harold Evans era. So, as Neil laid about him, the more admired became the subtle virtues of Donald Trelford.

The Observer, he said 'was undeniably displaying a caring and libertarian vision of the world. Trelford knew the sort of paper he wanted to edit, but he went after it by stealth. Whereas Neil charged headlong

forward like a mastiff – knowing that his master was right behind him
– Trelford showed the subtlety of a fox.'

• • •

One day in 1985 I was visiting New York when I took a call from Tiny.
He wanted me to go to the Bahamas, where many of his African leader
friends were attending a Commonwealth summit. My first reaction
was hostile: why should Rowland tell me to go anywhere? My second
reaction was more conciliatory: what was there not to like about a trip
to the Bahamas?

When the Queen's press secretary, Michael Shea, saw my name on
the list of accredited correspondents, he invited me for tea aboard the
Royal Yacht. I was on crutches again after another sporting injury, this
time on a cricket field. As I was piped aboard *Britannia*, a group of
journalists were having coffee nearby. One of them apparently quipped:
'Trelford must be getting a K.'

In Michael's cabin, we were interrupted by a visit from the Queen's
private secretary, Sir Philip Moore, a rather stuffy figure who didn't
seem too pleased to find me there. We talked about the Queen Mother.
I suggested that history would credit her with making a king of her
husband and a queen of her daughter. Moore looked unconvinced and
asked: 'Do you actually *know* the Queen Mother?' He was a bit startled by my reply when I said I had played snooker with her when she
opened new premises for the Press Club (she played left-handed).

As so often, sport came to my rescue. Sir Philip's attitude mellowed
considerably when I said: 'Didn't you play rugby for England?' I didn't
think it prudent to mention that he played only once, in 1951, and that
England had been beaten comprehensively by Wales, after which he
was dropped and never picked again.

I was invited to a reception by the Queen on board the *Britannia* and
joined the queue to meet her behind Lady Rothermere, who was wearing a red rah-rah skirt that failed to hide her prop forward's thighs.

When she was offered a drink from a tray, she declared: 'I thought I had made it absolutely clear when I accepted this invitation that I only drink Dom Perignon champagne!' At this, a white-uniformed flunkey appeared from behind a pillar with her ladyship's favourite tipple.

I had met Lady Harmsworth ('Bubbles' to the press, 'Patricia' to her friends) a number of times over the years and had always found her good company. On one occasion, Lajos Lederer, a long-time friend of the Rothermeres, had invited me with Pat and Vere to a Hungarian restaurant in Bayswater for dinner. They brought along young Jonathan (now the fourth Viscount), then a podgy teenager who, as I remember, tucked heartily into his meal.

I hope he wasn't listening when his mother whispered to me: 'Have you seen today's *Private Eye*? They say my husband is being tossed off by some Korean bint in Paris.' There is very little one can say in reply to this. What I managed to say was: 'Really? May I pass the salt?' (The so-called 'Korean bint' is now the Dowager Lady Rothermere, having married Vere after the couple divorced.)

I had also met Pat in 1975 in Canton when she had joined a group of Fleet Street grandees, led by Vere, who had just visited mainland China. She was talking to female members of the group when an imperfectly educated Chinese interpreter interrupted them and said – to general consternation and some amusement (on my part, at least): 'Ladies, it is time for you to shit.'

It so happened that Rupert Murdoch had been in the news that day, so when I met Her Majesty she said: 'Do you know Mr Murdoch, Mr Trelford?' When I said that I did, she asked: 'How would you describe him, Mr Trelford – in a word?'

Several words crossed my mind, none of them suitable to utter before a Queen, until I replied: 'In a word, ma'am, I'd say he was a gambler.'

'Ye-es,' she said thoughtfully. 'He seems to be winning, doesn't he?'

Then, moving away to greet the next guest, so that her words could hardly be heard, she added: 'So far, anyway.'

● ● ●

On the tenth anniversary of the Iranian Revolution, in 1989, Tiny invited me to join him on a trip to Tehran. I jumped at the chance, because few Western journalists were allowed into the country. I had nearly gone there some time before, during the reign of the Shah. Lord Barnetson had taken me for lunch with the Shah's suave ambassador, Parviz C. Radji, who wrote of me in a diary he published later: 'Trelford strikes me as a perceptive, intelligent individual with a probing mind and a generally sympathetic disposition.' I could have said the same about him. Despite all this goodwill, however, I couldn't finally make the trip. So, I was doubly glad to get another chance.

I hoped to secure an interview with one of the country's leaders. President Rafsanjani never gave interviews to the Western media, but I managed to have a long and rare discussion with the Iranian Foreign Minister, Dr Ali Akbar Velayati, who went on to serve sixteen years in the job, a mark of his standing with the country's religious leaders. We talked about the aftermath of the Iran–Iraq War and about the country's relations with the United States and Britain. He said he wanted to encourage more trade with Britain. I made a plea for the release of a British businessman, Roger Cooper, who had been held there for three years without trial as a spy and was to serve another two years before he was freed.

It was clear that Lonrho also had some serious business to discuss in Tehran, for Tiny was accompanied by Mahdi Al-Tajir, a former adviser to the rulers of Dubai and one of the world's wealthiest men, and by Wolfgang Michel, a German businessman who had close links to Gaddafi in Libya. I knew his daughter Caroline, who was a literary agent in London and was to marry the publisher Matthew (later Lord) Evans, of Faber & Faber.

On the flight, Al-Tajir and Tiny had a macho boasting contest about the respective size of their carpets. 'Mine is the size of a tennis court,' said Al-Tajir. 'Mine is the size of a football field,' said Tiny. Rowland also talked about owning a Columbian emerald mine, which he had been forced to sell because the miners stole most of the jewels. He went on to say that he kept a stash of the emeralds in his safety deposit box at Harrods. I recalled this remark some years later when Mohamed Fayed was accused of illegally breaking into Rowland's deposit box, setting off another legal dispute between the two men.

Tehran was not a comfortable place to be. There were anti-Western banners across the hotel lobby and in the streets. My hotel room faced the prison, where executions took place at dawn every day. On a drive through the capital I swear I saw a hamburger joint named after Bobby Sands, the IRA hunger-striker who was the first of nine men to die at the Maze prison at Long Kesh, near Belfast, in 1981. There was even a photograph of him outside the shop. I suppose it is possible that an IRA martyr would be celebrated in revolutionary Iran, but a hamburger joint in memory of a man who starved himself to death? It seemed like a sick joke.

On the flight back, Michel showed me a thirty-page dossier he had prepared about massive bribes being paid to members of the Saudi royal family by British Aerospace as part of the Al Yamaha agreement, described as the arms deal of the century, worth billions of pounds. The arms, he claimed, were not really needed by Saudi Arabia, but the commissions were; besides, the contract provided badly needed employment for British industry.

I thought the story was worth pursuing and showed the dossier first to Melvyn Marckus, the City editor, who said his staff were too busy on Fayed-related stories to carry out the checks and cross-checks that would be needed. I then involved Adam Raphael, an executive editor, who tried to interest David Leigh, the paper's chief investigative reporter, in the story. That is when the proverbial hit the fan. There was no love lost between Raphael and Leigh, which I suspect was a key part of Leigh's objection to the story.

He said it was wrong for the paper to pursue any story that emanated from Lonrho because there were bound to be hidden commercial motives and the paper was just being used to promote them. Raphael and I disagreed, believing that there are usually hidden motives behind all stories provided to newspapers, especially leaks from politicians. The test was whether the story was true and important, not who benefited from it.

Our inquiries revealed that there were indeed some hidden motives behind the leak to *The Observer*. Lonrho had links with Dassault, the French aircraft manufacturer, which had lost out when the contract went to British Aerospace. Rowland also hoped that exposure of the corruption would embarrass the chairman of BA, his old foe Professor Sir Roland Smith, who as chairman of House of Fraser had blocked his bids to get hold of the company. This knowledge did not deter us and Raphael published some strong stories about the Al Yamaha scandal.

Leigh decided to make it an issue of principle and took it to the NUJ chapel, who referred it to the independent directors. He argued that he shouldn't have been asked to cover a story supplied by Lonrho. In reply, I made the point that he could always refuse to cover it, which he did. It seemed to me that there was no problem in receiving a story from one's owner, as long as the paper was free not to publish it if the information was found wanting. At no stage had Rowland pressed me to publish the story.

The independent directors threw out the complaint, prompting Leigh to resign, complaining of 'a whitewash', and he returned to *The Guardian*, where the editor, Alan Rusbridger, was his brother-in-law. I was sorry to lose a first-class reporter whom I had once described as 'my hunting dog'. That was a phrase used by Lord Deedes, then editing the *Daily Telegraph*, when we shared a train journey to Oxford to speak at the Oxford Union. At one point in our conversation he said: 'A newspaper needs lapdogs and hunting dogs. At the *Telegraph* I need more lapdogs: at *The Observer* you need more hunting dogs.'

I suspect Leigh was looking for a reason to move on, anyway, just as he had left *The Times* and *The Guardian* earlier in his career. The final irony about all this was that he went on to publish under his own byline a number of stories in *The Guardian* about corruption on the Al Yamaha contract. When I teased him with this at a party some years later, he had the good grace to grin.

Like the Matatu non-affair, this was a manufactured crisis by individuals who simply hated the fact that *The Observer* was owned by Lonrho and wanted nothing to do with them. That was a luxury not available to me, because I knew, as many journalists did not, how vital it was for the paper's future that Lonrho should invest in new technology and provide the money to pay off redundant printers. As a director for two decades and latterly as chief executive, I knew just how important this was.

● ● ●

Yet another cloud over *The Observer*'s future began to emerge in 1990 as *The Independent*, flushed with its success with the new daily paper, turned its mind to a Sunday partner. Two factors seemed to be prompting its founder and editor Andreas Whittam Smith in this direction: the launch of a rival paper, the *Sunday Correspondent*, funded by a business consortium; and the need to find something for Stephen Glover, one his co-founders, to do.

The *Sunday Correspondent* was always going to be a failure, as I forecast on a TV programme at the time of its launch to Peter Cole, the paper's editor. (Cole, by coincidence, was to replace me, some years later, as head of the Department of Journalism Studies at Sheffield University.) There was no need for Whittam Smith to panic about the *Sunday Correspondent*, because it lasted just over a year.

Launching the *Independent on Sunday* turned out to be a colossal mistake, an act of vanity or hubris that led eventually to the end of the whole *Independent* dream. Before committing himself to the new paper, however, Whittam Smith had a better idea: why not buy *The Observer* instead and save on the costs of launching a new paper at all? Rupert Murdoch and David English had had the same idea thirteen years before.

I was invited to a breakfast meeting at Brown's Hotel with Whittam Smith and Glover. I was wary about the meeting, as Glover noted in a book he wrote later. He said I had 'displayed legendary political skills and a genius for survival', but that on this occasion my 'eyes darted nervously, as though we had laid a trap for him'. Whittam Smith's proposal was a merger between *The Independent* and *The Observer* into a new company – 85 per cent *Indy*, 15 per cent Lonrho. I said I doubted if Rowland would accept as little as 15 per cent. He said that was the statutory limit on the size of any outside shareholding.

I said I could see the commercial sense, from their point of view, of *The Independent* buying *The Observer* rather than launching its own paper: it would reduce the competition in the Sunday market and would give the joint paper a flying start by building on *The Observer*'s circulation and reputation. I also said that I had no interest in editing *The Observer* for very much longer. 'My only concern now', I said truthfully, 'is to secure the future of the paper.'

Whittam Smith then made a tactical error by assuring me that a financial contract for me would be included in the new arrangements. I was annoyed at the implication that I could be bought – cheaply too, by the sound of it – and resented his arrogance in suggesting it.

In fact, I was becoming more and more angry about the proposal, though I tried not to show it. It was clear that *The Independent* would dominate the joint paper and that *The Observer*'s existing staff and character would be submerged. Here was a man who had run a daily paper for four years, and knew nothing about Sunday papers, talking about taking over – and effectively destroying – the oldest Sunday paper in the world, just three years short of its 200th anniversary. I said I would report the conversation to Tiny Rowland. But I had already decided that the merger would never happen if I had anything to do with it.

The *Sunday Times* then ran a story about merger talks between *The Independent* and *The Observer*, prompting a firm statement from Lonrho that *The Observer* was 'not for sale'. Glover commented on this episode:

I interpreted this story as a leak from Donald Trelford. It seemed that Trelford had brilliantly drawn Andreas and me into talks which he had then scuppered by making them public, thereby inviting a denial of sale by Terry Robinson, one of Tiny's closest henchmen. If this was true, Trelford was more than worthy of his reputation. He was a wonder.

Having failed to secure *The Observer*, Whittam Smith went ahead with the launch of the *Independent on Sunday* in 1990. It caused me a number of problems, not just stealing some of our readers, but some editorial staff as well. I lost Blake Morrison from the literary department and Neal Ascherson, one of the very best writers on the paper. The *Indy*'s clarion call – that it had no commercial proprietor – was a powerful message to readers who distrusted the likes of Rupert Murdoch, Robert Maxwell, Conrad Black and Tiny Rowland.

The year of 1990 was a bad one for me, the worst in my time as editor. I was ready to quit, except that I needed to be sure that the paper would end up in good hands. It was also a bad time for Lonrho. As the 1990s progressed, it became clear that Tiny was losing control of the empire he had created, which made *The Observer*'s position highly vulnerable. The company's share price was badly hit (coming down from 259p to 59p) towards the end of 1991 when Robert Maxwell fell off his boat. There was a sudden loss of confidence among investors in companies that relied on a single charismatic leader and Rowland was targeted as one of the most prominent of these.

The lower share price attracted a new investor, to whom Rowland sold off many of his own shares, attracting criticism for receiving a higher price than the one available to other Lonrho investors. His new partner was Dieter Bock, a German property magnate, whose only interest seemed to be in selling off Lonrho's assets.

At that time Lonrho had debts of nearly £1 billion, which is what forced Rowland to sell the Metropole hotels group to a Libyan investment company, essentially to Gaddafi, who was seen by the City as an international pariah. This may have been essential to save Lonrho at the time, but it turned out to be a huge mistake, since it looked to the City as if the company was so desperate for cash that it didn't much care where it came from.

Bock had no interest in retaining a loss-making Sunday newspaper. Tiny (and now Nick Morrell) were the only Lonrho directors with any real interest in the paper. It was certain to be sold: Morrell's concern was not just to get a good deal, but to ensure that the paper found a good home. The only two real contenders were *The Independent*, which wanted to merge *The Observer* with its own Sunday paper, and the Guardian Media Group, which had no Sunday paper to partner its daily.

Some of *The Observer*'s journalists, led by Robert Low, wrote a personal letter to Rowland, thanking him for his stewardship of the paper over the previous dozen years, and begged him not to sell *The Observer* to *The Independent* because that would effectively be the end of the paper as a separate voice. Rowland was evidently moved by the letter, though Morrell's instructions were to get the best price for Lonrho.

The Independent had offered a price of £25 million. Morrell, a clever negotiator, told Harry Roche, the *Guardian* chairman, that they would need to go up to £27 million to secure the paper. He reported *The Independent*'s offer to Rowland and urged him to see *The Guardian* himself and find out if he could push them higher. This he duly did, settling at Morrell's projected figure of £27 million.

Morrell told me in strict confidence a couple of weeks before the sale that the paper would be going to *The Guardian*, which pleased me. So the *Sunday Times* story about the sale – that the editor was the last person to be told – was completely wrong.

I asked Morrell how Whittam Smith had received the news at 7 a.m. on the morning of the sale that *The Observer* wasn't going to *The Independent*. 'All I heard', he said, 'was a gurgling noise on the telephone, like somebody drowning.'

There was no party to mark the end of an era. I was 'banged out' by the journalists on my last day – an emotional ceremony in which

they all whacked filing cabinets or desks with bits of metal. This used
to happen in the composing room, when newspapers had composing
rooms. A couple of weeks later I had a card from the sub-editors' table
saying they didn't know if I was missing them, but they were missing
me. I used to fool around with them close to edition time, wearing a
cap with a flashing sign saying 'Editor' and comment on their headlines: 'Who wrote this rubbish?' and so on.

Much of the press comment described the sale to *The Guardian*
as some sort of failure by *The Observer*. That seemed to me to be
unfair: the miracle was that we had lasted so long as a stand-alone
Sunday paper.

There were two friendly comment pieces about me, both of which I
prized. One was by Peter Preston, who wrote:

> He was fated, for many years, to be a defender as well as a crusader; a
> bruising role where he sometimes felt himself beset on all sides. But
> Trelford was first and foremost a journalist and an editor: multi-talented,
> hands-on, a master of sport as well as news, shrewd and decisive. The
> paper, through his years, may often have been under attack, but it also
> won many awards and gathered together brilliant teams of writers who
> kept the flame of Astor alive. And Trelford, at the end, was there to pass
> *The Observer* on, unbroken and unbowed.

The other was by Gavin Young, one of *The Observer*'s greatest foreign
reporters and later a bestselling travel writer. He wrote in the paper on
my departure:

> It is an indisputable fact that, although Donald is quite unlike David
> Astor in a number of ways, he has proved to be a real chip off the old
> block, which David himself acknowledges. Donald is a journalists'
> editor. Like Astor, he appreciates good reporting and instantly recog-
> nises it when he sees it. And he has another great advantage over rival
> editors: he can write as well as his staff. He is an expert reporter with

a sensitive ear for words and a nose for news that would do credit to a beagle. These gifts are priceless.

He also managed to lay out the front page and write many of the best headlines himself – something beyond most editors these days – while simultaneously taking bets from the staff on every big race or rugby international. The queue of people outside his office door after first edition, waiting to hand over fivers, was like Russian serfs paying tribute.

• • •

Tiny's grip on Lonrho was slipping and it would only be a matter of time before he would be edged out of the company altogether – one he had created and built over thirty-four years. The *coup de grâce* came two years after *The Observer* was sold. He had started leaking stories against Bock, who was now the company's chief shareholder – a situation that clearly couldn't go on.

The Lonrho directors, now chaired by a former British ambassador, Sir John Leahy, voted him off the board, citing 'irreconcilable differences'. Leahy handed over the job of giving Rowland the bad news to Morrell, saying that as he had drafted the press announcement about Rowland's impending departure, he was the right man to read it to him. Rowland's only reaction was to point across the table at Morrell and say a single word: 'You!' Morrell never doubted that the board had made the right decision, but he liked Rowland and was upset by the task he had been given.

Bernard Levin wasn't the only person to find something tragically moving in the situation. He described Rowland, for all his faults, as a man who could never resist a fight – and nearly always won, even when the odds were stacked against him. He wished he had won his last fight against Dieter Bock, who had achieved nothing comparable in his life.

This is a fair point. Rowland had a vision of Africa that has sometimes been compared to that of Cecil Rhodes. The essential difference, however, is that Rhodes was building an Africa for whites; Rowland an

Africa for Africans. Lonrho became the second biggest food producer on the continent, which is no mean achievement. Rowland had also obtained some first-class assets for the company and its shareholders.

For his part, Bock built some apartment blocks for profit, before stripping Lonrho of the assets built up over three decades. He will be chiefly remembered for the manner of his death: choking on a steak in his own hotel. Rowland's monuments are all over Africa – in the tea and sugar plantations, the wheat fields, the cattle farms, the coffee estates and the gold mines.

●   ●   ●

Andrew Marr went much too far when he said that Rowland had treated me 'with cold brutality' and had been 'exceptionally nasty'. Bob Edwards, however, went too far the other way when he described him as 'an ideal press baron'. Tiny was what he was, beguiling and unpredictable, never easy to live with. But he really tried, in his own way, to help *The Observer* and achieved more than he has been given credit for, though it cannot be denied that the paper's public reputation suffered under his ownership.

He wrote a last message to the newspaper we had fought over for the past twelve years:

> And so farewell to *The Observer*. When Lonrho bought it, I thought we would soon be outselling the *Sunday Times*. I hope the new owners, *The Guardian*, will do much better. Donald Trelford will be leaving too. I'd like to say how well he did the job of preserving the paper's independence – perhaps too well. My interest was to bring in new life and increase its circulation. Apart from being allowed to start a profitable Business section under Melvyn Marckus, whom I greatly admire, ours was a one-sided love affair. Lonrho loved *The Observer*.

That wasn't altogether true. Tiny may have loved *The Observer* (even though he sometimes had a funny way of showing it) but few of his Lonrho colleagues shared that feeling. Nor is it true that the feelings were wholly 'one-sided'. I don't think I was alone at *The Observer* in becoming very fond of the remarkable, amusing and sometimes dangerous man who put us on a rollercoaster for so long, but kept the paper going through difficult times – and, also like a fairground rollercoaster, brought something into our lives that can best be described as fun.

CHAPTER 11

TOOTSIE

Tiny Rowland was in a sprightly mood as we arrived at the smart apartment block in Park Lane, next to the Dorchester Hotel. He was taking me there to meet an old friend of his, Mohamed Fayed. I was a bit put out at being dragged along and asked him why I had to be there. 'He wants to see you – I think he wants your advice,' he replied. When I asked him what Fayed was like, he did a surprising little jig in the apartment's gilt and marble hall as we waited for the lift, startling a posh-looking elderly couple.

Then, by way of an answer, he said, almost singing the words: 'If you knew Tootsie like I know Tootsie, oh, oh, oh – what a guy!' I gathered that 'Tootsie' was his nickname for Fayed, whom he seemed to regard as a bit of a joke, or maybe a joker. Which of them had the last laugh became a fraught issue between them. Tiny left me after introducing me to the squat middle-aged Egyptian in a room kitted out like Ali Baba's cave.

Fayed explained that he wanted a coffee table book, with stunning pictures, about the Ritz Hotel, which he owned in Paris. He wanted me to write the words, but I deflected that request by saying I would introduce him to Mark Boxer, who was then producing exactly that sort of book for publisher George Weidenfeld. He then invited my wife and me to stay at the Ritz as his guests, and I saw no reason not to accept the invitation.

We had a slightly odd, out-of-focus conversation about newspapers and about British politics, not helped by the fact that I could barely understand his accent and was distracted by the sheer number of expletives he managed to include in almost every sentence. When Rupert Murdoch's name came up, he said dismissively: 'He's a Jew from Alexandria.' I said: 'I think you'll find he's from Australia.' At this, he banged a little table and insisted: 'No, the Murdochs are f***ing Jews from Alexandria.'

As I stood up to leave, he asked me if I would like to stay on to see a new porn film that had just arrived from Beirut. I made my excuses and left. When Tiny asked me later what I thought of *Tootsie*, I used a phrase of my father's and said I thought he was a bit barmy. He laughed and added: 'More than a bit.'

Some time later, when DTI inspectors were appointed to investigate Fayed's purchase of House of Fraser, I reported the Murdoch conversation to them. In their report, the inspectors say Fayed denied the remark, describing me as 'a hired dog on a leash for Mr Rowland'. The inspectors concluded: 'We see no reason why we should not accept Mr Trelford's evidence, particularly as we preferred Mr Trelford to Mohamed as a witness of truth.'

My then wife and I accepted Fayed's offer of free accommodation at the Ritz – I didn't think it would be fair to land the bill on *The Observer* and we paid our own air fares. We stayed in a palatial room occupied the previous week, Fayed declared proudly, by the King and Queen of Jordan. I wasn't so much impressed as fearful on hearing this news, since the king was one of the world's prime assassination targets. I just managed to restrain myself from looking under the bed.

When my wife bought a few gifts for family and friends from the shops at the Ritz, she was told that as guests of Mr Fayed we were not allowed to pay for them. I took this up with Fayed when we left, but he repeated the edict and refused to allow me to pay for anything. These modest transactions, amounting in total to about €600, became an issue some time later, after he and Tiny had fallen out, when Fayed sent the bills to all the Fleet Street papers, claiming that my wife had been freeloading. Only *Private Eye* ran the story, the other papers having recognised it as the unfounded smear it was.

Fayed had offered a second visit to the Ritz as thanks for my help in getting his glossy book about the hotel into print. My wife refused to go again, saying she didn't trust Fayed and warning me not to trust him either. In her place I took my eldest daughter Sally, who, as a feminist, not to say an intelligent politics graduate, was not impressed when Fayed gave us tickets for a semi-nude review at the Lido. She was even less impressed when, after we had returned from Paris, he invited her back to his Park Lane eyrie and offered to set her up in a boutique at the Ritz. Sally, needless to add, is very attractive.

● ● ●

When Lonrho acquired the paper in 1981, they made a strong point of the fact that, unlike the *Sunday Times* or, especially at that time, the *Sunday Telegraph*, business people didn't take *The Observer* seriously, or at all. I had to admit they were right. Business had never been a high editorial priority for David Astor or for me and the section had never really recovered from the loss of Anthony Bambridge and Roger Eglin to the *Sunday Times* in the early 1970s. We had a brilliant share tipper in John Davis, a shrewd economics columnist in William Keegan, following in the great tradition of Sam Brittan and Andrew Shonfield, and an excellent adviser on personal finance in Joanna Slaughter. But our business news was weak and under-resourced.

Lonrho said we should have a strong business section and were prepared to pay for it, counting on a commercial return in additional readers and advertisers. To run the section, Tiny recommended Melvyn Marckus, then number three at the *Sunday Telegraph* business section, because he had found him reliable when he had dealt with him over Lonrho stories, and rather liked his crumpled appearance, which reminded him, he said, of Walter Matthau. I read Marckus's cuttings, which were very fluent, and was impressed by his ideas for the section when we had lunch. I was aware that some senior figures on *The Observer*, who didn't know or care much about business stories, were concerned at the idea of Rowland effectively appointing the paper's City editor.

Had I chosen not to appoint Marckus, Tiny would certainly have been disappointed, to put it mildly, but he would have accepted my decision, especially if I had been able to make a strong argument in favour of a candidate of at least equal quality and experience. In reality, however, this was an area of journalism I knew next to nothing about and none of my senior colleagues could come up with a better idea. Marckus seemed to be as good a City editor as we were likely to find – and he went on to justify his appointment with some cracking business scoops that had nothing to do with Lonrho, as well as some talented additions to his staff.

The Harrods story, which set Rowland and Fayed on a collision course that resulted in one of the world's most poisonous feuds, went back to 1981, when the Monopolies and Mergers Commission made two rulings affecting Lonrho: one approved the company's purchase of *The Observer*, the other prevented it bidding for House of Fraser, which owned Harrods and which Rowland had been pursuing since 1977.

Rowland was incandescent about the verdict on Harrods, but even more so at a ruling by the Secretary for Trade and Industry, John Biffen, that Lonrho must give undertakings not to buy more shares. It was then that he began to sell some of his Fraser holdings to Fayed, whom he had met when the Egyptian was briefly a Lonrho director.

Tiny once explained to me and to Marckus why he had chosen to 'warehouse' the Lonrho shares with Fayed in what he regarded as purely a holding operation. 'I look at you two,' he said, eyeing our manifestly non-Savile Row suits, 'and I can work out how much you are worth. I know your salaries, your houses and I can guess about your mortgages. The same was true of Fayed. I knew that Tootsie could never afford to purchase the whole of House of Fraser.'

And yet, of course, he famously did, in early 1985, in one of the

City's greatest 'stings'. Rowland was certainly motivated in his vendetta against Fayed by outrage at having been conned. But he was also convinced that his shareholders had been cheated. He believed Fayed had used a power of attorney he held for the Sultan of Brunei, then the world's richest man, to fund the purchase.

Furthermore, that he had lied to the government about the sources of his wealth, supported by lawyers and banks who took his word on trust without checking, that the government had failed to investigate Fayed's credentials and approved the sale without a reference to the Monopolies Commission (while Lonrho had faced three inquiries), and that the Trade Secretary, by then Norman Tebbit, had prevented Lonrho from bidding while the Fayed deal went through.

Between 1985 and 1987, Rowland led an extraordinary worldwide investigation into Fayed and his acquisition of Harrods. He employed several firms of accountants and solicitors, private detectives and freelance journalists in an operation, said to cost many millions of pounds, that was way beyond the scope of any newspaper inquiry. Illicit bugging devices were used and some of the money was spent on bribes to officials to unearth incriminating documents in Egypt, Haiti, Dubai, Brunei, France and Switzerland, allegedly proving fraudulent dealings by Fayed and showing his humble origins and limited net worth.

It was this incendiary material that Rowland placed at *The Observer*'s disposal. There were some editorial doubts about becoming involved in our owner's feud. I consulted Marckus and assured him of my backing if, as City editor, he didn't want to publish anything. He took the view, which I shared, that if a major British institution had been secured by fraud, and the authorities had been negligent in their regulatory duties, it was a matter of genuine public interest. We determined, however, that every line should be double-checked and not accepted simply on Lonrho's say-so. *Observer* business journalists travelled the world in pursuit of the facts – a sentence that could not have been written before Lonrho provided the funds to make it possible.

As it happened, on the day *The Observer* had to decide whether or not to publish the first instalment of what was to become an all-consuming campaign, I was away on a long-arranged holiday in Egypt, in the Valley of the Kings and on to Luxor and Aswan, oblivious of the drama being played out in the office about a modern-day Egyptian. Marckus told Anthony Howard, who was standing in as editor, that he wanted to proceed with the first of the anti-Fayed blockbusters.

It was Howard who made the historic decision to go ahead with *The Observer*'s Harrods campaign. It is worth remembering this when taking account of Howard's later claim that he had always opposed what he called Rowland's use of *The Observer* to pursue his company's vendetta. This is not to say that I would have reached a different decision.

Predictably, writs from Fayed soon poured in. I was shocked to learn from these that our own lawyers, Herbert Smith, had chosen to switch to the other side. Other newspapers, which had been supplied by Lonrho with much of the same material, did not dare to touch it for legal reasons, but were quick to follow up when we led the way. This was another reason that persuaded me to publish the material; *The Observer* was in effect indemnified against legal risks by our owner, which gave us a special responsibility denied to other papers.

We were campaigning for an inquiry into the takeover, something the government was reluctant to concede in case it opened a can of worms. Eventually, however, it launched an inquiry by Department of Trade inspectors, to which we all gave evidence. Their report was delivered in July 1988, but the DTI declined to publish it, on the unconvincing grounds that they didn't want to interfere with police inquiries into possible criminal charges that might arise from it. Eventually, after ten months of stubborn road-blocking, Tiny Rowland got hold of a copy. How he managed this I never discovered, but assumed that some policeman or civil servant would be sunning himself in the Bahamas on the illicit finder's fee.

Tiny rang me on Good Friday 1989 to say he had a copy of the report and asked if I would go to Hedsor to read it. It was a sensational document, justifying almost every charge *The Observer* had laid against the

Fayed brothers. 'We are satisfied', it stated, 'that the image they created between November 1984 and March 1985 of their wealthy Egyptian ancestors was completely bogus.' The report concluded that Fayed could not have found the £615 million asking price for Harrods from his own resources. It fell short of saying it was the Sultan of Brunei's money, for lack of definite proof.

For *The Observer*, this was total vindication. The inspectors contrasted our reporting with the 'lies' promoted by Fayed's PR spin machine and accepted by other papers. The last line of the report read: 'Lies became the truth and the truth became a lie.' We were facing three impending libel actions, so it was vital for us that the report should see the light of day. It was too late to publish it in detail in that Sunday's small Easter edition, so I suggested holding it until the following week. Rowland said we should meet at his London house in Chester Square on the Tuesday with the Lonrho board.

We immediately hit a brick wall. Sir Edward du Cann, the Lonrho chairman, insisted that the company's shareholders were entitled to know first about the report and he proposed to tell them at the annual meeting two days later. I pointed out that the government would then take out an injunction and prevent *The Observer* or any other paper using the material. We were snookered.

Eventually, the idea came up of a special edition of the newspaper to be published on Thursday morning, ahead of the AGM. I suggested it and Nick Morrell, the paper's managing director, worked out how to do it. It wasn't Lonrho's idea. This would at least put the inspectors' findings into the public arena, making them available for the paper's libel defence, and would hopefully pressure the government into releasing the report.

We set up a special unit within the paper to produce the sixteen-page issue, headlined 'The Phoney Pharaoh'. It was meant to be secret, but few secrets escape journalists in their own office and the NUJ chapel called a meeting. After I addressed them, the journalists voted overwhelmingly in favour of publishing the special edition.

I had no doubt that we were doing the right thing. The government had blundered and, by publishing the DTI inspectors' damning conclusions, we were ending the official cover-up and providing our lawyers with ammunition to beat off Fayed's legal assault on the paper. As with the Matabeleland story five years before, this was 'a story that had to be published'. None of my senior staff, including Tony Howard, said a word against publishing the special edition, though Tony suggested some changes to my introduction.

The special edition was given away free from 7 a.m. at news vendors' sites around London (the vendors got 10p a copy for their pains) and was soon being quoted on the radio and television. When du Cann stood up in the Barbican to quote the report to his assembled shareholders, lawyers representing the Department of Trade stepped forward with an injunction and ordered all copies of the special report to be handed over or pulped.

The damage, however, had been done. The papers on Friday morning hailed *The Observer*'s scoop. One or two, including David Montgomery, then editing the *News of the World*, rang me up to congratulate me; Tom Bower's claim that I was immediately reviled for publishing the special edition was simply untrue. I don't think a single newspaper criticised me at the time. They all saw that we had an important scoop. It was only later that Fleet Street's 'dog-eat-dog' instincts took over and I was regularly accused by rival papers of using *The Observer* to serve my owner's commercial interests.

Lord Goodman rang to offer legal support if I needed it. He added: 'I won't congratulate you, because what you have done is illegal.' It must have been around this time that he said of me (as quoted in the autobiography of Robin Lustig, my former news editor): 'Donald Trelford has a remarkable capacity for staying upright in a shipwreck.'

The report was eventually published officially in 1990, following heated demands by MPs and a declaration by Lord Justice Dillon that it was in the public interest for people in financial circles to know whether or not the owners of Harrods were 'fraudulent rogues'. Anyone who doubts the validity of *The Observer*'s reporting of the Fayed affair need only read the DTI inspectors' report.

Looking back, I think we were unlucky with our timing in two ways. One was the accident of the Lonrho AGM falling in the same week as Tiny procured the report, forcing us to produce the midweek edition to forestall a legal ban on its publication. The other was the Maxwell effect. Multimillionaire owners of newspapers were in disrepute at that time: Murdoch, Maxwell, Rowland – they all seemed to be tarred with the same brush. It was only when it came under the wing of *The Guardian* in 1993 that *The Observer* shook off that tainted label.

I remember meeting Roy Jenkins at a book launch around that time. He asked me: 'Do you think the Fayed business has damaged *The Observer*'s reputation? Has it damaged yours? And do you regret it?' I answered yes to the first two questions and no to the third, because I felt I had no alternative but to publish an important story when the facts were known to us. That remains my view.

When Fayed eventually sold Harrods to the Qatari royal family in 2010, some of the reporting amused me. After twenty-five years, despite an official report condemning him and revealing the lies he had told about himself, the media still accepted Fayed at face value. He was not, for example, entitled to the aristocratic prefix 'al-' Fayed, being the son of an impoverished schoolteacher, though he still appears in reference books as al-Fayed, as if the DTI report had never existed.

I feel the same about those who still, three decades on, criticise me and *The Observer* for running the anti-Fayed campaign. I want to say: just read the DTI report and you will see that we were right in nearly every respect. As the final line of the report said: 'Lies became the truth and the truth became a lie.'

●　●　●

In the summer of 1997, when reports came out about Princess Diana's affair with Fayed's son Dodi, Tiny rang me at home – something he had never done since we parted company four years before. He was very disturbed and unusually emotional. It was a year before he died.

> You know people in authority, Donald, more than I do. They will listen to you. Please warn them that this affair between Princess Diana and Dodi Fayed will end badly. It is bound to. If they stay at the Ritz together, or on his boat, Tootsie will have them filmed in bed together. Believe me, I know him. He used to boast to me about doing things like that. But it's more than just that. Something terrible will happen. I know it will. Please, please warn them that it will end in disaster.

CHAPTER 12

EDWARD

One afternoon I was summoned to Cheapside, where I found the directors of Lonrho waiting for me, all seated round the board-room table. Tiny Rowland was present, but he was keeping quiet. This was Sir Edward du Cann's show. 'Donald,' he said in his silky way, 'the Lonrho board are disturbed by *The Observer*'s figures and would like you to take some decisive action to correct them.'

'What do you have in mind?' I asked.

'Well,' said Sir Edward, looking round for support. When none of the directors offered any comments, he changed tack and said: 'Donald, we're not concerned about you. You are a good editor and we like you. It's Tony Howard we're worried about. Did you know', he went on, 'that he's a socialist?' – pronouncing the word with the kind of distaste people might show about the word 'paedophile'.

'Do you think you could find a way to get rid of him?' There were murmurs of assent around the table.

'If all you want is to get rid of Tony Howard,' I said, 'that's easy.'

I sensed the relief all round.

'Yes,' I went on, 'all you have to do to get rid of Tony Howard is to get rid of me first.' I swept up my papers and left the room.

Tiny caught up with me at the lift and said: 'This is nothing to do with me, you know. But if the paper loses money, I have to let them have their say.' He grinned at me, as if to say: 'Take no notice.'

●   ●   ●

I recall a journey to India with Sir Edward and Tiny on the company plane. As soon as we were seated and before the steward had come round with the drinks, the chairman announced: 'I had lunch the other day with Cecil Parkinson. He was asking about you, Tiny.' Rowland went ominously silent for a few moments, then exploded.

'So you entertained to lunch the man who, as Secretary for Trade, ordered a malicious inquiry into some of our share dealings that seriously delayed Lonrho's bid for the House of Fraser?! And I expect you did this at the company's expense?!' He sat there fuming with rage and curtly refused a drink when it was offered.

Sir Edward Dillon Lott du Cann sank in his chair and looked several years older. It was a Sunday evening and we had a long journey ahead. He was clearly a man who was used to a whisky and soda at that time of day. He desperately needed one now. But he couldn't have one unless I ordered a drink first, obviously unable to sit there alone sipping whisky after such an angry blast from his boss. I ordered a gin and tonic, not because his eyes were pleading with me, but because I wanted one.

●   ●   ●

Simon Hoggart used to tell a story, doubtless apocryphal, about a constituent in the lobby of the House of Commons who asked du Cann for the time. He is said to have put his arm round her shoulder and said: 'Tell me, my dear, what time would you like it to be?' I prefer Alan Watkins's description: 'Talking to Sir Edward du Cann', he said, was 'like descending a staircase in the dark and missing the final step. You are not hurt but you are mildly disconcerted.'

People have often wondered why Sir Edward was constantly being chased for unpaid bills and appeared to be permanently on the edge of bankruptcy. Lonrho paid him an extravagant salary as chairman and provided him with a vintage Rolls-Royce and driver, after a long career in Parliament and as a director of financial companies in the City. He wasn't a known gambler, so how could he have allowed his finances to have got into such a mess?

By 1991, he was so deeply in trouble, facing bankruptcy and possible criminal charges, that he had to resign as Lonrho's chairman. He had been deputy chairman of a company called Homes Assured, which provided loans for council house tenants to buy their properties. When the company collapsed, owing £6 million, the DTI sought to have him disqualified as a company director and he soon had to declare himself bankrupt.

The Lonrho board met to consider the situation this created for the company. Tiny was sympathetic to Sir Edward and came up with a bizarre proposal to help save him. He suggested that du Cann should submit himself to an examination by a doctor at the London Clinic, who would pronounce him temporarily out of his mind. Tiny offered to provide a doctor who would say this. Du Cann was summoned to the meeting and told to report to the London Clinic on Saturday morning.

He seemed remarkably unfazed by the proposal, then hesitated and said: 'Tiny, would you mind awfully if I went into the clinic on Monday?'

'Why?' asked Tiny.

'Because I'm due to open the Taunton Flower Show on Saturday.'

•   •   •

It seems incredible that du Cann, who had been described as 'incompetent' by a Department of Trade Inspectors' report into Keyser Ullman in 1976, ever became chairman of a FTSE 100 company. It was even more remarkable that he was seen as a serious right-wing challenger to Margaret Thatcher as leader of the Conservative Party around that time.

He was certainly a brilliant chairman of meetings, as he showed for twelve years on the backbench 1922 Committee and as chairman of the Public Accounts Committee. Rowland valued his ability to use his silky tones to pacify the unruly small shareholders at Lonrho's lively annual meetings. Tiny said he first spotted this quality in du Cann by hearing him on the BBC's *Any Questions?* programme. I suspect it also suited him to have such an eminent public figure financially dependent upon him.

I remember once going to see John Selwyn Gummer (now Lord Deben) when he was chairman of the Conservative Party. We had read English together at the same Cambridge college. I was asking for some help in a dispute with Lonrho. He looked doubtful, obviously thinking that *The Observer* was hardly a Tory sort of paper. Then I mentioned that Sir Edward du Cann was the Lonrho chairman. On hearing this, his attitude changed completely and he declared: 'If du Cann is your enemy, we're on your side.'

•   •   •

The Observer's finances fluctuated in the 1980s, sometimes in profit, sometimes at a loss, but nothing like the massive multi-million-pound losses that were to be run up later under *The Guardian*'s ownership. Whenever the figures came out, the board would look at me as if they were a judgment on editorial quality, when in fact it was the extravagant payments to the printers that distorted the company's balance sheet, just as they distorted the accounts of every paper in Fleet Street.

On one occasion I was summoned, along with Terry Robinson and Nick Morrell, to fly out to join Tiny on his yacht off Corfu. *The Observer*'s losses had risen that year and I assumed that was the reason for our trip. News of it somehow leaked out to the staff and thence to some other papers. Was Trelford finally getting the chop? We travelled in the company jet; unfortunately, Terry insisted on watching an Eddie Murphy film. Just before we were due to land at Corfu, the pilot was instructed to divert to the Turkish coast, to where Tiny's boat, the *Hanse*, had moved while we were in mid-air.

When we landed in Turkey, we were met by some men in smart white uniforms with peaked caps who saluted us and then steered us out on a small boat to the *Hanse* while standing up. No passport formalities seemed to be required. It felt as though we were in a James Bond movie. As always, Tiny was on the telephone when we went aboard, talking to Kenyan President Moi, with his back to the most wonderful view in the Mediterranean.

I had prepared an editorial plan for the coming year, but when I produced it Tiny waved it away. 'Do you think I care about *The Observer's* losses?' he said. 'They are nothing in the whole scheme of things. *The Observer's* value to Lonrho cannot be measured in money.' He explained that he had summoned us to the boat to create a bit of drama, so that Sir Edward du Cann and his board would think he was telling me off, which is what he wanted them to think. So we swam round the boat, had an excellent supper, slept comfortably on board and returned to London the next morning. Mission – whatever it was – accomplished.

When I got into the office, Tony Howard came in with a grave expression. 'How were things with Tiny?' he asked anxiously. 'Excellent,' I replied. 'Couldn't be better.' Surely that wasn't a look of disappointment I detected on his face?

• • •

Any editor spends more time on legal issues than he would like – not just libel, but contempt of court, official secrets, breaches of copyright or privacy. During the course of my editorship, I must have appeared in almost every kind of court in the land, from a magistrate's court to the House of Lords. Three of the best-known cases were also the most ridiculous.

Spycatcher, the book by a former MI5 agent, Peter Wright, described how the agency had tried to unseat Harold Wilson as Prime Minister because a Soviet defector had claimed that he was a Russian spy.

The British government tried to stop the book being published in Australia. When *The Observer* and *The Guardian* gave a brief report of these court proceedings, both papers were banned from saying any more. Our appeal against this decision went all the way to the European Court.

I spent two days in the witness box during the High Court hearing under Mr (later Lord) Justice Scott, from whom, I am pretty sure, I had once taken a beating at scrum-half in a Cuppers game at Cambridge, where he had won a blue as a marauding open-side wing forward. We watched each other warily during the hearing.

On the evening between my two days in the witness box, I returned to my old school in Coventry to hand out the speech day prizes. One of them, which I presented to a young woman, was a copy of the *Spy-catcher* book, which was already on sale in bookshops while we argued in court over whether *The Observer* had been entitled to publish, long before, a brief report of the court proceedings in Australia. As ever, the law was being an ass, assisted in this case by a boneheaded approach to the matter by the Thatcher government.

In another bizarre case, *The Observer* and Lonrho were charged with contempt of court by a law lord who had been offended by receiving a copy of one of Tiny's anti-Fayed missives when he was about to deliver a judgement on an aspect of the long-running feud. The booklet had been sent to all MPs; as a member of the House of Lords, the law lord had received one. Every director of Lonrho and every director of *The Observer* had to be defended by a separate QC, which must have cost the earth (I heard a figure of half a million pounds being mentioned).

It was soon established that there had been no contempt, because a judge is incapable, by definition, of being prejudiced by what someone else says or writes. The whole business had been a waste of time and money – but whose money? The law lords said they had no money to pay the costs and they didn't think it would be right to charge them to the government. So Lonrho would have to pay, even though the law lords had just established that they had committed no offence.

The nearest I came to jail was when the paper paid some expenses to a civil servant for information about a weapons programme in Bath, where a torpedo had landed on a golf course in a trial. The evidence had been kept from the MoD in London because the MoD staff in Bath feared for their jobs. We had only paid the man's expenses because the civil servant told us he had left government service, when it transpired that he was on his last day of terminal leave.

It was a ridiculous and vindictive case for the Attorney-General, Sir Michael Havers, to bring under the Prevention of Corruption Act 1906. In the Garrick Club bar, he talked across a group of members and guests to yell at me: 'I'm having you arrested!' Later, in a quieter mood, the garrulous Havers said the charges were being laid against the newspaper, rather than me personally, because he couldn't bring himself to charge a fellow member of the club, even though mine was the signature on the cheque. In the event, the jury dismissed the charges against *The Observer* anyway. Our informant, however, went to jail.

Michael Havers and I had 'previous' at the Garrick Club. I had been seated next to him at lunch during the Falklands War. I told him I thought the government had missed a publicity trick in failing to give a VC to Colonel H, who had been killed in a daring assault. Havers reacted as if he had been shot. 'How on earth could you know that?' he gasped. 'I've just come from a Cabinet committee that recommended it.'

I said no more, but slipped a suggestion into the Pendennis diary column that Colonel H might be so honoured. Havers reported the matter to the Garrick Club committee as a breach of club rules, but no action was taken. Kingsley Amis, then on the house committee, was quoted as saying: 'The committee took the view that Michael shouts, and if Michael shouts he shouldn't be surprised if non-members over-hear what he says.'

We won one famous libel action, brought by Labour politician Michael Meacher against Alan Watkins for saying he had pretended to be from a poor background when in fact his family were middle class. Alan, a qualified barrister, won that case for himself, charming the judge with his wit and his knowledge of the law. He wrote an entertaining book about it: *A Slight Case of Libel, Meacher versus Trelford and Others.*

We lost a libel case to the former Conservative minister, Edwina Currie, because she was inadvertently named in a magazine article about a film featuring a female politician who murdered her husband. It should never have come to court and even in court we might have won if our counsel, the legendary George Carman, hadn't gone over the top in his cross-examination of the former minister, annoying the judge by showing a *Sunday Mirror* feature of the lady in her underwear. He summed up against *The Observer* and the jury took the hint. I wished afterwards that I had allowed Michael Beloff to handle the case, as he had offered to do.

During her time in the witness box, Edwina had asserted that she was a faithful wife to her husband. Later, of course, she revealed her affair with John Major while he was in Downing Street. I had left *The Observer* by then. The paper rang to ask if they should revisit the case in the light of her admission, which appeared to contradict the evidence she had given under oath. I advised against it, since it would only line the lawyers' pockets and give her more publicity.

• • •

My last two overseas tasks for *The Observer* involved trips to Uzbekistan and to South Africa – one for Dieter Bock, who was gradually taking over the reins at Lonrho, and one for Rowland. I accompanied Bock to Tashkent, where Lonrho was planning mineral developments, because he hated public speaking. So, I had to do the honours. In return, Uzbekistan's dictatorial President, Islam Karimov, presented me with the country's traditional dress. The only possible caption to the comical picture taken of this ceremony would be: 'Prat in a hat.'

The other, more serious assignment, came as a result of a request made by Nelson Mandela to Tiny that Lonrho should fund a new ANC national daily paper. I was introduced to the great man by Tiny at a hotel in Piccadilly. I was disappointed that all they could talk about, apart from the newspaper project, was Gaddafi, both saying he was much misunderstood.

Tiny asked me to prepare a feasibility study, making it clear that Lonrho had no interest in funding the venture and would therefore welcome a report that offered them a way out. That wasn't a problem for me because – apart from the massive investment involved, with no guarantee of any early (or indeed any) financial return – I didn't think an ANC Pravda, pushing party propaganda and presumably protecting the ANC itself from criticism, was a good idea for a country that urgently needed uniting.

Nonetheless, it was a fascinating assignment, providing me with access to all the ANC leaders. I advised strongly against the project, but picked out Zwelakhe Sisulu, son of one of Mandela's companions on Robben Island, as a man capable of undertaking a major leadership assignment in the media. I was gratified to see that before long he was made head of the South African Broadcasting Corporation. The idea of an ANC daily was quietly dropped.

• • •

I later went to Pakistan to interview President Musharraf. This was not for *The Observer*, but was to appear in a supplement in the *New York Herald Tribune* and shown on a Washington TV news channel. Security was such at the time that no one left the hotel who could avoid it and I was never without a bodyguard. I travelled with the camera crew to Islamabad, where we struggled through layers of security to reach the President, who was also head of the army.

He and I sat a few feet away from each other while the crew set up their cameras and sound system. I felt obliged to say something. Finally, I said: 'Mr President, my country owes you an apology.'

'What for?' he replied. 'For colonialism?'

'No, sir,' I said, 'for the bad umpiring decision yesterday that gave your captain out.'

'That wasn't the only bad decision,' he said, eager to talk about the cricket. And so we broke the ice – so much so, in fact, that he must have been off his guard when I put the first question: 'Has Pakistan ever been a democracy?'

'No,' he replied, 'though it has had some civilian governments.'

When I returned to our hotel, I felt like a drink. I said this to an American businessman I met. He replied: 'There's only one way to get a drink here. You have to say that you are a registered alcoholic and that your doctor says you will be ill if you don't have a drink.' I thought I would try this and asked the hotel manager to come to my room.

He looked impassive as I went through this phoney alcoholic routine, then produced a form for me to complete and sign, having brought it with him.

When he asked, with a conspiratorial smile, what I wanted, I asked for five large gin and tonics. When these appeared, I rang the camera crew and invited them to my room. They were suitably astonished and grateful for my apparently magical achievement. They asked no questions about it, assuming, I suppose, that I had simply used bribery, the Open Sesame to most things on the sub-continent.

•   •   •

My last meeting with Sir Edward du Cann, long after I had left *The Observer*, was over lunch at Harry's Bar in London (I paid). He made a bizarre proposal that we should jointly write a biography of Mohamed Fayed. I said I doubted whether any reader or reviewer would regard such a book as – shall we say – wholly objective. I also told him I'd had rather more than enough of Fayed in my life already, thank you very much.

'Risk jail to challenge Secrets Act'

NEWSPAPER editors must test the reformed Official Secrets Act, by going to jail if necessary, *Observer* editor Donald Trelford, has said.

Trelford warned the proposed legislation was not a charter for liberty, as the Government claimed, but a "charter for state media".

He said many Britons did not realise how "deeply secretive" society had become under the Thatcher Government. Referring to the Prime Minister he said: "She is quite simply determined that in future she, and no one else (with the sole exception, perhaps, of Mr Bernard Ingham) will decide what the public is allowed to know."

The Home Secretary Douglas Hurd "has had the temerity to describe his new Bill as a 'charter for liberty' ", Trelford told industrialists in London last week. "If he were Pinnochio, his

Trelford: "society deeply secretive under Thatcher"

nose would grow longer for uttering such transparent whoppers.

"The truth is that the Bill does nothing to increase public access to information and a great deal to protect people in power even when they abuse that power."

Trelford said the guillotine imposed on parliamentary debate on such an important public issue was "nothing short of a scandal in a society that proclaims itself to be free.

"It is a mark of the arrogance into which a government without serious opposition can be tempted after too long in power by its own unshakeable sense of rightness and self-importance."

Three areas in the Bill were "still an insult to a society that prides itself on free expression", he asserted.

"We must be free to publish information about Britain that is freely available abroad. We must not Continued on page 3

Inside: Media Reporter on syndication

Challenging the secret state. The Thatcher years were grim for press freedom.

CHAPTER 13

TONY

S oon after the Lonrho takeover, John Cole came up to me with a serious look on his face and asked if we could have lunch together. In the car to the Garrick Club he was unusually quiet and seemed a bit jumpy, which wasn't like him at all. As we reached the club he told the doorman he was expecting a telephone call and would be in the bar. He remained restless until the call came and he went down to take it. When he returned he was more relaxed and said: 'Let's go in to lunch and I'll explain what this mystery is about.'

The call had been from Richard Francis, head of news and current affairs at the BBC, who had confirmed that the governors had approved John's appointment as political editor. I was delighted for John – and of course he went on to be an outstanding success, one of the BBC's most popular figures, affectionately satirised for his strangulated Northern Irish accent and his ubiquitous tweed overcoat.

For me, however, it presented an urgent problem. I didn't want Tiny Rowland or anyone else from Lonrho to be involved in the choice of his successor. I feared they might press for a deputy they found con- genial and that, in due course – if the paper's circulation fell sharply or its losses mounted, or my damaging evidence against Tiny at the MMC should come to light – he might drift into my editorial chair.

Some editors like a weak deputy who poses no threat. I took the view that strong editors want strong deputies. I certainly wanted a figure of some public standing who could not be brushed aside easily in the event that I had to leave – which, at that time, seemed more likely than not.

As luck would have it, the day following my lunch with Cole, 29 July 1981, was a public holiday to celebrate the ill-fated wedding of Prince Charles to Princess Diana. It gave me a day away from the office to think about John's successor. I consulted two people: Terry Kilmartin, the literary editor, and Alan Watkins, the political columnist. My then wife, Kate, commented on my choice of confidants: 'You've chosen the only two people in the country who won't be watching the royal wedding.'

I had a shortlist of three people, two from *The Observer* – Michael Davie (whose job as deputy editor I had taken twelve years before) and Adam Raphael – and one outsider, Anthony Howard. Howard was then editing *The Listener*, having had a successful spell as editor of the *New Statesman*, collecting around him a brilliant team of writers, such as Martin Amis, Julian Barnes and Christopher Hitchens – the first two of whom went on to write for *The Observer*.

I had first come across Tony Howard through his political column in the *New Statesman* in the early 1960s. One of my co-trainees on the *Sheffield Telegraph*, John Barry, later of the *Sunday Times*, had urged me to read it as one of the best things in British journalism. It was a beautifully crafted column, with many subsidiary clauses, reminding one of an elegant eighteenth-century essay, but with sharp observation of the current political scene and a refreshingly irreverent approach to the personalities on stage.

The *Sunday Times* had then hired him as Whitehall correspondent, giving him the daunting task of getting inside the civil service ('the people who really run Britain'). The appointment was blazoned so loudly, however, that Harold Wilson sent out an order forbidding civil servants to talk to him, thereby destroying his new job at a stroke. He moved onto *The Observer* as Washington correspondent and was doing that when I first joined the paper in 1966.

He blotted his copybook by being absent without leave (in Britain making a TV programme) when President Lyndon Johnson made an historic announcement on a Friday that he was seeking peace in Vietnam and would not be standing for a second term. KPO thought Howard should have been sacked, and on a less tolerant paper he would have been.

Kilmartin supported Howard as my deputy, though he had a hankering for Davie (who didn't want his old job back anyway, having settled into writing). Watkins, who was separated from Howard's sister, also favoured him, though he said he could panic in a crisis, and then added his cryptic warning: 'He'll be after your job.'

I rang Howard and arranged to meet him for breakfast the following morning at Sagne's, then a trendy café in Marylebone High Street, across the road from *The Listener*'s office. Howard almost snapped my hand off, as I knew he would, since *The Listener* was clearly living on borrowed time. I insisted on total secrecy and for all formalities to be completed within the day.

• • •

Then I turned my attention to Rowland, determined to present him with a *fait accompli*. He was in Africa, so I sent him a Telex message saying Howard was being appointed deputy editor unless there were any objections. According to Dick Hall, Tiny called him on his return and said bitterly: 'What could I do? I had to send back my approval. But I had never heard of Howard until that moment. Who is he?'

I had won my first battle without landing a blow. I had what I wanted: a deputy of some public standing who couldn't be brushed aside if I were to leave. Looking back now, however, I can understand why an owner might feel piqued at being ignored over such a senior appointment.

I was surprised that so many people assumed I would be leaving the paper, now that the dreaded Rowland had won the bitter fight to get it. One commentator suggested I should leave 'in a blaze of idealism'.

Abandoning *The Observer* and leaving my colleagues to Lonrho's tender mercies struck me as cowardly rather than idealistic, even though I was offered a couple of tempting jobs if I decided to make the big break – one from my friend Brian Wenham, then head of BBC Two, and one from Harold Evans.

When asked on *Newsnight* if I was going to quit, I replied: 'Certainly not. Editing *The Observer* is the best job in the world.' I especially enjoyed saying that in front of one of the panellists on the programme, Hugh Stephenson, a senior figure on *The Times*, who had been rumoured to be Lonrho's choice as my successor.

●　　●　　●

The 1983 general election was as problematic for me as the one in 1979. We still found it hard to support Margaret Thatcher, whom our readers heartily disliked; yet Michael Foot, whose manifesto was described by one of his colleagues as 'the longest suicide note in history', was hardly likely to make a convincing Prime Minister. As before, I would have fudged a straight choice, describing the strengths and weaknesses of both the main parties, with a mention for the Social Democrat–Liberal Alliance too, and leaving it to the readers to make their own minds up.

Tony Howard was very dismissive when I mentioned the Social Democrats, clearly afraid that I might give them the paper's backing, as Roy Jenkins had privately urged me to do. Howard had replaced Cole as the paper's political commissar and was determined that *The Observer* should give its support to Labour. That was the general view around the editorial conference table, but it wasn't backed with any great enthusiasm. Even Watkins, a lifelong Labour supporter, said he couldn't see Foot, 'the great bibliophile', ever reaching Downing Street. Howard, I could tell, was keeping a close eye on me for any sign of backsliding.

According to a passage in Tom Bower's biography of Rowland, presumably informed by Howard, Lonrho had been pressing for the paper to support the Tories and I had gone so far as to prepare a draft leader backing Thatcher. A horrified Howard had then, according to this version of events, reminded me that the paper had already committed itself to Labour at an editorial conference recorded by *Newsnight* earlier in the week. The BBC producer had been Howard's friend Robert Harris, later a political writer on the paper and later still a successful novelist. The broadcast item had ended with me apparently reading out the editorial on the telephone to Tiny Rowland.

This was a phoney call, which I should never have agreed to, because Rowland wasn't on the end of the line and he was cross when he saw the TV programme. In fact, as he pointed out, I had never consulted him about the position *The Observer* should take at the general election; nor had he ever shown much interest in knowing. In fact, Tiny had recently had a bitter row with Thatcher at Chequers at a lunch arranged by Lonrho's new chairman, Sir Edward du Cann. After that, Tiny had encouraged me to continue an anti-Thatcher campaign we were running in the paper, claiming that she had used her position to help her son Mark to secure a lucrative business contract in Oman.

There was certainly a *Newsnight* item about *The Observer*'s stance at the general election. But I had never drafted a pro-Thatcher editorial; nor had Lonrho ever pressed me to support the Tories. The whole episode, as relayed by Howard to Bower, never took place.

Long after I left *The Observer*, I discovered that Howard had been having regular lunches with Terry Robinson, the Lonrho director most involved with the paper, though my deputy had never thought it necessary to tell his editor about these occasions. I can only assume that Robinson may have argued Thatcher's case at one of the meetings and that Howard had assumed he was speaking for Tiny. The fact is that Tiny spoke for himself and didn't need Robinson to pass on his political messages; it was naïve of Howard to think otherwise.

At that time, I was a regular Sunday paper reviewer for David Frost's morning programme – we had known each other at Cambridge – and I was often partnered on the TV couch by Carol Thatcher. As we arrived at the studio, she said to me: 'What is *The Observer* attacking my mother for this week?' When I replied: 'It's not your mother we're after, it's your brother,' she had laughed and said: 'You can have *him*.'

• • •

Howard was chairing a Sunday TV election programme at the time called *Meet the Press*, generally known as 'Meet the Chums', since he always seemed to invite his friends. On the Sunday before the election I was a guest panellist on the programme myself, quizzing Cecil Parkinson, who was leading the Tory campaign as party chairman.

There was the usual after-show glass of wine, providing the journalists with a chance to quiz Parkinson off the record about the election. He was surprisingly talkative and seemed curiously reluctant to leave, especially for a man running the re-election campaign, and hung around while several bottles of wine were consumed. It was only afterwards that we realised why he was behaving like this. Just a few days later, on the eve of the election, he would have to tell Thatcher that his mistress, Sara Keays, was having a baby, that he had decided to stay with his wife, and that he would be resigning before an angry Ms Keays made the matter public and filled many tabloid pages with the scandal.

I became involved in the story later, when our photographer Jane Bown used a family connection to get access to the Keays household to take a photograph of Flora, the new baby. I ran it on the front page, attracting some criticism for an alleged breach of privacy. Ms Keays had raised no objection to the photograph being taken, so I thought I was in the clear.

On the Monday, however, the day after the picture appeared, *The Observer* happened to have a board meeting, at which several directors, led by Lord Shawcross, attacked me for publishing it. I shrugged my shoulders and said: 'I'm sorry you feel like that about it, but I'm a sucker for baby pictures (having a two-year-old daughter of my own at the time) and so are the readers. I simply couldn't resist it.' My detractors may not have been mollified by this explanation, but it certainly silenced them.

• • •

My biggest problem at the 1983 election was not *The Observer*'s editorial stance, but a battle provoked by the printers. When the presses failed to roll with the pre-election edition of the paper, I rang down to the machine room to find out why. Monty Berzinski, the machine room overseer, said some officials from the National Graphical Association night chapel wanted to see me.

Half a dozen huge men arrived and sat down heavily on the chairs in my room. When I asked them what the trouble was, their leader said: 'It's the Tory advertisement on page eight, Donald. Why isn't there an advert for the Labour Party? You always say *The Observer* treats all the political parties fairly.'

I replied: 'There isn't a Labour Party advert in the paper because they didn't book one. Perhaps they'd run out of money.'

NGA: 'In that case, Donald, we'd like you to drop the Tory advert in the interests of even-handedness.'

'I can't possibly do that,' I protested. 'They have paid for it and it helps to pay your wages and mine. It would be seen as censorship.'

NGA: 'We thought you might say that, Donald, so we'd just like you to take out the parts of the Tory advert that attack the trade unions.'

'You know I can't do that. They wouldn't pay for the advert, and they would be quite right not to. Besides, that would be political censorship and would make the paper and your union a laughing stock.'

NGA: 'We thought you might say that too, Donald, so instead we'd like you to carry this statement we've prepared for the front page, saying the NGA night machine chapel at *The Observer* wishes to dissociate itself from claims made in the Tory Party advertisement on page eight, especially the clauses relating to trade unions.'

'I can't possibly carry that statement, on the front page or anywhere else. Why should your chapel claim a special right to respond to the advert? It would reflect badly on your union and make me look a fool. So the answer is no.'

They were about to reply when Tony Howard put his head round the door and asked me to go outside. He said Len Murray, the general secretary of the TUC, was on the line, evidently having been put in the picture by one of the other print unions, and wanted to talk to the head of the NGA machine room chapel.

The conversation went on for some time and we could hear raised voices, even through the closed door. Eventually the father of the chapel took his men back to the machine room and they started up the presses. I rang Murray back to thank him. He said he had told the father of the chapel that he was stupid to stop *The Observer*, as it was one of the few papers likely to give Labour a fighting chance in the general election. If *The Observer* was stopped, the Tory papers would have the field to themselves.

• • •

'Howard and Trelford were an odd couple and Howard never made much secret of the fact that he was not among Trelford's greatest admirers.' The writer was Robin Lustig, my former news editor and later a highly regarded presenter on the BBC World Service. He added in his autobiography: 'Given his ambition, having edited two weekly magazines, it was only to be expected that one day he would try to find a way to take over the top spot on *The Observer*.'

Lustig described the divisive effect that my deputy had in *The Observer* office: 'Howard was a great gossip and an inveterate schemer, usually over lunch or a glass of red wine, puffing away at a miniature cigar. He was invariably kind to colleagues whom he respected, but could be cuttingly rude about those he did not.' 'He's got a tin ear' was a favourite put-down for anyone whose prose style did not impress him.

Robin continues: 'I was fortunate enough to be regarded as part of

what less favoured colleagues called "Tony's A-team", although knowing how he spoke of some of our colleagues behind their backs, I was
pleased that I never heard what he said about me when I was out of
earshot.' Knowing what Tony thought of me, I can guess what he said
to the A-team about their editor.

I was particularly annoyed at the way Howard openly derided
Angela Palmer, whom I had taken from her popular diary in *The Times*
to run *The Observer*'s news desk, where she was a big success, respected
by even the hardest of hard-nosed reporters. I had chosen her because
of the sharp news sense her diary displayed – not, as *Private Eye* insin-
uated, because I fancied her.

Tony called her 'Little Miss Muffet' and ran her down at every opportunity. She majored on topics like health and property prices, which
were novelties then but have since become part of the staple diet of all
news agendas. She went on to show great flair as editor of the colour
magazine until she was poached by *Elle* magazine. She has since forged
a new career as an ingenious artist and sculptor.

It also irked me to learn from another colleague that Patrick Bishop,
who had covered the Falklands War for the paper, then left to write
books, had approached Tony to ask about returning to *The Observer*
as a foreign correspondent. Tony had advised against it, saying it was
'never a good idea to go back'. I had a high regard for Pat Bishop and
would have taken him back like a shot, but Tony hadn't even thought
it worth telling me about. Bishop went to the *Daily Telegraph* instead.

When Nicholas Garland's book about the creation of *The Independent* came out, I was astonished to discover that Howard's name
appears on more than forty pages. He had been deeply involved in discussions about the paper's launch, yet had never once thought that he
should share this information with the editor of the paper that paid his
salary. I was both amazed and amused when his friend Roy Hattersley
wrote at the time of his death in 2010: 'Loyalty was one of Howard's
conspicuous virtues.'

We lost Mark Boxer, the great cartoonist and illustrator, when I refused to delete the mention of his wife, the news presenter Anna Ford, in a story about the role played by a resident MI5 man at the BBC in recommending the banning of staff with a radical past. I was amazed to hear Tony comment on the story on the radio, saying: 'It's very sad for *The Observer* to lose Mark. I only hope Donald thinks the story was worth it.' What I found so amazing about that remark was that Tony himself had provided the paper with the story – and with her name.

Apart from Alan Watkins, Tony's best friend in journalism was Paul Johnson, for whom he had worked when Johnson edited the *New Statesman* and who had written some of the most powerful pieces – notably the magazine's attacks on those hitherto sacred cows: the Labour Party and the trade union movement – while Tony sat in the editorial chair. This was the same Paul Johnson who went on, through-out the 1980s, to write a weekly media column in *The Spectator* which attacked any paper that dared to criticise the Thatcher government, especially the Iron Lady herself.

His main targets during this period were *The Guardian* and *The Observer*: Peter Preston and I still bear the bruises. When he wrote about *The Observer*, he seemed to be remarkably well-informed about the paper's internal politics and the current state of play in its relations with Rowland and Lonrho. It wasn't difficult to detect the hand behind these off-the-record briefings against the paper that employed him.

Finally, I reached the point where I knew Howard had to go. I was prompted into action by my secretary, Barbara Rieck, who came in to see me one morning in a tearful state and was very cross with me. 'You always pride yourself on your antennae and say that this is why you have survived as editor for so long. But your antennae are not working, Donald. You can't see what is going on under your nose.' I was clearly feeling the absence of Lajos Lederer, my 'house detective', who had died three years before.

The wall between Barbara's office and Tony's was so thin that she could hear every telephone call he made. 'Did you know,' she said in exasperation, 'that he has been seeing the paper's directors to try and get you sacked. Why don't you ask Nick Morrell?'

I rang Nick and asked him what was going on. 'Yes,' he said. 'Tony came to see me to ask for my support in getting rid of you. I told him that if he had a problem with his editor, why didn't he go and talk to you about it? I know he has approached several directors, but I don't know how they responded. Why don't you ask him?'

So I did. The next time he came into my office, I asked if he was free for lunch. We went to Gavvers, a junior branch of the Gavroche, on the north side of Chelsea Bridge. 'Any special agenda?' he asked as we looked at the menu. 'Yes, Tony, I gather you think it's time I went and that you have said as much to some of the directors.'

'Ah,' he said. 'Well, I have to be honest. I do think you've had enough. You've had a torrid time and you deserve a break. Nobody else could have done what you have done to protect *The Observer*, but I think you're getting tired and losing some of your fight and it's beginning to show. You're spending too much time away from the office writing books and living the high life.'

'Why didn't you come and tell me this, rather than going behind my back?'

'I didn't think you would listen.'

'Well, Tony, you are the most political person I know. You must realise that once you have said this, either I go or you go.'

'And are you going, Donald?'

'No, Tony.'

'So I'm going?'

'Yes, Tony.'

Long pause, then: 'Christmas, usual terms?'

'Talk to Morrell about it.'

After that we ordered our meal and never mentioned the subject again.

• • •

Looking back, I think I might have listened to Howard if he had had the courage to tell me to my face that it was time for me to move on. I had been tired of the constant strain for some time and only hung on through a sense of duty. I was drinking too much, which was damaging my marriage, and it was true that I was acquiring a reputation as a man about town. *Tatler* magazine had even run an article about me with a headline: 'Donald thinks that being editor of *The Observer* is an invitation to the cocktail party of life.' Tiny Rowland must have sensed my semi-detachment from the paper, for he asked me: 'Is it true that you're getting bored with editing *The Observer*? Because if it is, I'll get bored with owning it.'

But Tony enjoyed the intrigue too much to act in such a straightforward way. Watkins's warning seven years before had been proved apt: 'He'll be after your job.' I remembered with some amusement how, when Tony approached our table in the pub, Alan and I would suddenly start talking loudly about great prop forwards of the past to drive him away. His lack of small talk could be tiring and Alan and I went to the pub to escape from politics. Tony resented my friendship with Watkins, and upbraided him for treating me too kindly in his autobiography.

●   ●   ●

When Conor Cruise O'Brien died in 2008, Howard criticised me in *The Observer* for allowing Tiny Rowland to remove him. Instead of being criticised, I should have been praised for delaying the inevitable for so long. Rowland had promised Robert Anderson, as part of the sale agreement to Lonrho, that Conor would have to go. Because he had been hired originally as editor-in-chief, he was senior to me and not, therefore, a member of the editorial staff over whom I had jurisdiction. His contract was with the chairman – first Barnetson, then Bradshaw, Anderson, and finally Rowland.

Conor himself understood this, as he wrote in his memoir: 'Trelford held out against the proprietorial pressure to sack me for longer than I would have expected. But when a paper is making a loss, and the editor has regularly to ask the proprietor to make good the loss, the editor cannot hold out indefinitely against the proprietor's continual pressure. Trelford and I remained on good terms.'

Some years later we were both guests at a dinner with some Americans on the shores of the Bosphorus while attending a conference of the International Press Institute in Istanbul. Conor takes up the story: 'It emerged that both us had worked for *The Observer*. One of the Americans asked me why I had left. I nodded over at Donald and said: 'He fired me.' The Americans were quite upset. Why should one of these nice gentlemen have fired the other nice gentleman?

> The question was put to Donald, who replied calmly and truthfully: 'The proprietor made it plain to me that if I didn't sack Conor he was going to sack me. I thought if he sacked me, I might not survive. But I thought that if I sacked Conor, he *would* survive, and he has.'

In his autobiography, Alan Watkins wrote: 'When Trelford finally left the editorship, O'Brien predicted to me that history would judge him kindly for having maintained the standards of *The Observer* in the most difficult circumstances.'

• • •

I was amused to see Tony Howard quoted – and once heard him say the same thing on the radio – that he left *The Observer* because it was too much under the thumb of Tiny Rowland, especially in its coverage of the Fayed affair. The truth is that I sacked him for going behind my back to *The Observer*'s directors and trying to persuade them to get rid of me. He never once complained about coverage of the Harrods campaign, which, as related earlier, was actually launched when I was on holiday and he was in charge of the paper. He even stood up when Tiny Rowland rang him on the telephone, like a subaltern saluting a general. He told Robin Lustig that Tiny had 'beautiful manners' and was 'incredibly good-looking, like George Sanders', the film star.

A word often used to describe Howard by one of his less admiring colleagues was 'self-righteous'. The son of a clergyman, Canon Guy Howard, he had a faintly clerical air that sometimes came through in his manner and speech. Watkins told me that, when they had visited churches together in their younger days, Howard had always climbed up into the pulpit to survey an imaginary congregation and even declaimed from the Bible that was lying open there.

This clerical style sometimes showed in his writing too. I have a letter he sent to me when he was editing obituaries in *The Times* after both of us had left *The Observer*. Giving me what he called 'a gentle nudge' for being late with an obit he had commissioned, he wrote: 'The Christian Year moves on in its own imperturbable way. Could I hope to get your piece by at least Pentecost (or, as I still prefer to call it, Whitsun)?' At his funeral, he was said to have described himself as 'an agnostic, but a C of E agnostic'.

Howard's career in broadcasting was stalled by what a friend in the business told me was his old-fashioned orotund style of delivery that hadn't advanced with the times. The same was true of his return to writing a political column for *The Times* in the 1990s, three decades after his prime at the *New Statesman*. It was stopped for much the same reason, but also because he appeared to have lost touch with the modern political scene.

He relied too heavily on his two main political contacts, Michael Heseltine and Roy Hattersley, and to a lesser extent on Julian Critchley, the Tory MP.

Tony's real interest was in the politics of 1955–80, which made him an excellent reviewer of books about that period – and an obituarist of politicians from that time – but a less reliable commentator on more recent events. Watkins survived by employing a different technique – sitting on a stool in Annie's Bar in the House of Commons while MPs of all parties came to join him for a gossip.

Unlike Howard's, Alan's style was ageless. His comment when David Cameron came to power now looks prescient: 'Once a PR man, always a PR man.' His final published words were about one of the pre-election debates in 2010: 'Mr Clegg is adept at the soft answer that turneth away wrath. He does not have anything to teach Mr Cameron; still less poor Mr Brown, who chews gum even when he does not have anything to chew.' My favourite example of his style is worth repeating here. Talking to Sir Edward du Cann, he said, was 'like descending a staircase in the dark and missing the final step. You are not hurt but you are mildly disconcerted.'

Watkins had married Howard's sister, Ruth, who committed suicide; one of her daughters with Watkins also took her own life. Howard had a secret love affair over three decades with Corinna Ascherson (Neal's former wife) while staying with his wife Carol, a member of the Lloyds banking family. Both men died in 2010, their lives intertwined by politics, journalism, love and tragedy from the time they had met at Cambridge fifty-eight years before.

I wrote a column after Howard's death for *The Independent*'s media page that was badly cut (my fault, not theirs, as I wrote more than they had asked for). As a result, all the positive things I said about him were left out and all the negative points appeared. I had said that I didn't think he would have made a good editor of *The Observer*. A main reason was that he hated sport, which is often all that happens on a Saturday. Nor did he care much about what was going on abroad, apart from America, and then only at election times. He certainly had no interest in Europe, Africa or the developing world, all disturbing lacunae in an *Observer* editor. Nor did he have any interest in typography or make-up. I couldn't imagine him laying out the front page himself, as I always did – using a Barbie ruler my daughter Laura had given me.

This article offended Tony's acolytes. One of them wrote in the *Telegraph* diary that, unlike Howard's funeral, where distinguished figures like Lords Hattersley and Heseltine and Robert Harris had spoken, nobody would bother going to mine.

CHAPTER 14

PAMELLA

Pamella Bordes swanned into my life during a performance of *Swan Lake* at Covent Garden. Editors and their other halves had been invited there for a freebie hosted by the British Airports Authority. She turned up late, having missed the first act, on the arm of Andrew Neil, my rival editor at the *Sunday Times*. She made a striking entrance in red and black, looking as glamorous as a recent Miss India might be expected to look, though she didn't seem too pleased to be there. She and Neil were having some sort of argument, perhaps about him dragging her to the ballet when she would rather be somewhere else. Their disagreement became so obvious that one of our hosts said to me: 'Andrew looks as if he's having as much trouble with her as the Prince is having with Odile on stage.'

Afterwards we were all taken to dinner at L'Opera restaurant. I was seated next to Ms Bordes, with my then wife next to Neil across the table. We talked about *Swan Lake* and I compared the production with one I had seen in Moscow. She asked why I had been in Moscow and I told her I had been writing a book with Garry Kasparov, the world chess champion. She said that she and her mother were fascinated by Kasparov and could I possibly let her have a copy of the book. I said I would send her one and she gave me her card, in front of everyone, and that was that.

I posted the book with a corny inscription: 'For Pamella, a queen among pawns'. This was my standard inscription: for men I would write 'a king among pawns'. Nothing happened for a couple of weeks until I received a telephone call from her at the office. 'No man', she declared in an affronted tone, 'has ever failed to ring me when I have given them my card.' She said she was interested in finding work, ideally at the House of Commons, and would welcome my advice. Could we have lunch?

Such was the innocent beginning of what was in truth an innocent relationship. As she herself was to tell the *Daily Mail* when the Bordes scandal reached epic proportions: 'Donald and I were never lovers. We just used each other in our own ways to manipulate Andrew.' That was the truth. She used me to get back at Neil, who was trying to get rid of her; I was using her to find out what Neil was planning for the *Sunday Times*.

Believe it or not – and given her looks and my reputation, I realise many people won't believe it – my interest in Ms Bordes was commercial rather than erotic. It was at a time when Murdoch had smashed the print unions and given the *Sunday Times* the opportunity to spread its wings with more pages and new sections that gave it a big competitive advantage. *The Observer*'s management wanted to know about their plans and, when the story broke that I knew Neil's girlfriend, they encouraged me to use her to find out more, even suggesting that I put any entertaining or gifts on expenses.

When Neil discovered these gifts, which included a bracelet and a Cartier pen, he sent his chauffeur round to my office to return them. I sent them back to Pamella on the grounds that they were not Neil's property to dispose of. He may have guessed that some sort of industrial espionage was involved because he sent a solicitor round later to ask if I would return some of his papers or audio tapes, which had gone missing, in which reference was evidently made to the *Sunday Times*'s editorial and commercial plans. I told the solicitor honestly that I couldn't return the documents because I didn't have them; nor had I destroyed any audio tapes. This didn't mean, however, that I hadn't learned what they contained.

Marc Burca, who had published a flattering profile of me in

Boardroom, invited me to the opening of a nightclub to celebrate the sale of his business magazine to Pearl & Dean. Ms Bordes had also been invited. When the photographer came round, she held my hand for the camera – a picture that was to be used time and again by newspapers in the weeks, months and years ahead to imply that our relationship was not as innocent as I claimed. It even appeared in *Time* magazine in the United States under a headline: 'More sex please, we're British.' The whole Bordes episode was embarrassing for me because, unlike Neil at the time, I was married, and it caused distress to my family, which I shall always regret.

All this was happening, of course, before the *News of the World* splashed with the story that she was a call-girl, which came as a surprise to me and a massive shock to Mr Neil. It turns out that the notorious publicist, Max Clifford, now serving time at Her Majesty's pleasure, was pulling the strings on the whole Pamella story. A 'madam' who handled a string of prostitutes was being investigated by the *News of the World* and went to Clifford as a client to get the paper off her back.

When Max heard that Bordes was one of her 'working girls' and that she was the girlfriend of the editor of the *Sunday Times*, not to mention a friend of mine, he persuaded the paper to drop the investigation into his client in return for a much better tale. The story of two editors and a call-girl bears all the hallmarks of a Clifford special, too good for any paper to resist: 'SHOCK HORROR OF TWO POSH EDITORS IN LOVE TUG TANGLE SENSATION (*HONEST!!!*)', as *Today* newspaper calmly put it.

Once in the public domain, the story acquired wings and took off in some bizarre directions. It so happened that the film *Scandal*, about the Profumo affair, came out at the same time, so comparisons were made between Bordes and Christine Keeler. What the story lacked, compared with the original, was a political aspect, but that was swiftly supplied by the *News of the World*: 'CALL GIRL WORKS IN COMMONS'. The story was illustrated by a picture of Pamella arriving at the Tory Winter Ball as the guest of the Sports Minister, Colin Moynihan.

She had evidently achieved her ambition of becoming a research-er at the House of Commons, working for the MP for Dover, David Shaw. Her Commons pass had been counter-signed by another Tory member, Henry Bellingham, MP for North West Norfolk (later Sir Henry and a Foreign Office minister). Of course, neither man had known she was a prostitute; the word prostitute, though correct, seems a harsh word to use about Pamella; playgirl, courtesan, good-time girl – all seem more appropriate. The *Daily Express* evidently thought so, running a splash headline: 'PLAYGIRL HAS MPs BLUSHING', and the Tory grandee William Whitelaw wasn't the only one to find the episode 'very entertaining'.

What the story still lacked, however, to keep it going and to match up with the Profumo affair, was a security angle. This too was swiftly pro-vided – *The Sun* leading with a headline: 'PAMELLA DATED LIBYAN AGENT', while *Today* splashed with 'GADDAFI BOMBER AND MPS' BEAUTY'. The agent/bomber in question was Ahmed Gadaff al-Daim, a cousin of Colonel Gaddafi and a senior figure in Libyan intelligence who had been linked to terrorist attacks in Britain. As the *Daily Mail* wrote: 'The disclosures changed the atmosphere of the Bordes episode from that of a soap opera to a potential scandal.'

The Sun added fuel with the headline: 'PAM: I COULD BRING DOWN THE GOVT', prompting Labour's shadow Leader of the House of Commons, Frank Dobson, to call for an inquiry. MPs weighed in with parliamentary questions. According to the *Mail*'s political editor, 'the Westminster adventures of Miss Bordes almost overshadowed the Budget'.

Then, out of the blue, as if the story needed any more fuel, came a royal connection, when Buckingham Palace confirmed that Mark Phillips, then the husband of Princess Anne, had met Pamella at their home, Gatcombe, in Gloucestershire, though he denied any 'liaison'. All the tabloids led with the story, the *Daily Mail* screaming 'PAMELLA AND THE ROYAL FAMILY' and *Today* leading with 'COMMONS CALL-GIRL TORMENT FOR ANNE'.

The story ran on for weeks but came to nothing in the end as the political and security angles were found to lack any substance. However, as Thomas Babington Macauley, the nineteenth-century historian, put it, there is 'no spectacle so ridiculous as the British public in one of its periodic fits of morality.'

All this time I was trying to keep my head down, hoping the whole business would go away. But I made a bad error. Addressing a TUC media conference, I hit out at the Murdoch papers for highlighting my alleged part in the scandal. Someone with my experience of the media should have known better.

The Sun's resulting headline, 'I'M NO DIRTY DON', was undoubtedly true, but my ill-judged comments had served only to add extra mileage to the story, which appeared in every paper, mostly accompanied with that same stock photo of me holding hands with Ms Bordes. Neil was furious with me – but nothing like as furious as I was with him when he made a much bigger mistake in taking the whole business to court, thereby guaranteeing mammoth and seemingly endless publicity as the papers, not just the tabloids, gorged on the story.

The *Sunday Telegraph*, edited by Peregrine Worsthorne and prompted by that mischievous sprite Frank Johnson, had run an editorial called 'Playboy Editors', in which Neil and myself were roundly insulted for keeping 'inappropriate' company with Ms Bordes. Worsthorne got carried away, becoming 'inebriated with the exuberance of his own verbosity' (as Disraeli said of Gladstone). He admitted afterwards: 'How I enjoyed writing that leader ... vituperation can become an addiction ... I was no more restrainable than any wild animal which has once smelt blood.'

Had he written the article as a signed feature, rather than as a statement of editorial policy, I doubt if it would have caused so much trouble for him. He was basically saying something undeniable: that editors of serious newspapers used to mix with politicians in gentlemen's clubs rather than with women of dubious virtue in nightclubs. What prompted Neil to sue for libel was the implication, which Worsthorne says he never intended, that neither Neil nor I were fit to edit our newspapers.

Yet there had been no threat to his job or to mine. Murdoch funded the libel suit, albeit reluctantly. Rowland regarded the whole thing as a joke. Ironically, it was Worsthorne who fell off his editorial chair within days of publishing the offending article and months before the libel case came to court. So why Neil pursued the case is hard now to understand – for him too, I expect.

I liked Perry as one of Fleet Street's most attractive characters and as a writer who, while often wrong-headed, sometimes made a point that others had missed or hadn't dared to mention. I met him on a press visit to China in 1975. One bitterly cold night in a northern province we shared a room and he suggested cuddling together for warmth in our Chinese Army greatcoats. Remembering the story about him curling up at Stowe school with George Melly, for purposes other than warmth, I politely declined. The resulting articles on China that we published in our respective papers were praised by Bernard Levin for being 'implacable in the search for truth'.

What Worsthorne seems to have overlooked was that a court case – which he could have avoided if he had been ready to publish a reasonable apology or clarification – left him wide open to evidence being introduced about his own private life. His long extra-marital affair

with the actress Moira Fraser was bound to come out in disclosures
that his wife, Claudie, would hear in court. I remember one Saturday
evening when he took Mrs Lubbock (Ms Fraser's married name) for
what he hoped was a secret drink near St Paul's Cathedral, well away
from the *Telegraph* office in Fleet Street. He then looked up, startled to
find himself surrounded by journalists in one of *The Observer*'s favourite watering holes, the Rising Sun.

Although Neil got token damages of £1,000 ('RANDY ANDY GETS
A GRANDY'), this was no compensation for the leering headlines
we had both had to suffer, day after day, as the papers lapped up and
published every grubby detail. Both Worsthorne and Neil were said
afterwards to have 'ended up panting, dishevelled and bloody-nosed'.
The judge, Mr Justice Michael Davies, said the collision of the editors
was a matter of 'Greek meets Greek'. Neal Ascherson, writing in *The
Independent on Sunday*, responded: 'Only one member of the affair
acted Grecian, and that was the absent Donald Trelford, editor of *The
Observer*. The *Sunday Telegraph* article was much more insulting about
him but he had the sense to do nothing.'

It was George Carman QC who had advised me, as a friend, not to
sue. 'Anyone who knows you doesn't think any the less of you,' he said.
'Fairly or unfairly, it just enhances your reputation as a ladies' man. I
should be so lucky!' *The Observer*'s lawyers said I had a case against
any paper that accused me of having an affair with Ms Bordes, but I
took the view that the damage was done and any litigation would only
make things worse. But it was an uncomfortable and deeply annoying
experience to read lies about myself during the court case, many of
them projected in huge headlines, knowing that they would hurt my
family and yet unable to do anything about them. I accept, however,
that I had brought much of the embarrassment on myself.

It was simply untrue, however, that I had 'pursued' Ms Bordes, as
Neil claimed in court. I had already told him that firmly when he telephoned me to demand that I should leave the lady alone. He painted a
totally false picture of the two of us as rival lovers, he being the winner

and me having 'made several advances and been rebuffed'. That was complete nonsense or, as Worsthorne might have put it, balderdash.

When the whole business had died down, Pamella sent me a card from abroad, in which she apologised for dragging my name into the headlines. She added: 'If both Andrew and you were my boyfriends, I can assure you that if I had to choose in the end – it would be you. Because you are a lovely, lovely man, so kind, intelligent and witty … I also think that you are terribly handsome.' No, I didn't believe a word of it either.

The most famous headline in the whole affair resulted from Neil's evidence: 'DIRTY DON TRIED TO PULL MY PAM SAYS RANDY ANDY'. Even though it was a parody of the truth, I can now – after so much time and having happily remarried – see the funny side of it. So much so that a framed copy of *The Sun*'s front page now hangs in my study.

DIRTY DON TRIED TO PULL MY PAM SAYS RANDY ANDY

My only lasting complaint against Ms Bordes is that in an interview she described me as a 'pixie', a nickname seized on by *Private Eye* and applied to me with relish for many years to come. Still, I suppose there could be worse things to be called. When I made my debut in *Private Eye* in the early 1970s, I was described as 'the appalling Donald Trelford'. That same evening, I went to a dinner party in Blackheath and the host mentioned to another guest that I worked for *The Observer*. He came up to me and said: 'You must know the appalling Donald

Trelford.' I took immense pleasure in replying: 'I *am* the appalling Donald Trelford.'

At this year's *Oldie* awards lunch at Simpson's in the Strand, nearly three decades after the Bordes episode, I was rather startled to find myself seated next to Andrew Neil. I was even more startled when he whispered: 'Have you seen Pamella Bordes? I heard she was in London.' My answer was a very firm 'No'.

CHAPTER 15

FARZAD

Five box-files containing press cuttings, letters and other papers about Farzad Bazoft have followed me around the world for the past twenty-seven years, a perpetual reminder of my most harrowing time on *The Observer*. Going through them again and reliving that terrible period has been a painful but enlightening experience, especially in the light of some crucial facts which have only become available since the death of Saddam Hussein.

Farzad was thirty-one when he was executed in Baghdad. He had been born in Iran and came to England in 1975, at the age of sixteen, to complete his education. After the Khomeini revolution in 1979, he was allowed to stay on because Iran had issued a warrant for his arrest as an 'anti-revolutionary'. He became a freelance journalist and throughout the 1980s he fed *The Observer* and other media, including the BBC World Service, with items about the Iran–Iraq War.

He was a handsome and rather exotic figure with an Omar Sharif moustache. Although never on *The Observer*'s staff, or even on a retainer, he was welcomed in the office and allowed to use a desk and a telephone. Part of his attraction was his undisguised ambition to be a famous journalist like the *Washington Post*'s Watergate sleuths, Bob Woodward and Carl Bernstein. He carried around with him a copy of John Pilger's book, *Heroes*. His favourite film was *Killing Fields*, about foreign correspondents in Cambodia. He fought hard for a byline on his contributions. This naïve and romantic side of his nature was to have tragic consequences.

His opposition to the Khomeini regime made him accepted in Iraq and he was invited there five times and saw the front line of the war from their side. It is important to stress this, because after his execution I was virtually accused of his murder. This was in a *Sunday Telegraph* article of which John Pilger wrote: 'No finer example exists, not even in *The Sun*, of journalism's sewer.'

The paper equated investigative journalism with espionage and said I was 'culpably naïve' in sending an Iranian 'into the slaughter-house'. The fact is that I never even knew that Farzad had gone to Iraq. I didn't need to know. My deputy, Adrian Hamilton (son of Sir Denis of *Times* and *Sunday Times* fame), could authorise any expenses of the trip; fares and accommodation were paid for by the Iraqi Foreign Office.

This sixth, ultimately fatal invitation came in September 1989, to cover elections in Kurdistan. The invitation was not addressed to Farzad, but to Ian Mather, an *Observer* reporter who had been captured and detained during the Falklands War. Mather couldn't go, so he passed on the invitation to Farzad, who accepted it eagerly. On the day his press party arrived in Baghdad, *The Independent* led with a story about a massive explosion at a military complex in Iraq which had allegedly killed 700 people. There were suspicions that it might have involved chemical or even nuclear weapons. An ITN crew went to look but were sent away and their film confiscated.

Farzad met the deputy Foreign Minister, Nizam Hamdoun, and asked to visit the site. He also sounded out contacts at the Information Ministry about taking him there. Then, sensing that this might be the scoop of a lifetime, he enlisted the help of Daphne Parish, a British nurse he had met on a previous visit, to drive him to Al Hillah, 40 miles south of Baghdad. She agreed on condition that there would be 'no fence-jumping or James Bond stuff'. They went on successive days to take photographs and collect soil samples, though they always stayed on public roads.

When Farzad returned to Baghdad, he told the other journalists what he had been doing and showed them what he had found. Some of them were nervous on his behalf and urged him to leave the country. He was waiting for an Iraq Airways flight to London, just before midnight on 15 September 1990, when he was picked up at Baghdad airport and taken for interrogation by Saddam Hussein's notorious Mukhabarat secret police. He had either been followed, which was a common experience for foreign journalists in Iraq, or his telephone conversations with *The Observer* in London had been tapped.

He was held in solitary confinement for six weeks while this newspaper, the Foreign Office, the European Commission and many journalist organisations around the world campaigned for his release. *Observer* staff and other Fleet Street journalists joined a mass protest outside the Iraqi embassy.

Eventually, on 1 November, the Iraqis issued a tape showing him 'confessing' to being a spy for Israel. Earlier the Iraqis had claimed he was spying for Britain. When Farzad's *Observer* colleagues watched the tape together, we were shocked by his appearance. He had lost much weight and seemed to be exhausted, drugged or suffering from the effects of torture, or possibly all of these. His eyes were those of a sick and frightened man.

Worldwide appeals continued for his release, or at least a fair trial. I saw Iraq's ambassador in London twice. On my second visit, the ambassador was accompanied by a younger man in glasses, who sat with his long legs sprawled across his chair and looked contemptuous of our appeals for mercy. I assumed he was from the Iraq intelligence service and that they were calling the shots.

I went with Adrian Hamilton to see the head of the Middle East desk at the Foreign Office. He was dismissive of our requests for trade sanctions to be imposed on Saddam until Farzad was released. In Cabinet papers released in January 2017, Norman (now Lord) Lamont wrote in a memo to Douglas (now Lord) Hurd, the Foreign Secretary, that trade or credit restrictions would be 'ineffective in influencing the attitude of the Iraqi government', and would 'inflict disproportionate damage on UK industry'.

Hurd replied: 'Iraq would see any further action as a further political response to Bazoft. That would be bad for our wider commercial interests.'

Hamilton has made the shrewd point that, while the United States foreign service sees its role as protecting American people, British diplomats serve the interests of the British government and those interests were chiefly commercial. Only the toughest action by the British government might have saved Bazoft and that was not forthcoming.

In 1988, Saddam had sent war planes to attack the Kurdish town of Halabja with chemical weapons, gassing between 3,000 and 5,000 men, women and children. Just a year later, the British government relaxed controls on arms exports to Iraq. Why? Because Saddam's Foreign Minister, Tariq Aziz, had promised Sir Geoffrey Howe, then Foreign Secretary, that Iraq would not use chemical weapons again.

The Cabinet papers make clear that the Thatcher government's main interest in the whole Bazoft affair was protecting and promoting British arms sales. Lamont has since admitted that 'the decisive thing' in determining Britain's response was that, although he was a British resident, 'he wasn't a British citizen'. We now know that Farzad's fate was almost certainly sealed the moment he fell into the hands of Saddam's security police. But that is no excuse for the Thatcher government's failure to back up its strong words against Saddam with any kind of decisive action.

It has become clear now that they were never going to confront Baghdad over Bazoft. Many of Thatcher's ministers had made the trip to Baghdad to befriend Saddam and promote British trade with the Baathist regime. Hurd himself, William Waldegrave, John Biffen, John Wakeham, Alan Clark and David Mellor had all shaken the tyrant's hand. As Pilger put it, Bazoft's arrest and execution were 'the gravest inconvenience'.

We were shocked to learn that, even while Farzad was under arrest,

the Institute for International Affairs was hosting a conference to promote trade with Iraq. I told the organisers that the whole *Observer* staff
would descend on Chatham House in St James's Square to disrupt the
meeting unless they called it off. In the end we reached a compromise.
I agreed to call off our protest march if I was allowed to see the Iraqi
deputy Foreign Minister, Hamdoun, who was attending the conference.
He had met Farzad on his fatal visit, when he had sought permission
to visit the site of the explosion. Hamdoun, who seemed a decent man,
was sympathetic but he confirmed the view we had already reached that
Farzad's fate was outside the control of anyone but Saddam Hussein.

I was refused permission to attend the trial, as was the British QC
we appointed to defend him. His defence lawyer in Baghdad was given
one day's notice of the trial. It was conducted in Arabic, a language
Farzad didn't know. Sworn statements by *The Observer* and his press
colleagues on the trip were not admitted. On 26 November, the Revolutionary Court sentenced him to be hanged, with no right of appeal,
and Mrs Parish was given fifteen years' hard labour (she was eventually
released and returned to Britain after ten months).

In 2003, *The Observer* tracked down Kadem Askar, the colonel in
Iraq's military intelligence who had interrogated Farzad. He admitted
that he knew Farzad was innocent, but that he was powerless to ob-
struct Saddam's personal orders to have him convicted and executed.

The British Consul-General in Baghdad, Robin Kealy, had been
summoned to Abu Ghraib prison on 15 March 1990 and informed that
Farzad would be hanged in one hour, only to discover that the prisoner had not been told. He had to break the news, which Farzad bore
with dignity. He left letters for his family and friends and apologised
to Daphne Parish 'for having involved her'. His final words were: 'I was
just a journalist going after a scoop.'

I was informed of his execution by the BBC's *Today* programme
when they telephoned me at home just before 7 a.m. I went straight
on air and was unable to keep the tears and anger out of my voice.
When I got to the *Observer* offices on Battersea bridge, the staff in all

departments were in a state of shock. They couldn't think or talk of anything else.

When Canon John Oates, the Rector of St Bride's, rang with a message of sympathy, I asked him if he could come round and say some prayers. He held a deeply affecting ceremony around the paper's news desk, with staff from other departments looking on from a balcony. This seemed to calm the distraught atmosphere and allowed normal work to be carried on.

The Observer's management, working through the Foreign Office, tried hard to arrange for Farzad's body to be returned to his parents in England. Eventually, with no warning, the coffin arrived late at night at Heathrow airport, accompanied by a chilling message from an Iraqi official: 'Mrs Thatcher wanted him. We've sent him in a box.' The *Daily Express* ran a disgraceful front page, claiming that the absence of *Observer* representatives at the airport was proof that the newspaper, for all its public rhetoric, didn't care about its dead colleague.

His eventual burial in Highgate Cemetery, close to the grave of Karl Marx, was attended by his family and dozens of *Observer* staff. His office desk became a shrine, his picture surrounded by flowers and messages. Readers sent hundreds of sympathetic letters, some including poems or money. A permanent plaque and photograph remembering Farzad are now on display in the *Observer* newsroom.

Even now, nearly three decades on, it is hard to contain one's anger – not just at the insane barbarity of Saddam Hussein, but at parts of the British press that tried to shift the blame for his murder onto poor Farzad himself, onto *The Observer* and especially onto me. Some journalists came out well from the affair, notably Paul Foot, Hugo Young, John Pilger and Keith Waterhouse. Others, notably the *Sunday Telegraph* and *Today,* were guilty, to use Paul Foot's phrase, of 'vicious humbug and hypocrisy.'

News broke after his death that Farzad had spent twelve months in jail as a young man for attempted robbery (a surprise to us). It was splashed on the tabloid front pages and presented as if this was more important than his execution, even providing some justification for it. It appeared that, eleven years before his death in Baghdad, Farzad had found himself in financial difficulties and threatened to blow up a building society unless it gave him £475, the exact amount he was in debt. There was no bomb. He was arrested later that day.

We always wondered how the news of Farzad's criminal record had come out. The Cabinet papers released in January 2017 contain a note sent by Sara Dent, private secretary to David Waddington, then Home Secretary, to Charles Powell, Thatcher's foreign affairs adviser, while Farzad was under sentence of death. It sets out the facts of the failed robbery and adds: 'Although this has no bearing on his sentence in Iraq, it may be raised by the Iraqis or the press.' She said the Home Office 'proposed not to volunteer this information but not deny it if it is raised with us'.

There can be no serious doubt that the information was leaked from the Home Office to smear Farzad and distract press attention from the government's failure to help the *Observer* reporter. The smears succeeded to such an extent that several papers and columnists, including John Junor in the *Sunday Express* and Woodrow Wyatt in the *News of the World*, said the Bazoft affair should not be allowed to disrupt British trade with Iraq. One has to wonder who provided the *Mail on Sunday* with a story linking Farzad with Iraq's so-called 'doom gun' project. The documents the paper used were later shown to be forged.

The conduct of two Tory MPs was unforgivable. Terry Dicks said he 'deserves to die'. Rupert Allason said he was a spy. He had no evidence, other than that the name of an Israeli arms dealer was found in his diary. I had actually passed on that name and telephone number to Farzad myself as a possible contact for an investigation we had launched into the international arms trade.

Farzad's conduct in Baghdad, announcing his trip in advance to the Iraqi authorities and sharing the results with his fellow journalists, was hardly the stuff of espionage. As he said himself, he was 'just a journalist going after a scoop'. The deadly fact was that the story concerned Iraq's closest secret, its arms programme.

Ironically, Farzad Bazoft achieved his ambition of reaching the world's front pages. Sadly, however, his name was in the headline, not the byline. But his highly publicised death did highlight the evil of Saddam's regime in a way denied to the thousands of victims who died in silence. Only a year after his death, Iraq invaded Kuwait, sparking the First Gulf War and demonstrating the global threat that he posed.

Nothing will ever soften our rage at the injustice meted out to a dear friend and colleague, or our shame at the Thatcher government's collusion with Baghdad. But it does give added dignity and meaning to Farzad's death to know that it served, if nothing else, as a terrible warning to the world.

CHAPTER 16

MUAMMAR

I first went to Libya for *The Observer* nearly fifty years ago, when the country was still reeling from the discovery of the massive oil deposits which had raised it suddenly from one of the world's poorest countries to one of the richest. At independence in 1951, its total budget was £7 million; by the time I went there in 1968, a single housing project in Tripoli cost £400 million.

It was ruled by King Idris, whom I described in my report as 'a tall ascetic figure with a white beard in steel-rimmed spectacles, incubating a dignity that somehow refuses to hatch'. As I packed my bags in my hotel room on the Sunday morning on which this article appeared, I received a call from the Information Ministry, saying I must report there as a matter of urgency. Suspecting that this might for a rebuke for showing disrespect to His Majesty, I said I would go, but instead took a fast taxi to the airport and managed to get lift-off before I could be stopped.

King Idris – or El Sayyid Prince Muhammad Idris bin Muhammad al-Mahdi as Senussi, to give him his full name – probably didn't deserve to be ridiculed, having fought a tough guerrilla war against the occupying Italians in the 1930s and helped the British in the desert war against Rommel. The problem for me was that Idris was then a popular drink in England, often advertised on the London Underground ('Idris when I's dry'), which limited my ability to take him too seriously.

Besides, I sensed an impermanence about the country's current set-up and doubted if the old feudal monarch, who had chickens' throats cut in his honour whenever his cavalcade passed through a village, was the right man to share out the country's new booty. In my final paragraph, I mentioned the *Ghibli*, a hot searing wind that roars in from the Sahara, and said the people were expecting one to arrive any minute.

Blown in on the *Ghibli* was Colonel Muammar Gaddafi, who swept King Idris away in a military coup the following year. A handsome, dashing figure, often pictured on a horse in the sort of gown worn by Peter O'Toole in the film *Lawrence of Arabia*, he looked every inch the ideal Arab nationalist and a hero to old Arabists like Robert Stephens, *The Observer*'s diplomatic correspondent, who was dewy-eyed when he talked about him.

Two decades later, however, he had come to be regarded as public enemy number one, funding global terrorism and denouncing the West with a deep, religious-like fervour. He refused interviews with Western journalists, except at his windy press conferences, so when Tiny Rowland offered me the chance to meet him I seized it. Tiny insisted that I had to do the interview myself, but I took Colin Smith, a seasoned foreign correspondent, and photographer Sue Adler with me.

•   •   •

When we arrived at Gaddafi's desert camp it was almost dusk and the leader was playing volleyball with some of his guards, including his female guards, the Green Nuns. He was standing at the net in a claret-coloured track suit with white leather slip-ons. The troops wore drab olive uniforms and some had holstered .38 pistols in their belts. He was at once one of the boys and about as inconspicuous as a flamingo among a flock of pigeons.

Since the American attempt at aerial assassination in April 1986, ten months before, using F1-11s from RAF Lakenheath, Gaddafi, who had always prided himself on retaining his nomadic Bedouin ways, had become more of a moving target than ever. He rarely seemed to spend time in Tripoli now and his smashed living quarters in the Aziziya barracks, a two-storey house in the Italian colonial style, had already taken on the air of a museum. We were taken there first when we arrived in Tripoli.

Guides pointed to his children's exercise books among the fallen ceiling plaster on a dressing table and showed us the famous tent near the tennis courts where, they reminded us, the leader used to give audience to such coevals as Indira Gandhi and Fidel Castro.

The house, or what remained of it, was an impressive testament to pinpoint bombing. It was clear that the F1-11s were trying to do more than hurt Gaddafi's feelings. To remind one that surgical strikes exist only in the minds of air force generals, the Libyans were generous in their distribution of morgue and hospital pictures of civilians hit by the strays.

It had always been assumed that Gaddafi survived because he was sleeping in an underground bunker a few yards away from the house. He denied this to us, though, when we met him later. When we asked him to describe the raid, it became obvious that he had not been in the room where his wife, who has back trouble, was strapped to her bed in traction.

'All of a sudden the attack started on the house,' he said, 'so I put on my military uniform quickly because I was wearing my sleeping clothes, and so when I was sure the attack was on the house I ran to rescue the children.' The nearest bomb to the house seems to have fallen on the football field in front.

> The bombs were falling everywhere. You can see for yourself. The house was about to fall at that moment. Some of the children were pulled from under the ruins. The electricity was cut and we had to use hand torches. And there was nobody with me at the house except one relative. So we tried to rescue the children and the girl we adopted was killed.

Despite the extensive publicity Gaddafi had given his family from time to time, outsiders had not heard of fifteen-month-old Hanna until after the raid. Since then, Gaddafi had taken to wandering about Jamahiriya (the State of the Masses) in his custom-built yellow bus, a huge Daimler-Benz said to be armour-plated and complete with living quarters, conference and communication rooms.

To find the leader's bus involved us in a 45-minute flight in a Lear jet to a fair-sized military airfield somewhere in the desert that constitutes most of Libya apart from its fertile coastal strip. The men from the Ministry of Information assured us that we were going to a place in Gaddafi's home province of Sirte called Waddan.

If this was so, we took rather longer than we should have done, even bearing in mind that our Lear jet, which we picked up on landing at Tripoli, flew a circuitous route, first out to sea, then east along the coast instead of directly south-east. And if it was Waddan, the airfield must have been of recent construction, because it is not shown on maps.

It is possible that we were at Sabha, about 170 miles to the south-west of Waddan, which had had an airfield for years and was the place where Gaddafi was due to address the General People's Congress to mark his anniversary as Leader of the Revolution.

Wherever we were, we were fed heavily on mutton, spaghetti and chips in a little hilltop fort garrisoned by long-haired soldiers carrying paratroopers' Kalashnikov rifles. One of our escorts had invaded Israel with the Libyan Army in 1948 and another had acquired in Chicago a taste for whisky sours – a taste he could no longer indulge.

Immediately after the meal, a red telephone rang and we were told that the leader was ready to receive us. We set off in a couple of government Chevrolets – for the Jamariya not only bears no grudge against the American people in general but also retains a remarkable affection for their products.

The cars took us along a tarmac road and then suddenly lurched off left down a barely visible dirt track through the desert scrub. Soldiers leaning nonchalantly against their Ranger Rover watched us go by. On the skyline, to our left, was a single-storey building with what looked like a large radio mast. Nearby was the distinctive silhouette of ground-to-air missiles mounted on a tracked launcher.

But we veered to the right, were waved through a checkpoint by grinning soldiers in bush hats, and drove towards two single-storey buildings, one timbered and the other made of ferro-concrete. Next to the latter, a Bedouin-style tent was pitched. There were several vehicles parked around, including a mobile canteen for the troops. About 400 yards beyond this camp site, a large yellow bus was parked in a wadi.

The volleyball court was a few yards from the tent. 'The leader is playing,' said one of our escorts, obviously delighted at the show being put on for us: 'You can take pictures.' Sue Adler went to the net and so did a man with an old-fashioned film camera from Libyan television, who also took pictures of us.

Gaddafi leapt about in a fairly nimble manner for a man of forty-four and included some tomfoolery in the form of back-heel soccer kicks. It was enough to dispel any lingering rumours that he had been crippled by the American bombs, though there have been persistent reports that he was slightly wounded in the left arm. When the light began to fade, the game was deemed to be over and we were ushered into the tent.

Despite all the careful evasions and the very visible security we had witnessed in the four hours since we left Tripoli, all precautions now seemed to fade away. None of us was searched. The leader's only concern appeared to be that he should not be photographed in the tent in his tracksuit and summoned a dark-green burnous, the hooded cloak worn throughout North Africa.

He also summoned a brazier of hot charcoal, for it was suddenly getting quite cold. Inside the tent, Gaddafi sat in a quilted leather armchair below a low desk on which there was a red telephone and some writing equipment. Occasionally he would scribble a note in green felt tip and pass it to an aide. The tent was lit by electric light. Mattresses lay alongside its brightly decorated interior walls.

For the next hour – with a five-minute interlude for his evening prayers – we questioned Colonel Muammar Gaddafi, Leader of the Libyan Revolution, on subjects ranging from international terrorism to the American 'cowboy attack' on his house, and his thoughts on President Reagan and Margaret Thatcher.

During the course of this discussion we learned that he had increased aid to the IRA as a direct result of Britain's involvement in the American raid; that he welcomed Charles Haughey's success in the Irish elections; that the families of those killed in the air raids might wreak their revenge in Britain and the US; that he thought hostage Terry Waite might be a spy; that he thought the West was about to embark on another Crusade with the intention of re-colonising the East – and that he believed Americans and the British fell 'somewhere between monkeys and human beings'.

Throughout the interview Gaddafi seemed relaxed and calm – 'serene' was our photographer's description – and at times, it must be said, exuded a great deal of charm. Certainly, there was nothing of the 'mad dog' about his demeanour or any hint that here was a man who was running a regime which ruthlessly hunted down its exiled opponents abroad and had just televised the public executions of seven dissidents at home.

When we asked him about this, he said the condemned men had been American agents trained in Pakistan for the purpose of assassinating Soviet advisers. This, apparently, was explanation enough. They hadn't actually killed the Russians, he added.

By this time the heat and unaccustomed exercise were clearly having some effect on the leader's digestion, because a distinct and unmistakable aroma began to fill the tent. I didn't dare look at my colleagues as faint noises betrayed the source of the smell. Suddenly, Gaddafi rose to his feet and solemnly announced: 'It is time for me to pray.' The leader quitted the tent in some haste for what was clearly a five-minute comfort break.

●　●　●

What emerged strongly from the interview was the chilling naivety of a man who rarely seemed to think through the human consequences of his actions. A man who 'supports just causes everywhere' and passed round the plastic explosive, yet blocked out the reality of the bomb in the shopping mall, even though he screamed his head off when it happened near him.

Ten months later, his predominant emotion about the US air raid appeared not to be rage but indignation – at the fact that the Americans had not taken him seriously enough to grant him the immunity normally given to even hostile heads of state. 'I expended an attack, but I thought it would be on military targets,' he told us. 'I didn't think it would be concentrated on my family's house.' Like Wellington at Waterloo, he seemed to think that generals have better things to do than try to kill each other.

• • •

When I met Gaddafi again, five years later in 1992, it was also in a tent, but this time in the Aziziya barracks in Tripoli. The visit had been arranged by a shadowy Arab billionaire, Dr Ashraf Marwan, who flew me to Tripoli in his private plane. He had married the daughter of President Nasser of Egypt and was later chief of staff in the private office of his successor, Anwar Sadat.

By the early 1970s, when he met Tiny Rowland, he had risen to be head of Egypt's intelligence service, involved in arms trading, and was a friend of Gaddafi's head of security, with whom he had worked when Egypt and Libya were briefly united as a single country. When I met this grizzled head of security at Tripoli airport, I admired an ornamental stick he was carrying. When he said that it had been a gift from Tiny Rowland, my head began to spin.

Marwan became closely embroiled with Rowland, Fayed and Khashoggi and sold an airline to Lonrho. It was later discovered that while working for Nasser and Sadat he had been an Israeli spy, passing on advance intelligence about the coming war of 1973. He must clearly have become a marked man.

It was somehow unsurprising that he should eventually die in mysterious circumstances in 2007 by falling off the fifth-floor balcony of his apartment in Carlton House Terrace in London. The police assumed he was murdered, because two 'Arab-looking' men were seen by a witness looking over the balcony after he had fallen, but no charges were ever brought.

•   •   •

By the time I met Gaddafi for the second time, the revolutionary talk had stopped altogether – a change brought about, in my view, by the trauma of the bombing raid that nearly killed him in 1986. He admitted to 'errors' in the past. 'There were times in the mid-70s', he said, 'when we might have behaved in a way that was not in accordance with international law, but not now. Curiously, when I really was a revolutionary, an extremist, my image was not so black with the British and Americans as it is today.'

When I asked him if he was a changed man, he replied: 'By the passage of time everyone changes, through experience. In the 1970s we supported liberal movements without knowing which were terrorists and which were not. In the 1980s we began to differentiate between terrorists and those with legitimate political aspirations.'

So Gaddafi's 'conversion' to peace with the West – the 'conversion' which Tony Blair officially recognised and welcomed with a visit in 2004 – had already begun twelve years before. Gaddafi denied then that he had chemical weapons and told me he would consider renouncing international terrorism and allowing outside inspection of alleged chemical and nuclear installations as part of a deal with the West. His Minister of Planning, Omar Montazer, said such a deal might allow Western oil companies to return to Libya.

All this appeared in *The Observer* on 26 January 1992. Gaddafi might well have said to Blair when he welcomed him twelve years later: 'What took you so long?'

• • •

Much later, after the so-called Arab Spring, when David Cameron sent British troops into Libya, originally as a humanitarian act to save the besieged people of Benghazi, it seemed commendable. But when he went on, in total ignorance of the country's politics, culture and history – and against the firm advice of his military chiefs – to seek the destruction of the Gaddafi regime, he effectively destroyed the country as well, reducing it to ungovernable chaos and the status of a 'failed state'.

One could hardly mourn Gaddafi, just as one could never mourn Saddam Hussein, but one could mourn for the Libyan and Iraqi people and the destruction of their countries that followed the decision to have these leaders hunted down and killed. I couldn't help contrasting Libya's collapse with the country I had first visited nearly fifty years ago, a country full of riches, hope and ambition, all of which were eventually smashed.

CHAPTER 17

LEN

One of the many perks of being a national newspaper editor is that you get to meet, not just politicians, but some of your favourite people from the worlds of theatre, music and sport. Occasionally you make a new friend among them, as I was lucky enough to do with Len Hutton. I first met him when I was asked by the *Observer* sports desk to arbitrate on his contract with the paper; he wanted more money than their departmental budget could cope with. There had always been stories about Len being notoriously tight-fisted. I was thrilled to meet him because England's most famous cricketer had been one of my childhood heroes.

This good-natured negotiation became an annual event, eventually conducted on the golf course after Len said to me: 'I tell you what. I hear you live in Wimbledon. If you can get me a game on the Royal Wimbledon course, then we've got a deal.' I wasn't actually a member, but I had no trouble finding someone to sponsor us. The friendly relationship between us became warmer and more personal after I had interviewed him for the *Maestro* series on BBC Television to mark the fiftieth anniversary of his world-record score of 364 against Australia at the Oval in 1938.

I gave a lunch at *The Observer*, in a dining room overlooking the Thames, to mark that special anniversary. As well as Len himself, I invited two other former England captains who had also done some writing for the paper, Ted Dexter and Mike Brearley. Ted had co-authored a couple of thrillers in a cricket setting with Clifford Makins, the paper's eccentric and somewhat alcoholic sports editor. Makins, I recall, arrived at the lunch in a pair of trainers and promptly fell asleep over the soup, which nobody seemed to mind. At one point in the lunch Len appeared anguished for a few seconds when asked about a particular England batsman before delivering the verdict: 'He were just no good.'

I recalled a conversation I once had with Len about Brearley. Len had tapped his head meaningfully and said: 'Clever chap, that Brearley. Cambridge University, you know.' I said: 'Yes, Len, I know.' To which Len went on, with a deadpan face but with a wink in his voice: 'He's so clever, you see, that he never captained a team in the West Indies. That's what I call really clever.'

•   •   •

Len Hutton aroused remarkably strong feelings for a man who rarely showed emotion himself. Roy Hattersley remembers playing for Sheffield City Grammar School immediately after the Second World War: 'I touched the peak of my cap between every ball in the way that Len Hutton touched his.'

Playwright Harold Pinter also idolised Hutton and once wrote a poem about him and distributed it among his literary friends. It went like this:

> I saw Hutton in his prime.
> Another time.
> Another time...

Puzzled by the lack of reaction, Pinter rang a cricket-loving fellow playwright, Simon Gray, and asked: 'What do you think of my poem?'

After a pause, Gray replied: 'I'm afraid I haven't finished it yet.'

Pinter wrote more eloquently of Hutton in an essay:

He was never dull … His play was sculptured. His forward defensive stroke was a complete statement. The handle of his bat seemed electric. Always, for me, a sense of his vulnerability, an uncommon sensibility. He never just went through the motions; nothing was glibly arrived at. He was never, for me, as some have defined him, simply a master technician.

Pinter's obsession with cricket was such that he told an *Observer* interviewer: 'Cricket is the greatest thing that God ever created on earth … certainly greater than sex, although sex isn't too bad either. Everyone knows which comes first when it is a question of cricket or sex. All discriminating people recognise that.'

•   •   •

I got to know Pinter slightly. We had fallen out during the First Gulf War about a poem of his I refused to publish because it used foul language about George Bush and I didn't think readers of a family newspaper would like it. He cursed me so strongly that I never expected to hear from him again. But when I became involved in a public campaign about David Gower, who had been unfairly left out of an England squad to tour India, we made up.

There was a meeting at Lord's to persuade the campaigners to drop our demand for a costly special meeting of MCC members to vote on the issue. I was surprised when Pinter came in to the Long Room and immediately went to sit by my side. I whispered to him: 'I thought we were enemies and not talking.' He replied: 'Some things are more important than others, and cricket is one of them.'

At the special meeting, I quoted a comment by Sir William Haley, the former editor of *The Times*: 'There are some things in this life that are evil, false and ugly, and no amount of casuistry can turn them into something that is good and true and beautiful.' We won the vote in the hall, but lost overall because so many MCC members, who didn't even bother to turn up for the meeting, sent in postal votes supporting the committee. Pinter's widow, Lady Antonia Fraser, later attended a moving memorial meeting at Lord's at which his writings on cricket were read out.

•   •   •

Len Hutton had some other surprising disciples. I remember being astonished at Lord Goodman's seventy-fifth birthday party at University College, Oxford, where he was Master, to hear the great man – someone who had been loaded with virtually every honour available in British public life – declare that if he could have been someone else, 'I would like to have been Len Hutton.'

When John Major first met him at Lord's, introduced by Jeffrey Archer, he was completely overawed by the experience. Later Archer said to Major's son, James: 'Did your father ever tell you he met Len Hutton?' 'Daily,' replied the young Major.

•   •   •

Len sometimes surprised me with an unexpected telephone call that seemed to be motivated purely by goodwill. On one occasion, when I was engaged in a public dispute with Tiny Rowland, he rang up to say: 'I've only got one word of advice: keep your eye on the ball!' He had a great gift, certainly in later life when he had mellowed a bit after living half his life in Kingston-upon-Thames, for making everyone feel they were his special friend.

He was amused when Tiny Rowland's company, Lonrho, bought *The Observer*. The two men had met in 1948 on the *Durban Castle* taking the MCC team out to South Africa, when Rowland, having fallen out with the British tax authorities, was emigrating to Southern Rhodesia. Hutton later bought shares in his company. He recalled 'a remarkably handsome blond giant' who had placed wagers on the deck quoits and the squad's other shipboard games. Rowland had given Hutton a gold watch in exchange for one of his bats. Len recalled this one day and added wryly: 'Do you see him? Will you tell him the watch has run out?'

When, as described earlier, I attracted some unwelcome personal publicity about an alleged liaison with Pamella Bordes, the glamorous girlfriend of Andrew Neil, Len ran up out of the blue to say: 'Are you all right?' That was all, but it was enough encouragement, as it had often been enough for the younger players in his England sides.

•   •   •

Part of the explanation for Len Hutton's universal appeal relates to the circumstances of his legendary innings of 364 against Australia, when he beat Don Bradman's record with the great man staring into his eyes from short mid-off. This innings made him an instant national hero and is still a record for an English player. The endurance of this apparently frail young man, just after his twenty-second birthday – at the crease from Saturday to Tuesday for a total of thirteen hours and seventeen minutes, the longest innings on record – captured the public's imagination.

The innings seemed to symbolise the tenacious spirit of the underdog, the boy on the burning deck, the bulldog breed incarnate. He became a household name, part of the national myth, like Sir Francis Drake. The words 'Len Hutton' became synonymous with cricket in the minds of British servicemen during the six years of war. His name was as much a part of my war-time childhood as Spam and ration books.

He came to regret the fact that one single innings had dominated his life in this way. 'I sometimes wonder', he said, 'if it was not the second worst happening of my career to become a record-breaking national celebrity at such a young age.' Like other sporting and musical prodigies, Hutton had missed out on many of the normal pleasures of boyhood and youth, sacrificing them for the lonely hours refining his craft in the Winter Shed at Headingley. He said once: 'Almost all of my boyhood was spent with older men.'

The first 'worst happening' of his career was the appalling double fracture of his arm, just above the left wrist, while on commando training for the Dieppe raid in 1941. It happened when the mat slipped under him as he did a fly-spring in the gym. He returned to cricket two and a half years later, after several bone-graft operations, with the left arm – the guiding hand for a right-handed batsman – more than two inches shorter than before. The left arm was never again as strong as the right; it was thinner, with wasted muscles, as one could tell just by watching him use a knife and fork, let alone a cricket bat. No wonder it ached after a long innings.

There were times when he and his doctors thought he would never play again. Even when he recovered, the injury imposed severe limitations on his batting – no hooking, a schoolboy's bat, a restricted flow in stroke-making. Neville Cardus noted after the war: 'All his hits leave an impression of power not entirely expended … The sadness is that physical disability struck his career in its prime.' There are photographs showing him driving with the right hand alone when the pain was too much.

His Yorkshire and England captain after the war, N. W. D. Yardley, said: 'Had it not been for the war and the unfortunate injury to his arm, no record would have been beyond his grasp.' Len told me himself in our TV interview: 'I knew I wasn't the player that I could have become had there been no war.'

It wasn't just the injury, of course, that interrupted his career. The war itself deprived him of six seasons at his peak – from the ages of twenty-three to twenty-nine, nearly a third of his professional span. Bradman, in the equivalent period of his life, scored seventeen of his twenty-nine Test centuries, including two over 300 and eight over 200 – which is some measure of the potential loss to Hutton and to cricket caused by the war.

Len never betrayed any bitterness about the double deprivation he suffered, but once I thought I detected a faint sense of longing. It was over lunch at the Garrick Club, where a member had accosted him on the stairs and reminded him of a great innings he had seen Len play in South Africa in 1939. 'Ah yes, 1939,' he said wistfully as we sat down.

Everybody remembers 1938, but I was actually better in 1939. I was nearly as good as Bradman. After the war, of course, I was a different man. I'll never know how good I might have become in those lost years. I might not have got any better at all. The trouble is, you see, I'll never know.

• • •

Alan Ross, the poet and a former *Observer* cricket correspondent, wrote when Hutton died in September 1990:

There was about him always a wonderful stillness, an absence of hurry. The least theatrical of men, he nevertheless commanded attention in the way that a great actor does. You could not take your eyes off him, the slightly splay-footed, thoughtful walk, the nervous tugging of the cap peak, the fastidiousness of manner and line that marked his deportment and stroke-play as it does that of a dancer.

The dancing analogy would have appealed to Hutton, for he had an obsession about feet. He once told me: 'Bradman had us running all over the field for the whole of a day. Afterwards, on an impulse, I went into the dressing room and looked at his boots. Do you know, his feet were the same size as Fred Astaire's!' He used to propound the theory – how seriously I never knew – that the reason that players like Viv Richards and Colin Cowdrey, for all their talents, were not finally as prolific as Bradman was that they had big flat feet, which prevented them getting quite to the pitch of every ball and keeping it on the ground. Likewise, he thought the tiny feet of Sunil Gavaskar, the Indian batsman, were the source of his genius.

Len's own feet were 'moving all the time', said one former player. Another, Fred Trueman, said: 'He was so quick on his feet, like a ballet dancer.' Bob Appleyard, the former Yorkshire and England bowler, recalls walking behind Len down to a golf tee: 'I suddenly got this feeling that his feet weren't touching the ground.'

Hutton also had an obsession about hands, as a result of his wartime injury, which forced him to think deeply about the role of the hands in all forms of stroke-play. I can still remember a day playing golf with him. He played straight and tidy golf, unlike mine, and was immaculate with his short game, but he was plainly handicapped for length by his bad arm and used only a three-quarter swing. As I sprayed the ball all over the Royal Wimbledon course that day (and sometimes beyond it onto the Common), I could hear that gentle Yorkshire voice of admonition in my ear: 'It's all in the hands, Donald.'

Even now, nearly forty years later, when my golf has got even worse, I still hear that voice in my ear: 'It's all in the hands, Donald.' He explained how great stroke-players like Graveney and Cowdrey had a superb touch with the irons. He dissented strongly from the view propounded by pundits like Henry Longhurst that the secret of golf lay in the legs: 'It's all in the hands, Donald.'

Because of the problem with his arm, Hutton used bats weighing between 2lbs 2oz and 2lb 5oz, compared with the three-pounders wielded today. He once told me that he had been astounded to pick up Ian Botham's bat after his spell in the nets: 'It was like picking up a railway sleeper.' Hutton's relative lack of physical strength, compared with Hammond or Compton, denied him his full run-scoring potential. Even E. W. Swanton, a great Compton fan, admitted in Denis's annus mirabilis, 1947, when he scored 3,816 runs and hit eighteen centuries: 'If Len Hutton had been blessed with Compton's physical strength and vigour this summer he might have made 4,000.' Compton, always generous to Hutton, would not demur.

•   •   •

From 1963 until shortly before his death, he wrote a regular commentary in *The Observer*. One of Len's early articles began: 'I used to play this game a bit.' A sub-editor, with the insensitivity of his breed, had crossed this phrase out, but it was lovingly restored by Makins, the sports editor, who brought it to me for approval.

Many of Hutton's *Observer* pieces contained phrases like this, on a leg glance by Graveney, that deserve a better fate than being lost for ever in a newspaper library: 'This fine shot was played as a man would flick the ash off his cigar after a good dinner.' Or this, on the portly Cowdrey's temperamental reluctance to hammer the bowling: 'Perhaps a little less lunch, or a little less breakfast, would do the trick.' (As captain in Australia, Hutton once sent out the twelfth man with two bananas for Cowdrey just before lunch because he thought he was playing as if he must be feeling peckish.)

David Gower caused him the most exasperation. He couldn't understand how a man of such natural brilliance should fail to exploit his God-given qualities: 'David Gower's so talented he makes the game look easy, too easy. For me it was always very hard ... The price he pays for that languid fluency is a firm-footedness that often defeats him.'

His descriptions of players were sometimes like those of a quirky theatre critic, especially about West Indians: 'He may be descended from cane-cutters and slaves, but this Richards bats like a millionaire, as if he owned six sugar plantations'; 'Constantine's limbs appeared boneless'; 'Sobers and Kanhai play Calypso shots'; 'Walcott is such a giant of a man his bat looks like a toy, a father playing on the beach with his children. But when he hits the ball, it's like a punch from Joe Louis.'

In real life, too, Len Hutton had an eccentric turn of phrase that was often even funnier when you thought about what he'd said. His friends treasured these 'Lenisms'. Usually delivered deadpan with an unblinking stare from those wide-apart blue eyes, followed by a slow crease of a smile, they could be devastating. Take this one, for instance, repeated to me by Ted Dexter. Asked what he thought of a once fashionable

England player, Len replied carefully, wrinkling what Russell Davies called his 'knob of garlic' nose: 'Well, he lacks something at the highest level, some quality … there's a word I'm seeking … it'll come to me in a minute…' Then, with a twinkle and a flattening of vowels: 'I've got it. Ability … that's what he lacks … that's the word I'm looking for.'

I went over to him at the last MCC dinner he attended at Lord's and found him surrounded by Essex supporters, who were demanding that Len should give a public stamp of approval to their favourite Essex man. 'You've got to accept, Len,' one of them finally pleaded, 'that he knows a great deal about the game.' Len saw me approaching and winked. 'The thing is in this life', he declared, 'you can know a great deal about something – and still be wrong.'

● ● ●

David Sheppard, now Bishop of Liverpool, who made a century opening partnership with Hutton for England in 1952, surprised me once when we met at a dinner party by saying that the clue to Len's complex and elusive character was to be found in the Protestant movements of Bohemia. He was referring to his upbringing in the Moravian community at Fulneck, near Pudsey, Leeds. This sect, which had inspired John Wesley, was founded by Count Zinzendorf when he came over from Czechoslovakia in the 1730s.

It provided an austere upbringing – 'strict but caring', as Hutton later described it. The Huttons had been part of the Fulneck community since the end of the eighteenth century, and the house in which Len was brought up dated from that time. His father Henry and his three brothers all played for Pudsey St Lawrence Cricket Club. Len joined them in the first XI at the age of fourteen. He had been given a cricket bat for his second birthday. 'I took to this game', he once said, 'as naturally as a Sherpa to the mountains.' He also showed an early talent for soccer, though his career was abruptly shortened when he cut a knee and his doting aunts, solicitous of his cricketing future, threw his boots on the fire.

Fulneck would have instilled in him a stern sense of duty and social obligation that he carried into his cricket, qualities developed further in the austere rituals of the Winter Shed at Headingley. Graveney described Hutton's absorption: 'Len wasn't on this earth when he batted. He was in a trance. During an interval, he would just sit down and drink his tea and look into space while someone else unbuckled his pads.'

•   •   •

I am still baffled by the end of a profile of Hutton which appeared in *The Observer* in 1951. Although it paid fine tribute to his play, it was cool about his personality – 'He is the greatest living batsman and, behind this, he is the greatest living batsman' – and concluded that, like the poet Milton, he was 'not very lovable', if only because he didn't much care whether he was loved or not. As I wrote when he died in 1990, at the age of seventy-four: 'I think he did care, though he needn't have worried about it.'

He found it hard, even as captain, to offer more than token encouragement to young Oxbridge graduates like May and Sheppard, despite the fact that they hung on his every word, just as in his own youth he had revered giants like Sutcliffe and Rhodes. When he said anything at all, he seemed to be speaking in riddles, never quite finishing a sentence, then saying: 'See what I mean?' (which, of course, nobody did).

Len hardly ever spoke a word to his batting partner, but there are two known exceptions, both told to me by the men themselves. Peter May was batting with Len on the opening morning of a Test match in Jamaica when he 'lost' the ball completely as it left the bowler's arm. He did what he had been told to do in such an emergency by his coach at Charterhouse, the former England player George Geary, and played hard through what he thought was the line of the ball. It went for six over the sightscreen. May remembers Len being appalled at such levity on the first day of a Test match. 'He came up the wicket looking pale and asked in a sharp tone of rebuke: "What do you think you're doing?"'

Another was when Lindwall and Miller were giving Hutton and

Compton the treatment at Lord's in 1953. 'For about an hour and a half,' said Compton, 'Len and I were subjected to the fastest sustained spell by two bowlers that I've ever experienced.' Much to his surprise, Len summoned his partner to the middle of the pitch for a word. 'Yes, Len, what is it, old boy?' Len replied: 'Denis, I've been thinking. There must be a better way of earning a living than this.' He then returned to his crease and scored 145.

No wonder people found Len hard to make out. He was a bit of a mystery to himself at times and enjoyed people's bafflement about him. Trevor Bailey's verdict was succinct: 'Beautiful batsman, difficult man.' For Swanton, he passed two searching tests: 'Would you choose to take him as a model for any young cricketer? And would he have been great in any era?' Denis Compton, who played with him before and after the war, said: 'He was the most beautifully balanced player I ever saw, never ruffled, never without dignity – it was the same in his life, I reckon.' There was a kind of moral quality in the way he played and the way he approached the game.

It is a mark of the enduring respect and affection for Sir Leonard in Yorkshire that an annual lunch in his honour at Headingley is attended by more than 200 people – sixty years after his retirement from cricket and a quarter-century after his death. When I was a speaker there a few years ago, I found myself addressing an audience that included Ray Illingworth, Brian Close, Len's son Richard and others who had played with him for Yorkshire and England. It was rather intimidating to talk about Len, and even copy his accent in telling some stories, in front of people who had known him for much longer than me.

It didn't help either that the old geezer introducing me suddenly went blank and couldn't remember my name. He stuttered and finally said: 'Er, I hope he knows my name better than I know his.' Then, after an embarrassing pause: 'I know he's some sort of journalist – *Guardian*, *Sunday Times*, one of that lot. Here, I've got it – his name is Dan Trelford.' I was reassured when I sat down to hear from Close, a man not known for his generous attitude to southerners: 'That was great. You got Len bang to rights.'

•   •   •

Mike Brearley, a professional psychoanalyst, wrote when Hutton died: 'I suspect that behind the engaging surface was an unease, even a sadness.' In my own dealings with Len I sometimes detected the same thing, but I put it down to a wistfulness about what might have been – if the war hadn't interrupted his career in his prime, if he hadn't damaged his arm, if he hadn't had to bear the full brunt of the Australian attack in the immediate post-war years, if Yorkshire had behaved better toward him ... above all, a sense that he didn't know, and would never know, whether he had reached the peak of his talents.

But my impression was that he looked at that reality with the same straight gaze he applied to the bowling of Lindwall and Miller. Beyond that I sensed an enviable serenity, the wry fulfilment of a Conradic hero who had been severely tested by life and had finally come through, though he wished perhaps that he could have found a way to talk about these things more openly. A phrase by J. M. Kilburn, the Yorkshire cricket writer, stuck in my mind: 'Hutton's is a very romantic story, but Leonard wasn't romantic.' He said to me in our TV interview two years before he died: 'It's nice to be remembered for the 364 and so on, but really and truly I would like to be remembered for the sort of person I am, rather than for what I've done.'

Archbishop Runcie wrote in a letter of condolence to Lady Hutton:

> When you have idolised anyone in youth, it's sometimes a disappointment to meet him in later life. Of nobody was this less true than Len. Someone so modest, so free from cant or pretentiousness, was an inspiration. He seemed to me to have the highest standards for character as he did for the game of which he was such a master.

It is a mark of Len's human quality that he should have obliged such serious people to think so hard about him. When I produced a book about him, I was conscious of something Brearley also felt in writing

about him – an anxiety about intruding and thereby hurting or embarrassing him. It shows the unusual spell he cast that such considerations
should still have force beyond the grave. Len once offered these cryptic
words of advice to Tony Greig about leading an England team on tour:
'Don't say too much.' He might have said the same about this chapter,
but I hope not. Unlike most cricketers, Sir Leonard Hutton deserves to
be remembered for rather more than cricket.

CHAPTER 18

STANLEY

I was having lunch in a restaurant in Madrid when the call came from the *Daily Telegraph* sports desk: 'Donald, your column's a few inches short. Can you add a par or two?' I looked around the room in search of inspiration – and then I found it.

The wall above my lunch table was decorated by a framed photograph of two of the greatest footballers the world has ever seen: Stanley Matthews was shaking hands with Alfredo Di Stéfano, the Argentine genius who had played for Real Madrid. In 1956, when an award for European Footballer of the Year was first introduced, Matthews had beaten Di Stéfano by forty-seven votes to forty-four.

I scribbled down and then dictated a brief item, describing the photo and asking why one never saw pictures of Stanley Matthews in an English restaurant. A week or two later, a letter in spidery handwriting arrived from Matthews himself, having been sent on by the newspaper. He thanked me for the reference to him and said he would like to meet me. And so began my friendship with the man who was a schoolboy hero, not just to me but to every sports-loving youngster of my generation in the 1940s and 1950s.

• • •

I had started writing a weekly sports column in the *Daily Telegraph* as soon as I left *The Observer* in 1993. About eight years before that, Max

Hastings, the editor of the *Telegraph*, had sent me a note inviting me to write such a column if I ever left *The Observer*. He had been inspired to write, he said, by reading a book I had published about snooker. At the time, I was involved in a major public row with my owner, Tiny Rowland of Lonrho, and it didn't look as if I would survive for long in the editorial chair.

When I finally did leave *The Observer* in 1993, I wrote to Max reminding him of the letter he had sent and asking if he was still interested in me writing a sports column. He rang immediately and said he had arranged for me to have lunch the following day with his sports editor, David Welch. The following week my column made its first appearance and continued for fifteen years.

• • •

I happened to be in Madrid because I was doing some consultancy work for a Spanish-based company that produced supplements about individual countries. These supplements, which generated substantial advertising revenue, appeared in many of the world's major newspapers. My job was to open doors for the company into the offices of leading editors in Britain, Europe and America and to guarantee the editorial quality of the supplements.

I remember once ringing Conrad Black, when he owned the Telegraph group, to ask him to see the owner of the Spanish publishing company. The Canadian growled: 'What's in it for me, Donald?'

'He wants to give you a million pounds, Conrad.'

'In that case I'll see him.'

My introduction resulted in the *Telegraph* carrying the supplements for several years, and almost certainly producing the bumper revenues I had promised.

Matthews had said in his letter that he liked to meet people at a Crest Hotel off the M6, not far from his home in Stoke-on-Trent. At the time, I was travelling up every week from London to Sheffield, where I had launched a new Department of Journalism Studies at the university, so it was no problem to arrange a meeting with the great man. In fact, this became several meetings when we found we got on so well together. One reason for this was that I knew the names of the top players of his generation and he enjoyed being taken back in time to reminisce about them all.

My father had taken me to see Stanley play at Molyneux, the ground of Wolverhampton Wanderers, when I was ten or eleven years old. In those days, little boys rarely saw any action on the field, even on their father's shoulders. Descriptions of a goal or a special piece of skill were passed back through the crowd by word of mouth to those at the back of the terraces. One had to take Matthews's genius on trust, so to speak.

But I had managed to watch the famous FA Cup Final of 1953 on a flickering old 9-inch black-and-white TV set at the house of a friend. This became known for ever more as 'the Matthews final', though when I used the phrase Stanley said it failed to do justice to his friend Stan Mortensen, who had scored a hat-trick.

Their Blackpool team had beaten Bolton Wanderers by four goals to three, thanks mainly to mesmerising runs down the right wing by Matthews and his impeccably placed crosses into the penalty area. His team came from 1–3 down with half an hour to go to score the winning goal from a Matthews centre in the dying seconds.

The victory was all the sweeter because Matthews and Blackpool had lost the Cup Finals of 1948 and 1951. Stanley sent me an artist's depiction of the moment he crossed the ball for that winning goal. It still occupies pride of place in my study.

The year 1953, that of the Queen's Coronation, was also the year in which England's greatest jockey, Gordon Richards, finally won the Derby, the year Len Hutton won the Ashes against Australia for the first time since the war, and the year a British-led team conquered Everest. It seemed as though the country's sporting efforts were being blessed from on high.

●　●　●

When I entered the bar of the Crest Hotel, there was no mistaking the great footballing legend, even though he was approaching eighty at the time. He was wearing a sky-blue lightweight suit and skipped across the floor in loafers like a man several decades younger. His silver hair was wrapped around his head in a style that took one back to the 1950s.

I asked him about his fitness, which had carried him to British records that will surely never be beaten – of playing first-class football to the age fifty and appearing for England at forty-two. He said he had never smoked or drunk alcohol and stopped eating meat early in his career. He never ate at all on Mondays, drinking eight pints of water instead. His pre-match meal consisted of egg, milk and glucose powder.

Long before sports science was invented, he had taken vitamins and fruit juices and believed in the energising power of deep breathing. He used to run on Blackpool beach between 7 a.m. and 8 a.m. every morning – 'now I just stroll round the garden,' he added ruefully, though he could never completely break his lifetime habit of early-morning exercise.

He attributed his fitness regime to the example of his father, who had been known as 'the fighting barber of Hanley', a district of Stoke-on-Trent, where Stanley had been born and started and finished his football career. It was from his father that he acquired the dancing feet that were to leave despairing full-backs in his wake.

He told me that his aim had been to make himself the fastest man in the world over ten yards. He became known as 'the wizard of dribble' after practising his moves round kitchen chairs in the back yard at home as a boy. To improve his speed, he had ultra-light shoes made specially for him which lasted for only a few games at a time.

He was never booked on the field, never dived, never queried a referee's decision and never retaliated when he was roughed up by frustrated full-backs – a regular occurrence. He said to me: 'When a full-back kicked me, I knew I'd got him. It showed he was frightened of me.'

I asked if, these days, he would be marked out of the game. 'They tried that in my time, putting three big blokes onto me, and remember they wore heavier boots then. But concentrating on me just made it easier for the rest of the team.' These days, he thought, his talents would be best employed as a mid-fielder, spraying pin-point passes from deeper positions.

I asked which of his many achievements he was proudest of.

Well, the FA Cup medal, I suppose – my father had made me promise on his death bed that I would get one. But really and truly I'm proudest of other things – coaching boys in Africa and South America, for example, which I did for many years. They even had an all-black team called 'Stan's Men' in Soweto in South Africa, which was unheard of in the days of apartheid. I even took them to play matches in Brazil. The South African government didn't dare to stop us because of the publicity my name would have generated.

Was there anything he regretted? 'I'm still ashamed that we gave a Nazi salute in Berlin before playing Germany in 1938. The England team was ordered to do that by the Football Association.' He had many stories that reflected badly on the game's administrators. He said he was once the subject of an FA inquiry because he charged sixpence on his expenses for a scone and a cup of tea.

He said he despised the FA officials who denied a request from him and Tom Finney to stay on in Brazil to watch the World Cup after England had been eliminated in 1950. 'Tom and I were fascinated by the way the South Americans, in particular, were playing the game, their astonishing skills and tactics. They had so much to teach us. But the blazers said they could teach us nothing – after all, England had invented the game!'

Once, when he was already an England international, he knocked on the chairman's door at Stoke to ask for an increase on the basic wage of a few pounds in winter and even less in the summer. 'When I got no response I knocked again. Still no answer, so I tapped on the door and walked in. The chairman said: "Matthews, who invited you in? You can stand outside until I'm ready." That was the kind of attitude you faced in those days.' He told me that in the early days he had to perform with his brother as a touring music hall act to make ends meet in the summer.

Was he proud to have played as long as he did?

As a matter of fact, I could have played a couple of seasons longer. I called it a day because I was taking more and more time to get over minor knocks and niggles, but I regretted that decision afterwards. I actually played my last game of competitive football at the age of seventy, you know. It was a charity match in Brazil and some of their World Cup winners were on the other side – people like Amarildo, Tostão and Jairzinho.

● ● ●

Stanley's last league game was against a Fulham team containing Johnny Haynes, the star of the next generation. Even though Haynes was born in 1934, the year Matthews won his first international cap, they played together for England several times in the 1950s. Funnily enough (a phrase much favoured by my father), I got to know Haynes as well some years later when I moved to Majorca. A fan of his made a flat available to him and his wife on the seafront at Puerto Pollença every year at the same rent he had paid twenty years before.

We were introduced by a mutual friend and Johnny would come to our house and sit chatting by the pool. Again, I was able to indulge my unquenchable appetite for hero worship. I asked him if there was anything he regretted missing when he saw the game today. 'I don't envy them the money,' he said (he was the highest-paid player of his day, the first £100-a-week footballer). 'But I envy them two things: key-hole laser surgery' – his career never recovered from leg injuries suffered in a car crash in South Africa – 'and grass pitches prepared like lawns. I had to play on mud patches.'

I'm sure Stanley would have agreed with him on both counts. It's amazing to recall how much these great maestros of the art of passing a football managed to achieve in such terrible conditions. I have a vivid memory of Johnny cycling along Puerto Pollença's famous Pine Path to join me for a coffee and leaning his bike against a tree. A few weeks later he collapsed while driving his car and died in the resulting crash.

•   •   •

Stanley was visibly embarrassed when I quoted some lines about him from a poem by Alan Ross:

> Horseless, though jockey-like and jaunty…
> Expressionless enchanter, weaving as on strings
> Conceptual patterns to a private music,
> Heard only by him, to whose slowly emerging theme
> He rehearses steps, soloist in compulsions of a dream.

He claimed that he didn't know the poem (though I found that hard to believe) and asked me to send him a copy.

I actually gave him a copy of a book of Alan Ross's writings on sport, containing the poem entitled 'Stanley Matthews', when he invited me to his eightieth birthday party in Stoke-on-Trent. I was thrilled to receive the invitation and even more thrilled to find myself seated next to the legendary Tom Finney, who had so often played on the opposite wing to Matthews for England.

Finney was a delightful man, extremely modest and polite, who had worked as a plumber even while playing as one of England's greatest ever forwards. There were several of Stanley's former teammates from Stoke and Blackpool at our table and there was much laughter when someone said: 'Stan always counted the pennies.' I was reminded of Len Hutton, about whom the same used to be said, but then both were superstars in their sports when wages were closely controlled.

When I asked Finney about the modern game, he said he liked Marc Overmars, a Dutch winger then playing for Arsenal. 'He reminds me of me a bit, the way he takes the ball down the wing, then leaves the defence guessing whether he's going to cross the ball, run on to the byline or cut inside and have a shot at goal. I was like that.'

It was a magical evening, full of nostalgia and affection for a great man from friends who had known him for over half a century. When Matthews died five years later, 100,000 people lined the streets of Stoke-on-Trent, where a statue (in fact, two statues, one at Hanley) was built in his memory.

I was among the crowd of mourners, watching as people stopped working or shopping and children stopped playing in the street, men removing their headgear in respect as the cortege passed by. I feel greatly privileged to have known Stanley Matthews, even briefly, as a friend.

CHAPTER 19

GARRY

How I ever got involved in ghosting Garry Kasparov's autobiography I can't imagine. I hardly knew the moves on a chessboard when the world champion asked me to write the story of his dramatic life. My name must have been advanced by the publisher, because I had recently delivered another ghosted book – on Dennis Taylor, the world champion snooker player – to the same publisher. What had impressed them was that I had written that book in ten days. But moving from snooker to chess required a substantial change-up to a higher gear. Kasparov could reasonably claim to have one of the highest IQs in the universe; Dennis, with all respect to a lovely man, could not.

I had already written a book of my own on snooker, having followed the circuit for most of the season that culminated in the epic battle between Taylor, the man famed for his big glasses, and Steve Davis, until then the world champion. Taylor came from eight frames down to win by potting the final black in the thirty-fifth and final frame, having trailed for the entire match until that last shot. I had observed the match from a ringside seat. Eighteen million people had watched it into the early hours on television, a record at the time.

I got a call afterwards from Barry Hearn (the 'H', they say, is silent), the flamboyant sports entrepreneur, who was manager of both players – what you might call a win-win situation. 'Hey, Donald,' he said. 'I've got a contract for a book by Dennis now that he's world champion. The trouble is he can hardly read a book, never mind write one. Will you do it for him?'

'Barry,' I replied loftily. 'I'm the editor of a serious newspaper. Writing my own book on snooker was one thing, but I can't be seen ghosting a snooker player's book. That's a hack's job.'

After a pause, Barry asked: 'How much did they pay for you for that snooker book?'

When I told him, he said: 'I'll double it.'

'All right,' I said. 'I'll go this far. I'm off on holiday to Guernsey soon for three weeks. If Dennis can provide me with every cuttings book he's got about his career, and if I can meet him in Blackburn' – where he lived – 'and also in Coalisland, County Tyrone – (where he was born and brought up) – then I'll have a go. But if it doesn't work, then I'll back out. I'll know by the end of the three weeks if it's a runner or not. I won't sign anything until then.'

'Fair enough,' he replied. 'I'll get on to it.'

And so it all came to pass, and fortunately – from my point of view and the publisher's, but not of my family – the rain it raineth every day. I would write up about 7,000 words a day in longhand, then post them to Barbara, my secretary, in London, who typed them up each day and sent a copy to me and a copy to Dennis. We would then confer on the telephone. So the 70,000-word book was completed in ten days.

I remember saying at the end of all this: 'It's your life, Dennis. Are you sure I've got things right?' He replied: 'Well, Denise (his daughter) has read it and she says it's fine.' So I was never quite sure whether Dennis had read it at all.

The visit to Coalisland, a republican redoubt close to the Irish border, was quite dramatic. Dennis was taking me along to a snooker exhibition he was giving, and we were stopped several times on the way, and on the way back, by British troops, who sometimes seemed to emerge from bushes at the side of the road, with bits of the shrubbery still clinging to their uniforms. Dennis's snooker cue in its metal case attracted special attention. In the hall itself, Dennis introduced me as the editor of *The Observer*. We were both surprised when this news was greeted with prolonged cheering. Dennis then whispered: 'They think you're the editor of the *Coalisland Observer!*'

• • •

Writing Kasparov's book involved several visits to Moscow. I had first been there in 1970 on an inaugural flight by JAL, the Japanese airline, from London to Tokyo via Moscow. On the way back we stopped for a few days in Moscow. I had been reading two books on the journey: *Inside Russia Today* by John Gunther and a book on the Beatles by Hunter Davies. As we said goodbye to our Russian escorts, one of them whispered to me, asking if I could leave her the book I had been reading. I slipped her the Gunther, thinking she would want to read an outsider's picture of her country. 'No,' she said, 'the other one.' So I gave her the Beatles book.

My action in passing her a Western book on the airport runway was spotted by our minder. As a result, I was whisked away for questioning in a special room after being strip-searched. Back at the office a couple of days later, our lunch guest was John le Carré in his guise as David Cornwell. At lunch, when I told the story of being held by the KGB, le Carré peppered me with questions: 'How big was the room? Was there a window? What colour were the walls? Were there any pictures on the walls?'

• • •

When I was introduced to Kasparov and his English manager, Andrew Page, I had a question for them. I had heard that Dominic Lawson, an acknowledged expert on chess, had been lined up for the job, so why hadn't this happened?

'Garry didn't get on with him,' said Page. 'He felt Lawson was telling him about chess.'

Then I said to both of them: 'I really don't know much about chess, you know.'

Kasparov replied in his guttural voice, tapping his forehead: 'Not to worry, Mr Trelford. *I* know about chess.'

Page then said:

Garry is very impressed that someone of your standing as an editor is prepared to help him with this. He knows it will be intelligently written. Besides, the book won't be all about chess. It will be about his private life as well. Did you know that he has been invited to be a judge of the Miss World contest?

'Yes,' said Garry. 'Why do you think they asked me to do that?'

'Well, Garry,' I replied, 'maybe they think you're a world champion at that game too.'

They both laughed and Kasparov put his arm round my shoulder: 'Donald, I think we will get on.'

• • •

It was, of course, an amazing assignment, following the world champion to tournaments around Europe, Moscow, St Petersburg and Dubai, seeing all the matches close up. When I went to see him in Moscow I would often be met by a limousine at the aircraft steps and be borne off to see Kasparov without the need to show a passport or a visa. It was a far cry from being strip-searched by the KGB.

I soon became aware of the tense political atmosphere surrounding the game. Garry was campaigning for the overthrow of Florencio Campomanes, the Filipino head of FIDE, the world governing body, whom he suspected of being in league with (and very possibly in the pay of) the Russians. There would be conspiratorial meetings late at night in his hotel room at tournaments as he sought support from other grandmasters to have the FIDE chief removed.

Campomanes had halted his first world championship bid against the holder, Anatoly Karpov, in 1984 after Garry had recovered with an astonishing effort of will from a five-nil deficit (the winner needed to reach six points) to three to five, claiming that the players were exhausted – it was already the longest chess match in history. But in fact it was Karpov who had been fought to a standstill and the decision to stop the match had been made at the behest of the Russians to save their man. Karpov, from an uncomplicated Slavic background, was much preferred by the officials as their champion to the maverick and unpredictable Kasparov, who came from Azerbaijan, was half-Jewish and half-Armenian.

Garry was sure that the Russian officials had plotted to prevent him beating Karpov and had thrown every kind of obstacle in his way. In the rematch, however, Kasparov had taken the title at the age of twenty-two, but still felt himself to be under siege. It was a time of massive change in the Soviet Union, with Gorbachev struggling to introduce his *perestroika* reforms, so I presented Kasparov as the champion of change and Karpov as the representative of the old guard in the Kremlin.

Kasparov was wary of the association with Gorbachev, preferring Boris Yeltsin. This baffled me because Gorbachev seemed to be the more intelligent man, with a clear reforming agenda, whereas Yeltsin had never shaken off his reputation as a drinker. When I asked Kasparov about this, he said: 'They are both sitting on the fence. On one side is Communism, on the other side is democracy. Gorbachev's legs are still on the Communist side, while Yeltsin's legs are dangling on the democratic side.'

I remember an assembly of the International Press Institute in Moscow, where I sat with David English, the long-serving editor of the *Daily Mail*, while we watched Yeltsin make the opening address. His glass was being constantly refreshed with what we were meant to think was water. But David and I were seated in a position where we could peep round the screen at the edge of the stage and could plainly see the lackey who brought the 'water' on stage refilling the glasses from a bottle of Stolichnaya.

• • •

It was fascinating to watch how diligently Kasparov prepared for all his matches, even if they were relatively unimportant exhibitions. Once, I remember, Garry was due to play the whole Swiss team in Zurich in what is known as a 'simul', or simultaneous group of matches, where the grandmaster takes on several boards at once. Garry was concerned about the Swiss champion, who had recently beaten a Soviet grand-master. So he kept playing and replaying the key game on his computer until we had to tell him it was time for dinner.

He finished soon after and explained that he had found a counter to the Swiss player's attack that the Soviet grandmaster had missed. So the next day he led the Swiss champion into replaying that game, making the same moves that the Soviet player had used. His opponent must have thought it was his birthday, being invited to revisit the scene of his greatest triumph. That was the view in the grandmasters' room, where all the moves are carefully analysed. They couldn't understand why Kasparov was falling into the same trap. It was as if he was being pulled into a quagmire. Then, suddenly, in a flurry of moves, it was all over and Kasparov had won.

At a tournament in Brussels, which I watched in the grandmasters' room so that I could follow what was going on, the general verdict was that the game was heading for an inevitable draw. Then, to everyone's surprise, Kasparov found a way to win. I went up in the lift to his hotel room and plucked up the courage to ask: 'For how many moves had you been preparing that *coup de grâce*?' 'Thirteen,' he replied.

Kasparov introduced me to his mentor, Mikhail Botvinnik, who had been world champion throughout the post-war years. A tall man with a kindly countenance behind heavy glasses, he reminded me a bit of his fellow countryman, the cellist Rostropovich, but with a much calmer demeanour. When we talked, he said he had perfected a computer pro-gramme that would solve the problems of the Russian economy, but he couldn't get the authorities to listen.

• • •

Garry took me to Baku, a windy city on the Caspian Sea, the world's larg-est lake, to meet his formidable mother, Klara, who had been the driving force in his life after his father had died of cancer at the age of thirty-nine, when he was seven. Klara was a charming and very attractive woman with a powerful aura around her. His father had been an engineer from a family of musicians. Garry later had to escape from Baku, never to return, when the newly independent Azerbaijani government, having split with Moscow, started a pogrom against ethnic Armenians. Kasparov hired a Tupulov airliner to carry his family and friends out of the country.

This was a shattering blow to Kasparov, for his roots were in Baku and he used to retreat there for solace after his global travels. Parts of the city and neighbouring places like Sheki and Shemakha are like relics from Omar Khayam's world of *A Thousand and One Nights*, with donkeys pottering along the streets and women in highly coloured Azerbaijani headscarves drawing water from the well.

On my last night in Baku, Garry had said to me: 'Tonight, Donald, we have a party under our hotel. The heads of the KGB and the Com-munist Party for Azerbaijan will be there.' I asked: 'Why is the party *under* our hotel, Garry, and not *in* the hotel?' He replied frankly: 'Be-cause we don't want everyone to see how some of us live.'

The party started in the sauna bath, then we all had a plunge and wrapped ourselves in huge white towels which we kept on for the ban-quet that followed. We went into a room which had a vast number of trestle tables, all groaning with the weight of Caspian delicacies: red and black caviar, beans with walnuts, pickled tomatoes and egg-plants stuffed with herbs and garlic, smoked sturgeon and herrings, beef tongue, crab salad, pancakes with fish, meat and herbs inside, watercress, parsley, shalik or fish on a spit. We served ourselves then sat round a long table in our towels, looking like Roman senators.

The meal was interrupted by a constant stream of vodka toasts, all in Russian, but interpreters were sprinkled around the table so that the non-Russians present could keep up. Kasparov told me that he had always been puzzled by the habit in Britain of pouring glasses of vodka then putting the stopper back in the bottle, which never happened in Russia. Eventually there was a toast to me as their distinguished British visitor – at least, it was supposed to be to me, but the speaker added, rather surprisingly: 'And to Margaret Thatcher, greatest British Prime Minister since Churchill.'

I was a bit stunned by this and replied: 'Mrs Thatcher may be your favourite British Prime Minister, but she isn't mine, and I am certainly not her favourite newspaper editor.' There was general amusement at this, so I was encouraged to add: 'And I have news for you people. Margaret Thatcher isn't a Communist.' This was greeted at first in total silence, then a lonevoice came from along the table (afterwards I learned that it belonged to Kasparov's uncle, Leonid, a composer): 'Donald, we have news for you, too. Neither are we!'

At this the whole room erupted with applause and laughter. That this could happen in the presence of the local heads of the KBG and the Communist Party suggested to me that Communism in the Soviet Union was finished, despite Gorbachev's best efforts to keep a reformed version going. When I got back to *The Observer* in London, I told my foreign experts: 'By the way, Communism is finished in Russia,' and relayed the story. They were sceptical and one of them, Mark Frankland, had the cheek to say, jokingly: 'Leave the politics to us, Donald. You stick to snooker.' But, of course, it wasn't long before I was shown to be right.

• • •

One day, when he was in London, I took Garry to lunch with Tiny Rowland at Cheapside. The two giant egos eyed each other warily.

Finally, Tiny said: 'If you can put me in touch with the man who calls the shots in Russia's platinum business, I will pay one million pounds into any account of yours anywhere in the world.'

Kasparov was quite excited by this proposition and as soon as we got back into my office car he was on the telephone to Moscow to start finding out the name of the apparatchik who could make his fortune. Whether he ever got anywhere with this quest I never heard.

• • •

Andrew Page asked me to lay on a dinner at Zen, the Mayfair restaurant, for Garry to meet some celebrities. He particularly asked to meet Selina Scott, who had become a star with the arrival of breakfast television. At the dinner, however, he hardly addressed a word to her, apparently out of shyness, and as the evening went on he looked increasingly disgruntled. I put this down to the fact that nobody was talking about him. I had noticed before that he couldn't stand it if any of us started talking about a subject that excluded him.

His massive ego, which almost matched his IQ, couldn't cope with being ignored – a childish trait common, I gather, in people who had been infant prodigies in music or mathematics as well as chess. The talent for all these activities is said to come from the same specialised area of the cortex in the brain. Their personalities can become distorted as they grow up through lack of contact with other children and by the obsessive nursing of their particular talent to the exclusion of normal everyday life.

• • •

In order to complete the book, I had to find reasons for visiting Moscow that also suited *The Observer*. One of these was the publication of Andrei Gromyko's memoirs, which I had bought for serialisation in the paper, and on the strength of that sought an interview with the veteran diplomat.

Gromyko was one of the most important Soviet figures in the Cold War period, having served as Foreign Minister, ambassador to the United Nations, to the United States, to Cuba and to Britain. Gorbachev had finally given him the ceremonial role of head of state. Having been born eight years before the revolution in the time of the Tsars, Gromyko had served under Stalin, Malenkov, Khrushchev, Brezhnev, Andropov, Chernenko and Gorbachev.

I managed to secure the interview and he invited me to dinner in his dacha outside Moscow. The visit was filmed for the BBC's *Newsnight* programme. At dinner, attended by his Polish wife, no alcohol was served. Gromyko explained that when he was a boy, he and some friends had dug up an illicit whisky still in a field. After drinking from it, he was taken to hospital to have his stomach pumped. He had never drunk a drop of alcohol since. He told me that once, when as an ambassador he was greeting guests at diplomatic receptions, the smell from the tray of drinks nearby almost made him sick.

I asked him about the level of drinking in the Soviet Union, which Gorbachev had forlornly tried to halt, and I dared to ask whether it was true that Brezhnev had been an alcoholic. He paused for a while, staring at me closely, then took off his shoe and banged it on the table, shouting: 'Da, da, da!' ('Yes, yes, yes!') This was a deliberate inversion of his regular use of the word 'Nyet' to impose a Soviet veto at the United Security Council, where he had become known as 'Mr No'.

Afterwards we went for a walk in his garden to talk about world affairs. This appeared in *The Observer* over a long feature headlined: 'A Walk in the Woods with Gromyko', with a picture showing our two backs in heavy overcoats. Gromyko had been involved in every attempted global peace initiative since the Second World War and was a leading figure in the move towards détente between the Soviet Union and the United States. I had the feeling that, if asked, he could have listed the details of every arms agreement for the past half-century.

● ● ●

What I was very keen to achieve was getting an accredited *Observer* correspondent back into Moscow. Mark Frankland had been expelled as part of a tit-for-tat exercise in response to Britain's expulsion of a whole bunch of Soviet spies who worked on Highgate Hill. I didn't want to approach the press department at the Soviet Foreign Office because they would just follow orders and had no power to change them. I needed access to a more senior FO figure, which Kasparov helped me to find.

When I turned up at the senior apparatchik's office, the prospects did not look good. It didn't help that he spoke no English, or pretended not to. He was a huge bear of a man who sat behind an even bigger and distant desk. When I finally got him to understand that I was talking about *The Observer*, he suddenly came alive, but not in a good way.

He kept muttering, time and again while shaking his head: 'Observer, Nora Beloff, Observer, Nora Beloff,' as if he were recalling some great sadness in his life. Nora had recently driven through the country to report on the plight of Soviet Jews and had caused great annoyance to the Russians, mainly by what she wrote, but also by the way she had lectured them.

• • •

Nora Beloff had been *The Observer*'s long-time political correspondent and became a bit of a legend. She had joined the paper in Paris in David Astor's early days as editor, having worked in the Foreign Office intelligence department during the war and then for *The Economist*. She was a member of the distinguished intellectual family of Beloffs. Her brother was Max, later Lord Beloff, and her sister had married a Nobel Prize-winning chemist. Nora, not to put too fine a point on it, was an awkward customer.

When Mark Arnold-Forster had sent a story to *The Observer* from Paris in 1963, on the Saturday before General de Gaulle's historic Monday press conference, in which he vetoed Britain's entry to the

Common Market, he had forecast this outcome correctly. He had received confirmation from a lone junior French official in an otherwise deserted President's office. Nora had persuaded David Astor that this could not possibly be true, so *The Observer* had spiked a major scoop. Arnold-Forster resigned in protest and went back to *The Guardian*, where he had started.

Nora had a habit of acting as censor of other people's copy, especially if Israel was involved. John de St Jorre came into the office from the Middle East with a horrific story about the ill-treatment of Palestinian prisoners by Israeli soldiers. Nora and Lajos Lederer, the unofficial Israeli censors in the office, were opposed to publishing it. But they had to withdraw their objections when St Jorre produced some graphic pictures that proved his point.

Nora had appeared on the front page of the *News of the World* in the 1960s in a story claiming that Harold Wilson had called in Special Branch officers to follow her to find out who her contacts were inside his Cabinet, after a series of embarrassing revelations. In the '70s, she became obsessed with the idea that Trotskyists were infiltrating the Labour Party. Although she was forced to desist after the NUJ chapel had passed a resolution deploring this 'reds under the beds' campaign, it emerged some years later that she had been right all along. She had a reputation, as Alan Watkins put it, 'for grasping the wrong end of any stick that might be in sight'.

I once heard her talking on the telephone to Reginald Maudling, then Chancellor of the Exchequer. Her comments went something like this: 'Reggie, you're a coward. I'm not going to carry that anodyne quote you just gave me. I'm going to say this instead and that's what you must say in Cabinet' – then read out a much tougher quote she had just invented and put the words into Maudling's mouth.

Ken Obank, the managing editor, who handled production of the news pages on a Saturday, used to get angry with her on two counts almost every week: one was that she would dictate her story to the copytakers on Saturday afternoon because she couldn't type, at a time when they were at their busiest taking sports reports; the other was that she would wander over to the back bench, peep over Obanks's shoulder to see what he was putting on the front page, then say casually: 'I've just talked to Jimmy Margach (the *Sunday Times* political correspondent) and they are leading the paper with my story.'

When I was on the news desk, KPO would sometimes take me off for a quick drink after first edition. On this occasion we were joined in the Blackfriars by Clifford Makins, the eccentric sports editor, whose shirt tail had usually parted company with his trousers after a hectic day. KPO was swearing loudly about Nora Beloff as he passed the drinks from the bar counter to me. I will never forget the moment when Makins dropped his bombshell. I had drinks in mid-air in both hands when Makins said: 'She's pretty nippy round the bed.' KPO and I froze at the enormity of the image he had conjured up. To everyone's amazement, they soon got married: the ageing spinster and the unreformed alcoholic.

• • •

Soon after I became editor, I brought in Adam Raphael from *The Guardian* as political reporter and Alan Watkins from the *New Statesman* as political columnist. *The Spectator* was also trying to poach Watkins and we noticed that we were being followed to the Blackfriars pub by Geoffrey Wheatcroft, who made an unconvincing job of trailing us and ear-wigging on our conversation from behind a pillar. This comic episode was written up in the *Sunday Times*.

When I met Watkins a second time to confirm the arrangement, I had forgotten to bring the piece of paper listing all the points we had discussed. But I remembered them all and recited them to Watkins, who was so amazed at the exactness of my power of recall that he suggested that I would have made a good Chancery judge.

Having made these other appointments, I offered Nora Beloff the job of European correspondent. She was a strong Europhile and Britain had just joined the Common Market, so it seemed an exciting prospect for her. She replied by sending two letters, one to me and one to Douglass Cater, the American journalist who was the London representative of Arco, the American oil company which had just bought the paper from the Astor Trust.

She thanked me for the job offer and said she would be delighted to accept it. In her letter to Cater, however, she said the Americans should get rid of me as editor because I wasn't a patch on David Astor. Unfortunately for her, she put the letters in the wrong envelopes. As a result, her long career at *The Observer* ended on that very day.

•   •   •

Meanwhile, back in Moscow, the Soviet apparatchik was still muttering his little refrain: '*Observer*, Nora Beloff,' and shaking his head sadly. Then I had a brainwave. I was the man who, after all, had sacked Nora Beloff: surely that would carry some weight. When I finally got this point through the interpreter's head and into that of the apparatchik, there was a long silence while the news was slowly absorbed. Then the apparatchik came round his desk and gave me a massive bear hug in which I could hardly breathe. 'You sacked Nora Beloff,' he repeated several times in wonderment. I felt like the man who shot Liberty Valance.

So Mark Frankland got back into Moscow, where he did an excellent job. It was many years later when I began to wonder if I had been wise to appoint as our Moscow correspondent a man who had been in MI6 (do they ever leave?) and was also gay – not that I knew either of these things at the time. The opportunities for blackmail must have made his position hazardous.

•   •   •

I happened to be in Leningrad on one occasion when Kasparov called me and said it was important that I should see him in Moscow the following day. The hotel said all the flights to Moscow were fully booked and suggested that instead I should take the overnight train. This sounded fun, so I duly turned up at Leningrad's Moscow station just before midnight. On the platform, everyone was watching a fierce row between a man, obviously the worse for wear through drink, and a tall and very attractive woman, wearing thigh-high boots and with long hair down to her waist.

The whistle went for us to join the train and I thought no more about it. The babushka in charge of my carriage had few words of English. She showed me my compartment, pointed to the bottom half of a bunk bed and said sharply: 'You sleep here. Now.' I asked if there were any refreshments. She explained: 'First I bring tea. Then the light goes half off and you get undressed. Then the lights go off and you sleep.'

I was lying on my bed reading a Kingsley Amis novel and waiting for the train to set off when the rowing couple from the platform burst in. Seeing me lying there, the drunken man went into overdrive. He could see I was English from my book, so he yelled at me: 'You arrange this. You arrange to sleep with her. I will kill you.' I tried to reassure him: 'You've got the wrong end of the stick there, old boy. Never seen her in my life before.'

The Russian beauty then spoke up: 'Please don't worry. This man is a Finn. Therefore he is drunk. I meet him in a bar tonight and he wants to come with me to Moscow. I tell him this is impossible. But he is drunk. He is a Finn.'

The babushka had evidently been busy on the telephone, for the compartment was then invaded by two burly policemen, who carried off the noisy intruder to whatever gulag is reserved for drunken Finns in Leningrad. The beauty and I were left alone. The tea came, the tea went, the lights went half-off and we undressed with our backs to each other. Then the lights went out completely. She said she was a paediatrician called Olga, working in Moscow.

When I recounted this episode later in the bar of the Garrick Club, Melvyn Bragg had said: 'Well, your feet would be all right then.'

Another friend said: 'You slept with her, didn't you?' Clive James then intervened to say: 'No, Donald wouldn't be so stupid. She could have been a plant. He'd know the roof of the compartment might slide open silently and film all that was going on. If you went to Moscow so often, they'd be bound to put tabs on you.'

When they persisted in asking what happened between us, I said: 'It's like President Reagan said about the Contras.' (The Iran–Contra affair, in which the US covertly backed a rebel movement after Congress had banned such operations, was a highly publicised scandal at the time.)

'Well, what did Reagan say about the Contras?' they asked.

'He said he couldn't remember.'

• • •

Although he lost his world championship in 1993 and retired from competitive chess in 2005, Kasparov is still regarded as the greatest player in the game's history. From 1986 to 2005 he was world number one in 225 out of 228 months. He still has a remarkable record in the chess games he has played in retirement – and he reappeared for a US tournament in 2017, suggesting that he might play more comeback matches – but his interest moved on to politics more than a decade ago.

His is the strongest and bravest voice for democracy in Russia and he is Vladimir Putin's most vocal opponent. So much so that he no longer dares to live in Russia, for fear that Putin would have him killed – a belief shared by a former head of the KGB. Kasparov now has a Croatian passport and lives in New York when he isn't travelling, giving lectures and writing books.

I interviewed him for *The Observer* around the time the Berlin Wall came down. He said democracy would take root again in places like East Germany, Poland and Czechoslovakia, which had known democracy in the past. But he feared for Russia, since the country had moved straight from feudalism to Communism and had no concept of democracy.

His hatred of Putin is visceral. In 2005, he tried to run against him as a presidential candidate, but claims that the authorities put up too many obstacles to prevent him standing. When someone in America praised the Russian leader as 'strong', Kasparov replied: 'Putin is strong in the way arsenic is a strong drink.'

When Kasparov first told me he was going into politics, I feared for him. Of course, he has a devastating analytical brain and a forceful mode of expression, but he seemed to me to be too emotional and incapable of the compromises that politicians have to make. Also, as half-Armenian and half-Jewish, he was at a major disadvantage in a country riddled with prejudice.

But I had underestimated his courage and his will power, which are truly remarkable. I still think it is more likely that he will be assassinated rather than become President of Russia, but more probably neither will happen.

Once his enemy was the Russian authorities who sought to thwart his ambitions at the chess board. Then it was FIDE, the game's governing body, which appeared to be in cahoots with his enemies. Now it is Putin. He is still essentially the boy from Baku who has lost his father and will bravely take on anyone who threatens his ambitions and who has puzzled out for himself how to be the best in the world. Now that he has matured, he will take on anyone who spoils his dream of a democratic Russia.

At heart, though, he is the same small boy of remarkable brainpower, with shining moral courage and a saint-like purity, who will never back down in the face of anything he regards as evil. In chess terms, Kasparov plays the white pieces and Putin the black.

AFTERWORD

It was a great relief to me that *The Observer*, when it finally had to be handed over, was entrusted to the care of Peter Preston of *The Guardian* rather than Andreas Whittam Smith of *The Independent*. Merging *The Observer* with the three-year-old *Independent on Sunday*, with the *Indy* in charge of the merging operation, would have meant that most *Observer* journalists would lose their jobs. *The Observer* would have slowly lost its identity and the print edition of the world's oldest Sunday paper would have died in 2016, after 224 years, along with that of *The Independent* itself.

Preston was a fine editor, working like me through those dead days of the 1970s and early 1980s when the print unions strangled all enterprise, producing badly printed editions with terrible colour reproduction and frequent delays. Despite this, his *Guardian* was characterised by highly readable features, a strong social conscience and a sharper nose for news than it'd had in the past.

Peter and I had much in common, both grammar-school boys from the Midlands who had gone to Oxbridge, the same age, who had been elected by our journalists around the same time and had worked our way up through enthusiasm for the hurly-burly rigours of the newsroom and the technical challenges of pre-digital newspaper production. Peter also had a wicked sense of humour, sometimes so oblique that people could miss it.

I would have appointed Alan Rusbridger, then Preston's deputy, to succeed me as editor of *The Observer* (not that it was any longer my business). That way, I thought, he would have got to understand the quirks of running a Sunday paper by the time he took over Preston's job. He had spent some time on *The Observer* as TV critic in the 1980s. Instead, they chose Jonathan Fenby, a book-writing expert on France and China, who was essentially a news and comment man when a Sunday paper requires someone with a talent for features.

Fenby wrote an ill-judged letter to *The Times*, damning my regime for allegedly allowing Tiny Rowland too much influence over the paper. It seemed to me to be a bad idea for an editor to knock his own paper in public, especially when he didn't know the facts. My former colleagues told me that Fenby was 'like a man caught in the headlights' who had so much to do as editor that he couldn't decide what to do first.

The *Guardian* hierarchy took a long time to decide whether it wanted a Sunday version of its own paper or to let *The Observer* continue on the maverick way it had travelled over the two previous centuries. It was treated as the junior partner, yet it had always sold more copies than *The Guardian*.

I was followed by three editors in five years while Astor and I had racked up forty-five years between us. There were two short-term appointments as editor, Andrew Jaspan and Will Hutton, before Roger Alton, whom I had once tried to recruit as sports editor, brought some fresh energy to the paper before leaving after nine years, apparently over a dispute with *The Guardian*.

I was surprised that he threw the paper behind the invasion of Iraq in 2003 and wondered how much that had to do with memories of Saddam Hussein's brutal execution of Farzad Bazoft thirteen years before. I would have been tempted to do the same, but would have finally rejected it – or been talked out of it – on the grounds that we couldn't know what sectarian chaos might follow the fall of Saddam Hussein.

It is perhaps as well that I wasn't on board for the European referendum. With its long record of internationalism, *The Observer* had to be a Remainer. I was a strong supporter of Britain's entry in 1975. By

2016, however, I was in favour of Brexit – much to the consternation of my older children and the annoyance, even anger, of some of my journalist chums.

Alton's successor, John Mulholland, has served nine years so far and has imposed a distinctive character on the newspaper that is different from Astor's *Observer* or my *Observer*, but then it is serving a different generation in a different century. I always make this point when people ask what I think of *The Observer* today – that it isn't aimed at people like me.

What I mostly envy, not just about the modern *Observer*, but about all newspapers today, is the amount of editorial space they have, compared with the meagre rations on which we used to subsist in the old days. Editing was a constant process of cutting – choosing, say, one out of four possible articles for publication when there would be ample room nowadays for all of them, or cutting back a natural 1,200-word piece to 700.

Newspapers have Rupert Murdoch to thank for this, for destroying the print unions in the mid-'80s and thereby cutting production costs, allowing for more editorial space and more sections. But I doubt if the Dirty Digger gets the thanks he deserves, or if modern journalists remember or even care about it.

● ● ●

The Guardian was not sensitive in the way it handled the takeover, so that a number of staff chose to leave, notably Alan Watkins, who heard a *Guardian* team led by Hugo Young, the chairman of the Scott Trust, address *The Observer*'s journalists. 'They're like a conquering army,' he said. 'I'm off,' before moving his political column to the *Independent on Sunday* and writing a rugby column for the daily.

My friend Hugh McIlvanney was captured by the *Sunday Times*, where he built a brilliant second career over the next two decades, confirming his unassailable position as the best sports writer of the age. When Andrew Neil approached him after I had gone, he said he knew McIlvanney would never have left *The Observer* while I was at the helm.

Soon after I left the paper I was called by a former colleague who said *The Observer*'s files and other documents were being thrown into a skip outside the paper's old building on Chelsea Bridge. I drove round, climbed into the skip and rescued most of them, including letters from famous contributors such as Bertrand Russell, Graham Greene and Vita Sackville West, and accounts books from the 1930s with entries in copper-plate handwriting.

I arranged for them to be kept at Sheffield University, where I had launched a new Department of Journalism Studies. Eventually *The Guardian* got its act together and paid £25,000 to buy back the papers it could have had for nothing. They are now preserved in a wonderful new archive created by *The Guardian*. The paper deserves credit for this and for making much more of Jane Bown's brilliant and extensive portrait portfolio than we ever did.

Early in my time on *The Observer*, Jane went with me to interview Anthony Blunt, then director of the Courtauld Institute, taking the shopping bag in which she carried the day's vegetable shopping along with her cameras. The story was about a new collection of pictures the Courtauld had acquired.

All I saw when I interviewed Blunt was a remote patrician figure with a way-back accent and a rather disdainful manner towards a young reporter. Jane's camera, however, saw something more sinister, in a pose that made his eyes look evasive, even shifty, against a dark background. It was a portrait that was used extensively when he was finally exposed as a one-time Soviet spy.

• • •

At one stage during the Rusbridger era, when it looked as though *The Observer* might be sacrificed to pay for *The Guardian*'s over-investment in digital journalism, I received appeals from the *Observer* journalists to speak up on their behalf. I appeared with Harold Evans on *Newsnight* on BBC2 to fight for the paper's survival. It must have been a bizarre programme to watch: an octogenarian in New York and a septuagenarian in Majorca speaking from two large screens.

In Palma, where the time was an hour later than in London, I was being filmed on a bridge at closing time from the local bars, so shadowy drunken figures were staggering around while the TV crew and my wife were desperately trying to keep them away from the cameras. Because of this off-screen distraction I had some difficulty focusing on the questions Kirsty Walk was asking me from London. Thankfully, *The Observer* was reprieved.

Those of us who love *The Observer* and have devoted most of our professional lives to it should express profound gratitude to *The Guardian* and the Scott Trust for keeping the paper alive in what must sometimes have been very difficult times. More than forty years ago, when I was appointed editor, Lord Goodman had warned me that the paper might not last another six months.

Preston remains, even as he approaches his eighties, the shrewdest media analyst. I wrote on the media myself for many years after leaving *The Observer*, mostly for the *Evening Standard* and *The Independent*. I finally gave up when I read a lecture by the new *Guardian* editor, Katharine Viner, on the digital future facing the press. I could tell it was brilliant, but as I could hardly understand a word of it I decided that the time had come to stop pontificating on the media.

In any event, living in Majorca meant that I was missing all the Fleet Street gossip one used to pick up by meeting friends in the Garrick Club, El Vino's and on other licensed premises. But I remained in contact with the newspaper world as chairman and later president of the London Press Club and as president of the Media Society. I was also elected chairman of the European Federation of Press Clubs and the World Association of Press Clubs and hosted their meetings in London.

I was elected chairman of the judges for the British Press Awards and for the London Press Club Awards. I still write for newspapers and magazines – a weekly page on any subject I fancy for the *Majorca Daily Bulletin*, occasional features for *The Oldie* (which I once edited briefly in 1994 while Richard Ingrams was away writing a book) and for *The Observer* and the *Daily Mail*, but more often obituaries for the *Daily Telegraph*, where I specialise in media figures and old rugby players.

Even though I couldn't keep up with digital developments, I still maintained an active interest in the ethical issues surrounding newspapers, and actively joined the debate about press regulation. From the time I became an editor over forty years ago I had urged British governments to reach a deal with the press. Essentially the deal consisted of an exchange: better conduct by the newspapers in return for greater access to information.

In Britain, public information had always been regarded as the property of the state, to be divulged when it suited the interests of the ruling party, rather than something that belongs to the people as a basic right to know what is being done or planned in their name and with their money. The Freedom of Information Act has squeezed the orange on specific issues, but the official mind-set on information is still largely unchanged.

Britain is still some way from the ideal set out by James Madison in the United States in 1822, as inscribed over the main entrance to the Library of Congress in Washington:

A popular government, without popular information, or the means of acquiring it, is but a prologue to a Farce or a Tragedy; or, perhaps, both. Knowledge will for ever govern ignorance. And a people who mean to be their own Governors must arm themselves with the power that knowledge brings.

And has the press met its own side of my proposed bargain by improving its conduct? Yes and no. There is still more harassment and triviality than many people would like, but at least the editors are now held to account by what I regard as a stronger system of self-regulation. Government attempts to force newspapers into a state-backed system are bound to fail.

Although I have been critical of the tabloids – to the extent of once enraging *The Sun* into running an editorial called 'Dozy Don' denouncing me on page two, facing a topless 'Ship-Shape Tina' on page three – at the end of the day I have always argued that if the choice lay between a shoddy-but-free press and a state-controlled press, then the free press must prevail.

The recent debate over press regulation got itself into a twist from the beginning because of David Cameron's weak position as a man who had hired a phone hacker as his director of communications in 10 Downing Street. Phone hacking, in fact, had nothing to do with regulation. It was a criminal offence and a number of journalists, notably Andy Coulson, went to jail for engaging in it.

But Cameron's enforced silence on this issue was exploited ruthlessly by Labour in the form of Ed Miliband and the ineffable Tom Watson, by Nick Clegg of the Liberal Democrats, and by a well-organised campaign of newspaper critics called Hacked Off. Cameron was in no position to resist the setting up of the Leveson Inquiry or the crude machinations that followed it. Nor did it help that many MPs, seeking revenge for the newspaper campaign which had exposed their fraudulent expenses claims, were unwilling to defend the press when it came under siege.

Self-regulation, rather than some form of imposed system, has to be the right way, but this can still involve a majority of adjudicators who are completely independent of the press. Having served for six years on the Council of the Advertising Standards Authority and learned to admire the quality of its judgments – and the staff work that lay behind them – I would like to see a similar balance of professional and independent members making the key decisions on complaints.

I also spent six years on the Competition Commission's newspaper panel, being called in to advise on whether proposed newspaper mergers would threaten freedom of expression. This gave me a rare insight into the finances and operational methods of various kinds of newspapers as they entered the digital age.

Sheffield University had approached me while I was at *The Observer* to advise them on the creation of a new Department of Journalism Studies. I made a number of visits to the city – where I had been trained as a journalist myself thirty years before – to talk about teaching courses and research objectives. Senior members of the university, including the then Chancellor, Vice-Chancellor and the Registrar, also attended a dinner at the newspaper, at which they invited me to become the first head of the new department, with the title of Professor. Initially I declined because I wanted to see *The Observer* through a difficult period, but when, soon after, the newspaper was sold, I accepted the university's renewed offer.

Having grown weary of university media departments that produced ill-informed left-wing critiques of 'the capitalist press', I wanted a department that really understood the way newspapers worked and the natural tensions that were bound to exist between commercial and editorial needs. I also wanted one that mixed academic study of media history and ethics with basic training in the practice of journalism, such as writing, sub-editing and design. That meant recruiting a staff that contained both academics with a serious interest in the media and former professional journalists. We finally got there, but not without some teething problems in the early years, and Sheffield's Department of Journalism Studies is now, twenty-three years after its launch, one of the most highly respected in the country.

From my own experience as an editor, I wanted research that measured the performance of newspapers, especially in covering big events. I had been prompted in that direction by a number of major stories *The Observer* had covered in my time, but one particular event had stuck in my memory and nagged at my conscience. That was the riot of Red Lion Square in London in June 1974, when police and groups of left-wing demonstrators clashed over a rally by the National Front.

Kevin Gately, a twenty-year-old mathematics student from Warwick University, died from a blow to the head, delivered in circumstances that were never fully established. Although non-political himself, he became the first person to die in a political demonstration in Britain for fifty-five years. He was 6 ft 9 in. tall, prompting speculation that he had been hit by a truncheon from a mounted policeman. This theory was seized on in the next day's papers, including my own, which all blamed the police for causing the disorder that resulted in the student's death.

A public inquiry into the rioting, headed by Lord Scarman, thought this 'unlikely' but failed to discover firm evidence of how, or from whom, Gately received his fatal wound. The inquiry also revealed for the first time that a group of marchers from the International Marxist Group had attacked the police cordon and had thereby been responsible for setting off the rioting.

When I read the report I was struck by the contrast between the papers' immediate reporting of the riot and the facts established by Scarman after taking evidence from all parties for over a month. There have been many (and worse) cases of misrepresentation in newspapers in the years since then, but Red Lion Square was the one that made me focus on the problem. I began to wonder how often newspapers got such things wrong. I also developed doubts about the way journalists from various newspapers tended to seek a consensus about what had happened – a consensus which in this case had misled readers and set off a public debate based on a false premise. Above all, I distrusted the sense of omniscience that newspapers conveyed.

It is, of course, impossible for any newspaper, no matter how well resourced, to produce a definitive account of complex events so soon after they have taken place. I thought editors should therefore value the results of an independent review of their papers' performance if it revealed weaknesses in the way news was collected, assessed or presented – weaknesses that could be corrected for the future. If the right lessons were learned, I thought it should be possible, and highly desirable, for newspapers to edge their way nearer to the truth.

I would like to see an annual audit of press performance – an idea I am happy to credit to my late friend Sir Louis Blom-Cooper QC. Clearly a university would be an appropriate body to conduct such an audit. The difficulty would be getting newspapers to pay for it, or even give evidence, if they thought they might be reprimanded afterwards. I would hope the audit could be conducted in a spirit of seeking enlightenment or learning lessons rather than attaching blame. It would be useful, for example, to see an audited review of the press's performance in its coverage of the referendum campaign or of Donald Trump's election as President of the United States. Even if only one or two major stories a year were to be reviewed in this exhaustive way, the results, whether positive or negative in outcome, could only bring benefit to journalists who care about the accuracy of what they report and to those who direct and publish their efforts.

When I look back on the periods I covered as a newspaper editor, I am sometimes shocked or disheartened when the truth that emerges decades later shows how we got things wrong – or missed the big story completely. I have felt this particularly about coverage of governments in the 1970s, a troubled time when nobody seemed to be telling the truth. Reading books about that period by Dominic Sandbrook or Francis Wheen, I discover all sorts of things I didn't know – and should have known – about what was really going on. The experience can be humbling, and reinforces my view that the posture of omniscience adopted by most newspapers, whether tabloid or not, will be shown in time to be comically absurd.

● ● ●

Running a newspaper for many years isn't always good for the soul. An editor is often treated like a god within his office – understandably so, in my opinion, since he (or she) is the person who ends up in court, and sometimes in jail, if the paper gets things badly wrong. But I have to say I found it rather disconcerting to move from a newspaper conference room, where the editor's decision is final, to a university environment, where everybody wants to go on and on talking. It felt a bit like Wellington's experience when he moved from the battlefield into Downing Street. 'I gave the Cabinet their orders, but they insisted on talking about it!'

I found faculty meetings especially trying. There was usually a simple decision to make – whether or not to promote someone to senior lecturer, for example – and the answer was nearly always clear from the paperwork provided in advance of the meeting. Yet people would rabbit on – often past the time for me to catch my train to London – because they liked the sound of their own voices. Like academics, journalists are also articulate folk, but in their case I could shut them up – very often a stare would be enough.

• • •

The internet revolution has brought about the greatest changes in journalism, both positive and negative, since Rupert Murdoch challenged the power of the print unions in the mid-1980s. The surviving regional newspapers, having seen swathes of their classified advertising move online, have cut their staffing to the bone, with groups using reporters to write for several papers at once. It seems incredible that when I joined the *Sheffield Telegraph* in 1961, there were seventeen general reporters signing in every day on the news desk – about twice the number I had available at *The Observer* when I became editor fourteen years later.

One of my persistent arguments over many decades is that journalism will survive – and for the sake of an informed democracy has to survive, especially in these days of 'fake news' – in whatever technical form it appears. For no matter what is wrong with a society – whether it be corrupt businessmen, corrupt politicians or even corrupt judges – if the press is free, the facts cannot be concealed for ever. While that is true, everything else is somehow correctable.

That high claim for the press may seem hard to justify in the face of some of our trade's more extravagant confections. As a character says in Tom Stoppard's play *Night and Day*: 'I'm with you on the free press. It's the newspapers I can't stand.'

Aleksandr Solzhenitsyn evidently shared that low opinion of the press. When I was introduced to him as a journalist on his first visit to London after his expulsion from the Soviet Union, he just glowered at me, said nothing and turned his back. Yet the reason his publisher had invited me to meet him was because I had serialised several of his books.

In his Harvard address, the Nobel Prize-winning novelist claimed that 'hastiness and superficiality are the psychic diseases of the twentieth century, and more than anything else this disease is reflected in the press.' Hastiness has to be conceded. It is the business and function of journalism to bring the news to people as fast as possible, and some errors are an unavoidable part of that process.

Superficiality, however, Solzhenitsyn's other charge, the press *can* do something about. The really significant shifts in our rapidly changing world are not on the surface. They are not physically there to be photographed or filmed. The printed word – the medium of our poets, novelists and philosophers – is still the best equipped to chart those hidden currents beneath the surface of contemporary life.

John Maynard Keynes put it like this:

The events of the coming years will not be shaped by deliberate acts of statesmen, but by the hidden currents flowing continually beneath the surface of political history, of which no one can predict the outcome. In one way only can we influence those hidden currents, by setting in motion those forces of instruction and imagination which change opinion, the assertion of truth, the unveiling of illusion, the dissipation of hate, the enlargement and instruction of men's hearts and minds.

'The unveiling of illusion, the dissipation of hate, the enlargement and instruction of men's hearts and minds.' That is a tall order for a newspaper, which is mainly concerned with the rapid recording of current events before they pass into oblivion. But it expresses in an ideal form what a newspaper should aspire to achieve if it is to deserve to be more than the lining of a sock drawer or wrapping for fish and chips.

It requires what David Astor once described as 'a whiff of old-fashioned idealism'. Or, as an old editor once told a budding reporter: 'A newspaper needs a lot of young fools, foolish enthusiasm and foolish ideals.'

•   •   •

As every year goes by, however, newspapers as we have known them seem less and less likely to survive. Some papers will continue to be printed on paper, but with dwindling circulations and with little chance of making a profit on their own. I thought it was a significant moment when my friend Brian MacArthur, a highly experienced newspaper man and one of the best-informed media commentators, gave up reading newsprint last year and now acquires all his information online.

I have to read some papers online – *The Guardian* and *The Observer* don't send hard copies abroad, and the papers that do, some of them printed in Madrid, charge about a fiver for a much-reduced edition. But I still enjoy the tactile feel of a newspaper that you can carry around, much as Len Hutton enjoyed the feel of a cricket bat even in his old age or Yehudi Menuhin the touch of a violin. I also remain a keen student of the layout and typography of news and features, which is something you miss online.

I can't help reflecting that during my active newspaper career, for the three decades from 1960 to the early 1990s, we had the best of it. It was not just that newspapers really mattered then, but that working for them was a daily pleasure, with ample expenses to fund pleasant and sometimes riotous living. The days of sandwich lunches at the desk were just coming in as I left. I used to rage at reporters to go out and discover what was happening in the world outside.

• • •

I was privileged to work with some of the most talented journalists of the post-war period. I could perhaps have made more use of my position to get to know more politicians. But I took the view, rightly or wrongly, that the best use of an editor's time is talking to his journalists and reading their copy. Maybe that's a matter of horses and courses.

I wish I had written more for the paper myself, especially editorials. On Saturdays, I gave priority to reading news and feature proofs and laying out the front page. Instead of working on leaders drafted by office pundits, I should have written more of them myself.

Another regret I have as I look back on more than half a century since I first climbed the Dickensian staircase to join the *Coventry Standard* in 1960 is that I was promoted so quickly through the ranks that I never got the chance to be a sports editor or a magazine editor on the way to the top. I would also have enjoyed making more documentaries for television. Still, I can hardly complain about the life I have been immensely lucky to enjoy and which has taken me to so many parts of the world.

After leaving *The Observer* I spent some time presenting the breakfast show on LBC radio, which meant rising at 3 a.m., reaching the studio at 4 a.m. to prepare the programme and write a daily press review, then go on air from 6 a.m. to 9 a.m. It was both exhilarating and exhausting, especially as I then frequently caught a train to Sheffield to supervise the launch of the new Department of Journalism Studies, returning to London the same day to resume this punishing regime. Part of me – the part that needed more sleep – was grateful that the job ended after nine months when the company lost its franchise.

• • •

As for the Rowland period, which I have described in detail earlier, I saw my role as taking any flak myself and keeping him off the writers' backs, so that they didn't feel that the owner was looking over their shoulder all the time. I mostly succeeded in this, though it became harder in my final few years in the editorial chair, after the publication of the special edition on the DTI report into the Harrods affair had brought so much public attention and made the staff ultra-sensitive to the slightest sign of interference.

Friends tell me the special edition was a mistake, and they may be right, certainly as far as my reputation and that of *The Observer* were concerned. But, as I have already explained, I didn't feel I had any choice in the circumstances. I didn't actually do it to benefit Lonrho, as people assume, but to get lawyers off *The Observer*'s back.

● ● ●

I have visited twenty countries (so far) to lecture on journalism or join panel discussions or conferences, mostly about the threats to a free press. The list (not in any order) includes Spain, Egypt, Germany, Italy, the USA, Canada, India, Turkey, South Africa, Argentina, Kenya, Trinidad, Barbados, Lebanon, Russia, South Korea, Peru, Belgium, Singapore and Ethiopia.

In Ethiopia, I found myself at a welcoming drinks party, given by the British Council, with about two dozen would-be journalists – mostly press officers, in fact, since the country had no independent media to speak of – who were standing around in glum silence. I broke the ice by announcing: 'Will Manchester United supporters please come to this side of the room and Liverpool supporters go over there?' The effect was remarkable, causing a buzz of excitement and chatter that lasted all evening.

The follow day I was asked by one of the audience what 'spin doctor' meant. I struggled with a cricket analogy, but they wouldn't have that, pointing out that the phrase was also used in America. Finally I spluttered: 'Bend it like Beckham!' – at which they all stood up and cheered. Once again sport had provided the key to global communication.

After I had completed the course, I was asked if I would address the whole Ethiopian Cabinet. I gave them my usual spiel about the need for a free flow of information to make a country efficient and for its people to feel they have a real stake in the society. The grey-looking men in suits looked back at me blankly through their shades. I left with the feeling that I had made no impression whatsoever, and the country has shown absolutely no sign since of opening up. Even so, it was extraordinary that they were even prepared to listen.

When I flew to present the annual West Indian journalism awards, I was met at the airport in Barbados by my hosts, who insisted that I should be whisked off immediately to the studio, since the event was being shown live on television and was already behind schedule. With difficulty, I persuaded them to allow me to stop off at my hotel briefly for a shower and a change of shirt before I could face the cameras.

In Calcutta, I took part in a panel discussion in a football stadium in front of an estimated 14,000 people. As it happened, *Private Eye* accused me of absenting myself from the office on that particular Saturday to get up to no good. On my return, I was able to tell Richard Ingrams that I could produce 14,000 Bengali witnesses and a newspaper picture to prove that I was in India. He agreed to publish an apology.

The Calcutta event was arranged by my friend M. J. Akbar, one of India's most distinguished journalists and authors. We had first met at the home of Mark Tully, the veteran BBC correspondent in New Delhi. I remember Tully, wearing a white kaftan like an Old Testament prophet, walking around with a drink in his hand and warning his guests that the West didn't understand the force of religion in Asia and the Middle East and that one day we would feel the force of it.

• • •

The most serious event I took part in was a conference in South Africa during the final days of apartheid, organised by Harvey Tyson, an energetic South African journalist who attracted fellow editors from all over the world to provide support for the country's beleaguered press. I was asked to 'evaluate' the conference at the end; no easy task, especially as I had to criticise in their presence two speeches by ministers of the apartheid government.

The opening address had been given by Katherine Graham, Watergate heroine and by then chairman of the *Washington Post*. Some of her comments are still relevant now:

'Governments are too quick to cry national security when often they only want to make their own job easier, to protect themselves from embarrassment, or carry out a policy or programme that could not win public support.'

And again: 'When governments or their leaders try to persuade people they are suppressing information in the interests of the people themselves, I tend to believe that's precisely the information the people most need to know.'

I had first met Mrs Graham in 1975, soon after I was appointed editor of *The Observer* and a few years after the Watergate scandal had forced the resignation of President Richard Nixon, thereby conferring everlasting global celebrity on the *Post* and on her and her executive editor Ben Bradlee. It was a dramatic day when I went for lunch with them in Washington, with helicopters on the office roof carrying newspapers to defeat a strike by print workers.

I quoted another conference speech that seemed to me to hit an important note. It was from Bill Kovach, who went on to be Washington bureau chief of the *New York Times* and one of America's most respected journalists. Although clearly directed at apartheid South Africa, his comments are just as valid today:

Conflict which cannot be resolved by debate is likely to be resolved by force, for the truth is always there. It pounds like the surf against the shore, relentless and irresistible. Like a rock which stands before the wave, a government which stands against the truth is eaten away, its credibility undermined, and its form will eventually collapse.

I ended my speech with a quotation I have used many times from the same Tom Stoppard play, *Night and Day*, which I quoted before. A seasoned foreign correspondent says: 'I've been around a lot of places. People do awful things to each other. But it's worse in places where everybody is kept in the dark. It really is. Information is light. Information, in itself, about anything, is light. That's all you can say, really.'

And, of course, he's right: that's all you can say, really.

ACKNOWLEDGEMENTS

I must first thank my wife Claire for encouraging me to write this book and for providing an invaluable sounding board while it was being written – and especially for the forbearance she has shown in taking on additional domestic chores while I was failing to do my fair share of basic parental tasks. There are several friends, too many to mention by name, who should also be thanked for pressing me to write; one even suggested that I should invent an affair with the Queen Mother to add some spice to the book.

I am eternally grateful to my *Observer* secretary, Barbara Rieck, now back in her native Australia, for the ultra-loyal support she always gave me and for organising my papers so well that even I, the least organised of men, could usually find what I needed when I needed it. Barbara typed up many of the original diary entries I have relied on to prompt my memory. My thanks are also due to Gina Hallam, who typed up some diary entries I had written in a barely legible scrawl and also input a number of articles and documents produced in a pre-digital age.

I am grateful to Nicholas Morrell for reading and correcting some chapters involving Lonrho. Parts of the chapter on Dr Banda ('Kamuzu') were taken from a talk I gave on BBC Radio 4 about my time as an editor in Malawi, which was later reproduced in *The Listener*. Some stories in the chapter on my late colleague Lajos Lederer are derived from his private papers and from some articles he wrote about himself in *The Observer*. I am immensely grateful to Randolph Lederer for unrestricted access to his father's archive. Some of the material in this chapter about Sir Robert Mayer appeared in an article I wrote for *The Oldie*.

In the chapter on Farzad Bazoft I have made use of some recent material unearthed by *The Observer* in Iraq, more than twenty-five years after Farzad's execution. The chapter on Colonel Gaddafi ('Muammar') relies partly on a joint article I wrote for *The Observer* with Colin Smith after we had interviewed him together; the best phrases were undoubtedly his. The chapter on Mohamed Fayed ('Tootsie') contains some points from an article I wrote for *The Observer* when Harrods was sold to its new Qatari owners in 2010. Some parts of the chapter on Len Hutton appeared in an introduction I wrote for a book of tributes after his death.

Finally, I owe a profound debt to the dozens of *Observer* journalists, living and dead, who wrote and edited the many thousands of articles that appeared in over 900 editions of the newspaper during my editorship. I hope I have done them justice.

BIBLIOGRAPHY

Bower, Tom. *Tiny Rowland: A Rebel Tycoon*. Heinemann, 1993.

O'Brien, Conor Cruise. *Memoir*. Profile Books, 1998.

Brivati, Brian. *Lord Goodman*. Richard Cohen, 1999.

Chisholm, Anne & Davie, Michael. *Beaverbrook: A Life*. Hutchinson, 1992.

Christiansen, Arthur. *Headlines All My Life*. Heinemann, 1961.

Clifford, Max & Levin, Angela. *Read All About It*. Virgin Books, 2006.

Cockett, Richard. *David Astor and The Observer*. Andre Deutsch, 1991.

Cole, John. *As It Seemed to Me*. Weidenfeld & Nicolson, 1995.

Edwards, Robert. *Goodbye Fleet St*. Coronet, 1988.

Evans, Harold. *Good Times, Bad Times*. Weidenfeld & Nicolson, 1983.

Frayn, Michael. *Towards the End of the Morning*. Faber & Faber, 1967.

Garland, Nicholas. *Not Many Dead*. Hutchinson, 1990.

Glover, Stephen. *Paper Dreams*. Jonathan Cape, 1993.

Goodman, Arnold. *Tell Them I'm On My Way*. Chapman, 1993.

Greenslade, Roy. *Press Gang*. Macmillan, 2003.

Gross, Miriam. *An Almost English Life*. Short Books, 2012.

Hall, Richard. *My Life with Tiny*. Faber & Faber, 1987.

Harris, Kenneth. *Conversations*. Hodder & Stoughton, 1967.

Hoggart, Simon. *House of Fun*. Guardian Books, 2012.

Kasparov, Garry. *Child of Change*. Hutchinson, 1987.

Lester, Anthony. *Five Ideas to Fight For*. Oneworld Publications, 2016.

Lewis, Jeremy. *David Astor*. Jonathan Cape, 2016.

Lustig, Robin. *Is Anything Happening?* Biteback, 2017.

Marr, Andrew. *My Trade*. Macmillan, 2004.

Neil, Andrew. *Full Disclosure*. Macmillan, 1996.

Porter, Henry. *Lies, Damned Lies and Some Exclusives*. Chatto & Windus, 1984.

Preston, John. *A Very English Scandal*. Penguin Books, 2016.

Pringle, John. *Have Pen, Will Travel*. Chatto & Windus, 1973.

Radji, Parviz C. *In the Service of the Peacock Throne*. Hamish Hamilton, 1983.

Randall, David. *The Great Reporters*. Pluto Press, 2005.

Sandbrook, Dominic. *The Way We Were: Britain 1970–74*. Allen Lane, 2010.

Shawcross, William. *Rupert Murdoch*. Chatto & Windus, 1992.

Stoppard, Tom. *Night and Day*. Faber Paperbacks, 1978.

Trelford, Donald (ed.). *Len Hutton Remembered*. Witherby, 1992.

Tyson, Harvey (ed.). *Conflict and the Press*. Argus, 1987.

Watkins, Alan. *A Short Walk Down Fleet Street*. Gerald Duckworth, 2000.

Wheen, Francis. *Strange Days Indeed*. Fourth Estate, 2009.

Woods, Donald. *Asking for Trouble*. Victor Gollancz, 1980.

Worsthorne, Peregrine. *Tricks of Memory*. Weidenfeld & Nicolson, 1993.

INDEX